70
GREAT
CHRISTIANS

Changing the World

Most of the material in this book was first published in the Christian Herald weekly newspaper, under the title, *Footprints of Faith*. The author's purpose was to give an overview of the flow of church history illustrated by the lives of men and women of different denominations who significantly affected its development.

70

GREAT
CHRISTIANS

Changing the World

Geoffrey Hanks

Christian Focus Publications

Published by
Christian Focus Publications Ltd
Geanies House, Fearn, Ross-shire,
IV20 1TW, Scotland, Great Britain.

Cover design
by
Seoris N. McGillivray

Printed in Great Britain by
Bookcraft (Bath) Ltd.

He is the head of the body, the church; he is the beginning, the first-born from the dead, that in everything he might be pre-eminent (Colossians 1:18 RSV).

To
Celia,
my wife

Charts

Maps

CONTENTS

Sadhu Sundar Singh, Evangelist to India and Tibet; Dr Ida
Scudder, Founder of Vellore Medical College; Amy Carmichael,
Founder of the Dohnavur Fellowship; Watchman Nee, Chinese
Pastor and Preacher; Gladys Aylward, Missionary to China;
Geoffrey Bull, Missionary to Tibet; Jackie Pullinger, Missionary
to the Walled City.

The Vins Family in Russia; Richard Wurmbrand, Romanian
Pastor; Brother Andrew, Ministry to the Communist World; Nate
Saint, Mission to Headhunters; Janani Luwum, Archbishop of
Uganda; Corrie ten Boom, Ambassador for Christ.

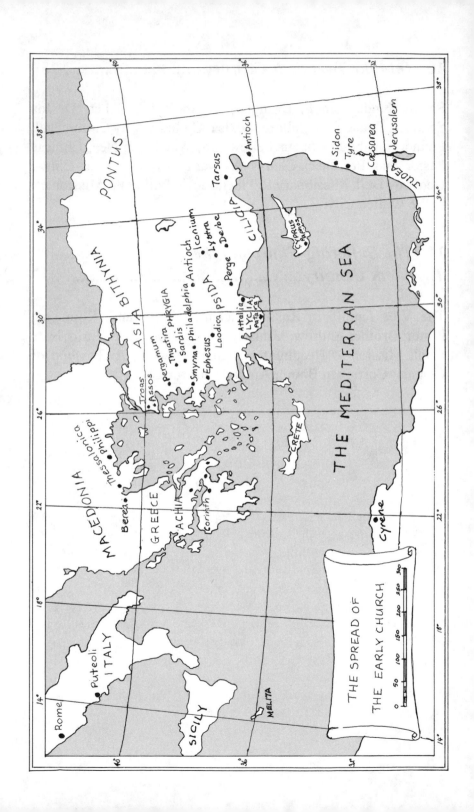

THE SPREAD OF
THE EARLY CHURCH

THE MEDITERRAN SEA

ITALY
SICILY
Rome
Puteoli
MELITA

MACEDONIA
Thessalonica
Philippi
Berea
GREECE
ACHAIA
Corinth
CRETE

PONTUS
BITHYNIA
ASIA
Troas
Assos
Pergamum
Thyatira
PHRYGIA
Sardis
Smyrna
Philadelphia
Ephesus
Laodica
PSIDA
Antioch
Iconium
Lystra
Derbe
Perge
Attalia
LYCIA
Patara
CILICIA
Tarsus
Antioch

CYPRUS
PAPHOS

Sidon
Tyre
Caesarea
Jerusalem
JUDEA

Cyrene

ONE

The Early Church

Throughout its history the Christian Church has been subject to divisions and heresies, quarrels and wars, and no century has passed without it being troubled by enemies. Worst of all, countless numbers of believers have suffered torture and been cruelly put to death for their faith in Jesus. Warned that they would be betrayed and brought before governors and kings, they were stirred to great deeds of heroism and paid the ultimate price rather than deny their Lord. Not only did the early Church survive this terrible onslaught, but it increased in strength and by the fourth century was firmly established throughout the Mediterranean world.

Beginning in Jerusalem
Although Jesus was put to death by the Romans, it was the Jewish authorities - who rejected the claim that he was the Messiah - that mounted the first attacks upon the Church. Beginning in Jerusalem, followers of *the Way* were imprisoned and beaten, while others such as Stephen and James were executed. Paul also relates how he was imprisoned, stoned and exposed to death for the sake of the gospel.

At first the Romans were unaware of the differences between Christianity and Judaism, and they regarded Christianity as a Jewish sect. It was Roman policy to allow freedom of worship to the national religion of the peoples they conquered, and for a while Christians were granted the same rights and privileges as Jews. In fact, the New Testament makes reference to a number of occasions when Roman officials gave legal protection to believers and saved them from harm.

As the number of Gentile Christians in the Church greatly increased, however, points of difference between the two religions began to emerge. The Church was no longer a Jewish ethnic group, and the process of separation between synagogue and church was accelerating. Awareness of these developments may well have been brought to Nero's attention as a result of Paul's trial in Rome.

The Romans eventually classed Christians as atheists, because they

---

Emperor worship

Emperor worship can be traced back to the reign of Julius, when in BC 42 the Senate gave him a place among the Roman gods. The Emperor Caesar Augustus (BC 29 - AD 14), who was in power at the time Jesus was born, prohibited worship of himself in Italy, but the practice spread in the provinces to become the official religion of Rome. Worship was offered to his *genius*, or guardian deity, and he was addressed as 'lord'. After his death, his name continued to be honoured, and Nero, who was his great-grandson, also accepted the title of 'divine'. Christians who refused to offer incense on an altar to the divine Emperor were considered unpatriotic and became a target for persecution.

---

had no gods - they did not display any idols and they refused to worship the Romans' gods. Believers came under increasing suspicion from the populace as they tended to keep themselves separate: they refused to attend the games at the Circus (because they started with a procession of the gods), it was difficult to do trade with them, and they often withdrew from the normal round of society.

Each week they held 'secret' meetings at which they spoke of another kingdom; they partook of a communal meal at which they were said to 'drink blood and eat flesh', a practice which led to charges of cannibalism and witchcraft. When finally they refused to offer incense on an altar to the divine Emperor or to address him as 'lord', they were regarded as traitors to Rome. Christianity was declared to be a *religio illicita* - a religion not recognised by the state - and Christians became outlaws.

Christians in Rome

By now the believers formed a large, prominent body in Rome and public feelings against them were mounting. Things came to a head during the reign of the Emperor Nero and local attacks broke out against the Christians. For the next two and a half centuries the Roman government attempted to stamp out Christianity, though opposition merely served to stiffen resistance. By the fourth century the Church emerged intact into a period of calm, albeit increasingly swayed by worldly influences.

Nero, who reigned from AD 54-68, was the first of a line of Emperors who tried to destroy the Church. He came to power at the age of eighteen and for the first five years ruled with clemency and justice, though privately he was a licentious and depraved young man. His lust for power, however, led him along a path of senseless destruction. To further his political ends he arranged for his mother to be clubbed to death, and had his brother, wife and other members of his family killed as well; in AD 65 he forced his tutor and aide, Seneca, to commit suicide.

He was a 'playboy' Emperor who enjoyed all kinds of pleasures. As an accomplished musician and poet, he wrote his own compositions; he was also keen on chariot racing and had his own private hippodrome next to the palace gardens in the Vatican valley. When in AD 62 he took sole charge of the government of the Empire, things took a turn for the worse.

In July AD 64 a great fire destroyed two thirds of Rome. Rumour had it that it was the Emperor himself who had started the blaze in order to provide a scenic background for the recitation of his poems about the burning of Troy, though there is no evidence to this effect. Surprisingly, in fact, he showed concern for the people who had lost their homes during the fire: he started a relief programme and opened up his gardens as a place of refuge for the homeless.

But the rumours persisted, so to divert this suspicion he made a scapegoat of the Christians, already a target of public dislike, and accused them of being the culprits. A large number of believers were arrested and charged, not on religious grounds, but with arson; others were quickly implicated as confessions were obtained under torture. According to the Roman historian, Tacitus, who wrote some fifty years later, the charge against the Christians was gradually changed to that of 'hatred of mankind', meaning disloyalty to the Empire. Soon, anyone

'Nero fastened the guilt and inflicted the most exquisite tortures on a class hated for their abominations, called Christians by the populace. Christus, from whom the name had its origin, suffered the extreme penalty during the reign of Tiberius at the hands of one of our procurators, Pontius Pilate; and a most mischievous superstition, thus checked for the moment, again broke out, not only in Judaea, the first source of the evil, but even in Rome, where all things hideous and shameful from every part of the world find their centre and become popular.'   Tacitus, Annals

who acknowledged the name of Christ was accepted as guilty and hundreds more were subjected to a most barbaric death.

In order to provide amusement for the citizens of Rome, Nero turned the occasion into a show, and details of how the Christians were made to suffer have been passed down to us by Tacitus. The Emperor dressed himself as a charioteer and, mounted in his chariot, mingled with the crowds who had gathered to witness the spectacle. Christians were covered in the skins of wild animals and were then torn to pieces by dogs; some were crucified, others were nailed to crosses, their bodies covered with tar and set alight, so that when darkness fell they burned as human torches. Although Tacitus had a low opinion of Christians, he felt pity for them and described how 'there arose a feeling of compassion for them (i.e. among the Roman people), for it was not for the public good... but to glut one man's cruelty'.

PETER and PAUL (died AD 65-68): Apostles in Rome

Among the martyrs at Rome were the apostles Peter and Paul, though there is no direct evidence to prove it. Little is known of Peter's movements after his escape from prison under Herod's persecution in Jerusalem, except that he eventually reached Rome. The claim that he founded the church in Rome cannot be supported, though he was certainly active there in ministry. One suggestion is that he visited Rome at the request of Paul, to try and heal a breach among the Christians.

Paul was arrested in Jerusalem, and following his appeal to the Emperor reached Rome around AD 59-60. He was in custody for two years until his trial before Nero. During that period he lived in rented accommodation under guard, but was given freedom to receive visitors.

After his acquittal in AD 62 he probably travelled to Spain and later visited the churches of Asia Minor. He was at some point re-arrested, by which time the tide of opinion had turned against Christians and being a follower of Christ now carried the death penalty. The date of his execution is unknown, but it was sometime between the years AD 65-68.

Both apostles wrote stirring epistles while they were in Rome. Peter penned his first epistle in which he spoke of the possibility of persecution and called on his readers not to be ashamed of suffering for the name of Christ. He was joined there by Mark who, according to Papias (c140), wrote down Peter's recollections of what Jesus had said and done. Woven into the fabric of the Gospel of Mark is the theme of Christ's sufferings, possibly written to encourage Roman believers under attack.

At the height of Nero's persecution, Peter was arrested and crucified, though the circumstances of his death are shrouded in mystery. One apocryphal account tells that he was crucified head downwards because he did not believe he was worthy of suffering as his Master had done.

According to tradition - which is quite likely correct - he was buried on Vatican hill and a chapel erected over his tomb. This was later replaced by a basilica which was pulled down in the sixteenth century to make way for the new basilica of St. Peter's that we know today.

When Paul was arrested and brought to trial a second time, he had no illusions about being set free, and wrote to Timothy that 'the time had come for his departure.' As a Roman citizen he would have been beheaded rather than crucified, and the place of his execution was quite likely outside the city walls on the road to Ostia. In the fourth century the Emperor Constantine had a basilica built over his burial place, where the church of St. Paul's Outside the Walls now stands.

The attacks on the Church continued up to the death of Nero, when the Emperor was declared a public enemy by the Senate and forced to commit suicide. For the next thirty years the Church enjoyed comparative peace until the reign of the Emperor Domitian, when in AD 95 a second wave of persecution broke out.

The martyrdom of these early believers proved a testimony to Christians throughout the Empire, and the church in Rome, which continued to flourish and grow, became a church 'worthy of God, worthy of honour and worthy of congratulations'.

IGNATIUS (died 110-117): Bishop of Antioch

The followers of Jesus were first called Christians at Antioch, the third largest city of the Roman Empire and capital of the province of Syria. The term was a nickname probably invented by the pagans to identify the disciples of Christ. It appears to originate from the Latin word *Christianoi* meaning 'followers' or 'soldiers' of Christ, and came into common usage during the AD 40s.

The first known use of the term 'Christianity,' *Christianismos*, comes from the works of Ignatius. It was allegiance to the name of Christ that brought believers into conflict with the Roman authorities, and anyone who professed the name was liable to be put to death.

The Emperor Domitian (AD 81-96), perhaps even more ruthless than Nero, demanded that he should be worshipped as both 'lord and god'. Those who refused - Christians and Jews - were punished, which led to the execution of members of his own household who were accused of 'atheism'. After Domitian's death the Empire fell into the hands of a number of good and able rulers, and following a two year respite under Nerva, the Emperor Trajan (AD 98-117) appeared anxious to be fair to Christians and continue his predecessor's policy. His attitude to the matter was set out in his correspondence with Pliny the Younger, Governor of Bithynia in north-west Asia Minor.

The Governor wrote to the Emperor asking how he should proceed against the people accused of being Christian. Is the very name of Christian to be punished or only the criminal practices that go along with it? (This was a reference to rumours about cannibalism and incest at the Lord's Supper.) Because he had never been present at a trial of Christians or had experience in dealing with them, he described to Trajan what rule he applied and enquired whether his action was right.

When brought before him, he first asked if they were Christians. If they said 'Yes,' he asked them a second and a third time, warning them of the penalty of professing Christ. If they persisted in their confession they were led off to an immediate execution. Some were only too ready to curse Christ and offer incense to the Emperor's image, while others denied ever belonging to the Faith or that they had any connection with it, and so were released. But many refused to do either of these things, to the annoyance and the amazement of the Governor.

In his reply, the Emperor agreed with Pliny that he had taken the right line and explained that there could be no set way of dealing with them. He ordered that they should not be specially searched out nor should anonymous charges be accepted against them. If they were charged and convicted, they were to be punished; if they denied being a Christian they were to be set free. So even though there was no law against it, professing Christ was still considered to be a capital offence.

Godbearer

The persecution that struck Bythinia and Pontus also reached Syria, where the aged Bishop Ignatius of Antioch was an obvious target. Hardly anything is known of his early life, though some fragments of tradition have been preserved.

Born of pagan parents, it was said that he was the child that the Lord took in his arms to bless (Matthew 18:2), though this may have been an attempt to explain his baptismal name, Theophorus ('Godbearer'). It was also claimed that he was ordained bishop at Antioch by Peter.

What is sure, however, is that he was once a disciple of the apostle John, and that he was the Bishop of Antioch at the turn of the first century where he held office for about forty years. Details of the last month or so of his life can be gleaned from the seven letters he wrote while on his way to Rome to face death.

Why Ignatius should have been singled out for special treatment is a puzzle. Perhaps it was because he was the leading bishop at Antioch and his witness for Christ was widely known. Whatever the reason, he was apparently the only Christian arrested at Antioch and he had to stand trial alone. It happened at the time of Trajan's visit to the city, and Ignatius - at his own request - was brought before the Emperor.

The Emperor asked Ignatius, 'Who are you, who possessed with an impious spirit are so eager to transgress our commands and persuade others to do the same, to their own destruction?'

Came the answer, 'Theophorus, he who has Christ within his breast.'

'Do you mean the one who was crucified by Pontius Pilate?' asked the Emperor.

'Yes,' was the reply, 'I mean him who was crucified for my sin.'

When the examination was over, the Emperor pronounced the sentence: that he be taken in chains to Rome, to be devoured by the lions 'for the gratification of the people'.

'I thank you, Lord that you have thus honoured me, like the apostle Paul,' he prayed, and commended himself to God.

The reason for his removal to Rome rather than being executed on the spot is a matter for conjecture, but he may have been too popular a figure to be dealt with in his own city.

Escorted by ten soldiers and in the company of two other prisoners, Ignatius was taken in chains, not by sea - as Paul before him had travelled - but by an overland route. They followed the northerly road through Asia Minor, via Philadelphia and Smyrna to Troas. Although allowed considerable freedom by his guards (on payment of a fee), they treated him roughly. He described it as being 'bound to ten leopards, whose usage grows still harsher when they are liberally treated'.

During the course of the journey Ignatius was permitted to receive guests at a number of stopping places, and at Smyrna had a chance to spend time with his friend Polycarp, the leading elder of the local church.

There was also opportunity to dash off a few letters, which give us insights into his pastoral concerns and the problems facing the Church. His letters bear the mark of having been written in great haste, but they sparkle with life and ring true to the Scriptures.

Five of the seven letters were addressed to churches in Asia Minor and were delivered by Christians who had been sent to greet him on his

way; another letter was sent on ahead to the church at Rome and he wrote
a farewell note to Polycarp.

The letters reveal that Ignatius had a working knowledge of what we
now acknowledge as the Scriptures: he quotes from both the Old
Testament and the Gospels, though he showed a preference for the
writings of Paul.

False doctrines

He was especially concerned about the false doctrines put about by two
groups of people who were upsetting the faith of some of the believers.
The matter was urgent, and he took up his pen in order to counter their
teachings.

One group was the Judaisers, Jewish Christians who maintained that
it was necessary to observe Jewish practices such as circumcision and the
dietary laws in order to be saved.

The other, called Docetists (from the Greek *dokein* meaning 'to
seem'), denied the Incarnation and taught that Christ was not real, that
he only seemed to be a man; therefore his sufferings on the cross and his
resurrection were an illusion. Ignatius replied by saying, 'Suffer he did,
truly and indeed; just as he did truly and indeed raise himself again. His
Passion was no unreal illusion.'

To further counter these heretical teachings, Ignatius stressed the
importance of unity in the Church and urged Christians to obey their
bishop in all things.

Some of the believers had been in the habit of administering the
sacraments themselves, without the bishop; to baptise or celebrate the
Eucharist without the consent of the bishop was not lawful, he chided
them. 'Let that be considered a valid Eucharist which is under the bishop,
or one to whom he commits it,' he wrote to the church at Ephesus. In this
way, he not only hoped to remain true to the Scriptures, but also to
promote the role of the bishop as the sole leader of the local congregation.

But Ignatius' mind was fixed on martyrdom, and his motto - *The
nearer the sword, the nearer God* - only served to underline his determination to face death. In his letter to the church at Rome he begged them
not to intervene on his behalf, as he died willingly for God.

Death for him would be the crown of his endeavour and the
attainment to Christ and to true discipleship. 'I am God's grain and I am
ground by the teeth of wild beasts that I may be found pure bread,' he
wrote.

From Troas, Ignatius was taken to Philippi and thence to Rome. He was brought to the Flavian Amphitheatre, known today as the Colosseum, an almost circular building with seats in three tiers. Opened in AD 80 during the reign of Titus, it was intended as a place of amusement for Roman citizens and had seating for 50,000 spectators. People from all over the Roman world flocked to attend the games, to see wild beasts tear each other apart and gladiators duel to the death.

What happened to Ignatius at the end is not exactly known. It is said that he was scourged and then tortured in a most cruel manner, and his flesh was torn apart with hot pincers. At last the lions were let loose on him and soon all that was left was his bones. The remains were gathered by the Christians who made provision for his burial at Antioch. The accepted date of his martyrdom is 19th December, some time between the years 110-117.

Hundreds of other martyrs are believed to have gone to their death in the Colosseum, though the evidence is unsure. In medieval times, sightseers to the Roman amphitheatre were asked the question, 'Do you want martyr relics? Then take up the dust of the Colosseum - it is all the martyrs.'

LAST PRAYER OF CHRISTIANS THROWN TO THE WILD ANIMALS

POLYCARP (c69-156): Bishop of Smyrna

By the second century Christianity had spread to the outer limits of the Roman Empire - Asia Minor, Europe, North Africa and beyond Palestine as far as Mesopotamia. But one of the strongest bastions of the faith was in Asia Minor, known today as Turkey and a land now almost closed to the preaching of the gospel.

The origins of the Church in Asia Minor go back to the apostle Paul who visited the area on each of his three missionary journeys. It was at Antioch (in Pisidia), when the Word of God was rejected by the Jews, that Paul made his dramatic decision to turn to the Gentiles, giving a further impetus to the gospel. He preached in a number of cities, mostly in the southern and western provinces, from where Christianity spread to the surrounding rural area.

Towards the end of the first century the church at Ephesus was encouraged by the presence of the apostle John. During the persecution, he was banished to the island of Patmos, where he wrote the Book of Revelation to the seven churches in Asia Minor. Later he was able to return to Ephesus where he lived until the days of Trajan and was the last of the Twelve to die.

In the second century, the Romans were forced to recognise that Christianity was a thriving and widespread force to be reckoned with. It had taken such a firm hold in Asia Minor that Pliny, the Governor of Bithynia, complained to Trajan that 'this contagious superstition had spread not only through the cities, but through the villages and countryside, so that the pagan temples had been near-abandoned'. As a result, sales of fodder for the sacrificial animals had dwindled, causing an economic crisis!

The policy of persecuting the Christians had done little to diminish the fervour of the believers and the Church in Asia Minor stood firm. Emperors such as Hadrian (117-138) and Antoninus Pius (138-161) tended to follow Trajan's more lenient attitude, and fewer martyrs were sent to their death.

Pagan respect

During the reign of Antoninus there occurred the most famous of all martyrdoms, that of the aged Polycarp, Bishop of Smyrna (69-156). Polycarp was a man of simple yet deep faith. He was regarded with much reverence and affection by his flock, and many of them were happy just to have the privilege of removing his shoes as a sign of their respect.

Even the pagans of Smyrna respected him, and described him as 'the Father of the Christians, the destroyer of our gods, teaching men not to sacrifice or worship!'

Polycarp was the Church's last link with the 'Apostolic Age'. In his younger years he had been a pupil of the apostle John and had enjoyed the company of many who had seen the Lord. The bishop often recounted to his pupils what he had heard about the Lord concerning his miracles and teaching, always emphasising that he had received it from eye-witnesses. Polycarp was recognised as one who had adhered to the Scriptures and preserved the apostolic tradition received from John.

This is illustrated by an incident during his visit to Anecitus, Bishop of Rome, in 155. On one occasion he came face to face with the heretic Marcion who was originally a member of the church in Rome but was excommunicated in 144 as a consequence of his heretical teachings. (Marcion had rejected the Old Testament on the basis that the Creator-God had nothing to do with the God of love revealed in Christ Jesus. He only accepted ten of Paul's letters and an edited version of Luke's Gospel as canonical. And like the Docetists, he taught that Jesus' appearance on earth was entirely unreal and that he did not actually die.) 'Do you recognise me?' asked Marcion. 'I do recognise you - the first born of Satan!' he retorted.

The Church enjoyed a time of relative calm under the Emperor Antoninus Pius (138-161), who took a lenient view towards Christians. At Smyrna, however, there arose a local outbreak of persecution and twelve Christians were condemned to die in the arena.

One man, Quintius, who had originally exhorted the others to face martyrdom, lost heart at the sight of the beasts and was persuaded by the Romans to offer incense to the Emperor. The other eleven held firm under torture and were thrown to the wild beasts; one of them actually goaded the beasts into attacking him, and his courage incensed the

---

'They were in the habit of meeting on a certain fixed day before sunrise and reciting an antiphonal hymn to Christ as God, and binding themselves with an oath - not to commit any crime, but to abstain from all acts of theft, robbery and adultery, from breaches of faith, from denying a trust when called upon to honour it. After this, they went on, it was their custom to separate, and then to meet again to partake of food, but food of an ordinary and innocent kind.'

Pliny, Governor of Bithynia, A.D. 112

crowd. They began to clamour for the bishop: 'Polycarp to the lions!' they shouted, 'Search out Polycarp!'

The believers, anxious for his safety, urged the bishop to withdraw to a farm in the country. Though unafraid of death, he realised he would be needed to minister to the flock, and so agreed. But the Lord revealed to him that his end was near. Three days before his death, Polycarp had a dream in which he saw his pillow on fire. Believing it to be prophetic, he informed the Christians, 'I must be burned alive,' which caused much alarm. Although he still had the opportunity to escape, he refused, saying, 'God's will be done.'

One of Polycarp's servants was seized and tortured, and he betrayed the whereabouts of his master. When the Roman officials arrived to arrest Polycarp, he treated them with the utmost courtesy, and invited them to eat and drink as his guests. It seems as if they too were awed by his presence, and were amazed at his great age and bearing.

He asked the men to give him one hour in which to pray, and he spent some time in commending his friends to God and asking for courage to face the coming ordeal. When he was ready, the officials mounted him upon an ass and led him into the city. As they travelled, the men tried to persuade him to deny Christ: 'Why, what harm is there in saying "Caesar is lord," and so save yourself?' they argued.

But the purpose of their pleas was not to save him from death, rather the honour of breaking down a champion of the Church.

In the Arena

As Polycarp was entering the stadium where the games were being held there came a voice from heaven: 'Be strong, Polycarp, and play the man.' Some of the believers standing by heard the voice, but they saw no one; perhaps it was the voice of God?

In the arena the wild beast show was over and the crowd had grown restless and angry. Polycarp was brought before the proconsul who began by urging him to deny his faith. 'Have respect for your old age,' he told the bishop, 'Swear by the divinity of Caesar; repent, and say "Away with the atheists".' Polycarp solemnly waved his hand towards the pagan crowd and repeated 'Away with the atheists!' But the proconsul pleaded further with him, 'Take the oath and I will let you go; revile Christ.' To which the bishop nobly replied, 'Eighty-six years I have served him, and he has done me no wrong - how can I blaspheme my King who has saved me?'

Despite further entreaties and threats of wild beasts and fire, the bishop remained firm in his resolve. At last the proconsul called the herald and told him to announce three times, 'Polycarp has confessed to being a Christian.'

Without waiting for the wild beasts, the crowd demanded that Polycarp should be burned alive, fulfilling the prophecy. Hurriedly, logs were gathered together and a funeral pyre built. The bishop put off his cloak, loosened the girdle of his tunic and endeavoured to untie his shoes. At his request, he was spared being nailed to the stake. 'He who gives me power to endure the fire will also give me the power to withstand the flames,' he declared.

As the flames leapt around him, Polycarp looked up to heaven, praising God and thanking him that he was counted worthy to take the cup of Christ. When the onlookers saw that the body was not being consumed in the fire, a gladiator was sent to despatch the bishop with a dagger thrust through the heart.

Afterwards the Christians requested his bones for burial, but were refused, 'in case they should abandon the crucified one and worship the martyr'. 'We worship Christ the Son of God,' came the reply, 'but reverence the martyrs as disciples and imitators of the Lord.' Later the remains were released and placed in a tomb, giving the believers the opportunity to gather and celebrate his 'birthday' each year.

Polycarp's martyrdom brought to an end this local outbreak of persecution and there was a period of rest for the believers. It would have been simple for anyone charged with being a Christian to have escaped death, as some did, by outwardly conforming to the Roman requirements.

But the believers were aware of the true nature of the ceremony of offering incense to Caesar and were faced with a choice: Who was Lord in their lives? The majority could not deny the Lord, despite the consequence, and chose rather to die and receive the crown of glory.

IRENAEUS (130-200): Bishop of Lyons

Almost from the beginning of its history the Christian Church has been plagued with the problem of heresy and several of the New Testament letters were written to combat false doctrine. By the second century, the Church was seriously being threatened by heretical groups such as the Gnostics and the Docetists, and its position weakened. In God's goodness, however, the heresies served more to benefit the Church rather than the heretics. It was during this period that a number of scholarly men were converted to Christ who were able to use their gifts to confront the new movements.

Men such as Justin Martyr, Irenaeus, Tertullian and Cyprian found themselves at the forefront of the battle. They not only defended the faith but also strengthened the Church by attempting to define Christian belief and to produce some kind of statement by which doctrine could be known. In this way all heresy - a Greek word meaning 'choice' - could be seen for what it was.

Defender of the Faith

One of the most remarkable Christians who defended the Faith during the second century was Irenaeus, Bishop of Lyons in Gaul. He was a gifted author and contributed much towards the development of Christian doctrine. A native of Smyrna, a seaport in Western Asia Minor, he was a member of the church which had received one of the apostle John's letters recorded in the Book of Revelation (2:8-11).

Smyrna was a prosperous city; it had a large Jewish population with a synagogue whose members were hostile to the Christians. It was here that the aged Polycarp was martyred, and Irenaeus may well have been in the city at the time. When Irenaeus was a teenager he had studied under Polycarp and remembered hearing how the bishop had heard the apostle John preach in Ephesus. In a letter to his friend Florinus in Rome - a man who had lapsed into heresy - he wrote about 190, 'I can tell you the very place where the blessed Polycarp used to sit as he discoursed, his goings out and his comings in... with John and with others who had seen the Lord, how he remembered their words, and what the things were which he had heard from them concerning the Lord...'

This evidence is important as it shows that towards the end of the second century Irenaeus was only one remove from those who had known the apostles; he had been a disciple of Polycarp who had been taught by the apostle John who in turn had known the Lord.

Irenaeus later moved to Rome where he was probably a pupil of Justin Martyr, one of the great apologists of the second century. Born of pagan parents in Palestine, Justin was the first Christian writer to try and reconcile the claims of faith and reason. His *First Apology* was written AD 155 to the Emperor Antoninus Pius, in which he defended Christianity as the only truly rational creed; his *Second Apology* was written to refute specific charges against Christians. When accused of being a Christian he refused to sacrifice to the Emperor Marcus Aurelius (AD 161-180) and was consequently scourged and beheaded during the persecution set up about AD 163.

THEATRE REMAINS, LYONS.

This may have been a signal for Irenaeus to leave Rome, and he moved westwards to Gaul where a Greek colony from Asia Minor had settled in the valley of the River Rhone. They had established a strong church, served by some of their own leaders. He moved to Lyons and became a presbyter under the aged bishop Pothinus.

The persecution of Marcus Aurelius raged on for some years and in 177 reached southern Gaul. Again, Irenaeus found himself dangerously close to what was possibly the worst outbreak of persecution ever suffered by the Church at the time. It arose without any special cause when a mob attacked some Christians and brought them before the magistrate. Despite torture, a number of believers remained faithful to Christ while others broke down under the beatings. Conditions in prison were terrible and many died there from suffocation, including the Bishop of Lyons, Pothinus, who was over ninety years of age. Altogether some forty-five believers died, including a boy aged fifteen called Ponticus. Their bodies were burned and the ashes thrown into the Rhone in an attempt to deny a claim to 'resurrection'.

The bravest of the martyrs was a slave-girl called Blandina who under torture confessed, 'I am a Christian and we have done nothing vile.' She was scourged in an attempt to force her to renounce Christ and was finally tied to a stake and gored to death by a wild bull in the amphitheatre. The courage of this young girl encouraged the Christians and amazed even the hardened pagans, as it was something they could not understand. An account of the persecution was written probably by Irenaeus, who took it to their fellow countrymen in Asia and Phrygia.

On his return to Gaul he was chosen bishop of Lyons and was faced with the task of re-building the Church. For many years he worked hard at writing a treatise defending the Church against the heretical sect of Gnosticism which was pervading the country. Although his monumental work, running to five volumes, was probably written for the Christians of Gaul, it had a much wider readership.

Irenaeus had studied Gnostic teaching in detail and became both the leading authority on the subject and its chief opponent. The book, entitled *Against Heresies,* was written to show heretics 'the teachings that have been kept dark until this present, but have now in the grace of God been made manifest.' Of the five volumes, two deal with heresy and the remainder consider the question of Christian theology and the need to maintain the Christian tradition.

Heresy

Of all the second century heresies, Gnosticism was the most subtle and dangerous. A mixture of Christianity and pagan philosophy, it rose to prominence between the years AD 80-150. The term comes from the Greek word *gnosis*, meaning 'knowledge', and its followers claimed a special knowledge of the 'way of salvation'. Gnosticism is a modern term to cover a variety of sects, each one gathered round its own leader, the most famous of which were Marcion and Valentinus. Many groups had their own special writings (in a rather similar way to some modern cults), whilst others used a selection of Christian writings - parts chosen from our New Testament - that suited their own theories.

Irenaeus' strongest argument against the Gnostics was to emphasise the basic Christian doctrines under attack. He put forward a *Rule of Faith*, a simple statement summarising the fundamental Christian beliefs. He was the first to draw up a clear summary, and it later became a basis for other creeds. In this way, anyone could test heretical beliefs and determine what was true.

In his creed, drawn up about 180, he stressed that the world was made by the one God, that Jesus the Son was made flesh and died, and that the Holy Spirit made known God's plan of salvation. Included also was reference to the resurrection and ascension of Christ, and to his future appearing from heaven. His emphasis on Jesus as fully man and fully God was intended to refute the Gnostic heresy that Jesus only 'seemed' to be a man, an idea similar to that taught by the Docetists.

The Gnostics claimed to possess a 'secret knowledge' reserved only for the elect, and passed down by the apostles of which they were the keepers. Irenaeus countered by arguing that the 'body of truth' (i.e. accepted beliefs) was attested by the four Gospels, handed down from the apostles through the bishops without alteration and drawn from all corners of the Church. From his own experience he could vouch for succession of the tradition, just as the church at Rome could show a line of teachers going back to Christ and the apostles. It could not be added to or diminished by any 'secret knowledge'.

Although Irenaeus had been able to write about the universal Church and its affirmation of apostolic doctrine, there was not complete unity on all matters. An internal controversy arose in the second half of the century concerning the date of the Easter celebration.

It was the practice of the Church in Asia Minor to celebrate the Lord's Passion at the same time as the Jewish Passover, the 14th Nisan, the day Jesus was crucified. Other churches celebrated on the Sunday following Passover. As the Passover was a moveable feast, churches in Rome, where visitors from Asia Minor were staying, found they ended their fast at a different time to the other believers, causing confusion.

The matter flared up again about the year 190. The Bishop of Rome determined to resolve the argument and banned the Asian Churches from Christian fellowship. It raised a storm of protest and Irenaeus (whose name means 'peace') was despatched to Rome to act as mediator. The Roman bishop's attempt to assume authority was overturned and the two parties agreed to allow the different practices to continue. In fact, some years later the Asian practice fell into disuse and the matter ended.

At the end of the century, the time of Irenaeus' death, the Church though shaken remained strong and resolute. While the *Rule of Faith* had provided the Church with a measure of orthodoxy, the more definite and formal creeds of the fourth century were still nearly 200 years away. Yet Irenaeus had been God's man for God's time. He had responded to the challenge and provided the Church with a useful breathing space.

TERTULLIAN (150-212): Theologian from North Africa

Martyrdom is the bait that wins men for our school... the blood of Christians is seed,' declared Tertullian, one of the great writers of the Early Church, towards the end of the second century. Tertullian had lived through a time when Christians were being persecuted and was aware of the powerful effect the death of martyrs had on unbelievers; it was this very witness that brought him to faith.

Rather than destroying the Church, the death of the martyrs actually increased admiration and respect for the believers and numbers were won to Christ. Pagans were at times amazed at the courage (some said foolishness) of men, women and children who faced death in the arena. In enforcing the death penalty, however, the aim of the Roman government was not to create martyrs but to persuade Christians to deny Christ. Whilst many abandoned the Faith, others were ever ready to face death.

Some even coveted martyrdom, and over-zealous believers ignoring the warnings of Jesus, gave themselves to the wild beasts in their eagerness to obtain the 'martyr's crown'. By the second century a cult of martyrdom had developed in which the martyrs were elevated to the rank of 'Heroes of the Faith', and to confess Christ in death was to win the highest accolade of approval. The occasion of the martyr's death became known as the 'birthday' (a phrase invented by Tertullian) and in some instances became an annual festival almost as important as the celebration of Easter.

Influenced by believers

Tertullian was born in Carthage, modern Tunis in North Africa, about 160, and grew up in a Roman city that had a strong and vigorous church. His well-to-do pagan parents gave him a sound education; he was fluent in Greek and Latin, well-read in history and philosophy and studied law. Later he moved to Rome where he practised as a lawyer and began to make a name for himself. It was while he was in the capital that he became a Christian, about 195, influenced by the way he saw believers face martyrdom.

He afterwards gave himself to the study of Christianity and its literature, then began to use his legal and writing skills to champion his new-found faith. Some time following his conversion he returned to Carthage and threw himself into the life of the local church.

After a short time as a layman, he was ordained as a presbyter; he became a preacher and teacher, and several of his writings that remain are in sermon form.

The Church throughout North Africa had benefited by a period of calm under the Emperor Commodus (180-192), but his successor Septimius Severus (193-211) turned against Christianity. In 202 he issued an edict forbidding his subjects to embrace either the Christian or Jewish Faiths, leading to another outbreak of persecution. The presbyter Tertullian felt that believers should not go into hiding, as some had done, and though he survived the trouble many were arrested and executed in the arena at Carthage.

At some point - some think it was in 202, at the time of the persecution - Tertullian left the church in Carthage and joined an ascetic break-away group called the Montanists. The founder, Montanus, believed himself to be the mouthpiece of the Holy Spirit, the Paraclete, and taught that the second advent of Christ was at hand. Tertullian was probably attracted by the exact moral standards demanded by this movement, which prohibited second marriages and denied that serious sins committed after baptism could ever be forgiven. He also argued that Christians should not undertake military service, or attend the theatre or other public amusements, as they involved pagan religious practices.

Although Tertullian had developed a rigid attitude to certain moral issues, he was essentially a man of compassion. He delighted in the pagans' comment upon the believers: 'See how these Christians love each other,' as they witnessed the care for the poor, the widows and orphans, and the generous hospitality displayed often from meagre resources.

For the remainder of his life, Tertullian spent his time in Carthage where he continued his literary activity and acted as the Church's spokesman against the heresies within Christendom. Towards the end of his life it appears he left the Montanists and formed his own sect known simply as the 'Tertullianists'. The sect survived for over two hundred years after his death before finally being re-admitted into mainstream Christianity.

Apologist

Tertullian is remembered as the most prolific Christian writer of the second century and the major theologian of the West until the time of Augustine in the fourth century. He was the first of the African Church Fathers to write in Latin instead of Greek, and there are thirty-six treatises attributed to his name. He wrote with considerable zeal and passion, and adopted an aggressive style of writing that earned him the title 'the fierce Tertullian'.

Early in his Christian life Tertullian took up his pen in defence of Christianity. He was one of a group of second century writers known as 'apologists', whose vocation was to put forward a defence of Christianity on intellectual grounds. Up to this point, believers had suffered without protest; now the apologists countered by explaining the case for Christianity and refuting the false charges made against them.

In his defence of Christianity, Tertullian protested about the treatment of Christians under the Roman law. He questioned the legality of not allowing Christians to speak in their own defence and the assumption that they were criminals worthy of death. Christians, he asserted, were good people who were loyal to the Emperor and prayed for him, in contrast to the hypocritical honour paid to him by pagans.

To make a point, Tertullian was not afraid to use sarcasm when defending Christians against the accusation that they were the cause of catastrophes. 'If the Tiber rises too high or the Nile too low, the cry is "The Christians to the lion!" ' he inveighed. 'What, all of them to a single lion?'

Of his many other works, one was an attack on heretics such as the Gnostics, who did not accept that Jesus was fully divine, and another a treatise on the Trinity explaining the difference of the 'Three Persons in One'. His writings are a valuable source of information about ecclesiastical affairs, and his study on baptism is important as it is the only serious treatment on the subject during the early history of the Church.

Christianity is indebted to Tertullian for introducing many theological terms that are in common usage today. He coined the term *Trinity* and formulated the doctrine of 'Three Persons held together in unity of one Substance'; he was the first to use terms such as *sacrament, resurrection* and *penitence*, and even the use of the term *New Testament* to describe the latter part of the Bible was his invention.

Some of his theological arguments have weaknesses and at times he treads on dangerous ground. For example, he speaks about baptism as a means of regeneration and salvation, as though the rite itself had magical powers, an idea that opened the way for the baptism of babies - and corpses! Yet for all his faults he was undoubtedly a writer of great ability and proved a tower of strength in serving the Church.

Tertullian will probably be best remembered for his vigorous defence of Christianity, when the might of the State was pitched against the fervour of the Church. 'The more you mow us down,' he thundered against Rome, 'the fuller is the harvest. The blood of Christians is seed.'

CYPRIAN (200-258): Bishop of Carthage

The Roman province of North Africa extended from Egypt along the Mediterranean coast as far as present day Morocco. Perhaps surprisingly to us today, it was crowded with people and cities, and its fields supplied Italy and Rome with corn. Its main language was Latin, and Roman civilisation was deep-rooted at all levels of society.

Roman religion, however, had not taken a firm hold and Christianity made in-roads throughout the province and into the country districts. It was said that the believers there were 'full of African emotion and zeal' and generated more heat than light!

Little is known of the origins of the Church in North Africa. It burst suddenly to prominence towards the end of the second century when twelve Christians from the town of Scilli near Carthage were executed for refusing to sacrifice to the state gods. Despite a chance to change their minds, they remained loyal to Christ, declaring: 'We render honour to Caesar as Caesar, but worship and prayer belong to God alone.'

Further executions also took place in 202 at Alexandria (Egypt), and at Carthage two young women - Perpetua and Felicita - went hand in hand to death in the arena. The Church in North Africa took a rather rigorous stance towards the Faith and regarded martyrdom as the Christian ideal; this attitude often led to disputes and divisions, damaging the unity of the Church.

Second Birth

Cyprian was one of a group of able and devoted Christian leaders in North Africa during the third century. He ranked alongside Tertullian and Augustine as a pillar of strength in the Roman province, and exerted a tremendous influence on the Church far beyond the confines of his native Carthage.

Details of Cyprian's early life are unknown, but he appears to have come from a well-to-do pagan family in Carthage. He became a successful teacher of rhetoric and a wealthy lawyer, famed for his learning and eloquence, and was a man of high social position. He was

---

Carthage martyrs (c 202)

The most memorable of martyrdoms at Carthage was that of a 22 year old widow, Perpetua. Her mother was a Christian but her father remained a pagan. At the time of her imprisonment she was nursing a new-born baby. Her father pleaded with her to renounce her faith, but she refused. Baptised while in prison, her cell (she related) 'became as a palace.' At her interrogation, the Procurator entreated her to offer a sacrifice to the Emperor, if only for the sake of the child, but she refused. She was taken with four other Christians to the amphitheatre where they were first savaged by wild beasts; after giving each other the kiss of peace they were put to death by the sword.

converted to Christ in middle age, probably in the year 246, as a result of a friendship with a church elder. After he was baptised, he wrote describing his experience, 'A second birth created me a new man by means of the Spirit breathed from heaven.'

The change in his life was marked, and he started by selling his pleasure gardens in order to give the money to the poor. Touched by his generosity, his friends bought back the gardens and restored them to their former owner! It seems he abandoned his occupation and social position, and gave himself to a life of celibacy, poverty and Bible study. He refused to read any secular literature and devoted himself entirely to the Bible. Such was his progress in the Christian life that he was soon chosen as a presbyter, and within two years was elected bishop of Carthage, the most important Christian community in North Africa.

His elevation to bishop was a rare compliment and reflected his standing in the church of his home city. But it also earned him many enemies, including presbyters who had been overlooked for the office. Cyprian was a great admirer of his fellow-countryman, Tertullian, whom he always referred to as 'the Master'. But he was a man of wider outlook and more practical ability than his hero, and brought qualities of administration, wisdom and dignity to his position.

Into Hiding

A year after attaining to his new office yet another outbreak of persecution took place throughout the Empire. The Emperor Decius, who reigned for two brief years (249-251), issued an edict requiring all his subjects to obtain a certificate (*libellus*) to prove they had sacrificed to the gods. Cyprian, realising the threat, heeded the words of Jesus and left the city to go into hiding in the country; he continued to care for his flock from a distance by sending secret letters. Many other church leaders, however, chose to stay on and suffer for their faith in Christ. It was at this time that the bishops at Rome, Antioch and Jerusalem all went to a martyr's death.

As always, there were those who could not face the prospect of persecution and looked for a way out. Many Christians lapsed from the Faith and, sometimes by purchase or by deceit, acquired a *libellus* affirming they had sacrificed. But there were some Christians known as 'confessors' who, having suffered in prison, issued their own sort of *libellus*, re-admitting their weaker brethren back into the fellowship of the Church.

When peace came it was necessary for the bishop to re-establish his authority at Carthage and especially to settle the question of whether the 'lapsed ones' should be restored to the Church. For Cyprian it was an awkward question, as he also had left the city during the persecution, though for pastoral reasons.

In 251 he called a council of African bishops and encouraged them to come to a moderate decision. They decided to ignore the certificates issued by the 'confessors' and to treat each case on its own merits. In the end they agreed that the 'lapsed ones' who were penitent should be allowed back, but only on their death-bed; and clergy were to lose their office permanently though they could be restored to communion.

The following year the threat of further persecution broke, and so to encourage them Cyprian proclaimed a general pardon to all who at that time were 'doing penance'.

Another controversy in which Cyprian became involved concerned the re-admission to the Church of heretics and others who had joined breakaway groups. If they had been baptised within one of these groups, was their baptism valid or should they be re-baptised on their return? Cyprian argued that there is no baptism outside the Church just as there is no salvation outside the Church, for 'he cannot have God for his Father

RUINS OF CARTHAGE

who has not the Church for his mother'.

While Cyprian's teaching was intended as a safeguard, it was obviously open to some misinterpretation. His view was supported by the North African bishops but opposed by Stephen, the new bishop at Rome, who argued that all who were baptised in the name of the Trinity were to be accepted, and attempted to assert his authority by claiming to be the successor to Peter. A compromise was reached and Stephen backed down, but by the beginning of the next century only Trinitarian baptism was accepted.

A third matter of contention was to do with the election and authority of bishops. Again Cyprian turned his mind to the matter and set out his teaching in a treatise *Unity of the Church*. He argued that the unity of the Church rested upon the foundation of the bishops, each one exercising his powers and functions within the whole. He spoke of Peter as the 'prince of apostles' and the one to whom Christ had conferred the 'keys of the kingdom', in which case the bishop of Rome occupied a special position among the bishops. Despite this, he did not accept that Rome could dictate matters to other bishops, but each one should act according to his own discretion.

An Example

In 254 a new Emperor, Valerian (254-259), came to power in Rome and issued two edicts in an attempt to destroy the Church. One ordered all subjects to worship the Roman gods, and Christians were forbidden to hold meetings or to have access to their cemeteries. The second, issued a year later, condemned all clergy to death.

On this occasion Cyprian refused to leave Carthage; he was arrested and brought before the proconsul. At first he was only sentenced to exile, but a year later a new proconsul had him recalled for a further trial. A crowd of believers gathered round the villa where he was being kept, probably for moral support. The trial was brief. Cyprian was invited to conform to the Roman rites; he refused.

The proconsul pronounced sentence: 'You have long lived an irreligious life... and professed yourself to be an open enemy to the gods and the religion of Rome... you shall be made an example... It is the sentence of this court that Thascius Cyprianus be executed by the sword.'

The bishop was straight away led out, accompanied by a great crowd. Because his hands were unsteady, the presbyter Julian fastened a handkerchief around his eyes. So Cyprian died. His body was removed by night to a burial ground, accompanied by a procession carrying torches.

During his ten years as a bishop much of Cyprian's time and energy was spent in dealing with troubles within the Church as well as facing the constant threat of persecution. He stood the test well and departed this life in a blaze of glory. He will be remembered for his insistence on the bishop as a God-appointed ruler in the Church, for his concept of the clergy as sacrificing priests and for his support of each bishop's right to reach his own decisions. But above all for the pastoral concern of his flock, for whom he cared above all else.

As for the Church in North Africa, it later fell prey to the Muslim invasion of the seventh century. Hundreds of churches became mosques or were destroyed and only a few Christian communities survived here and there. It was rather like 'a removing of the candlestick out of its place'.

PERSECUTION OF CHRISTIANS UNDER ROMAN EMPERORS

EMPEROR and LOCATION	PERSECUTION	MARTYRS
NERO (54-68) Rome (65-68)	* Fire in city - Christians made scapegoat * Large numbers arrested and convicted - subject to horrendous treatment	* Apostles Peter and Paul
DOMITIAN (81-96) Rome and Asia (96)	* Emperor demanded to be worshipped as 'Lord and god' * Not an attempt to crush Christianity, but aimed at a few individuals * The Apostle John banished to Patmos around this time	* Flavius Clemens, Domitian's cousin * Others also executed
TRAJAN (98-117)	* Spread of Christianity meant pagan temples nearly emptied * Christianity illegal, though no properly defined law against it * Christians not to be hunted out, but to be punished if refused to recant * Many denied their faith and offered sacrifices	* Ignatius, Bishop of Antioch
HADRIAN (117-138)	* Pursued Trajan's policy * Hadrian requested popular clamour and decreed that investigations should be properly investigated * After death of Polycarp, Antoninus sent rescript to East, ordering use of legal processes and forbidding attacks on Christians	* Polycarp, Bishop of Smyrna
MARCUS AURELIUS(161-180). Rome (165) Lyons and Vienne (Gaul), (177) North Africa (180)	* New decrees against Christians led to severest outbreak yet * 90 year old Bishop of Lyons tortured, died in prison	* Justin Martyr in 165 * 45 believers in Gaul, including Blandina, a slave-girl, in 177
SEPTIMIUS SEVERUS (193-211) Egypt and North Africa (202-211)	* In 202, passed decree forbidding citizens to become Christians or Jews * Persecution of Alexander regarded as sign of anti-Christ	* 5 catechumens martyred at Carthage, in 203, including Perpetua, 22 years old and Felicitas, a slave

PERSECUTION OF CHRISTIANS UNDER ROMAN EMPERORS

EMPEROR and LOCATION	PERSECUTION	MARTYRS
MAXIMINUS (235-237) Confined to a few provinces	* Introduced repressive measures against Church leaders * Localised attacks - Christians able to escape by moving to another province * Two rival bishops exiled to Sardinia.	* Fabian, Bishop of Rome * Babylas, Bishop of Antioch * Alexander, Bishop of Jerusalem.
DECIUS (241-251) Rome, Antioch and Carthage	* Most successful and systematic attempt to stamp out the Faith * Christians commanded to sacrifice to gods, or suffer torture and imprisonment. Many died, including Origen of Caesarea.	* Xystus, Bishop of Rome * Bishop of Tarragona * Cyprian, Bishop of Carthage, beheaded in 258
VALERIAN (253-260) Rome, Spain, North Africa (257-260)	* Edict in 257 banned Christian meetings under threat of death * Second edict condemned clergy to death.	* Alban, Roman soldier in Britain * Romanus, deacon of Caesarea * Peter, Bishop of Alexandria * Countless others burned alive or beheaded.
DIOCLETIAN (284-305) Eastern Empire and Africa (303-311)	* The Great Persecution - longest and most severe * Isolated cases of martyrdom, especially in army * Edicts for suppression of Christianity: - churches and property to be destroyed - Christian meetings banned, clergy to be arrested - all compelled to sacrifice to gods - forbidden to profess Christianity.	* A few recorded deaths in army. * Some Christians murdered by pagans.
JULIAN (361-363) Confined to a few provinces	* A heathen Emperor, though baptised as a child * Attempt to discredit Christianity and restore heathen religion * Temples re-opened but churches not destroyed * Christians forbidden to act as teachers	
VALENS (364-375) Eastern Europe 370	* Of Arian persuasion - opposed to orthodox Christianity *Attempted to propagate Arianism	* 80 protesters imprisoned on ship and burned to death

TWO

The Christian Empire

The greatest onslaught the Church had ever endured took place during the closing years of the reign of the Emperor Diocletian (284-305), which was a final attempt to wipe out Christianity. As before, there were countless martyrs; but many gave up their faith as church buildings and books were burned, believers tortured and drowned, men despatched to the mines and women condemned to a life of prostitution.

In a remote outpost of the Roman Empire, a young man was at that time rising to prominence who was to become one of the greatest Emperors Rome had ever known. His reign proved to be a turning point in the history of both Church and Empire, inaugurating a period of peace and stability together with an abundance of mixed blessings.

CONSTANTINE THE GREAT (died 337): Emperor of Rome
Constantine was the son of a nobleman, Constantius Chlorus, who had married a simple serving maid called Helena, though was later forced for political reasons to abandon her. As a junior Emperor, Constantius ruled Spain, Gaul and Britain and was regarded as a successful general. When Diocletian abdicated he became the western Emperor, but ruled for only one year. He died at York in 306, his son at his side.

The Roman troops immediately proclaimed Constantine as the new Emperor, much to the consternation of the court at Rome. It led to some considerable intrigue and in-fighting, and Constantine took the opportunity to march on Rome to secure the title for himself.

As he approached the capital he had two remarkable experiences that convinced him of the truth of Christianity and altered the course of his life. So far he had worshipped the 'unconquered sun' as the sole god, but from his father had gained some idea of a supreme being that governed the world.

The first experience happened at about midday as he was praying to his father's god asking him 'to tell him who he was ... and to help him in his present difficulties'. As he prayed, a most incredible sign appeared to him and he saw a cross of light in the heavens, with an inscription, 'By this sign conquer' attached to it. That night in his sleep Christ appeared to him and commanded him to make a likeness of the sign and use it in battle against his enemies. Later, while camped at the entrance to Rome, he was directed in a dream to mark 'the heavenly sign of God' on the shield of his soldiers. This he did, using the *Chi-Rho* symbol which are the first two letters of the Greek word for Christ.

From then onwards it appears that Constantine thought of himself as a Christian and in his letters often spoke of himself in such terms.

When battle began, Constantine won a complete victory at the Milvian Bridge outside Rome (312) and became the Emperor of the western half of the Empire (Licinius remained Emperor of the eastern half). He credited his success to the God of the Christians; he had challenged the Christians' God, and that God had kept his pledge.

Subsequent events, however, raised doubts about whether his 'conversion' was genuine, as alongside his new-found belief in God he continued his allegiance to the gods of Rome. As Emperor he was officially 'Pontifex Maximus', the chief priest of the state religion. Some Roman coins of the period carried the image of pagan gods (others had the Chi-Rho symbol) and he erected statues of Roman gods in the new city of Constantinople.

Favoured Position

Yet after his victory at the Milvian Bridge his attitude towards Christianity changed. State sacrifices to the gods were discontinued; he gave the Church a favoured position and pursued a policy of humanitarian reforms that suggested a genuine concern.

His first gesture was to allow all citizens the right to choose their own religion, placing Christians on equal terms with Jews and pagans. At the same time, all property confiscated during the persecution was to be returned to believers. This ruling is usually known as the 'Edict of Milan,' though no copy of the edict has ever been found so it may simply have been a general proclamation.

In the following years further laws were enacted which introduced a truly Christian morality and in which nearly every relation in human society was altered. It was forbidden to brand slaves and criminals on the face because 'men were made in the image of God'; crucifixion of slaves was abolished; gladiatorial shows were prohibited; unwanted babies were no longer put to death; and attempts were made to stabilise marriage by severely punishing cases of sexual immorality.

The Church also benefited financially and materially from the Emperor's patronage. New copies of the Scriptures were made available, members of the clergy were given positions of state importance and were exempt from taxes on their lands (a privilege already accorded to pagan priests); and a fixed proportion of state revenue was set aside for Church charitable works.

Many new church buildings were erected on sites where martyrs had died. In the Holy Land the name Jerusalem was restored (the Romans had renamed it Aelia Capitolina) and the Emperor made an effort to locate the exact spot of Christ's crucifixion, where he built the Church of the Holy Sepulchre. At Rome two basilicas were built to commemorate the deaths of Peter and Paul, on the Vatican Hill and on the Ostian Way just outside the walls.

Constantine encouraged pilgrimages to the Holy Land and his mother, Helena, restored to a position of honour, zealously searched for the ancient Christian sites. She was responsible for the foundation of basilicas at Bethlehem and on the Mount of Olives and, according to tradition, discovered the true cross on which Christ had been crucified.

Christianity Fashionable

Because of the preferential treatment of the Church, Christianity became fashionable. Many pagans started to attend church and became nominal members, perhaps to enjoy some of the benefits Christians had gained. Correct doctrine became more important than right behaviour, and there was a lowering of moral standards.

Other changes were taking place that tended to wean believers away from the personal 'Faith once delivered to the saints'. Formalism in worship appeared; priests repeated set prayers and the congregation listened to a performance; the use of vestments, candles and incense was introduced. A form of ritual gradually crept into services, replacing the simplicity of earlier years. The Church responded by allowing Constantine the opportunity to exercise spiritual authority. On two major issues, Church leaders appealed to the Emperor for a ruling on matters which they themselves should have decided upon.

In 313 a group of Christians from Carthage begged his support in a dispute with their bishop. The Donatists, who refused to accept Caecillian as Bishop of Carthage because they felt he had been a traitor during the persecution, championed their own nominee, Donatus. The Emperor called a council of bishops at Arles (Gaul) in 314 which dismissed the charges and decided in favour of Caecillian.

A further opportunity arose in 325 when the Emperor called and presided over another council of bishops at Nicaea in north-west Asia

Minor. Nearly three hundred bishops attended and it was the first ever ecumenical council of the Church. The dispute originated in Alexandria, where a presbyter called Arius was teaching that Jesus was neither God nor man but something between, denying the power of the cross.

The debate centred around the true nature of the Person of Christ and the need to adopt a statement of faith that would clearly define what Christians believed about Jesus. Arius and his creed were condemned by the bishops and the one put forward by Athanasius was accepted. The crucial phrase in this creed involved use of the Greek word *homoousion,* where the Son was declared to be 'of one substance' or 'essence' with the Father. Although the term is ambiguous, it secured the assent of all but two of the bishops and achieved a temporary sort of unity. Afterwards, credal professions of faith came to be used as standards whereby orthodoxy was measured.

Pomp and Splendour

Constantine now saw himself as ruler of both Church and Empire. His quest for power was reflected in his craze for pomp and splendour. From the time he became sole Emperor he began to wear a diadem, his imperial robes were adorned with pearls and jewellery and he carried the ceremonial regalia.

His thoughts of aggrandisement led to the founding of a new capital for the Empire. In 324, tired of Rome, he began the creation of Constantinople, 'the new city of Constantine'. When completed in 330 it rivalled Rome for its glory and survived until it fell to the rule of Islam in 1453.

But Constantine was not to live long enough to enjoy the pleasures of his new city. As he lay dying he was at last baptised into the Church and spent the remaining days of his life arrayed in his baptismal robes. He died at the Feast of Pentecost in the year 337 and was buried in Constantinople amid universal grief.

Constantine was afterwards accorded the title of 'Great', an honour rarely bestowed throughout history. As an Emperor, he was adroit and skilful; he created a single, centralised Roman Empire in which all peoples were 'subjected to one peaceable sceptre', and his creation of a New Rome was a masterly move.

As a churchman his attempts at unity were without lasting success and the controversy at Nicaea continued after his death. In the Eastern Empire he was made a 'saint' and still bears the further title 'Equal of the Apostles,' though the benefits he conferred were of doubtful consequence.

MAJOR HERESIES OF THE EARLY CHURCH

HERESY and LEADING TEACHERS	HISTORICAL BACKGROUND	TEACHINGS
EBIONITES 2nd century	* Development of Judaizers in New Testament * Ascetic sect of Jewish Christians, flourished east of River Jordan * Name probably derived from Hebrew and means 'poor' * Rejected Paul's letters, used gospel of Matthew	* Emphasised Law of Moses, including sabbath and circumcision * Regarded Jesus as greatest of the prophets, the natural son of Joseph and Mary, but not the Eternal Son
GNOSTICISM 2nd century Cerinthus Alexandria Basilides Valentinus Tatian Marcion	* Complex religious movement based on pagan philosophy * Rejected Old Testament and Judaism * Pre-Christian in origin, later formed into sects * Refuted by Irenaeus who wrote *Against Heresies*	* Based on 'gnosis' i.e. knowledge of a way of salvation, a mystical enlightenment * Claimed to have derived this 'gnosis' from the Apostles * A form of dualism: matter is evil and salvation available only to those who had 'gnosis' or were 'spiritual' * God remote and unknowable, approached through series of 30 emanations or aeons.
MONTANISM 2nd century Montanus Prisca and Maximilla	*Originated Phrygia, spread to Rome and North Africa * Trend in Church towards formalism and worldliness *Tertullian an adherent, but withdrew later	* Millenium close at hand, outpouring of the Holy Spirit expected * Return to ascetic practices e.g. celibacy, fastings, abstinence from meat
ARIANISM 2nd century Arius, priest in Alexandria Eusebius bishop of Nicomedia	* Heresy condemned (319), Arius excommunicated * Council of Nicea (325) called to deal with controversy * Arius recalled from exile (334) but died suddenly	* Denied divinity of Christ * Son of God not eternal, but created by the Father as instrument for creation of world * Inferior to Father in nature and dignity
APOLLINAR-IANISM 4th century Apollinarius, bishop of Laodicea	* Church in West accepted conception of full deity and full manhood of Christ * Ideas in East confused, led to discussion, relation of human and divine in Christ * Heresy condemned by Council of Constantinople (381)	* Denied true humanity of Christ * Jesus had a human body but no spirit - was replaced by 'Logos' (Word) * He could not redeem human nature, only its spiritual elements

EARLY CHURCH COUNCILS

LOCATION and EMPEROR	KEY FIGURES	POINTS OF INTEREST, MAIN ISSUES, COURSE OF EVENTS
NICAEA (Bithynia) 325 Constantine (313-337)	Eusebius, Bishop of Caesarea Athanasius Arius Alexander	* First ecumenical council - attempt to bring all parts of Christian Church together. * Drafted original form of Nicene Creed. * Arian heresy condemned; Eusebius presented orthodox creed for discussion * Use of term *homoousios* (the Son is of 'one substance with the Father') accepted * Four anti-Arian anathemas added
CONSTANTINOPLE (Thracia) 381 Theodosius I (379-395)	Meletius Gregory, Bishop of Nazianzus Gregory, Bishop of Nyssa	* Second ecumenical council (though only Eastern bishops present) * Called to end Arian controversy * Ratified doctrine of Christ formulated at Nicaea * Affirmed deity of the Holy Spirit * Condemned Apollinarianism
EPHESUS (Asia) 431 Theodosius II (408-450)	Cyril, Bishop of Alexandria Nestorius, Patriarch of Constantinople John, Bishop of Antioch	* Summoned to settle Nestorian controversy * Nestorius banished to Upper Egypt, his documents condemned * Creed of Nicaea reaffirmed * Use of term *theotokos* ('God-bearer') upheld
CHALCEDON (Bithynia) 451 Marcian (450-455)	Pope (Leo) sent four legates Dioscurus, Patriarch of Alexandria	* Largest council to date, 520 bishops present * Acknowledged Christ's two natures in one person, he was fully God and fully man * Formulated the creed of Chalcedon, regarded as the 'orthodox' solution of the Christological problem

EUSEBIUS (263-339): Father of Church History

The Acts of the Apostles covers a period of about thirty years, from Pentecost through to Paul's release from prison in Rome around the year 62. For the next three hundred years we are indebted to the work of Eusebius of Caesarea, who painstakingly gathered information from a remarkable number of sources to complete his monumental *History of the Church*. He gave us a knowledge of those early years that would otherwise have been lost.

All the documents referred to in the *History* are no longer in existence and are known only second hand through Eusebius' work. The reason for this is quite interesting. During the first three centuries, authors wrote on papyrus which was a perishable material and had only a short life. It was not until the beginning of the fourth century that vellum - made from skins of calves, kids and lambs - was substituted for papyrus, giving a longer life. At the same time, most literary works were presented in codex (book) form rather than a scroll.

Eusebius' work has consequently survived whereas those of most of his predecessors perished. The result is an authoritative account of the story of the Early Church, its persecutions and martyrdoms, its heresies and divisions.

Wealthy and Educated

By the third century many converts to Christianity came from the wealthy and educated classes and this was probably the case with Eusebius. He was born in Palestine around the year 263, during the reign of Emperor Gallienus. The persecution of Valerian (253-259) ended with his death in 259. His son made amends by restoring Church property, ushering in a period of peace.

Hardly anything is known of Eusebius during his early years. There is no indication that he was brought up in a Christian family, but he received Christian instruction and baptism at Caesarea, the city founded by Herod the Great. In 296 he saw - and may even have met - the youthful Constantine who was touring the Eastern Empire with the Emperor, Diocletian (284-305).

The major influence on his early life was that of the presbyter Pamphilus at Caesarea. Pamphilus was a scholar of considerable repute, dedicated to the spread of sound learning. He had emigrated from Alexandria and founded a notable library and theological school at Caesarea. It seems that Eusebius studied under Pamphilus and the two became firm friends. Indeed, Eusebius always spoke of his master in the highest terms of praise and affection. During this period of study Eusebius gave much time to reading both pagan and Christian authors, reading that was later to bear rich fruit in his own writings.

Under Pamphilus he also copied and corrected portions of the Scriptures, and made copies of books, especially those of the theologian Origen. It was during his time as a student that he began to gather material for two of his major works. First was his *Chronicle* which was a history of the world up to that time, then his *History of the Church* which eventually ran to ten volumes. With Pamphilus he also composed a *Defence of Origen* who in 230 had been deposed as a priest and afterwards settled in Caesarea.

Great Persecution

In February 303 the 'Great Persecution' of Diocletian broke out and continued intermittently for ten years. The events witnessed by Eusebius were recorded in his *History* and also in his *Martyrs of Palestine*. By now he had been ordained presbyter and was therefore under threat of arrest. In March the persecution reached Caesarea and a number of believers paid the supreme penalty for their faith.

Over the next two years further edicts intensified the persecution; church buildings were destroyed, copies of the Scriptures burned and believers tortured and executed.

Towards the end of 308 Pamphilus was arrested and tortured. Eusebius may have been in prison with him, but certainly he had access to his friend in the prison where they continued their writing together. In his *History* Eusebius wrote of this time, 'We saw with our very eyes the very houses of prayer cast down to their foundations from top to bottom, and the inspired and sacred Scriptures committed to the flames in the midst of the market places, and the pastors of the churches, some shamefully hiding themselves here and there.'

Early in 309 Pamphilus was executed and Eusebius was free to travel to other parts. It may be that like Cyprian before him, he decided that for a time it was wiser to avoid the persecution by being absent from Caesarea. He first visited Tyre and then moved south to Egypt, where again he was confronted with the threat of death. He witnessed the arrest of many Christians who were maimed, blinded and mutilated before being sent off to the mines. Eusebius was also arrested and thrown into prison, but by the following year he was free and back again in Caesarea. Nothing is known of the circumstances of his imprisonment or why he should have escaped unscathed.

A quarter of a century later, at the Council of Tyre, a bishop taunted Eusebius and charged him with cowardice and apostasy: 'Pray tell me, were you not with me in prison during the persecution? And I lost an eye on behalf of the truth, but you appear to have received no bodily injury, neither have you suffered martyrdom, but have remained alive with no mutilation.'

His writings give no indication what happened in prison, except to suggest he endured suffering yet without apostasy. If this were not so, he would not have been appointed as bishop. After 311 the persecution petered out and two years later Constantine's edict of toleration was introduced.

Literary Activity

Amazingly during these past ten traumatic years Eusebius experienced the most fruitful period of his literary activity. As well as making additions to his *Chronicle* and *History Of The Church*, he wrote a *Life of Pamphilus*, began his *Martyrs of Palestine* and completed some ten other books on Christian topics. All this was accomplished while on his travels with the need to undertake research in libraries at both Caesarea and Jerusalem!

In 314 Eusebius was elected bishop at Caesarea and his literary activity ceased for a while. His time became taken up with urgent ecclesiastical affairs; after the years of persecution he needed to spend time in rebuilding the Church and its properties.

Before long, however, his work was interrupted by a doctrinal dispute of ecumenical proportions, the most widespread heresy in the history of the early Church. It started in Alexandria about 318 when a priest called Arius expounded the idea that Christ was not completely God, that there was a time when he did not exist and that he was capable of evil as well as virtue. The heresy caused a serious split in the Church and the Emperor, anxious to maintain a semblance of unity, called a council of bishops at Nicaea for May 325.

Meanwhile the matter was raised earlier in the year at a local council at Antioch. When Eusebius explained his views, which were much in sympathy with those of Arius, he was provisionally excommunicated. What happened at the Council of Nicea, where Eusebius was given the chance to repent, was described in his *Life of Constantine*, written after the Emperor's death.

The council was presided over by the Emperor, with Eusebius, who gave the opening address, at his side. The main contestants were Arius and his powerful supporters, opposed by Athanasius (who became the greatest opponent of Arianism), secretary to the bishop of Alexandria, with the third group of 'conservatives,' represented by Eusebius, who preferred to remain neutral.

First Arius was examined and his ideas quickly condemned. Then Eusebius submitted his baptismal creed in use at Caesarea; it was amended by the inclusion of the anti-Arian phase 'of one substance with the Father' (Greek, *homoousis*) and accepted. (Seemingly his name was now cleared.) The Caesarean creed was then used as a basis for further discussion. More amendments were made and four anathemas added, totally safeguarding the teaching about the Trinity.

Eusebius was not completely happy with the new creed and signed the document unwillingly. In his account of the council, he not surprisingly omitted the details and concentrated simply on the externals.

High Esteem

By now the bishop had become a firm friend of the Emperor and their admiration was mutual. Constantine held Eusebius in high esteem, and Eusebius was given to frequent eulogies of the Emperor! Further evidence of the regard came when the Emperor offered Eusebius the bishopric of Antioch, which he had the humility to turn down. But he accepted the position of president of the next synod, at Tyre in 335.

Despite the heavy pressure of ecclesiastical duties, Eusebius again took up his pen and produced further literary works in the years after Nicaea. In addition, he prepared for the Emperor fifty copies of the Scriptures - 'on parchment (i.e. vellum), in a legible manner and in a convenient portable form' (codex?) - for the use of the church in the new city of Constantinople. The relationship flourished further, as Eusebius was given the honour of addressing the Emperor and his bishops assembled for the dedication of the Church of the Holy Sepulchre at Jerusalem in 335.

In return the bishop composed a flattering oration, *In Praise of Constantine,* for the Emperor's thirtieth anniversary, in which he spoke of the Christian Empire with the Emperor as the living image of Christ!

When Constantine died, Eusebius wrote a *Life of Constantine*; it was not so much a biography as an extended obituary, assessing the importance of the Emperor - whom he believed to be God's representative on earth - and proclaiming his virtues. Eusebius died two years later, on 30th May 339.

His greatness lies essentially in his work as a historian, which remains of inestimable value to the Church, and he was the first writer to attempt a history on a grand scale, setting the pattern for future historians. But while his political ideal helped to create the Christian Empire of Byzantium, his theology was as suspect as that of some of his heretical contemporaries.

EARLY CREEDS

TITLE	ORIGINS	BACKGROUND DATA
APOSTLES' CREED	* Probably formulated in Rome between 150-175 * Based on confessions of belief in Gospels, and especially on Great Commission (Matthew 28:19-20)	* Reaffirms facts of the Faith and is a summary of what apostles believed and taught * Taught to catechumens and used as a baptismal creed * Gained wide acceptance in Western Church * Regarded as having apostolic authority by time of Tertullian * Title first discovered c 390 in letter of Ambrose, Bishop of Milan
NICENE CREED	* Council of Nicaea 325	* Based on creed used by Eusebius at Caesarea * Drawn up to defend orthodox Faith against Arianism * Clauses about the Holy Spirit added at Council of Constantinople, 381 * Expresses a maturer Christian experience than the Apostles' Creed * Longer formula used in Eucharist, both Eastern and Western churches
ATHANASIAN CREED	* Probably composed by a theologian from Spain, 5th century	* A Latin hymn, beginning 'Quicunque vult...', became known as 'The Faith of St Athanasius' * An exposition of the meaning of the Nicene Creed, focusing on the Trinity and the Incarnation * Intended as a means of instruction, warning against false doctrine.

AMBROSE (340-397): Bishop of Milan

Towards the end of the fourth century the most prominent figure in western Christianity was Ambrose, Bishop of Milan. He was in his day the supreme defender of the true Faith and, it has been suggested, 'the greatest force of his time for righteousness'. Yet until the age of thirty-four he had not taken up any ecclesiastical office or even been baptised.

Ambrose came from a Roman noble family which had a long Christian pedigree. His father held high military office and was the Prefect of the Roman province of Gallia, which included Britain, Gaul and Spain. Ambrose's family was close knit and developed a strong love and respect for each other.

When his father died, the family went to live in Rome where Ambrose was educated. He studied law - the usual path in those days to the highest civic positions - and was appointed to the court of the Praetorian Prefect of Italy. Promotion soon came and he was appointed as Consular Magistrate (i.e. governor) of the Roman province of Liguria and Aemilia, centred on the city of Milan. His qualities as a magistrate were widely recognised and he became known as a conscientious and genuinely religious official.

In 374 a most astounding event occurred that speedily changed the whole course of his life and profoundly affected Church history. The Arian Bishop of Milan died and two opposing factions met in a church to debate the appointment of his successor. Agreement seemed impossible and a serious squabble developed. The Consular was called to the church to mediate; as Ambrose addressed the crowd, a voice - some said it was that of a child - was heard above the strife calling, 'Ambrose for bishop!' The crowd warmed to the idea and the cry was heard resounding round the church: 'We will have Ambrose for bishop!'

Baptism

Ambrose resisted the pressure and eventually managed to escape from the church. After several days, however, he yielded to the call; he gave up his government post and prepared himself for his new office. His first action was to dispose of his wealth and property, then he began a course of theological study. Arrangements were made for his baptism, a step he had deliberately avoided because of its awesome responsibility, and on the eighth day after his call he was consecrated bishop.

Ambrose became famous as a preacher, a duty he took seriously. In his sermons he aimed to build up the believers, to safeguard them from heresy and to encourage them in purity of living. His preaching reflected practical, moral concerns and he spoke without compromise on matters affecting public life. He brought to his office his skills as a government official and became renowned as a Church administrator. And he ruled his diocese with the firmness of a secular governor - of the best type!

With his flair for poetry, Ambrose began to compose hymns and became known as the founder of Latin hymnody. Twelve of his compositions have remained in use right up to this century, including *O splendour of God's glory bright,* and *O Trinity, most blessed light.*

Much of Ambrose's greatness, however, lies in the spiritual authority and influence he wielded over the Emperors of his day. As the Bishop of Milan (the city where the western Emperors now resided), he became the equivalent to the 'court bishop' - the power behind the throne.

He enjoyed a special relationship with the young Emperor Gratian who ruled in the West (373-383) and then with Theodosius in the East (379-395), as well as with other Roman rulers. Under Gratian he presided over the downfall of paganism in the Roman Empire. Gratian was the first Emperor ever to refuse the title of Pontifex Maximus, the high priest of the state religion, a title Constantine held dearly.

Two years later he struck at the very roots of paganism by removing the altar (and perhaps the statue) of the goddess 'Victory' from the Senate House. Symmachus, a leading senator, was sent from Rome to plead for its return, but in vain; Ambrose staunchly supported the Emperor in the matter and the ban remained. Although a few years later a temporary reprieve was won, the Emperor Theodosius finally defeated the old Roman religion.

The True Faith

By the end of the fourth century, paganism had bowed to the power of Christianity. The Church would no longer tolerate any other form of Christianity than that permitted by law; only the *catholic* Faith was allowed.

Since the second century the term *catholic* had been increasingly used to denote the true Faith as laid down by the apostles. With the rise of heresies such as Gnosticism and Arianism, it had become necessary to distinguish between the true Church and the false. Those Churches throughout Christendom that held to an accepted Rule of Faith and subscribed to a recognised body of sacred literature were considered members of the *catholic* (i.e. universal) Church.

In 380, the Emperor Theodosius published an edict in which he ordered that the Faith taught to the Romans by Peter should be accepted by all nations. The title of *catholic* was henceforth to be reserved for those churches which adhered to the creed declared at the Council of Nicaea, and it became the legal religion of the Romans. Already the church in Rome was claiming spiritual authority over the other churches, and the bishop there began to assume the title of *Pope*.

The chief opponent to the true religion was, as in the time of Constantine, the heresy of Arianism. It even had a foothold in Milan where Ambrose was in residence. Matters came to a head in 385 when the Empress Mother, Justina, mother to the young Valentinian II, requested the use of a church building in Milan for Arian worship. When refused, the Arians tried to take it by force. Ambrose organised a sit-in and the Christians spent their time singing some of the hymns he had composed. This attempt to re-establish Arianism failed, and except for some minor pockets of resistance among the barbarian troops, the heresy faded away.

Church and State

The Christian Empire was now firmly established and the State was responsible by law for maintaining the Faith. Under Theodosius Church and State were united. But it was as a result of Ambrose's stand against the Emperor that the Church gained the ascendancy. As the bishop affirmed: 'The Emperor has no rights over what belongs to God.' Two incidents serve to illustrate this point.

When in 388 a group of Christians, led on by the bishop, robbed and burned down a synagogue, the Emperor ordered it to be rebuilt at the bishop's expense. Ambrose felt this amounted to apostasy and wrote to the Emperor, arguing that 'the maintenance of civil law is secondary to religious interests'. He even preached a sermon on the matter in Theodosius' presence. Under the threat of with-holding communion from him, the Emperor withdrew the order.

Two years later a commander of the imperial troops executed a popular charioteer from Thessalonica. A mob retaliated by murdering the commander. In response - and rather out of character - Theodosius ordered a massacre of the offenders. Ambrose's protest came too late, and seven thousand citizens were put to death.

The bishop remonstrated with the Emperor who, it was said, kept away from church for eight months. When he attempted to enter the church on Christmas Day he was met by the bishop who reproved him, and would not allow him to be present at the Eucharist until he had done penance. Whether or not the story is entirely true is unsure, but it illustrates the power of Ambrose's position.

To the end of his days Ambrose remained a statesman as well as a bishop, and was distinguished as a ruler by his wisdom and common sense. He had a genuine humanitarian concern, not only for his own flock but for the universal Church, and his sermons reveal a practical turn of mind. Most of all, he established the principle of the authority of the Church above that of the State, and fought successfully for orthodox doctrine and a Church based on the deity of Jesus Christ.

His death marked the end of the fourth century - an age of martyrs and creeds, the fall of paganism and the rise of the Church. His life brought the era to a fitting close.

JEROME (331-420): Scholar Of Bethlehem

The fourth century Church in the western half of the Roman Empire had not developed to the same degree as its counterpart in the East. The Greek-speaking East could boast of its great scholars Eusebius and Origen, but the Latin Church had nothing yet to parallel their achievements. It was not until Jerome that the West produced one of its most eminent sons, a man who exercised a wide influence both in his lifetime and afterwards.

Jerome's parents were well-to-do Christians who owned considerable land and property in northern Dalmatia (modern Yugoslavia), where he was born. As a child he was given an expensive education and also taught the rudiments of the Christian Faith, though he was not baptised until he was of more mature years. He was educated in Rome where he studied under the most famous teacher of the day, and then graduated to a school of rhetoric, the ancient equivalent to a university. It was in Rome that he developed an interest in language and classical literature, reading such authors as Cicero and Virgil, which in later life influenced his writings.

Slippery Paths

Like many teenagers when free from parental control, Jerome faced all the temptations of a cosmopolitan city and could not cope. He soon found himself in the grip of 'passions' and fell on to the 'slippery path' of youth, though he gives no further explanation of what happened.

Eventually he was filled with shame and seems at this point to have made a Christian commitment. In 366 he offered himself for baptism and received the 'vesture of Christ' (i.e. baptismal robes). After that he spent his Sundays in the company of Christian friends, touring the catacombs and looking for the tombs of martyrs.

In the fourth century it was common practice for Christians who took their faith seriously to break with the world - career, marriage and wealth - in order 'to hold themselves free for God and Christ'. This attitude reflects the ascetic strain then present in Christianity and spreading throughout the Church. Like Ambrose, there were Christians who set a premium on celibacy and in some circles the practice was becoming increasingly fashionable.

After completing his education, Jerome decided to renounce his secular ambitions and live a life of contemplation. He moved in 370 to Aquileia in Italy, not far from his family home, where he joined a number of young men in a religious community who were intent on leading an ascetic life. The experiment lasted three years; Jerome's uncontrollable tongue and his passionate temperament caused some strained relationships and forced him to withdraw. He also appears to have fallen out with his family who evidently disapproved of his monastic practices.

His next move was to Antioch (Syria) in 374, travelling in the company of friends and taking his whole library with him. He fell ill with a fever and in a dream saw himself before the throne of God where he was accused of not being a Christian but a disciple of Cicero, for 'where your heart is there is your treasure'. When the Judge ordered him to be flogged, Jerome pleaded for mercy and on a promise never to read worldly books again, was released. The effect was dramatic, and he began an even more zealous study of Christian books than before.

He joined a colony of hermits living in the Syrian desert in an attempt 'to find God.' Each hermit lived in a separate cave, but they met together on Saturdays and Sundays for worship. In addition to his Bible studies, Jerome began to learn Hebrew, a decision that was to have a great impact upon his future.

Once again, however, he ran into trouble with his companions who looked upon him as an intruder, so he returned to civilisation. He settled in the Eastern capital of Constantinople and became a disciple of Gregory of Nazianzus. He mastered a second language, Greek, and launched into a new activity - translation. He prepared a Latin version of Eusebius' *Chronicle*, with additions, and translated some of Origen's works.

In Rome

As a result of an invitation, Jerome returned to Rome where he became a secretary to Bishop Damasus and was able to make further use of his translation skills. At the bishop's suggestion, he prepared a revision of the

---

The canon of Scripture

The Greek word *canon*, originally a rod or a bar, came to be used of a list of rules or books. While the Jewish Scriptures (the Old Testament) were written over a period of nearly 2000 years, the list of recognised books was not completed until after the time of Jesus, about the end of the first century AD. The Church very quickly recognised some of its own writings, especially those of the Apostles, as of equal authority and inspiration. The Gospels and most of the Epistles were accepted in all quarters of the Church by the second century; the list of twenty-seven books was first mentioned by Athanasius (365) and Jerome (383). They were accepted as canonical by an ecclesiastical council at Hippo Regius (393), North Africa.

Psalter and made a special study of the Old Testament, comparing the Greek and Hebrew versions.

While in Rome he was introduced to a number of noble families and became a special friend of one, Paula, and her three daughters. The family used their home for study of the Scriptures and Jerome became their teacher; he also encouraged their interest in ascetic observances.

In 383/384 Bishop Damasus asked Jerome to undertake a revision of the existing Latin texts of the Bible and the production of a single standard version. Since the second century there had existed a confusing variety of Scripture portions in Old Latin and it was felt necessary to have a new version based on the original languages. He started by translating the Four Gospels and soon completed the task. When the work was published it was greeted with howls of protest and he was accused of tampering with the inspired words of the Gospels. At the same time he had managed to win a lot of enemies among the clergy of Rome, mostly for his criticism of their expensive and worldly habits, and decided to leave the city.

The Holy Land

Accompanied by a band of devout women, including the wealthy Paula, he journeyed to the Holy Land and in 386 took up residence in Bethlehem. Using Paula's wealth, he built a monastery which became a centre for his work of teaching and translating; a convent was also built for the women, with Paula in charge.

Despite further possible hostility Jerome started work on the Old Testament, making a fresh translation based on the Hebrew. Progress was slow and there were frequent interruptions - his responsibilities at the monastery, preaching in the Church of the Nativity, his involvement in several theological controversies that demanded much correspondence, including with the scholar Augustine of Hippo, and writing Bible commentaries.

His translation was not finished until 405/406, and even then it is not sure that he actually completed the whole Bible, there is evidence to suggest it was finished by another hand. Yet again his work was criticised except for a few friends who applauded his efforts. In time, however, his Bible - known as the Vulgate (i.e. in common use) - became accepted as the standard translation, though it was not finally accepted as 'authentic' by the Roman Catholic Church until 1546.

By now Jerome was about seventy-five years old, yet his mind and pen were constantly active. He produced Bible commentaries on the prophets, and corresponded with a number of individuals about their spiritual problems, especially exhorting them to follow after chastity. He also debated with a British monk, Pelagius, who was the leader of a heretical group.

At Rome, storm clouds gathered over the Empire as the barbarian armies marched down from the north; to Jerome it seemed like the advent of the Antichrist and the end of the world. In 410 the Roman army was defeated and the city fell to its enemies; its glory was no more. King Alaric's Goths were Arian by religion and they showed the utmost reverence towards the churches and Christian treasures. In the provinces the news about Rome was greeted with gloom, but life went on as before.

Jerome, now without his companion Paula, became more and more depressed and overtaken by 'the feebleness of old age'. When he died in 420 he was buried in the Church of the Nativity, a few yards away from the grotto in which Jesus was supposed to have been born.

Jerome was an eccentric writer with a passion for quarrelling with most people with whom he came into contact. Fame came to him late and it was not until many years after his death that the value of his translation of the Bible began to be appreciated. He is now recognised as the greatest of early Christian scholars and has earned for himself a place in history as one of the four 'Doctors of the Early Church'.

The Vulgate Bible

Although Latin was the language of Rome, most of the New Testament books were originally written in Greek. The spread of Christianity led to translations into other languages, and by the second/third century there were New Testaments in Latin, Syriac and Coptic. Jerome's Vulgate was a revision of a number of 'clumsy' Old Latin versions, but the separate portions were not collected together within one cover until the sixth century. This version remained the standard Bible of the western world throughout the Middle Ages and the basis for the first English translations.

AUGUSTINE (354-431): Bishop of Hippo

Since the middle ages certain Christian theologians have been accorded the title 'Doctor of the Church', and up to the present day over thirty such awards have been made. Possibly the most outstanding holder of this title is Augustine, one of the most important figures in early Christianity since the apostle Paul, and one whose influence on Western Christianity still lingers on today.

Augustine's parents were quite contrasting personalities and both of them exercised a deep influence on the young boy, causing conflict and unease in the family. His pagan father, Patrick, was a man of modest means and owned a few acres of land. A hot-tempered man, he was often unfaithful to his wife and his wayward example no doubt contributed to his son's errant behaviour.

Yet it was the consistent witness and the persistent prayers of his believing mother, Monica, that finally brought about his salvation. As a young woman, Monica was given to drink and was one day rebuked by a servant for her drunkenness. This reprimand brought her to her senses and under the conviction of sin, prepared her to receive the gospel. She became a devout Christian and soon became known for her godly living and faithfulness in prayer.

Fortunately Augustine's father had enough sense to give his intelligent son a decent education at a local school. Their home, in Thagaste, (modern Algeria), North Africa, was not many miles to the west of Carthage, so his upbringing and education were completely Roman. Though his school days were not happy ones, he developed a passion for books and read many of the Latin authors. He also learned Greek, and though he did not enjoy the discipline he reached a high level of competence.

His mother made what endeavours she could to bring him up in the Christian Faith. As a child he was enrolled as a catechumen (baptismal candidate) and as a teenager went unwillingly to church, but paid more attention to the girls than the sermon!

Carthage

Anxious to further his education, Augustine moved to Carthage in order to study at a school of rhetoric, paid for by a generous neighbour. He studied philosophy from the writings of the Greek thinker Plato and was greatly influenced by the works of the Latin author, Cicero.

At Carthage, Augustine formed a relationship with a servant girl and they lived together for thirteen years without ever getting married. She

St. Augustine 360-430

produced an unwanted child, but the child later became much loved. For some reason they gave him a Christian name Adeodatus, which means 'gift from God'.

Reading Cicero at school started Augustine thinking seriously about ethics and religion. 'From henceforth began my upward way,' he later explained. But he rejected the Bible and was attracted to the Manichees, a religious sect with which he stayed for ten years before finally becoming dissatisfied with its teachings. His prayer at this time reflected something of a conflict that was beginning to trouble him: 'Give me chastity and continence...but not yet.'

In 383 Augustine moved to Italy, first to Rome and then to Milan where he became a professor of rhetoric. He was accompanied by his girlfriend and their son, and followed by his mother who was still praying for him to believe. By now he had become an ambitious man and felt he might even become a provincial governor. To further his ideas he decided he must part with his girlfriend, whom he sent back to Carthage, and became engaged to a young heiress. Deep within him, however, there was an unhappiness, a longing for peace.

One day in Milan he passed a beggar who was laughing. 'That poor wretch is happy and has what I cannot attain to,' he ruefully told himself.

For consolation he turned to yet another partner, but had no heart for the relationship. Where should he go next?

He was at last persuaded by a Christian friend to accompany him to church to hear the scholarly Ambrose, Bishop of Milan. As he came under the influence of the gospel he began to sort out some of the religious problems that troubled him - the origin of sin and evil, and the nature of Christ's person. He turned from philosophy to the Scriptures, especially the writings of Paul, to find his answers.

Then he came one day to recognise 'how sordid, how full of spots and sores' he was, and wept bitterly. As he did, he thought he heard a child's voice speaking - 'Take and read.' He turned to the Scriptures and his eyes fell on the words '...not in debauchery and licentiousness... but put on the Lord Jesus Christ'. Conscious of his sin, Augustine turned to Christ and was born again. He was baptised a Christian the following Easter 388, together with his son, Adeodatus.

Augustine was thirty-two at the time of his conversion. He gave up his post at Milan and returned with his son to Thagaste. His mother lived long enough to see the answer to her many years of prayer and died before they left Italy. Back home Augustine entered a semi-monastic life of reading and writing together with a group of like-minded Christians, and three years later was ordained priest. In 395, eight years after becoming a believer, he was appointed coadjutor bishop to Valerius and a year later became sole bishop of the see of Hippo.

Influence

Next to Carthage, Hippo was the most important town in North Africa. As bishop, Augustine's influence soon spread and he was recognised as the ablest and saintliest bishop of his time. For the remainder of his life he was engaged in administering the Church, preaching in the cathedral and combating heresy.

During his first years as bishop, Augustine wrote one of his most famous works, *Confessions*, published in 400. This work was a prose-poem in the form of an address to God and included his autobiography down to the time of his mother's death in Italy. His other outstanding treatise was *The City of God*, written over a period of fourteen years following the fall of Rome in 410. This work was a response to the accusation that the fall of Rome and the disasters besetting the Empire were due to forsaking the old religion and taking up a new Faith.

In this new book Augustine wrote about his whole philosophy of history. He argued that God's blessing could not be experienced by a society that would not submit to his rule. There were, in fact, two cities - one earthly and one heavenly. He went on to distinguish between the city of Rome and the city of God (a title he took from the Psalms), showing that the city of God endures forever while the earthly city must pass away.

It has been said that Augustine was the Father both of medieval Catholicism and of modern

> **Pelagius**
> Pelagius was an Irish monk who settled in Britain. When he visited Rome in 384 he was deeply shocked by what he considered to be the low tone of Roman behaviour, and he began to teach the need for higher ethical standards. He rejected the doctrine of original sin and argued that people are sinners because they follow their own free choice; there was no need for God's grace - it was simply a matter of choosing what was good. In 410 the approach of the barbarians forced him to leave Rome for Carthage, and the following year he moved to Palestine. Although cleared of the charge of heresy at a Jerusalem synod, he was condemned and excommunicated by the African bishops in 416.

Protestantism, and that the Reformation represents a revolt of his doctrine of grace against his doctrine of the Church. While this contention bears an element of truth, it is not to be taken at face value. He developed his doctrine of grace partly as a result of his own conversion experience and partly in response to the teaching of the heretic Pelagius, a British monk in Rome, who taught that man was basically good and could lead a good life if only he made the effort. He rejected the need for God's grace.

Augustine replied to this false teaching in two treatises, *On The Spirit and The Letter* and *On Nature And Grace*, in which he denied the popular English creed of 'justification by decency'. He described his own enslavement to sin until the grace of God had freed him, and spoke of the need to be born again. For Pelagius, relying on God's grace meant a denial of man's free will and his ability to make his own choice. He also took exception to some words of Augustine's in his *Confessions*, when he wrote, 'Give what you command and command what you will,' which seemed to deny man the right to exercise his own free will.

The other controversy that engaged his attention for many years was the Donatist heresy, which led Augustine to formulate his doctrine of the Church. The Donatists were a schismatic group which had broken away from the catholic communion during the reign of Constantine. Small bands of Donatist followers roamed North Africa, destroying churches and attacking the clergy, and they were particularly active around Hippo.

The Donatists were strong on martyrdom and wanted a 'pure'

Church, from which all regarded as apostates were excluded. Augustine pointed out that the parable of the wheat and tares, in which the two were to grow together until the harvest, suggested to him that the city of God and the city of Rome were to co-exist until the end of the world. Meanwhile Christians should obey the government unless commanded to do evil. There was grace available for all sinners.

But this idea that the Church was a mixture of true and false Christians and that they should be allowed to co-exist pandered more to Augustine's feelings than to a correct view of Scripture. Under the threat of government military action and the offer of an amnesty, many Donatists returned to the catholic Church and hardly anything further is heard of them.

During his thirty-five years as a bishop, Augustine wrote over one hundred treatises and opposed five different heretics. His teaching has been described as the highest attainment of religion since apostolic times, and the Church is indebted for his defence of the gospel. And while many passages in his writings are seized upon by Roman Catholics to support their own doctrines, Protestants can rejoice in his stalwart defence of the gospel of grace.

THREE

Christianity comes to Britain

The First 400 Years

No one is certain when or how Christianity first took root in Britain. There is hardly any documentary material available until the fifth century, and archaeological remains are scanty and inconclusive. In the thirteenth century lack of historical knowledge led to the rise of legendary accounts of visits to Britain by the apostle Paul and Joseph of Arimathea, but there is no foundation for these claims.

The first hint of Christianity in Britain comes in the writings of Tertullian and Origen at the beginning of the third century. Both mention Britain as among the places where Christianity was to be found, but give no indication about the strength or distribution of the Church. Perhaps the first tangible evidence is the martyrdom of the soldier Alban who, according to the Church historian Bede, was from the city of Verulamium.

He was arrested and condemned to death after giving shelter to a Christian priest hiding from his persecutors. As a result of his conver-

Bede (673-735)
Known as 'the Father of English church History', Bede entered the monastery of Wearmouth at the age of seven. He transferred to Jarrow probably at its foundation in 682, where he spent the rest of his life with the exception of occasional visits to York or Lindisfarne. At the time, he was probably the most learned man in England and wrote books on theology and Scripture (including numerous Bible commentaries), natural phenomena and chronology. His most famous work was *The Ecclesiastical History of the English People*, which is our chief source of information regarding early Christianity in England. The story is told that he died as he was completing his translation of John's Gospel. 'Now,' said his scribe, 'it is finished.' 'True,' replied the dying Bede. 'Take my head between your hands and raise me, that I may call on my Father.' Then, 'Glory be to the Father, and to the Son and to the Holy Ghost,' and he breathed his last. In the ninth century he was honoured with the title of 'Venerable'.

BEDE

sation with the fugitive he was converted to Christ. The date is generally thought to have been 304, during the persecution of Diocletian, but revised opinions now suggest it was more probably during the reign of Decius (249-251). By the beginning of the fourth century, there is definite evidence for the existence of a Church in embryonic form.

Toleration

Following Constantine's declaration of toleration at Milan in 313, whereby all religions were given equal rights under the law, the Church in Britain (sometimes referred to as the Celtic Church) emerged into the open. In 314 we learn that three bishops - Eborius of York, Restitutus of London and Adelphius of Lincoln (or Colchester?) - attended a Council at Arles in Gaul to discuss the Donatist controversy at Carthage.

Although there were no British bishops at the Council of Nicaea (325) they afterwards gave their assent to its findings, affirming for Britain its commitment to the orthodox creed. The Council of Rimini (359) was attended by several British bishops, perhaps suggesting some expansion of the Church; but three of them were so poor they had to claim travelling expenses from the imperial treasury! By the fourth century the Church was organised on a firm foundation and was part of the Latin-Western tradition.

Christians were found mostly in Roman towns and at forts, and in the houses of the rich Romans in out-lying country districts. They were Romano-Britons (those who had come under the influence of Roman civilisation), together with some of the Roman colonists.

Archaeological evidence from the same period helps shed further light on the problem. Remains of the earliest known church building in Britain, dated about 360, are to be found at the Roman fort of Silchester (Hampshire). It was a small building in basilica form, with an apse at the western end of the nave. The altar was made of wood, and outside the church was a trough where worshippers washed before entering. Remains of another church from the same period are to be found at Caerwent, in South Wales.

Baptismal Tank

A recent archaeological find is a fourth century baptismal tank, recovered from the bottom of a well at Caversham (Berkshire). It is one of only six such tanks known in the Roman Empire, all of them from Britain. The tank, which displayed the Chi-Rho monogram, is unusually complete, but squashed by the weight of the ground above.

The earliest material monument of Christianity has been found at a Roman villa at Lullingstone, Kent, dating from about 350. The villa contained a number of upper rooms apparently used for Christian worship, evidenced by two wall paintings. One included the Chi-Rho symbol, and the other showed ornate figures which were believers with their arms raised in prayer. A second Roman villa at Hinton St. Mary in west Dorset of the same date also shows signs of Christian activity.

But how Christianity came to Britain poses an even more difficult question and it is possible only to conjecture an answer. The idea that it was brought by Roman soldiers is for the most part now discarded.

Mithraism

Mithraism, which originated in Persia, was one of a number of 'mystery religions' that were in vogue in New Testament times and afterwards, and had certain characteristics in common with Christianity. The 'mystery' was a 'way of salvation' through a redeemer-god who died and rose, and who shared his divine nature with his followers through partaking of a symbolical meal. Mithras was a legendary figure who offered cleansing from sin by the blood of a bull, by which the initiate was 'reborn forever'. The religion was especially popular among soldiers, and evidence of the worship of Mithras has been discovered at some of the forts along the Hadrian Wall and in the city of London. Mithraism had spread so widely by the third century that it proved a serious rival to Christianity.

Surprisingly, perhaps, many soldiers were adherents of one or other of the variety of mystery religions of the day, and Mithraism was especially popular among the troops. It is quite likely some soldiers were Christians, but their presence would appear to have been slight.

The most appealing suggestion is that Christianity was brought to these shores by ordinary people. Like most religious ideas in the first three centuries, it may have been brought by traders who heard the gospel in other parts of the Empire. The churches at Lyons and Vienne in Gaul, for example, were probably founded by immigrants from Asia Minor in the second century, and the message could easily have been carried further to Britain by merchants. It is also possible that Britons travelling abroad could have become Christians and on returning to their native land shared their new faith with others. Whatever the case, it is certain the Church in Britain was not founded as the result of an evangelistic mission, but because ordinary people shared the good news of Jesus with their friends and neighbours.

Towards the end of the fourth century there was considerable unrest

among the Germanic tribes on the Continent. In 401 Alaric the Goth
turned against the Western Empire and launched an invasion of Italy.
Roman troops had already left Britain in 383; now further soldiers were
withdrawn to defend Rome. On 24th August 410 Alaric captured Rome
and the Empire came to an end.

Roman Officer

The Roman population of Britain, however, remained and Christianity
continued to flourish, though not without its problems. The Pelagian
heresy, which had originated in Rome, made inroads into the British
Church, causing alarm among Christian leaders on the Continent. A
council of bishops from Gaul met in 429 to consider the situation and
decided to send two bishops to assist the Church. The leading bishop was
Germanus of Auxerre, who, took a particular interest in the British Isles.

Before becoming a bishop, Germanus had been an officer in the
Roman army and had lost nothing of his flair for commanding men. Not
only did his mission to Britain succeed in checking the Pelagian threat
- though only temporarily - but he also led a force of Britons against the
invading Picts and Saxons. He organised an ambush and his troops
rushed at the enemy shouting, 'Alleluia, Alleluia.' The Picts fled in fear!
This probably took place near Mold (Cheshire), in 430.

By 447 Germanus had to pay a return visit to Britain, to encourage and
strengthen the British against a revival of Pelagianism. Though he again
enjoyed some success, the situation was not helped by the attacks of Saxon
invaders. Although much of the Roman culture was destroyed, peace was
eventually restored and the Church entered into a period of rest.

Many Britons fled westwards and settled in either the mountains of
Wales or in Cornwall. Eventually the Christian Church was weakened
by the invasion and little is heard of the Faith in Britain for about 150
years. Its place was taken by the heathen religions of the conquering
Jutes, Angles and Saxons. But while the gods Wodin and Thor replaced
Christ, the Church in the West continued to survive, especially in Wales.

Hard historical fact is difficult to come by and we have to rely on the
writings of Gildas, a British monk and historian who wrote in Brittany
in 547. This period of Church history produced two famous Welsh saints
- Illtyd and David, later the patron saint of Wales. David (520-588) was
a pupil of Illtyd and a native of Wales. He belonged to one of the chief
royal families of Britain and in his youth became a monk. He settled in
Pembrokeshire and founded a monastery at Glyn Rosyn, the site of the
present-day St. David's Cathedral.

He was a typical Celtic abbot-bishop, a founder of monasteries and an evangelist, the most influential Christian in sixth-century Britain. Yet the Church historian Bede complained that the Welsh Church made no attempt to evangelise the Saxons. For further missionary expansion into Scotland and Ireland, we have to look elsewhere. And it was left to missionaries from Rome to bring about the conversion of the Angles and Saxons.

THE CHURCH IN BRITAIN

Scotland

When the Romans invaded Britain they penetrated as far as the High-lands of Scotland, but then withdrew after defeating the Caledonians. Because of the continued threat of an invasion from the Picts it was decided to build a 'wall' of forts across the North, from the Solway Firth to the mouth of the River Tyne. Completed about 120, it was named Hadrian's Wall after the reigning Emperor. Despite the Wall, trade was carried on across the border, but Scotland remained untouched by the gospel, except for a Christian enclave that existed in Galloway (in the south-west), towards the end of the fourth century. It is here that the story of Christianity in Scotland begins, with the mission of Ninian.

NINIAN (c 360-c432)

Ninian was of royal birth, the son of a Christian king in Cumbria, and spent his early years in the valley of the Solway. As a child he was instructed in the Christian faith and was baptised. In his teens he made a pilgrimage to Rome and stayed there for some years to study the Scriptures. He was consecrated bishop in 393/4 and was sent to Britain to minister to the needs of his own people.

On his return journey he spent some time with Martin, Bishop of Tours (Gaul), who greatly influenced his thinking. Martin was an evangelist, and when he founded his new 'Greater Monastery' at Marmoutier, it was not as a place of withdrawal but as a centre for the spread of the gospel.

When Ninian reached Galloway he founded a church and monastery based on Martin's ideas of evangelism. The buildings were of stone and white washed so that they would be conspicuous. He named it *Candida Casa*, or White House; today it is called Whithorn from the old English *hwit-aern*. In 397, following the death of his master, the monastery was dedicated to the memory of Martin (it was a regular practice in Celtic Christianity to name a monastery either after its founder or the founder of the parent monastery).

Although by the time of Ninian's arrival Roman troops had been withdrawn from the Wall, Galloway still enjoyed a period of stability and peace. Ninian was able to go about his mission evangelising the southern Picts who 'abandoned the error of idolatry... and accepted the true Faith,' and many became Christians.

His most notable convert was a local prince, Tuduvallus. Ninian laboured for over thirty years preaching the gospel and furthering the work of the Kingdom. His preaching tours took him along the Roman

Wall and up the east coast of Scotland. The gospel was also taken across the sea to Ireland, where the Scots of north-east Ulster lived (a tribe that was later to give its name to Scotland).

The monastery of Candida Casa, rather than a church, became the centre of the episcopal see, as was usually the case in Celtic Christianity. It became the chief seat of early Christian learning and believers from Wales and Ireland came there to study.

When Ninian died about 432 his body was buried in the monastery, where the ruins of the chapel can still be seen today. He was described by Bede as 'a most revered bishop and most saintly man.' The work of Whithorn continued and greatly influenced the life of the Church in Ireland during Patrick's day, later in the fifth century.

The evangelistic work and training at Whithorn was eventually curtailed by the barbarian invasion of the fifth and sixth centuries. For nearly a hundred and fifty years the Celtic Church went into recession as the invaders introduced their own gods and Britain almost reverted to paganism.

Remnants of the Faith survived in the western parts of Britain as many ordinary Britons fled from the attacks. But much of Roman civilisation and the benefits that accompanied it were lost. The Church in Ireland, founded by Patrick, remained untouched by these continental invaders and in the next century produced Scotland's second most influential missionary, Columba of Iona.

COLUMBA (c 521-597)

Columba was born of royal descent and could trace his line back to Niall, high King of Ireland, at the beginning of the fifth century. He was educated at the monastery of Moville and studied under the scholar Finnian who had graduated from Whithorn. From Moville he went to Clonard in Meath, where he was ordained presbyter. At the age of twenty-five he founded a monastery in Derry, followed about six or seven years later by another at Durrow. Many other foundations are attributed to his name, including the monastery at Kells.

He was known, apparently, as Columba the Dove, though his passionate temperament could strike terror into the heart of an opponent. In about the year 560 he became involved in a petty dispute over the ownership of a manuscript, which developed into a tribal conflict. He gathered an armed force and in the ensuing battle defeated his enemies, leaving three thousand of them dead. Forced to flee the country, Columba vowed not to return until he had won as many pagans for Christ

22222222

as he had killed on the battlefield.

With twelve companions he set sail and headed northwards and finally landed on an island off the west coast of Scotland then called Hy or Ioua, today known as Iona. Now out of sight of Ireland, they decided to bury the boat and make the island their home. The island lay close to the Scottish kingdom of Dalriada, ruled by Columba's kinsmen. Conall, the Dalriadic king, granted him the island for the foundation of his monastery, though it was necessary to have the gift confirmed by the Pictish king, Brude, who was their overlord.

They built the monastery based on the usual Celtic pattern - a church made of wood, with beehive-shaped huts and a wall surrounding the whole enclosure. Their time was spent in cultivating the ground, fishing and copying manuscripts, as well as the normal call to prayer. Later, many Psalters and Gospels were required and considerable time and zeal was given to copying the Scriptures to meet this need.

Columba's mission was to bring the gospel to the northern Picts and he began by attempting to win over the king. Brude lived near Inverness, and after two years on the island the missionary determined to meet him. Despite the king's reluctance to receive him, Columba persisted and, according to Bede, 'turned the nation to faith in Christ by word and by example'.

Changed Life

The fact is that some kind of change had happened in Columba. The head-strong 'soldier' of Ireland had become, according to his biographer, a lovable person, full of religious devotion, a man of great kindness with a concern for the poor. His reputation spread far and wide, and Iona was visited by many who were sick or troubled but who went away healed.

He preached to the pagans, 'My Druid is Christ the Son of God,' as he challenged the people's belief in magic and the supernatural. He met with fierce opposition from the Druids, but even they had respect for the power of his God and they did him no harm.

When Brude died in 585, Columba was quick to establish relations with his successor at Abernethy, and then followed this up with a mission to the tribes along Tayside. He also knew the king of the Britons in Strathclyde, who sent to ask whether he would die in a battle with his enemy, the English king of Bernicia (Northumberland). Columba replied that he would probably die a peaceful death, which he did.

Other Christian missionaries were also involved in bringing the gospel to Scotland in the sixth century, notably Kentigern, who evange-lised the Strathclyde region and fixed his episcopal see at Glasgow. His work radiated out towards Galloway in the south, and north towards Aberdeen and even to the Orkneys.

But there was no one to compare with Columba the Dove, who not only evangelised the Picts but also laid down a foundation of a consolidated Scotland and a united Scottish people. He died at Iona on 9th June 597 at the age of seventy-six. It was the same year in which the Roman missionary Augustine landed in Kent to convert the English.

Ireland

Christianity was probably introduced into Ireland during the fourth century, but the evidence is slight. The chances are it was brought by immigrants and traders from Britain and the Continent, who sowed the seeds of faith which gave rise to the several scattered Christian commu-nities on the island.

The first certain date in Irish Church history is the year 431 when Celestine, Bishop of Rome, sent Palladius as the first bishop to 'the Scots believing in Christ'. Palladius, a deacon at Auxerre (Gaul), was able to visit some of the Christian communities and to establish contact with Ninian's monastery in Galloway before he died the following year. Ready to take his place was another deacon from Auxerre, Patrick, who had some years previously received a call from God to evangelise the people of Ireland. He was consecrated by the Bishop of Auxerre and left immediately to fulfil his vocation.

PATRICK (390-461): Apostle of the Irish

Little is known about Patrick's early life and the facts are mostly gleaned from his *Confessions*. His Latin name was Patricius, though he was also known by a British name Succat or Sochet. He was a native of Britain and his home was near the west coast, somewhere between the Bristol Channel and south-west Scotland.

The village of his birth, Bannavem Taberniae, has never been identified, but must have been close to a Roman settlement where his father, Calpurnius, was either a magistrate or held some other civil position. His family, who were Roman citizens and held the rank of 'freeborn', were Christians; his father was a deacon and his grandfather had been a presbyter. Patrick, however, did not regard himself as a believer despite his family advantages.

As a boy, he would appear to have spent more time working on his father's farm than studying his lessons. When he was older, he regretted his lack of education and described himself as 'illiterate'. In 405 a band of Irish raiders landed on the coast and seized a large number of captives, including the sixteen year old Patrick.

What happened to the rest of his family is not known and there is no further reference to them in his writings; perhaps they were killed in the attack. In Ireland Patrick was brought up as a slave by a heathen farmer from Slemish, near present day Ballymena in County Antrim, and for six years worked as a swineherd. The days were long and hard, and Patrick had plenty of time in which to seriously consider his life and his relationship with God.

Perhaps something from the Scriptures that he had learned in his early years came back to him. But he tells how in time 'the Lord opened the understanding of my unbelief, that, late as it was, I might remember my faults and turn to the Lord my God with all my heart'. He went on to praise God that in the land of his captivity, after having been chastened, he had come to the knowledge of God. God had kept guard over him, and had strengthened and comforted him as a father does his son. In time he found the love of God and the fear of him increased more and more, and as he walked about the woods and mountains he learned to pray. Sometimes he prayed as many as one hundred prayers a day.

Heavenly Vision

One night in his sleep he heard a voice telling him he was to leave the farm and make for the coast where a ship would be ready for him. He obeyed the heavenly vision, and on reaching the coast found a ship soon to cast off its moorings. The master refused to take him on board, but after praying to God, Patrick returned to the ship and was this time taken on as a member of the crew. After a journey of two months he left the ship and found his way to the island of St. Honorat off the south coast of Gaul, where he spent several years studying at a monastery. He returned to his home in Britain in 414/5 where he stayed with relatives.

It was during his stay in Britain that a friend from Ireland called Victoricus came to him in a vision. He gave Patrick a letter to read and that moment he heard the voice of those who were beside the wood at Focluth near the western sea, calling, 'Please, holy boy, come and walk among us again.' Their cry pierced his heart, and Patrick awoke from his dream. (The account of this vision raises a question about Patrick's captivity: was it at Slemish near the east coast, or at Focluth in the west? The text is inconclusive.)

Believing this to be a call from God to take the gospel to Ireland, Patrick left for Auxerre for further study and to prepare himself for this work. He was ordained deacon, but when a bishop was needed to minister to the small Christian community in Ireland, Patrick was overlooked in favour of Palladius.

It was not until a replacement was needed that Patrick was at last enabled to fulfil his calling. He was consecrated bishop by Germanus, the new Bishop of Auxerre, and sent out as the 'apostle of Christ'. Over twenty years had elapsed since his escape from captivity in Ireland.

At the time of Patrick's mission, Ireland was a pagan country, though there were known to be a few scattered Christian communities, some founded by his predecessor Palladius. His aim was to encourage these believers and to reach the outlying regions as yet untouched by the gospel. Politically, Ireland was not part of the Roman Empire, but Patrick was a Roman citizen and Christianity was the religion of the Empire. His purpose, however, was not to spread the religion of Rome but to preach the gospel to those who had previously worshipped idols and who now were 'prepared a people of the Lord... called children of God'.

He landed in Ireland in 433 on the east coast and was welcomed by a local chief, Dichu, whose fortress was Downpatrick. Dichu received the gospel and became Patrick's first convert. The chief gave Patrick a barn to serve as a church building at a place now known as Saul, from the Irish word *Sabhall* meaning 'barn'.

In the hope of also winning his former master to Christ, Patrick travelled north to Ulster. But Miliucc heard of his coming; determined to have nothing to do with the missionary, he apparently committed suicide by setting his home on fire. After this, wherever Patrick went he

---

Worship of relics

When Patrick returned to Ireland from Rome he carried with him a number of relics for the new cathedral he intended building. The cult of relics began around the middle of the second century and by the reign of Constantine was a well-established practice within the Church. It was believed that veneration of the remains of martyrs and 'saints' or the objects that had been associated with them, brought special merit to the worshipper and gave access to God in prayer. Relics claimed to be discovered included the bones of martyrs, the true cross (found by Queen Helena in 326), the head of John the Baptist, the chair of James, the Lord's brother, plus all manner of other objects. The cult was so deeply entrenched that the Seventh General Council (787) declared that any bishop who consecrated a temple without relics was to be deposed.

STATUE OF ST. PATRICK

first tried to win the local ruler for Christianity in order to gain entrance into the rest of the tribe.

Ireland at this time was divided into tribal groups, each ruled by a chieftain who in turn owed allegiance to an overlord or king. One of the kings held the title of 'high king' of Ireland and he ruled from Tara in County Meath. Patrick went to meet the high king, Laoghaire (pronounced Leary), who listened to his message. Though he did not accept the gospel, one of his brothers - Conall - and one of his sons were converted to Christ. Despite his rejection, the high king was prepared to tolerate the new Faith and the way was open for Patrick to continue his mission.

From Meath, Patrick travelled west to Connaught where he met and baptised the two daughters of Laoghaire. He spent seven years in the area and must surely have visited the village he had seen in his vision. In 441/2 he paid a visit to Rome to consult the bishop about setting up a see, but soon returned to his mission.

The following year he visited Ulster and then went to Armagh where he built his cathedral upon a hill. From here he set up his episcopal organisation of the whole island. Because of the lack of any cities, he based his system on the tribal divisions of the country. This meant that the monastery rather than the cathedral became the centre of the see, ruled over by an abbot rather than a bishop.

As Patrick travelled through Ireland he established many monasteries, some of them housing several thousand monks. Each monastery had its own rule, as it was thought necessary to exert a strict discipline over the thousands of pagans recently turned Christian. In the early Irish Church the monastery was the centre from which the missionaries went out to preach, and where pupils came to study the Scriptures and make copies of the Gospels and where art flourished.

Much of our knowledge of Patrick's life is gained from two of his own works, *Confessions*, written fairly late in his life, and his *Letter To The Subjects of Coroticus*, who was the British king of Strathclyde. Both were written in Latin, a language at which he was not very proficient, but it was the language of the Church.

Towards the end of his life Patrick spent most of his time in the north and about 457 stepped down as leader of the Irish Council. Four years later he died, on 17th March, now celebrated as St. Patrick's Day, and was buried at Downpatrick.

Patrick had the distinction of establishing the first Church in the West that was outside the Roman Empire. His mission also gave an impulse to the urgency of evangelisation, and the Celtic Church sent out many monks to take the gospel to western Europe. In his *Confessions* Patrick concludes by asking his readers to receive his writing, 'that no one ever say it was my ignorance that did whatever trifling matter I did... but judge and let it most truly be believed that it was the gift of God'.

England (1)

Augustine's mission to England gave birth to a Latin Christianity which was rapidly acquiring all the hallmarks of the Roman Catholic Church as we know it today. When King Ethelbert and the people of Kent accepted the Faith, they came under the spiritual authority of the Pope and became members of the Roman Church.

During the fifth century changes were taking place in the Church whereby the authority of Rome was being established throughout the whole of Christendom, in both the eastern and western halves of the Empire. The custom had grown up of addressing the bishop of Rome as 'pope' and, with the exception of the Celtic Church, this was confirmed by Pope Leo the Great at the Council of Chalcedon in 451. Other practices such as making the sign of the cross, private confessions and the use of vestments were creeping in, and the sacrifice of the mass and the adoration of Mary were already accepted.

But the Pope was not only the spiritual leader of the Church; at times when Emperors lacked political strength, the Pope assumed the role of secular leader as well. When the Vandals from Africa attacked in 455 and Rome was defenceless, it was Leo who was able to meet the invaders and to prevent a senseless massacre.

In Britain, the Anglo-Saxon invaders destroyed much of Christianity along the eastern side of the country and the Church was forced to retreat to the west. Christian countries on the Continent were also over-run by the Barbarians and were lost to paganism. Pope Gregory the Great (590-604) was anxious to win back the lost tribes and restore them to the 'Christian Commonwealth'.

His attention was drawn to the plight of the British by a delightful incident that happened in the forum at Rome, probably in 586. It was related by the historian Bede and seems to be based upon fact. The story goes that Gregory saw some fair-skinned boys for sale in the slave-market; he learned that they were Angli from England, and that they were pagans. He gave the famous reply, 'They look like Angels not Angles.' He was also told that they were subjects of King Aella; 'In which case,' he replied, 'they should sing Alleluia.'

From that time he determined, when he could, to send a mission to England. He made several unsuccessful attempts and once set out himself, but was recalled to Rome. His chance finally came when he was elected Pope, and he chose Augustine, Prior of St. Andrew's monastery in Rome, to lead a team of forty monks.

AUGUSTINE (died 604): First Archbishop of Canterbury

Augustine's expedition set out for England in 596 and travelled as far as the south of France before the fear of facing the barbarians in England caused them to turn back. But Gregory encouraged them and sent them on their way again. The party reached England and landed at Ebbsfleet, near the mouth of the River Stour in Kent.

To his surprise, Augustine was well-received by Ethelbert, the most powerful king in the south of England, who came out to meet them. The king was advised by his priests not to meet the missionaries under cover for fear of magic, so a conference was held in the open-air.

Augustine's fears were completely unfounded and it seemed as though God had gone before and prepared the way. In the first place the king was a civilised man and a strong ruler, not ignorant or ruthless as had been imagined. He had a Christian wife, Bertha, the daughter of a Frankish king, who had been praying for the English and had appealed for missionaries to come and teach the gospel.

Moreover, the heathenism of the Saxons was losing its power and there was no opposition to the new God. The king laid down one condition, that Augustine should not use compulsion or force in making converts. The door was open for the missionaries to begin their work.

Augustine and his monks marched in procession on the city of Canterbury, holding aloft a banner bearing the figure of the crucified Christ. Bede describes how as 'they drew near the city, after their manner, with the holy cross and the image of our sovereign Lord and King, Jesus Christ, they, in concert, sang this litany: "We beseech thee, O Lord, in all thy mercy, that thy anger and wrath be turned away from this city and from thy holy house, because we have sinned. Hallelujah." '

Queen Bertha was in the habit of praying daily in a little church given to her by the king; St. Martin's had first been used by Roman Christians and now became the centre of Augustine's mission. The monks began to meet there - to sing, pray, say mass and to preach. Great numbers began daily to flock to hear the Word of God; they left their pagan gods 'by faith to unite themselves with the holy Church of Christ'.

Writing to a Bishop Eulogios, Pope Gregory described how 'many thousands' had been baptised by Augustine at the first Christmas after his arrival in England. Certainly, small Christian communities were established and Augustine had to send to Rome for more helpers.

Archbishop

Because the mission was proving successful, Augustine felt it necessary to have himself consecrated bishop. Sometime in the autumn of that year (597) he travelled to Arles (Gaul) for the ceremony - a long journey so soon after his arrival. Later, on Gregory's instructions, he was recognised as Archbishop of England. On his return to Canterbury, King Ethelbert gave Augustine land for building a church and palace, and for a monastery outside the city.

The bishop had a new church built, quite likely of wood, which he called Church of the Holy Saviour. Here he began to 'imitate the apostolic life of the primitive Church, in continued prayers, fastings and vigils' and 'in preaching the word of life'. These buildings formed the centre of the episcopal see of Canterbury, and the present Christ Church cathedral was built around them.

In time, Ethelbert warmed towards the new religion. The 'pure and holy life' of the missionaries especially commended itself to the king and after witnessing miracles considered the God of Christianity to be more powerful than his own. He was converted to Christ and baptised, probably at Easter in 601, in St. Martin's Church.

As no trace of a baptistry has been found in the church, it has been assumed that the baptism must have taken place in a shallow lead tank, usual at the time. These tanks, inscribed on the side with the alpha and omega symbols, marked the transitional stage between the traditional stone Roman baptistry and the medieval font found in many churches today. The candidate stood in the tank, water was poured on him and the cross signed on his forehead. The ceremony concluded with the celebration of the mass.

What was particularly endearing was the king's attitude towards those converted to Christ. Bede wrote, 'For the king showed himself pleased with their faith and conversion but he did not compel any man to be a Christian. Rather, he loved the believers more fervently as fellow citizens of the heavenly kingdom.'

Authority

Meanwhile in Rome, Gregory was eager to move ahead with the evangelisation of the rest of England. He proposed setting up two metropolitan bishoprics, at London and York, each to have twelve bishops.

Augustine was to be in overall charge and had authority over the British bishops, in order to bring them into the Church of Rome. Gregory's plans, however, did not materialise. In deference to Ethelbert, Augustine decided against going to London but stayed in Canterbury to supervise the work from there. The see of York did not appoint an archbishop until 634, after Christianity had eventually reached Northumbria.

In 603 Augustine made his first attempt to meet the Celtic bishops; he wanted them to accept Roman Church practices and to assist his efforts in evangelising the English. The meeting took place under an oak tree, known as 'St. Augustine's Oak', near Dyrham (Gloucestershire). The Celts were suspicious of the Roman bishops and no agreement was reached.

A second attempt was made when seven British bishops and some of their learned men journeyed to North Wales for a conference near Bangor. Before they went, the bishops consulted a hermit and determined they would only listen to Augustine if he were truly a man of God. If he were, the hermit suggested, he would rise from his seat to greet them.

When the British arrived, Augustine remained seated; feeling despised by the Roman, the British refused his overtures for not showing them common Christian courtesy. The hope of bringing the Celtic Church under the wing of Rome was deferred until towards the end of the century.

On his return to Canterbury, Augustine continued his mission and tentative steps were taken towards evangelising the East Saxons of Essex. A see was established at London where Mellitus, one of his original helpers, was consecrated bishop. Another monk, Justus, was sent as bishop to the people of west Kent and a new see was set up at Rochester.

As the work expanded, more churches were built and old church buildings repaired. Just as the work seemed to be gathering momentum, however, Augustine died in 604; he was buried out of doors (it was not yet permitted in Roman law to bury within a building) next to the church of St. Peter and St. Paul. His ministry in England had lasted hardly more than seven years.

Augustine was a monk and not an evangelist; in coming to England he had not received a call, like Patrick of Ireland, but was merely obeying the command of his Pope. Yet he left behind him a flourishing Church which, despite a minor resurgence of paganism, remained firm in the Faith.

REMAINS OF ST. AUGUSTINE'S ABBEY

When King Ethelbert died in 616 his position as Bretwalda (Britain-ruler) passed to Edwin, King of Northumbria. Edwin married Ethelberga, a Christian princess from Kent and Ethelbert's niece. She was accompanied by Paulinus, one of Augustine's Roman monks, thus opening up the way for the spread of Christianity to northern England.

England (2)

Augustine's mission to Kent had been successful, but England was still very much a pagan country and there was more ground to be gained. After Kent, the next kingdom to receive the gospel was Northumbria, which consisted of Bernicia (Northumbria) and Deira (Yorkshire), and stretched from the Cheviot Hills in the north to the River Humber.

The customary strategy of first endeavouring to win the local ruler proved effective, and was invariably the means whereby Christianity spread throughout the rest of England. When Ethelberga, a Christian princess of Kent, was married in 625 to Edwin, King of Northumbria, it was on the understanding he would allow her to continue the practice of her religion. He went even further and vowed that if he found Christianity to be good, he would embrace the new Faith himself.

The Roman monk, Paulinus, who accompanied Ethelberga from Canterbury was consecrated bishop in anticipation of opening up new lands to the gospel. His efforts soon began to bear fruit, and the following Easter not only was the new baby princess baptised but eleven members of the royal household as well.

Paganism Denounced

True to his word, the king summoned the Witan (royal council) to discuss the new religion. Starting with his chief priest Coifi, he invited each member to give his own opinion. They all denounced paganism and agreed they should follow the new religion. The king agreed with their decision. He renounced paganism and ordered all temples to be destroyed. He accepted Christianity and was baptised on Easter Day 627 in a wooden church specially built for the occasion.

Paulinus made York the centre of his missionary activity. The wooden church he had erected was later built-over by a larger stone building, the site of the present cathedral. For the next six years Paulinus preached throughout Northumbria, moving from one royal estate to another, establishing churches.

Yet his efforts appeared short-lived. Edwin was killed in battle in 632/633 near Hexham, and Northumbria was laid waste. Queen

Ethelberga and other members of the royal family, together with Paulinus, were forced to escape; they went by sea to Kent, never to return.

The outlook in Northumbria seemed bleak as the kingdom reverted to near paganism; the work of Paulinus was apparently destroyed during what was described by Bede as 'the disastrous year'. Then the new king, Oswald, defeated the enemy Cadwallon at a battle near Hadrian's Wall, heralding a restoration of peace. To commemorate the occasion the king set up a wooden cross at Heathfield, affirming his belief in the Christians' God.

Oswald was a member of the royal family but had spent seventeen years in exile on the island of Iona. He was brought up by the monks from whom he learned the Christian Faith. When he received back his kingdom, Oswald was determined to restore Christianity to Northumbria. He appealed not to Canterbury, but to Iona for a missionary to evangelise his people.

The abbot sent the monk Corman who arrived in 634 and stayed barely a year before returning to Iona to report his lack of progress. The people had not responded to his preaching and few came to hear him. On his part, he found them to be 'wild, ungovernable men of harsh and barbarous disposition'.

At Iona, the fathers were perplexed and one of the monks, Aidan, was outspoken in his criticism of Corman. 'You did not after the apostolic precept: first offer them the milk of more gentle doctrine, till by degree through the nourishment of God's Word they might have strength to receive and practise God's more perfect and exalted counsel.' The fathers recognised that here was a true missionary and so Aidan was chosen to take up where Corman had left off.

AIDAN (d 651): Bishop of Lindisfarne

Aidan was consecrated bishop in 635 and left for Bamburgh where Oswald had his castle. The king gave Aidan the nearby island of Lindisfarne as a centre for his mission. For some time, Lindisfarne rather than York became the episcopal capital of Northumbria and was established as a second Iona, a monastic centre of learning and mission.

Bede describes how people flocked to hear Aidan preach the Word and many were won to Christianity. On his preaching tours he was often accompanied by the king who acted as his interpreter, and the two men worked in harmonious partnership. Aidan always travelled on foot and frequently stopped on his journeys to speak to other travellers, urging them to accept Christianity. If they were already Christian, he exhorted them to live godly lives and so commend the gospel. As he went, he baptised and confirmed many; he even ordained some as clergy, presumably to lead the churches he founded.

Known by all to be a saintly man, Aidan was not one for wasting time or idle chatter. As he walked around the countryside with his monks they repeated the psalms or meditated on sermons. When he was at the king's table, he would sometimes hurry away to read and pray, and he followed the practice of fasting each Wednesday and Friday (except during Eastertide) until the ninth hour.

He was not a man given to wealth, as some of his successors were, and many of the gifts he received were used for the poor. Sometimes the money was given to redeem captive slaves, especially those he felt had been sold unjustly. And he was never afraid of rebuking vice or oppression in the rich and powerful. Once, King Oswin - Oswald's successor - complained when Aidan gave a poor beggar the horse he had given him. 'What sayest thou, O king? Is that son of a mare more dear to thee than the son of God?' At this, the king fell at Aidan's feet, confessed his sin and vowed never again to begrudge the monk's generosity.

Prayer

It seems that Aidan was also a man who believed in the power of prayer. On one occasion when the pagan king of Mercia laid siege to Bamburgh, the town was set on fire and the flames were heading towards the king's castle. Aidan prayed and the wind changed direction, bearing back on the besiegers!

King Oswald was killed in battle near Oswestry in 642 and Aidan lost a faithful co-worker in the gospel. He continued his preaching tours and also sent groups of monks to other parts of the land. Aidan led a mission to Lindsey (Lincolnshire) where a number of churches were built, and his monks were said to have reached as far south as the River Thames.

He also encouraged the founding of monasteries for both men and women, such as the ones at Melrose and Gateshead. The most famous one was at Whitby where, as at Lindisfarne, the monks and nuns lived in individual cells in order to spend some of their time in meditation, fasting and penitence.

In September 651, while on a tour, Aidan was seized with a violent illness. The monks pitched a tent against the west wall of a church and Aidan died with his head leaning against a post which served as a buttress. He was buried in the monastery at Lindisfarne.

Despite the brief reversion to paganism, Aidan re-established Christianity in Northumbria and his mission sent 'gospel ripples' throughout other parts of the land. Lindisfarne was influential in the spread of Christianity to several kingdoms, either by royal marriage alliances or by direct contact.

Soon after the death of Aidan, monks from Lindisfarne were able to visit the kingdom of Mercia (the Midlands) led by the missionary Cedd. Some of the royal family were already Christian, which benefited the work of the mission.

Mission

Cedd next moved to the kingdom of the East Saxons, where Augustine's mission some fifty years earlier had failed to make much headway. He was consecrated Bishop of the East Saxons with his see at London. His mission was more successful than that of Augustine, possibly because King Sigbert was a Christian; he established both churches and monasteries, the most famous one being that at Bradwell-on-Sea.

In the south, the kingdom of Wessex was evangelised by Bishop Birinus, who was specially sent by Pope Honorius. The bishop promised to 'sow the seeds of the holy faith in the hearts of those English who lived beyond the others, in other parts where no teacher had preceded him.' His mission was successful; the king of Wessex believed and was baptised, and gave Dorchester-on-Thames to Birinus as his see. Towards the end of the century Wilfred of Ripon visited the kingdom of the South Saxons and preached the gospel there. He was responsible for turning many from paganism to Christianity.

By the eighth century, England was virtually a Christian country and the last vestiges of paganism were fast receding. The Church that Aidan had established in Northumbria, however, was according to the Celtic tradition and at variance with the Roman Church of Kent. They differed on several issues, such as the wearing of crowns by bishops, the cut of the tonsure (shaved head) and particularly the date of Easter.

In 664 the Synod of Whitby - probably the most famous of all early English ecclesiastical gatherings - met to settle the issues. The northern king Oswy presided and finally pronounced in favour of Rome, as he was more prepared to obey St. Peter than St. Columba! It seemed as though the discipline of the Church of Rome was about to take a firmer hold on the country.

BONIFACE (680-784): Apostle to Germany

Missionary zeal is the mark of a healthy church life. Towards the end of the seventh century the Church in England, growing in strength, soundly organised and administered and respected by the secular rulers, began to reach out to the pagan tribes on the continent of Europe. The impetus came from the monasteries which were not only evangelistic centres, but also places of learning where men and women were being trained for playing a part in the spread of Christianity.

The conversion of the English in the seventh century came about through the missionary efforts of monks from Rome, Scotland and Ireland; they inspired the English to carry the Christian message through the rest of the country. Soon the young Church in England began to show a concern for its neighbours in Europe and before the end of the century had launched an evangelistic outreach to the Germanic tribes.

Christianity first reached Germany in the fourth century. Some of the tribes along the Rhine and the Danube had been converted to Arianism, while others came under the influence of the Catholic Church. But the gospel did not take a firm hold and the work had later to be repeated. Towards the end of the sixth century missionaries from the Celtic Church of Ireland started evangelistic tours on the Continent. Most important was Columban (543-615) who went to France (590) and then into Italy; he also worked for a while in the Rhineland area.

Again the work was not adequately consolidated and it was left to English missionaries, after the Synod of Whitby in 664, to lay the foundations of a strong German Church, bearing the imprint of Roman organisation and sense of order. In 678 the first missionary from the Church in England, Wilfrid of Ripon, visited Frisia (modern Holland) to begin sharing the gospel with pagan tribes and he stayed for two years.

His work was continued in western Frisia by his pupil, Willibrord, in 690, who laboured faithfully until his death in 739. He gained Papal support for his mission, and in 695 was consecrated Archbishop of the Frisians, with his see at Utrecht.

More important, however, was the work of Boniface, a modest monk from England. It was chiefly as a result of his activity that thousands were converted to Christ, churches and monasteries built and the foundations of an ecclesiastical organisation laid.

Christian Upbringing

Born of Christian parents in Crediton, Devon, Wynfrith - the name of Boniface was given him later by the Pope - was allowed at a very early age to join the monastery at Exeter. He was apparently a likeable and clever pupil and at the age of fourteen was admitted into the full membership of the community. By the time he was twenty-two, he felt he had learned all he could at Exeter and was moved to Nursling, near Winchester, for more advanced studies. His ability was quickly recognised and he soon began to make a name for himself; he was ordained first as deacon and then presbyter.

In 715, at the age of thirty-five, Wynfrith made it known to his Abbot that he felt a call to serve God overseas. The prospect of losing so notable a scholar, particularly to go and work in distant and dangerous lands, filled the monks with dismay. Over the years he had taken a special interest in the activities of Wilfrid, Willibrord and other missionaries, and believed God wanted him to play his part in spreading the gospel. It was only after some months of prayer and persuasion that the monks gave him their blessing.

It was arranged that a small number of companions should escort Wynfrith, who was to assist Archbishop Willibrord in West Frisia; after a while he would be able to visit East Frisia and hopefully the Old Saxons of northern Germany, who were his main concern. The expedition lasted only four months and he did not even manage to meet up with the archbishop. To his surprise, he found the churches in the area destroyed, including the one at Utrecht, and paganism once again on the increase. He decided to venture no further and returned to England.

At that point it was rumoured that the new Pope, Gregory II, had an interest in the Germanic peoples. Wynfrith determined to go to Rome and seek permission from the Pope for his missionary plans. He arrived in December 718 and was granted an audience. The Pope was impressed with Wynfrith and his eagerness to evangelise the Saxons, and commissioned him to carry out the work of Christ over a large area of Europe. He also gave him a new name, Boniface (there is no explanation for the choice) and sent him off to join Willibrord in Frisia.

Willibrord (658-739)

A native of Northumbria, he was educated under Wilfrid at the monastery at Ripon. In 678 he moved to Ireland where he spent twelve years in an abbey at Rathmelsigi and was ordained priest. With twelve companions, he went as a missionary to Frisia in 690, and after gaining Papal support was appointed Archbishop of Frisia and was granted land outside Utrecht for a cathedral. He founded the monastery of Echternach (Luxembourg) in 698, and worked also in Denmark, Heligoland and Thuringia. He was known as 'the Apostle to the Frisians'.

Boniface stayed two years with Willibrord, during which time he learned the Frankish language, and then decided to move on. Journeying up the Rhine and along the Lahn Valley, he discovered a place where he could make his base. At Amoneburg he came upon a small Christian community which had strayed from the Faith, and felt this would be a good starting point.

Success

There was an encouraging response to his preaching; people believed and backsliders recanted. His work in Germany had begun. Hearing of Boniface's success, the Pope elevated him to the rank of bishop so he could more properly care for the flock and confirm those who believed. But still Boniface had no defined diocese, and was answerable only to God and the Pope.

The work at Amoneburg progressed; churches were built, men prepared for ordination and the Faith re-established. Yet not far away the Borthari tribe were worshipping the old gods and he felt drawn to preach to them. At Geismar there was an ancient oak tree sacred to the god Thor, which proved a stumbling block to the progress of the gospel. Boniface realised he would have to tackle this problem before he could make any headway.

In front of a hostile crowd of heathens, he struck the tree one blow with an axe and it fell down (assisted at that moment, according to the story, by a great wind). The onlookers were impressed and started to praise the Lord. Afterwards the pieces of the tree were used for making a chapel on that spot.

The next years were taken up with missionary journeys, particularly to Hesse and Thuringia, organising the growing Church and corresponding with friends in England and with Rome. On his travels he occasionally discovered long-established Christian groups that had erred from the Faith or gone 'underground'. He was able to encourage them in their faith and help them sort out their problems.

In 732 a new Pope decided to recognise him as archbishop, though still without a see, so that he could set up proper dioceses in the areas he had evangelised. Boniface felt the loneliness of his position as an itinerant bishop and his elevation did little to relieve his sense of frustration. He had failed to win the full support of the king of the Franks, 'Charles the Hammer', and had been unable to set up a proper diocesan system.

His correspondence with friends and other ecclesiastics in England proved a source of great comfort to him; he discussed his problems, asked advice and requested prayer for himself and for 'those Germans who are given over to the worship of idols.'

By now his mission field had widened and had spilled westward over the Rhine into Frankland (France). He had also made contact with the Saxons, the tribes most dear to his heart. His flock was numbered in thousands and there was a constant need for pastoral care. He also continued his evangelistic outreach, administered the Church and re-formed those sections that had fallen into disarray.

The work of establishing religious houses went ahead, and monasteries and convents were set up where the 'work of God' could be continued. The most famous one was at Fulda in Hesse, founded in 744 by one of his disciples. A parcel of land was allocated to them and a cross raised; within a year a form of monastic life had been started, though it took ten years to complete the building project. As with all his houses, it was under the rule of Benedict.

FULDA: THE CATHEDRAL, ONE OF GERMANY'S MOST BEAUTIFUL BAROQUE CATHEDRALS BUILT BY JOHANN DIEZENHOFER.

Renewal

Towards the end of his life Boniface was finally able to enlist the support of the Frankish kings. Previously, Charles the Hammer had aided the Christian missions, and the Church had been grateful for his success when he defeated the Muslem invasion at Poitiers in 732. Later, Charles' two sons helped Boniface to carry out a major reform of the Frankish Church, bringing about a renewal of religious and intellectual life in Frankland.

Unable to make any further progress among the Saxon tribes, Boniface once again turned his attention to Frisia. He was now seventy-four and his eyesight was failing, but the threat of the danger among the heathens did not deter him. After Pentecost 754 he gathered a group of over fifty volunteers for the missionary tour which started off as a great success.

One night they camped by the River Boorn where next day the new converts were to be baptised. In the early morning they were awakened by 'harsh and violent sounds'. The monks ran out of their tents and were attacked by a heathen mob; Boniface called on his followers not to fight but 'to follow the example of our Lord in Gethsemane'.

In a matter of minutes the whole band was martyred. Boniface, protected until the last, was killed with one blow to his skull despite shielding his head with a book. His body was later recovered and taken to Fulda for burial, and the Abbey became a shrine and place of pilgrimage.

More than any other he can rightly be called the 'Apostle of Germany'. Although he reaped where the Celtic Church had sown, it was largely by his efforts that the German Church was re-established.

ALFRED THE GREAT (849-899): King of Wessex

England is a Christian nation and many of the institutions and customs interwoven within its history are derived from the Faith. In the ninth century Christianity was severely challenged by another wave of heathen invaders, the Vikings of Denmark, who were even more fierce and ruthless than their Saxon predecessors. Yet England was saved by the leadership of Alfred, King of Wessex, who during his reign of twenty-eight years drove back the enemy, united the English peoples and re-established Christianity.

Alfred was born at Wantage (Oxfordshire) in 849; he was the youngest of four sons of Ethelwulf, King of Wessex, one of the four main kingdoms of England. His parents were of the Christian faith and they gave their sons a religious training. As Alfred grew older he took his religion more seriously, so that his life and role as king were influenced by his faith.

As the favourite son, Alfred was kept at court for his education. He was taught many of the hymns written by Aldhem of Malmesbury, but did not learn to read until he was twelve or thirteen years old. When he did, it opened a new world for Alfred and he developed an appetite for books. He began to learn the daily services of the Church, some of the psalms and a number of prayers.

At some point in his early life he visited Rome, though the dates are unsure. On the first occasion he was sent by his father and stayed several months at the English College. The next time, the two of them went together and stayed as long as a year. They took with them gifts of gold and silver for the Church of St. Peter, and probably visited the tombs of the apostles Peter and Paul.

After the death of his father in 858, further tragedy struck the family and Alfred's three brothers died, possibly from some congenital complaint. At the age of twenty-two Alfred inherited the throne of the kingdom of Wessex, coming to power at the darkest hour in his nation's history.

Since Lindisfarne was pillaged by raiders in 793, England had been increasingly subject to attacks from the Vikings of Denmark. At first they attacked the towns near the coast, plundering and destroying churches and monasteries; they seemed determined to stamp out Christianity and restore heathenism. In 865 a great Viking army under Ivar the Boneless landed in East Anglia, intent on conquest. They captured York in 866, subjugated Northumbria and occupied most of Mercia; in 872 they captured London.

Victory

Alfred became king in 871 as the Vikings were mounting an offence against Wessex, and in his first year he fought nine battles against the enemy. In 878, after spending the winter at his camp on the marshes at Athelney, he re-grouped his forces and engaged the Vikings in battle at Edington, south of Chippenham. He won a decisive victory and forced the Vikings to make peace. It proved to be the turning point in his campaign against the Danes.

As a result of his defeat, the Viking king Guthrum and twenty-nine of his chieftains accepted the Christian religion. They were baptised and Guthrum was given the Christian name of Athelstan by his godfather,

Alfred. Soon Alfred was accepted as the leader of the free people of England, all except those who were under the power of the Danes. This recognition outside the kingdom of Wessex marked an advance towards the founding of a united English nation.

The peace with the Danes enabled Alfred to set about re-building his kingdom and strengthening his defences. First, he built new fortifications of ditches and banks surmounted by a stockade, and in places made use of the Roman Saxon shore forts such as at Porchester or the Roman defences at Chichester.

Then realising the need to meet the enemy at sea, he created a navy of ships built to his own design, which proved more than a match for the Danish long-boats. At first he had to man his ships with seamen from Frisia until he could train his own fighting men. Despite the peace, raiders continued to harry the coast of Wessex, but towards the end of his reign his galleys and long-ships formed a genuine English navy that was able to command the Channel. Today, Alfred is remembered as the 'Father of the English Navy'.

Whatever ambition Alfred may have had of becoming a king of a great kingdom, he seems to have set it aside. His purpose was to devote himself wholly to the welfare of the people of his kingdom. He was especially anxious to restore the Christian Faith to its proper place in the life of his people and to encourage his subjects to live according to the precepts of the Bible.

As a Christian king, Alfred endeavoured to set his people an example. On one occasion, a Viking chieftain broke his promise to him. Alfred attacked him, captured his family and then showed them mercy; instead of holding them as hostages, he sent them back with gifts of money.

Alfred began a programme of re-building those religious places destroyed by the raiders. Unfortunately, there is no evidence to link his name with any of the Saxon churches still standing, but he is known to have founded the abbey at Winchester, a monastery at Athelney and a nunnery at Shaftesbury. His efforts to fill his houses with English monks failed, however, and he had to send abroad for volunteers. He pressed into his service scholars, teachers and ecclesiastics from other countries, whose learning enriched the life of Wessex.

Generous
He gave half of his income to God and divided its use into four parts - for the poor, his monasteries, his school and lastly, for neighbouring

KING ALFRED

monasteries in Mercia and beyond. Following his father's example, he made generous gifts to Rome and each year sent an embassy to the Pope with offerings for the Church and the English College.

Essentially a practical man, Alfred used his ingenuity to aid his devotion to God. He is credited with the invention of the candle, which he used to measure time. He also introduced the lantern, which had doors made of white ox-horn planed so thin that they were like glass. In this way he was able to allocate half his time to God and dutifully complete his service.

It was Alfred's desire that his people should be properly and justly governed, and he was determined to rule his kingdom wisely. As king, he was assisted by the Witan, a council composed of nobles, the higher clergy and important laymen, which tended to take on the appearance of a synod. Towards the end of his reign he introduced a new code of laws, with a preface written by himself in which he quoted the Ten Commandments and the 'Golden Rule' of Jesus. The purpose of this was to show his people the Christian basis of the law and to indicate the relationship between religion and life.

The laws he established were not his own, for he had collected together the ones he thought to be the most just from the kingdoms of Wessex, Mercia and Kent. In dealing with offenders, the purpose was to show mercy, and each offence was dealt with by a fine imposed by the synod. Hopefully, the people would see that an offence against the law was also an offence against God.

Despite his late start in life along the path of literature, Alfred developed a passion for culture and achieved a high level of scholarship. Some would even go further and claim that we owe to Alfred the foundation of our English literature. He collected and preserved poems based on the Saxon traditions and legends, and stories of the deeds of mighty warriors who fought dragons and wild boars.

Between 892 and his death in 899 he produced English translations of five Latin works, the most famous known as *Cura Pastoralis*, a treatise by Gregory the Great describing the responsibilities of bishops. He also translated Bede's *History of the English Church* and the *Soliloquies of St. Augustine*. His most delightful work was the one he called his *Manual*, a book of meditations upon the Scriptures which is no longer in existence.

Needless to say, Alfred valued education highly. His youngest son, Ethelwerd, was sent to one of the schools the king had by that time established. He was taught to write and read both Latin and Saxon books. Alfred hoped that this pattern of education would be available for all free-born children, but it was not to be.

The respect for Alfred grew during his reign and his position as leading king was firmly established. In 884 he re-captured London which, following the Roman occupation, had fallen into disrepair. He re-built the walls and re-peopled it, making it a strong defensive point along the Thames. This action proved of historical importance, preparing London to become the future capital of the country.

It is not surprising that Alfred was accorded the title of 'Great' when the breadth of his achievements are considered. He not only stemmed the tide of barbarianism, but laid down a foundation for the Christian kingdom of England. When he died, his body was buried first in the Cathedral at Winchester and afterwards in the Abbey which he had founded. The name of Wessex has almost been forgotten, yet the name of Alfred will long be remembered as one of the greatest monarchs of our history. His own words can serve as his epitaph: 'I have desired to live worthily while I lived,' he wrote, 'and after my life to leave to the men that should be after me a remembrance of good works.'

FOUR

The Growth of Monasticism

Origins

The practice of going apart for the purpose of prayer and meditation and in the pursuit of God has for many centuries commended itself to religious people. Since the third century Christians have withdrawn from society in order to search for God and to lead a more Christ-like life unhindered by worldly pleasures. Some have sought the sanctuary of a place where their love for God could be expressed in daily devotions and in service to other people, usually in a monastery or convent.

The word monastery and other related terms are derived from the Greek word *monos* meaning 'one' or 'alone,' and conveys the idea of solitude and isolation. The first monks were hermits who lived an ascetic kind of life in the deserts of Egypt, cutting themselves off from society. Later, monks began to live together in a community, practising the 'coenobitic' life (from another Greek word, meaning 'living in common with others'). Although monks do not now live in isolation, the term has continued to be used of men who belong to a religious order.

For some Christians, the origin of this idea goes back to the Gospels. They recall how Jesus spent forty days in the wilderness, where he ate nothing and was hungry. On other occasions he went by himself to a solitary place to pray, sometimes staying out all night. It seemed he was challenging his disciples to follow an austere life, with an emphasis on self-sacrifice and self-discipline, where material possessions were a stumbling block rather than an asset. Taking this teaching out of context led a number of Christians to take up a monastic life.

The most influential of these monks was Antony (251-356), who as a youth of eighteen gave away all his possessions and went to live as a hermit in the deserts of Egypt. Before long a number of disciples had gathered around him, each living in a separate cell but under his rule. The monks devoted themselves to prayer and fasting, Bible study and meditation. The problem of living alone was too much for Antony; he suffered from hallucinations and was said to have fought demons in the guise of wild beasts. Nevertheless, he lived to over a hundred and became known as the 'Father of monasticism'.

Community-type monasticism was founded by Pachomius (290-

346) who was converted to Christ after leaving the army in 313. He lived for a while as a hermit then gave it up to found a monastery at Tabennisi on the banks of the Nile, where at one time some three thousand monks resided. His code of discipline, or 'rule', specially designed for monks living together under the same roof, formed the basis for similar rules of later monastic orders.

But monasticism in the Eastern Church is chiefly indebted to Basil of Cappadocia, later Bishop of Caesarea. His rule, which is still followed in the Greek Orthodox Church today, laid more stress on the pursuit of sanctification and the love of one's neighbour, rather than on certain religious practices. In addition to prayer and Bible study, the monks engaged in practical concerns such as agriculture, poor relief and nursing, and although strict, they avoided the more extreme austerities of the hermits.

In the West, monasticism grew more slowly. It was introduced by Athanasius, Bishop of Alexandria (296-373), friend of Pachomius and an ardent admirer of Antony. Yet there was already in the Roman Church an established interest in the ascetic life, and Ambrose of Milan and the scholar Jerome of Bethlehem did much to foster it.

The laxity of sexual relationships among Roman and Greek pagans in the fourth century caused many Christian young men and women to withdraw from society to lead a celibate life.

In Gaul, a further stimulus was given by Bishop Martin of Tours who has been credited by some with being the real founder of western monasticism. Certainly he founded the first monasteries in Europe, at Ligugé and later the 'Greater Monastery' at Marmoutier, which he developed as a centre for evangelism.

This vision was taken up by the Celtic Church in Britain, and Ninian of Whithorn, Columba of Iona and Patrick of Ireland all used their monasteries for missionary work.

Yet it was Benedict of Nursia, in north-central Italy, who one hundred years later probably became the true 'Father of western monasticism' and whose rule helped establish medieval monasticism on a sound basis for the next few centuries.

BENEDICT (480-550): Father of Western Monasticism

Benedict lived in an age of violence and change, when the Roman Empire was in its death throes. As a young man he left home to study in Rome, but found the life there too corrupt. He abandoned his studies and went in search of God. East of Rome, near Subacio, he found a cave in a hillside above a lake where he was able to live the life of a hermit. His only company was provided by a monk, Romanus, who brought him his food.

In time his reputation grew, probably spread by the local shepherds, and other men came to join him. He founded a monastery at Vicovaro and became the abbot, but when he attempted to impose high standards on their way of life, he met with considerable disapproval. The monks tried to kill him with poisoned wine but failed, so he decided to return to Subiacio.

His next move was to establish a monastic work in the Aniane valley, and he gathered enough monks to set up twelve small communities who devoted their lives to prayer. His growing reputation for holiness, however, provoked the jealousy of a priest who lived nearby. A further attempt was made on Benedict's life when the priest tried to poison him, and the abbot once again felt compelled to move on. He settled at Monte Cassino, halfway between Rome and Naples, and in 529 founded a monastery within the walls of an ancient fortress. He remained here until his death around 550.

Extraordinary Lives

While he was abbot at Monte Cassino he drew up his essentially practical *Rule of Benedict*, which became widely adopted throughout Europe. There had been various codes of monastic rules for nearly two hundred years and Benedict drew upon these when writing his own, but he considerably modified them in the light of his own experience and his understanding of human nature. He was aware that monks were 'ordinary people called upon to live extraordinary lives'. He referred to his rule as a 'beginner's rule', and it was a document that combined practical rules for living in community with 'pages of sublime spirituality', the whole being firmly rooted in Scripture.

The *Rule of Benedict* is divided into seventy-three chapters, which not only lays down a code of conduct but also sets out his philosophy for his monastery. He envisaged a self-sufficient family unit under the care of the Abbot, devoted to the *opus Dei*, the work of God. The three main activities were prayer, reading the Scriptures and work, but mostly the *opus Dei*, the daily offering of praise and prayer to God. At first, the work was manual - growing food, preparing the meals and maintaining the monastery; later it included writing and copying books, illustrating manuscripts and teaching.

As today, the monks took three vows; of stability: whereby a monk remained with the one monastery; of conversion of manners, that is living a celibate life whole-heartedly for God; and of obedience to the Abbot and the other monks.

The communities of Benedictines, or Black Monks (from the colour of their habit), were discouraged from the extreme forms of asceticism and unlike the hermits, wore proper clothing, ate sufficient food and enjoyed adequate sleep. Although Benedict's rule was strict, it was 'marvellous in its tenderness'.

Within a short time after his death, the *Rule of Benedict* was the principal form of monastic rule in the Western Church. Gregory the Great was a Benedictine monk, so under Augustine the order became established in England and it spread to Germany where Boniface also founded Benedictine monasteries. It finally became the standard rule by imperial decree when Emperor Charlemagne declared that it alone should be used.

To the dismay of his monks, Benedict had a prophecy that 'Almighty God has decreed that this entire monastery and everything I have provided for the community shall fall into the hands of the barbarians'. Before the end of the century, the prophecy was fulfilled and Monte Cassino was sacked by the Lombards from the north.

Benedict had not intended to found a monastic order, but the gentleness of his rule, drawn up 'for monks that functioned imperfectly', had a wide appeal. Many religious houses adopted his rule, forming a confederation of self-governing monasteries. Over the years, many of the monasteries increased in wealth, while their ardour for God waned; until in the twelfth century a new voice was heard, Bernard of Clairvaux, calling the monks back to their vocation.

BERNARD (1090-1153): Abbot of Clairvaux

The spirit of revival in the eleventh century Church resulted not only in an increase in papal power over secular rulers, but also in the formation of new monastic orders. Following the foundation of the Order of Cluny (910), the most influential monastic movement was that of the Cistercians, founded in 1098.

Since the sixth century the Benedictine Order had achieved popularity and attracted the attention of the rich nobility, who had endowed the monasteries with wealth and grants of land. With prosperity came a decline in religious fervour, and abuses crept in. The Order of Cluny was founded with the object of reform and was based on a return to the strict Benedictine rule. Education and culture were abandoned, emphasis was placed on liturgy with an increase in the number of daily services and masses, and churches were built on a grander scale.

Towards the end of the eleventh century a further attempt at reform was made when a Benedictine monastery was founded at Citeaux in Burgundy (France). It led to a new order which took its title of Cistercian from the name of this monastery. The object was again to keep the original Benedictine rule and to seek God in simplicity, silence and poverty.

The monks at Citeaux wanted to get away from the world and were ordered to build their monasteries 'in places remote from habitation'. They were to receive no gifts of land or money and could have no personal possessions. The churches were to be plain; stained glass windows and mosaic pavements were forbidden as was gold and silver church plate, and altar fronts and habits were to be simple and without embroidery.

The greatest of these monasteries was at Clairvaux, founded in 1115 by Bernard, who became the most influential preacher and writer of the medieval Church and the main force behind the Cistercian expansion.

Brilliant Pupil

Born near Dijon, Bernard's father was one of the Knights of Chatillon, of ancient stock yet not of the highest nobility. His mother, a woman of strong character, devoted much of her time to the poor, yet without neglecting her six sons and one daughter. While still a child Bernard was marked out by his parents for the Church. He was given a suitable education and studied the trivium, which consisted of rhetoric, logic and grammar. He was said to have been a brilliant pupil, and although sensitive and shy, was at times full of high spirits.

It was his mother who had inspired his desire to enter the Church but when she died in 1104 he lost his sense of purpose for a while. Yet in 1111, at the age of twenty-one, he suddenly decided he wanted to become a monk; he intended to join the poor and relatively insignificant abbey at Citeaux rather than the well established one at Cluny. 'I chose Citeaux in preference to Cluny,' he explained, 'because I was convinced that my weak character needed strong medicine.'

Despite his family's attempts to dissuade him, his mind was made up; in fact he was afire with enthusiasm and set about persuading others to join him. When he entered Citeaux he took with him thirty companions, plus his brothers and a cousin. News of his recruiting campaign spread far and it was said that 'mothers hid their sons and wives their husbands' for fear of Bernard.

Life at Citeaux was demanding, but the greatest difficulty
for the young nobleman was
probably the complete obedience demanded by the Rule.
Bernard never enjoyed robust
health and on one occasion collapsed under the strain of
harvesting. After prayer, however, his strength returned and
he was able to continue with the
work.

In 1115 the Abbot decided
to expand the order and to make
two more foundations. The
young Bernard, who had shown
great promise, was chosen to be
the Abbot at the one in the
'Valley of Light', or Clairvaux,
north of Bar-sur-Aube. With
twelve other monks, he chose a

BERNARD

desolate spot in the valley of the Saone to build his monastery. As usual,
a temporary wooden structure was erected prior to a building of stone.

At first there was little money or food for the monks, and their habits
were thread-bare and shoes worn out; some of the brothers were getting
quite ill and losing heart. Then one morning as Bernard was at prayer,
he had a vision in which he saw the whole valley with men of every age
streaming towards the monastery. His faith was encouraged; he told of
his vision to the monks and exhorted them to trust God and he would
supply all their needs.

Bernard found that as he prayed, God opened up a way so the work
could go forward. Once the cellarer told him that there was no money
left. 'How much money do you want?' asked Bernard. 'Eleven pounds,'
was the reply. Bernard prayed about the matter and shortly a woman
arrived with a gift of twelve pounds as a thanksgiving for the cure of her
husband.

Despite the early problems, Clairvaux began to expand and in 1118
founded its first daughter house. The increase continued throughout
Bernard's life until by the time of his death in 1153 there were sixty-five

daughter houses in Europe. Although Cluny continued to hold an acknowledged place of esteem, monks were seeking something less ritualistic and Clairvaux fulfilled that need. The White Monks of Citeaux won the admiration of the ordinary people, so that the Black Monks of Cluny (who were Benedictines) became envious. Rivalry between the two groups sadly turned their relationship quite sour.

As Bernard toured the neighbourhood preaching - and persuading men to join his monastery - his reputation grew. He was extremely busy, receiving visitors and messengers, and travelling to distant places on ecclesiastical business. Soon the fame of the young Abbot reached Rome and Bernard found himself involved in papal affairs.

He was also increasingly called upon to arbitrate in disputes. In 1125, for example, he was asked to intervene in a quarrel between the canons of Chalon and their bishop, and when the two popes claimed the Chair of Peter at Rome, splitting the Church, it was Bernard's eloquence that won the day.

Meanwhile, he became involved in the foundation of the Order of the Knights Templar, formed for the purpose of protecting pilgrims in the Holy Land. As a result of Bernard's persuasion, they were given Church approval at the Council of Troyes (1128) and it is thought that Bernard also drew up their Rule. His apologia, *In Praise Of The New Knighthood*, declared that 'God had chosen these men to serve him and to guard the most holy sepulchres of the Church'.

Controversy

As a defender of the Faith, Bernard became involved in a controversy with a brilliant Benedictine monk, Peter Abélard of Paris, whose views on faith and the Trinity he considered to be heretical. The two men met in public debate in the presence of the king and the bishops of France, but Abélard's opposition fell apart at the last moment. 'I will not answer the Cistercian,' he declared, 'I will appeal to Rome.' The Pope condemned Abélard and his books were publicly burned.

By now Bernard was fifty-four years old and had reached the zenith of his powers. His name had become a household word throughout Europe and he was the friend of kings, princes and bishops alike. He intervened in their troubles and dealt with affairs of state. At one point he even wrote to the Pope, 'Men are saying it is not you but I who am Pope, and from all sides they are flocking to me with their suits.'

A resurgence of Islamic forces at this time led to the formation of the Second Crusade and Bernard took it upon himself to stir the nations of

Europe to action. In 1145 he wrote an encyclical letter warning the churches of 'the enemy of Christ' and calling for action. He persuaded the King of France and the Emperor of Germany to mount an expedition, which left in 1148. It was a fiasco and ended in defeat; within two years the Crusade was forced to return home. The blame fell on Bernard who was heart-broken.

By now his life was drawing to a close. A number of his dearest friends died and then Bernard himself was taken seriously ill. For many years he had been plagued with illness and his ascetic way of living was now taking its toll. He rallied for some months but finally passed away on 20th August 1153.

Throughout his life Bernard radiated immense charm and personality. He had great powers of persuasion and attracted many men to his order. Yet he could easily lose patience and was quick to flare up in anger. He loved his friends dearly; it was said he could never see any good in his enemies and no evil in his friends. He was a supporter of lost causes and no problem was too small for him.

Like many other scholars, he left behind a large number of letters and other works, the most famous being his essay on *The Love of God*. He also wrote eighty-four sermons on the *Song of Solomon* where he speaks of the mystical meaning of the text, and numerous sermons in praise of Mary.

Without doubt, Bernard was the most influential man of his age, but despite his success the Cistercians had begun to lose their effectiveness by the end of the twelfth century. Although the order grew to include

---

The Crusades

A series of military expeditions were mounted between the years 1095-1291 intended to free the Holy Land from domination by Islam. In 638 Muslims captured Jerusalem from the Byzantines after a two year siege and finally took control of both Palestine and Syria. Although pilgrimages were allowed to continue, pilgrims came increasingly under attack and when the Seljuk Turks seized Jerusalem in 1071 they desecrated the holy places. Following an appeal from Pope Urban 11 the crusaders set off overland to defeat the 'infidel' and restore access to the ancient sites. En route, they massacred 12,000 Jewish people in the Rhineland, though Bernard made valiant attempts to shield them, and in the Holy Land the inhabitants of Jerusalem were ruthlessly put to the sword. The first Crusade was a success in that the Latin Kingdom of Jerusalem was established and pilgrimages were safely resumed. But later expeditions failed, interest waned and the Arabs finally re-captured the Land in 1291.

some seven hundred and fifty monastic houses, the importance of cloistered monasteries declined and new groups of monks appeared.

FRANCIS (1182-1226): Founder of the Franciscans

During the twelfth and thirteenth centuries the monasteries began to lose their influence as a result of their wealth and worldliness. Faith was questioned and false beliefs were spreading. At the same time there was a 'population explosion' throughout western Europe and towns and cities were developing fast. It was the need to combat these problems that led to a new monastic movement; its members were not monks, however, but friars, who instead of being confined to a religious house went out into the world to preach and to care for the sick and the poor.

One such group was the 'Poor Men of Lyons', founded by Peter Valdes, a rich merchant who gave his wealth to the poor. Later there were the Dominican Friars founded by a Spaniard Dominic de Guzman in order to preach in schools and universities against the Albigensian heresy, which disputed Christ's death and resurrection.

But the most famous order was the Friars Minor founded by Francis of Assisi, which captured the admiration of the people and proved to be the most influential. When he died, Francis left not one but three religious orders that adopted his ideals.

Francis was the second son of a wealthy cloth-merchant in Assisi, a city in Umbria, north-central Italy, and lived a life of ease and luxury. His father, however, was a harsh and avaricious man and a domineering husband, ill thought of in the town. Over the years Francis grew up to hate his father and yet constantly sought his approval.

High Living

Following an adequate education by the canons of a nearby church, Francis went into his father's business at the age of fourteen. He was clever and quick to learn the trade, and his father showed his satisfaction by allowing him all the money he wanted. The youthful Francis became a spend-thrift, squandering his money on gambling and high-living, wasting his time, yet always generous to the poor and the beggars.

He was very conscious of being the son of a merchant and not of the nobility, and used his money to win friends among the upper classes. Although for a time his money bought him companions, he never reached the rank of nobility to which he aspired.

One possible method of entry was by joining one of the Crusades to the Holy Land, but he returned home depressed after only a few days into the journey. It may be that a reaction set in, but he began to take an interest in the Catholic Church. When he went on a pilgrimage to Rome, he forced himself to overcome his loathing for lepers by greeting them with a kiss. Later he retired with some companions to seek out remote and solitary places.

One day he visited the church of San Damiano and knelt before the altar to pray. He heard a tender voice speaking to him, 'Francis, do you see that my house is falling into ruins? Go and repair it for me.' Amazed, Francis blurted out, 'Gladly I will do so, O Lord.' But using his father's money for religious purposes caused a family quarrel. To teach him a lesson, his father arraigned him before an ecclesiastical court, where the bishop told Francis that if he wished to serve God he must first return the money to his father.

Francis, who for some time now had been labelled a 'madman', removed all his clothes (despite the cold winter winds) and gave his belongings and the money back to his father. 'I am resolved to serve God,' he told an astonished crowd, 'and from now on I will say, "Our Father which art in heaven" and not "my father Pietro Bernadone".' Bursting with anger, his father snatched up the clothes and the money and returned home.

One of the bishop's farm-hands gave him his own tunic, upon which Francis inscribed the sign of the cross. He was now definitely alone, not knowing where his future lay. For some while Francis continued to restore ruined churches, and with no income had to beg for stones and other materials; he even had to beg for his food, bringing further disgrace upon the family.

Destiny

One feast day in February 1208, Francis was struck by the Gospel reading about Jesus' instructions to his disciples when he sent them out among the people. His command not to take any money or even extra clothing and to preach the kingdom of heaven came as a challenge. 'This is what I long for with all my heart,' he declared. He had at last found his destiny.

To signify the change, Francis discarded his girdle, shoes and staff; he put on a rough grey tunic, worn over breeches, with a cord round his waist. He repaired no more churches but began to go around preaching. His message was rather low-key and whenever he met anyone he simply greeted them with, 'God give you peace.'

The people of Assisi warmed towards Francis and their attitude changed; the 'madman' became accepted as part of the local scene. He was soon joined by his first helper when a wealthy merchant gave away his riches to be with Francis; others quickly followed, including two men from noble families, and by the following year there were twelve Brothers. The men lived in a hut close to one of Francis' restored churches outside Assisi. They rose at midnight for prayer and spent their days working or begging. Sometimes they would go out to preach to passers-by, urging them to fear and love God, and to do penance for their sins.

With the possibility of further expansion, it seemed important for the growing movement to gain official recognition. In 1210 Francis and the twelve Brothers went to Rome - walking barefoot - to meet the Pope, who was eventually persuaded to give them his blessing. Francis wrote a simple form of life and rule for the order, using the words of the Gospels, as they were to be under no rule except that of the Lord. They had to give to the poor, have no possessions and to take up the cross. Francis insisted on complete poverty, as only in this way could they be relieved from the cares of the world and be joyful before God.

Poor Clares

In 1212 Francis' preaching attracted the attention of a young lady from one of Assisi's noble families. Despite his vocation, it is possible Francis formed some attachment with Clare, though the friendship was always discreet. She expressed her desire to join Francis in his way of life, and one night secretly left her home and was taken into a local convent. Both her family (who tried to get her back) and Francis were presented with a *fait accompli*, and there was no turning back.

Other noble ladies were attracted by her example and came to join her. Within three years Clare was made the abbess of the group and Francis gave them the Church of San Damiano, which he had restored, as their headquarters. They became known as the Poor Clares, and accepted Francis' rule of poverty and chastity. Given to good works, they were particularly concerned with the sick, which later paved the way for a study of medicine.

There are many legends about the life of Francis and it is not always easy to get at the truth. But for sure, Francis had a love of nature and was known to preach to the birds and animals. Once on a preaching tour he left his companions, saying, 'Wait here for me on the road, I am going to preach to our sisters the birds.' It was said the birds in the trees came down to listen to him; he told them to 'praise the Lord,' and as they flew away they sang a wonderful song. He also loved having pets, especially birds, lambs and rabbits, but they were later forbidden in his Second Rule.

Towards the end of his life he wrote his *Canticle To The Sun* in which he taught his friars to sing as they went around preaching. In the song he praised God for Brother Sun, Sister Water and Mother Earth; and before he died, he added a verse to 'our Sister, bodily Death.'

On several occasions Francis attempted to make a preaching tour beyond the shores of Italy. In 1214 he started a journey to Morocco, to convert the Moors and hoping to achieve the prize of martyrdom. He was forced to turn back to Assisi by a prolonged bout of illness.

In 1219 he made a second attempt to reach the Holy Land and preach to the Muslims, and although he managed to visit both Egypt and Palestine he returned home sad and disillusioned. He had presented himself at the Sultan's camp in a rather foolhardy attempt to convert him, offering to prove the truth of Christianity by ordeal of fire. The Sultan received him kindly but declined the offer.

The Stigmata

On his return to Assisi Francis discovered that a number of changes had been made in the order during his absence, so he gave up the leadership of the Friars and retired to live a hermit's life in the hills. His health was deteriorating, due to his long journey to the Middle East, and his eyesight was getting worse.

During a time of fasting in the month of September 1224, Francis allegedly received the stigmata, the first known example of such an experience, in which the wounds of Christ's passion were reproduced on his body. He had wounds on his hands and his feet, which he kept bandaged; after that, he was no longer able to walk barefoot, but had to ride a donkey.

The last days of his life were spent in a small hut built by Clare. He was taken finally to the Church of San Maria degli Angeli where he died at nightfall on 3rd October 1226. His body was laid to rest in a basilica specially built after his death.

Before he died Francis warned the Brothers about accepting churches or houses, but to 'conform to holy poverty'. After his death, the order continued to grow, but it became more difficult to maintain the vow of poverty, dividing his followers and the Church for more than a century.

Francis had an attractive and winsome personality that endeared many people to him and to his cause. He frequently gave the impression of being an eccentric, but for some he was the most Christ-like figure that ever lived. Perhaps his remarks about his tenderness towards leprosy sufferers best illustrates this: '...the Lord himself did lead me among them, and I had compassion upon them. When I left them, that which had seemed to me bitter had become sweet and easy.'

MEDIEVAL MONASTIC ORDERS

ORDER	FOUNDATION	IMPORTANT FEATURES	LEADING FIGURES	CHIEF BRITISH HOUSES
BENEDICTINES (or Black Monks)	* Benedict of Nursia (c480-550) Monte Cassino, Italy, 529	* First of monastic orders * Drew up own rules: - combined practical living in community with spirituality; - self-sufficient family unit under care of Abbot * Main activity: Opus Dei - praise and prayer to God * Prosperity led to decline in religious fervour	* Pope Gregory the Great * Augustine of Canterbury * Venerable Bede * Boniface	Canterbury Dunfermline Gloucester Westminster Winchester
CLUNIACS	* Williams the Pious, Duke of Aquitaine Cluny, France, 910	* Under direct control of Pope * A return to Rule of Benedict * Origin of 10th century revival of Church * Emphasis on liturgy and elaborate ceremonies * Influence declined 12th century	* Hugh of Cluny * Pope Gregory VII * Pope Urban II	Few in number, include: Lewes, Bermondsey, Castle Acre, Pontefract
CISTERCIANS (or White Monks)	* Stephen Harding (d 1134) and Bernard of Clairvaux (1090-1153) Citeaux, France, 1098	* Austere form of Benedictine Rule * Monks were 'soldiers of Christ', disciplined and drilled * Monasteries built in remote places - each one autonomous	* Ailred of Rievaulx * Pope Eugenius III * Pope Benedict XII	Beaulieu Fountains Kirkstall Melrose Tintern Waverley
AUGUSTINIANS (or Black Monks)	* Arose out fo communities of clerics, in North Italy and South France in the 11th century	* Lived a common life of poverty, celibacy and obedience * Adopted Rule of Augustine of Canterbury * Spread Western Europe 12th century over 140 houses in England * Known in England as Austin Canons	*Dominic de Guzman * Thomas a Kempis * Martin Luther	Carlisle Cirencester Colchester Holyrood, Oxford St Andrews Waltham

ORDER	FOUNDATION	IMPORTANT FEATURES	LEADING FIGURES	CHIEF BRITISH HOUSES
DOMINICANS (or Black Friars)	* Dominic de Guzman (1170-1221) Spain, 1216	* An order of friars - travelling preachers who also cared for the sick * Practised poverty and lived by begging * Attracted intellectuals - taught in schools, universities * Preached against heresies * Conducted Inquisition, 1232	* Thomas Aquinas * Albertus Magnus * Johannes Eckhart * Savonarola	* Over 70 houses but few material remains
FRANCISCANS (or Friars Minor)	* Francis of Assisi, (1182-1226) Italy, 1209	* Laid down own Rule - life of simplicity and poverty, following the Lord's example * Churches simple and designed for preaching * Friars went out among people, tending the sick and preaching * Received stigmata in a vision 1224	* Bonaventura * William of Ockham * Roger Bacon	About 50 houses, but few remains Canterbury Chichester Kings Lynn Kirkcudbright Lincoln
JESUITS (or Company of Jesus)	* Ignatius of Loyola (1491-1556) Spain, 1534	* Two aims - to encourage reform within the Church of Rome; - to undertake mission work * Members regarded as 'soldiers' devoted to the Pope's service * Established successful missions from South America to the Far East * Implicated in plot to assassinate Queen Elizabeth I, and accused of interference in secular affairs of state * Suppressed by Pope, 1773, restored 1814	* Francis Xavier * Robert de Nobili	

FIVE

The Reformation

The Church of Rome

By the fourteenth century the medieval Church had sadly fallen into a state of decline, so that political and economic interests had overtaken matters of faith. The Church, seeking to establish its authority, especially over secular rulers, put itself above the laws of God and man; corruption was rife, false religious doctrines and practices increased and Scriptural teachings were disregarded.

The wealth of the Church was particularly noticeable in the monasteries, where rich noblemen often made large grants of land to the monks in exchange for pardons and services of mass for the souls of the dead. In England, the monasteries were the country's greatest land-owners and held over one third of the land; the Cistercians, for example, raised large flocks of sheep, bringing in immense wealth. Bishops, abbots and monks sank into worldliness, forgetting the purpose of their calling and indulging more and more in secular pursuits.

The Papacy was equally at fault, and spent huge amounts of money in vying with kings and emperors in maintaining a lavish and resplendent court. Church taxes were levied and bishoprics and divorces 'sold' to support the papal patronage of the arts. An extravagant building programme was set up, which later included building the Sistine Chapel in Rome.

Further disgrace was brought upon the Papacy when the 'Great Schism' (1378-1417) rent the Church with the election of two rival popes, one residing in Avignon and the other in Rome.

Discontent grew as a result of a number of teachings and practices that were contrary to Scripture.

The doctrine of transubstantiation, which teaches that the bread and wine at the Eucharist become the actual body and blood of Jesus, was accepted by the Fourth Lateran Council (1215), which also laid down that every Christian should confess his sins at penance at least once a year.

The cult of the Virgin and the teaching of the Immaculate Conception, which declared Mary to have been free from all stain of original sin, were also gaining ground, though not without opposition. Practices such

as auricular confession and the sale of indulgences whereby the penalty
for sin was remitted by the priest (on behalf of the Church) became
common, and in 1232 the Courts of Inquisition were set up to deal with
heretics.

As the sole dispenser of salvation, the Church of Rome seemed to be
in an impregnable position. Yet the seeds of discontent were already
sown; many Christians were growing restless under its yoke and signs
of resistance gradually began to appear.

We have already cited the Albigenses of southern France and the Poor
Men of Lyons as protest movements against the Catholic Church. In the
Netherlands, the Brethren of the Common Life was formed to foster a
higher level of Christian conduct and devotion, working through schools which offered free education. One of their members was Thomas à Kempis who wrote *The Imitation of Christ* to encourage Christians to follow the pattern of Christ's life and teaching.

There were also individuals who opposed the Church from within its ranks. Marsiglio of Padua (1275-1342) wrote his *Defensor Pacis* in 1324 to defend the Bible as supreme in matters of faith. Similar ideas were expressed by William of Ockham (1285 -1347) from Surrey, a leading Franciscan later excommunicated by the Pope.

Probably the most prominent opponent of the Church

Albigenses

Centred on the town of Albi in the south of France, the Albigenses were an heretical sect which reached its zenith around 1200 when they were supported by large sections of the population. In Italy the movement was known as the Cathari (Greek, 'Pure ones'), and their strength was such that at one point they were a threat to the Roman Church. They taught that all matter was evil, in which case Jesus was merely an angel - he did not have a real body and did not suffer or rise again, and his work of redemption was simply by way of his teaching. Under Pope Pius III a crusade was launched against them in 1208 which led to twenty years brutal and destructive warfare. The Dominicans were given the task of countering their heretical teachings and they mounted an Inquisition. There was no trace left of the sect by the end of the 14th century.

at this time, however, was John Wyclif, a Roman Catholic priest and a philosopher and theologian of Oxford University. The greatest scholar of his day, he has been described as 'the morning star of the Reformation,' though the extent of his contribution has not been fully determined.

JOHN WYCLIF (1320-1384):
The Morning Star of the Reformation

Little is known about his early life, except that he was born in north Yorkshire and his father was the lord of the manor at Wyclif. He may have gone up to Merton College, Oxford, in 1345, and from 1360-1362 he was the Master at Balliol College. He spent nine years reading for his doctorate, which he was awarded in 1372. At the University he was described as 'the flower of Oxford, in philosophy second to none, without rival in the discipline of the schools.' Seemingly the academics held him in high esteem, which may account for his entry into the king's service in 1366 under the patronage of John of Gaunt, Duke of Lancaster.

Though his foray into politics was not successful, it led to the formulation of his teaching on lordship, or 'dominion', which highly displeased the Church. He put forward the idea that the king's authority was derived from God, and therefore as God's vicar he had dominion over the clergy. As dominion was founded on grace, then sinful Popes need not be obeyed and it was the king's duty to reform the Church.

Wyclif used this theory to attack the abuses of the Church and to limit the authority of the Pope, an idea that appealed to secular clergy and laity alike. Condemned by the Church, Wyclif was summoned before a council of bishops at St. Paul's in 1377 to answer charges against his new teaching, though a mob intervened and the meeting had to be abandoned.

So far Wyclif had not disputed the primacy of the Pope, only to deny those not in 'a state of grace'. His break with the Papacy came in 1378 when he launched an attack on the central doctrine of the Church, transubstantiation. While believing in the real presence of Christ in the mass, he declared it to be spiritual rather than actual; that the bread and wine did not become the body and blood, but that Christ was received by faith. In which case, there was no need to be dependent on a priest, as each believer could receive Christ for himself.

His doctrine on the sacraments was determined by his view of the Church, which he defined as consisting of all of God's elect, those predestined to be saved, 'who cannot cease to be such... even by mortal sin.' On this basis, the Pope was not necessarily the head of the Church as it was not certain that he was even a member of it! Wyclif based his views on the absolute authority of the Bible, God's law, which he distinguished from the teaching of the Church. He further argued that every man had the right to examine the Bible for himself, in which case the Scriptures had to be translated into the common language.

His ideas about the eucharist, however, proved unacceptable and

provoked an up-
roar at Oxford. In
1381 he wrote his
Confession in
which he defended
his ideas, but was
deserted by many
of his supporters
and forced to leave
the university.
Many of his en-
emies would
gladly have had
him burned at the
stake, but he was
protected by John
of Gaunt. He re-
tired to Lutterworth
where he had been
given a living in
1374 for his sup-
port of the Crown
against the Pope.

JOHN WYCLIF

Wyclif was by now seriously ill, yet despite his condition the
remaining years of his life were among his most fruitful. He was visited
by a group of friars who had once been his friends, who now came to
advise him to repent. He told them, 'I shall not die, but I shall live and
declare the works of the Lord.' He did. In partnership with Nicholas of
Hereford, he began the first translation of the Bible from Latin into
English, which they rendered in a Midland dialect.

After his death this 'Wyclif Bible' was revised and written in a more
common dialect of the day. At the same time, Wyclif began a thorough
organisation of his Poor Priests, or Lollards (meaning 'mumblers', a
term used of heretics). The work had originated while he was at Oxford,
where some of his followers had preached his ideas. These followers
were 'unauthorised preachers', i.e. not licensed by the bishop. They
went out into towns and villages where they preached in the market
places or wherever people congregated, and distributed his tracts and
sermons, now written in English instead of Latin.

The Lollards worked mostly in the Midlands, but reached beyond to such places as Bristol, Amersham and Windsor. They established cells of believers from which to continue their outreach and received much popular support. The movement was condemned at the Blackfriars Council in 1382, but this failed to make any impact on its progress.

For the last two years of his life Wyclif was paralysed by a stroke and while attending Mass in December 1384 received another setback. He died three days later. Although Wyclif initiated no reforms, his ideas lived on and proved to be the rumblings of a disturbance later to erupt into the Reformation.

On the Continent, Wyclif's writings were taken up by Jan Hus (1374-1415) of Prague University in what is now Czechoslovakia. Hus preached the importance of the Scriptures in matters of faith, and condemned practices such as the use of images and sale of indulgences. When ordered to stop his preaching, he refused and declared, 'I will defend to the death the truth God has vouchsafed me, especially the truth of the Holy Scriptures.' He was put on trial and then burned at the stake.

MARTIN LUTHER (1483-1546):
Founder of the Reformation

The Protestant revolution owes its birth and initial development to the faith of one man - Martin Luther. Although there was widespread discontent within the medieval Church, it was ultimately Luther's challenge of papal power that brought about a reformation of the Christian religion in Europe. Others before him had made their protests, but Luther's attack on the sale of indulgences, or 'holy trade' as it was

---

Writing the Bible

The books of the New Testament were written on papyrus rolls and the writing arranged in columns. The letters were small, the words not separated and there was very little punctuation, which gave rise to misunderstandings. Separation of words did not appear until the Middle Ages and punctuation followed the invention of printing. Writing on vellum, in use by the fourth century, was in large capitals known as uncial, and resulted in cumbersome volumes. A new style of writing called minuscule or cursive, which used smaller letters linked together, remained in use between the ninth and fifteenth centuries. The division into chapters and verses first occurred in the Hebrew Old Testament in 1448 and in the New Testament in 1451, devised by a certain Stephanus as he travelled from Paris to Lyons; the first complete edition of the Bible with divisions was published in 1555.

known, caught the imagination of the ordinary people and found an active response.

The son of a miner, Luther was born in the village of Eisleben in Thuringia. His father was a determined, independent man who became part owner of six mine-shafts and two foundries. He also became a town councillor and owned a large house in the main street. The young Martin was brought up in the Catholic religion, in a world dominated by superstition, the fear of evil spirits, eternal damnation and in purgatory, as well as the hope of heaven for those who did good. The mass had lost its original meaning and had become merely a required ritual, and salvation depended upon the blind acceptance of the Church's doctrine.

In 1501, when Martin had reached the age of eighteen, his father sent him to the ancient university of Erfurt where he read for a Bachelor of Arts degree. He considered training as a lawyer, but the course of his life was changed one day when riding in the forest his companion was killed by lightning. Luther was shocked by the event; he gave up the idea of becoming a lawyer and, despite his father's protests, joined the Augustinian Hermits at one of Erfurt's five monasteries.

He received the tonsure in 1505 and became a novice, but his superiors had enough sense to recognise his preaching and teaching ability, and encouraged him to pursue the higher academic life. He was ordained a priest in 1507, he became lecturer in moral philosophy at the new University of Wittenberg where, in 1512 he was chosen as Professor of Theology, with the option of occupying the chair for the rest of his life. His time at the university was so fully occupied that at one point he felt he needed two secretaries in order to cope. He lectured on the apostle Paul, preached almost daily in the parish church, acted as the district visitor and wrote endless letters. Then in order to be able to read the New Testament in the original language, he set himself the task of learning Greek.

Outwardly, Luther lived the life of an industrious and successful friar; yet inwardly he was in turmoil and his mind filled with endless questions. Like thousands before him, he had entered the monastery to put himself right with God; but the usual prescribed methods of confessions, penances, prayers, fasting and vigils had failed to bring him the peace he longed for.

Pilgrimage
In 1510 he went on a pilgrimage to Rome, though it was ostensibly on monastic business. He took the opportunity to make confession and

MARTIN LUTHER THE AUGUSTINE MONK

celebrate mass (he once saw seven masses performed in one hour), he sought pastoral advice, but to no avail. He crawled up the twenty-eight steps of the Scala Sancta, supposed to be the staircase of Pilate's house which Jesus descended after his condemnation, saying a Pater Noster on each step (reckoned to free a soul from purgatory), yet he had no sense of forgiveness.

While ascending the steps, so his son later recounted, a verse from Habakkuk came to his mind: 'The righteous shall live by his faith', but an inner voice challenged him, 'How do I know all this is true?'

He returned to Germany greatly saddened by his failure to find peace; the thought struck him that 'the Church had lost the key to the kingdom.' He said later, 'Like a fool, I took onions to Rome and brought back garlic.'

Under the conviction of sin, Luther was obsessed with a sense of guilt and felt that he could not survive the judgement of God. At the university his mentor Staupitz, a philosopher, tried to soothe his mind and endeavoured to remind Luther of God's forgiving mercy, yet pointing out that it was also necessary to work hard to deserve God's salvation -

advice that brought little comfort. The matter came to a head in 1513 when Luther was preparing his lectures on the Psalms and he read the familiar phrase, 'Deliver me in thy righteousness' (Psalm 31:1).

Previously he had understood righteousness to be the punishment of a holy God towards sinful man, an idea that caused him considerable unease. But then his thoughts turned to Romans 1:17 where he read that man was made right with God by faith and not by works. He began to realise that the New Testament idea of righteousness was not one of punishment, but that it was God's nature to show mercy and forgiveness. 'When I realised this,' wrote Luther, 'I felt myself absolutely born again. The gates of paradise had been flung open and I had entered. There and then the whole of Scripture took on another look to me.'

Luther had re-discovered a Gospel truth that had lain dormant and hidden for hundreds of years, that salvation is the gift of God and no amount of religious ritual can reconcile the sinner to the Almighty. No longer was he under the threat of eternal damnation, for God had declared him to be righteous in Christ.

Indulgences

Four years elapsed before a situation arose that provoked the new-born Luther to challenge the false doctrines and practices of the Church. The occasion was the sale of indulgences in order to raise money for the re-building of St. Peter's in Rome. As medieval man was anxious about the state of his soul in purgatory, the idea of being able to buy remission of sins had appeal; it side-stepped the need for repentance and faith in Christ and supposedly offered a less painful entrance to heaven.

When Tetzel, the Pope's emissary, visited a town close to Wittenberg offering absolution of all sins, plus a plenary indulgence for the souls of the dead relatives who would straight away be released into heaven, Luther felt it was time to act.

On All Saints' Eve, 1517, he nailed his famous 95 theses to the door of the Castle Church at Wittenberg, condemning the sale of indulgences. He also sent printed copies to his archbishop and bishop, hoping to force them to show their position and make them respond. Luther's action, in fact, was nothing unusual; it was common practice to post such matters for academic discussion and he was drawing the Church's attention to his objections.

The thrust of his argument was that although an ecclesiastical indulgence may remit a penalty imposed by the Church, it could not bring about the release of a soul from purgatory. 'Those who assert that a soul straight away flies out (i.e. of purgatory) as the coin tinkles in the collection box are preaching an invention of man,' he declared.

The following day was All Saints' Day (1st November) and Frederick, the Elector, had secured an indulgence for all who came to the services at the Castle Church to see his collection of holy relics (he claimed to have 5,005 relics, giving an indulgence of 127,799 years and 166 days). Luther's attack was not only levelled at the Pope, but more immediately at the Elector. Despite this criticism, the Elector was concerned over the safety of his young professor as the storm burst, and urged him to be cautious.

To Augsburg

At first it seemed as though the affair was a squabble between two monastic orders, the Dominicans (to which Tetzel belonged) and the Augustinian Friars. But news of the protest soon reached Rome and the Pope, Leo X, summoned Luther to meet him. Luther, however, would only agree to appearing before the papal legate at Augsburg, where the Imperial Diet was meeting.

Despite great pain in his digestive system, Luther struggled to Augsburg, journeying the last three miles on a cart. Cardinal Cajetan, whom Luther respected, informed him that the Pope required him to

Martin Luther nails up his 95 theses

recant and never to teach again. Luther claimed that he had not taught anything that was contrary to the Bible and offered to submit to open debate. The dispute reached a state of impasse and Luther, threatened with the possibility of excommunication, waited for Cajetan's verdict. His supporters, fearful for his safety, whisked him away in the dead of night, 'without breeches or boots', and sent him back to Wittenberg.

Cajetan ordered Frederick either to send Luther to Rome or to banish him from the country. As Luther awaited his fate, he held a supper party to say farewell, believing that Frederick would no longer protect him. Yet before the meal ended, a letter came asking him to stay and offering him protection.

It is uncertain why the Elector had second thoughts, but he had changed his mind and even demanded a fair trial for his professor. Humanly speaking, Luther was secure and the Reformation intact. Tetzel was discredited and accused of embezzlement and immorality. He died a year later, and the only comfort he had was a letter from Luther urging the friar not to blame himself.

The year 1517 is regarded as the official starting date of the Reformation, but God had been working out his purposes long before. Men like Wyclif and Hus had called the Church to restore the Bible to the central position in its doctrine, creating a movement towards a more personal religion; and the Renaissance had ushered in a revival of learning and a spirit of inquiry, causing Christians to look again at the New Testament origins of their Faith.

But the Reformers such as Luther did not create the Reformation - they were simply the instruments through which it was expressed. Luther's challenge to the papal authority had thrown the Church into disarray and he found himself engaged in a fierce theological battle. His ideas spread quickly throughout Germany and the rest of Europe, and he gained support not only from ordinary people but also from a number of German princes who offered him their protection.

In 1519 a debate was arranged between the Catholic theologian John Eck and the Wittenberg School, who were accused of being followers of Hus. Luther caused an uproar when he declared the Pope's supremacy was based on false decretals and was not known in Scripture - the idea had only grown in the previous four hundred years. Furthermore, the Greek (or Eastern) half of the Church had nothing to do with the Pope or councils that had drawn up the Catholic Faith. 'A single layman armed with Scripture is to be believed above the Pope or a council without it,' he asserted.

Battle For Reform

Luther was now at the forefront of the battle for Church reform; he had denied the authority of the Pope as well as the infallibility of a general council; and even the politicians were beginning to see the benefits of a Germany independent of Rome. Not only was freedom of religion at stake, but the freedom of Germany itself was at issue.

The invention of printing (credited to Gutenberg, who published a Latin edition of the Bible in 1455) enabled Luther to produce a never-ending stream of tracts and books clarifying and defending his position. In 1520 he published his three most famous pamphlets, followed by theological treatises, Bible commentaries and devotional works. Indeed, from the age of forty (1523) he turned out books at the rate of one every two weeks!

At the instigation of Eck, a condemnation was drawn up in Rome (July 1520) in the form of a papal bull (this is a papal edict sealed with a *bulla* or red seal): Luther's works were to be burned and his followers to be excommunicated; he had sixty days in which to recant.

The bull met with a mixed reception in Germany and many towns refused to accept it; attempts to burn his books also met with limited success. In Mainz, the task was given to an illiterate gravedigger and fifty students piled the fire with anti-Lutheran tracts instead.

At Wittenberg, at 9 o'clock on 10th December, Luther together with other professors and students, made a pile of volumes of the Church's canon law plus some of Eck's works, and set them on fire. Then Luther stepped forward and publicly threw the papal bull into the flames, signifying his rejection of the Pope's authority.

Following the normal procedure, Luther should have been arrested and executed, but the Elector Frederick insisted that he should have a fair hearing in Germany. The young Emperor, Charles V, King of Spain, a devout Catholic, ordered an Imperial Diet to meet at Worms (April 1521). He was anxious to maintain the unity of the Church and would have gladly suppressed this dissenting movement.

'Here I Stand'

Although Luther was granted a safe conduct and a covered cart for the journey, his friends urged him not to travel. 'Even if there were as many devils in Worms as there are tiles on the roofs I would enter anyway,' he replied. All along the route to Worms he was received with great honour by the crowds, who turned out to hear him preach. Efforts were made by enemies to delay his progress and the Elector wrote to say that he thought that his time was up.

When brought before the Diet, presided over by the Emperor, he was shown a pile of his books and asked to renounce them. He asked for time to reply, and the next day told the council that unless he was proved wrong on the basis of Scripture and sound reason, he was bound in conscience to the Word of God. An account of the Diet published later that year disclosed that he also declared, 'I can do no other. Here I stand. May God help me!'

The Emperor's attempt to condemn Luther had failed. He gave him twenty-one days in which to return to Wittenberg, after which he was to be regarded as a convicted heretic - and excommunicated. Further, Luther was placed under a ban of the Empire, which meant that for the rest of his life he would be restricted to living in Saxony. The next morning, two wagons pulled out of Worms escorted by twenty nobles, heading for Wittenberg. Before the party could reach its destination, however, it was ambushed and Luther 'captured'. He hurriedly collected his Hebrew Old Testament and Greek New Testament, and was whisked away to the castle of Wartburg. For a long time his enemies thought he had perished; in fact he was in the Elector's safe-keeping.

During the year of his captivity, Luther used the time to make a translation of the New Testament into German, but was unable to finish the complete Bible until 1534. He finally felt it necessary to leave the castle and return to Wittenberg, for he had heard that the young Evangelical Church, as it was called, was facing difficulties. Some of his followers were causing problems by bringing in extremist measures, and there were reports of disorder. Within a week, Luther had cleared up the problems and those who had declared themselves to be 'prophets' had left the town.

Luther stayed at Wittenberg and was quite safe under the protection of Frederick; as the Reformed religion spread to other towns and cities, a number of other princes joined the cause and the Evangelical Church grew. But while pressing ahead with a reform of the Church's faith and doctrine, Luther still had respect for some of the Catholic traditions, church buildings, robes, candles and even the crucifix.

Changes

Having re-asserted the doctrine of the centrality of the Scriptures and salvation through Christ, he began to introduce changes in the forms of worship, especially the mass. He drew up a treatise on *Divine Worship*, in which he emphasised the reading and exposition of the Bible; he also outlined the shape of a reformed mass, aiming at simplicity and doctrinal purity (a form of service similar to that of the Anglicans). In addition, he wrote books for pastors on the practice of confession, marriage and baptism, on the Litany, and a service book of twenty-four hymns - his most famous hymn being *A Safe Stronghold Our God Is Still*, the battle hymn of Protestantism.

The Emperor, Charles, had not yet given up his attempt to halt the spread of the reform movement. He called a Diet at Speyer in 1526 which, surprisingly, came out in favour of toleration (probably the result of Charles' quarrel with the Pope). This meant that each state in Germany would be allowed to hold the religion of its ruling prince.

A second Diet was convened to meet in 1529, in the hope of uniting the Church and also to find a policy against the threat of a Turkish attack on the Empire. Luther had written a book in which he argued that it was the responsibility of the Emperor to defend Christendom, and for the Germans to support this cause. The Catholics at the council concentrated on Church affairs, however, and forced through an order whereby the Reformed states were allowed to keep their religion, but the other states should remain Catholic, which prevented any further expansion of the Reformation. The Evangelicals, led by Luther's successor, Melanchthon, protested against this move, but to no avail; they refused to accept this decision and asserted the authority of the Word of God and of the conscience.

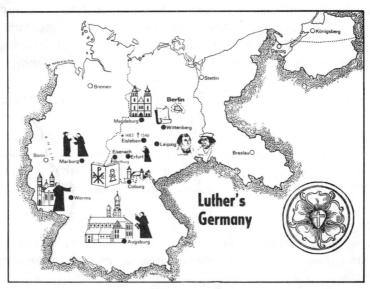

LUTHER'S GERMANY

New Movement

The protest mounted by the Evangelicals at Speyer gave us the term 'Protestant'; it became the title of the new movement and has remained to this day. The Reformation had by now spread beyond the boundaries of Germany and other Protestant groups emerged. The Anabaptists, who stressed believer's baptism, came into being after the break with Luther at Wittenberg in 1521.

There was also Zwingli and his followers in Zurich who, like Luther, accepted only the gospel as the sole basis of authority. Regretfully, Luther and Zwingli disagreed over the true meaning of the eucharist and attempts to find a basis for unity failed; Luther's belief in consubstantiation, a position somewhere between Rome and Zwingli, drove a wedge between them. The *Confession of Augsburg* drawn up by Melanchthon in 1530 listed the articles of the Reformed Faith and became the Lutheran statement of belief.

Meanwhile, Luther's private life had also been 'reformed', since he had renounced celibacy and taken a wife, Katie, an ex-nun. Their marriage was definitely successful, and they had six children as well as caring for four orphaned relatives. He was a true family man and enjoyed romping with his children, teaching them and making music; he was kind and generous and always hospitable.

Yet he could also be a man of moods, given to fits of depression and elation. In the Peasants' War he counselled peace, and when this failed he urged the magistrates to take harsh measures; the slaughter of peasants that followed was terrible, and the Romanists blamed it on the Reformer. Similarly with the Jews, when they spurned his invitation to 'come over to us' he bitterly turned against them. Admittedly it was towards the end of his life when he was a sick man, but he wrote, 'Burn their synagogues and schools... break into and destroy their homes... Forbid their rabbis to teach, on pain of life and limb.'

Despite his faults, he comes down to us as one of the great men of God, who spent his life in bringing the Church back to its gospel beginnings. Worn out and weary, Luther died at Eisleben as he prepared to journey home to his beloved Katie. As he breathed his last, he was heard repeating John 3:16, the foundation of his life and work.

Lutheranism spread from Germany to Scandinavia, where it was later recognised as the State Church; the Swiss also had their Reformation, but were not so easily bound by medieval traditions, and their ideas reached France, Holland and Scotland.

JOHN CALVIN (1509-1564): Reformer and Theologian

It is important to realise that the Reformation did not altogether originate with Luther, though the major impetus may have come from him. Lefèvre in France and Zwingli in Switzerland had been preaching a 'pure gospel' before him; and while both the Swiss and French Reformations met in Calvin, Lutheranism followed a separate path. Both movements, however were united in seeking to restore the Church to its New Testament basis and encouraging a return to scriptural truths.

Chief of the reformers of German-speaking Switzerland, Zwingli studied at Basle under the humanist Wyttenbach who taught him the sole authority of the Scriptures. Ordained in 1506, his reputation as a preacher and scholar led to his appointment in 1518 as the People's Preacher at the Old Minster in Zurich. The beginning of the Swiss Reformation dates from 1519 when Zwingli gave a series of lectures on the New Testament, followed by attacks on Catholic doctrines and practices.

The civil government took the churches into their own hands and ruled that 'the pure word of God' was alone to be preached. In a debate on sixty-seven theses, his attacks on Roman teachings was upheld by the civil authorities, and in 1524 images, relics and organs abolished. The movement for reform spread to other parts of Switzerland and Zurich was regarded as the head of the evangelical cause. But when an attempt was made to force evangelical preaching on the Catholic cantons, war ensued in which Zwingli was killed.

After his death in 1531, leadership passed to Geneva where Calvin tried to establish a theocratic regime based on biblical teaching. Although that idea was eventually bound to fail, he was responsible for setting out a complete statement of Christian doctrine that is still relevant to us in the twentieth century.

Calvin was a Frenchman, raised in the ancient cathedral city of Noyon, north east of Paris, where in 768 Charlemagne was consecrated king. His father, Gérard Cauvin (the Reformer latinised his name to Calvinus), rose from among the artisans to become procurator-fiscal of the cathedral chapter and secretary to the bishop. He had great ambitions for his son and wanted him to train for the Church.

At the age of twelve the young John received a Church benefice and the money enabled him to further his education at a local college, the Collège des Capettes. For two years his fellow pupils were from among the nobility of the district and some remained his companions in later years. In 1523, at the age of fourteen Calvin was sent to the University of Paris to continue his education, he studied first at Collège de la Marche where he was fortunate in having the famous Mathurin Cordier as his Latin tutor, laying the foundation of an expert knowledge of the language.

Two years later he moved to Collège Montaigu, a place of greater repute but noted also for its medieval methods. Life was harsh and his days were taken up with worship and study; he rose at 4am

JOHN CALVIN

and began the day with worship and retired to bed at 8 pm after his study was finished. The beds were hard and the food frugal and punishments took the form of whippings.

The college principal was an enemy of the new Reformation ideas that were spreading from Germany, but Calvin was at least introduced to the writings of the Church Fathers and particularly those of St. Augustine, which were later to strongly influence his thinking.

Under the impression that a career in law would reap better dividends than one in the Church, Calvin's father sent him to the University of Orleans. Although he remained at Orleans until he received his doctorate in 1533, he also spent some of this time at the University of Bourges (1529) where he came under Humanist and Lutheran influences.

Conversion

No one is quite sure at what point Calvin experienced conversion and took his stand on the side of evangelical views. In the preface to his *Commentary On The Psalms*, dated 1558, Calvin writes, 'I was so obstinately given to the superstition of the papacy... yet by a sudden conversion he (God) tamed my heart and made it teachable.' Certainly by 1st November 1533 he had obviously espoused the evangelical cause and because of his views was forced to leave Paris. Initially he spent time in wandering through parts of France; he went to Poitiers, where he formed a small congregation, then moved to Strasbourg where he was introduced to Martin Bucer, one of the great scholars of the Reformation. In 1535 he settled in Basle as a refugee and continued his studies.

At this point Calvin had in mind writing an elementary manual of doctrine, but an outbreak of persecution in France led him to prepare a clear defence of Reformation beliefs. In 1536 he published his *Institutes of the Christian Religion*, the first systematic exposition of Reformed teaching, described as 'the masterpiece of Protestant theology'. The work was based on the Apostles' Creed and showed how the Reformers were leading believers back to the beliefs and practices of the Early Church. The first edition, published in Latin, was a small work of six brief chapters, but subsequent editions enlarged its original size; it was translated into the languages of Europe and the final edition was written in French (1560).

Calvin's journeyings brought him to Geneva, *en route* for Strasbourg, where he met William Farel. He had only intended staying one night, but Farel - 'by a fearsome adjuration' - persuaded him to stay and help establish Protestantism in the city. Geneva had in 1535 broken free from allegiance to the Duke of Savoy in whose territory the city was situated, and by decree of the city council and under the preaching of Farel, had formally become a Protestant city. But although the Catholic clergy had left, there were many citizens who had no desire to see them replaced by another Faith.

The city was governed by a series of councils which had already made some attempt to reform the moral life of the people, but with little success. When Calvin arrived the situation was unsettled and the relationship between the Church and the State not resolved.

Between 1536 and 1538 Calvin drew up a list of articles of faith, teaching the people that they should live according to the New Testament. He also proposed that Church members should be excommunicated (which involved loss of citizenship) if they were not prepared to live by God's Word.

The question of Church discipline was to prove a real bone of contention throughout his ministry. Many people attended the Lord's Supper just as they had attended mass, and not out of true conviction. Calvin therefore wanted to protect the Lord's Table from being pro-

---

Calvinism

The theological system of John Calvin is generally noted for three characteristics.   First, its doctrine of predestination holds that certain people are infallibly destined for salvation, based on an understanding of the writings of Paul and Augustine.   Calvin wrote in his *Institutes*, 'We assert that by an eternal and immutable counsel God hath once for all determined both whom He would admit to salvation and whom He would admit to destruction.'   Second, based on the equality of all believers before God, its Presbyterian Church government recognises three permanent offices: pastors, elders and deacons (entrusted with care of the poor). Third, its austere attitude towards certain social practices and moral standards.   In Geneva, while adultery was punishable by death, the emphasis on the sanctity of marriage helped to improve the relaxed morals of the day.

---

faned. He set up a system of reproof and control, and the city council appointed elders whose job was to keep an eye on people's conduct and to check any faults. But the council objected to Calvin's attempted excommunication powers and declared that no one should be barred from the Lord's Supper. In April 1538 both Farel and Calvin were ordered to leave the city.

Calvin was invited to take up a ministry at Strasbourg, where there were some French refugees driven out by persecution. For three years he worked as pastor and teacher; he produced another edition of his *Institutes* and introduced the singing of psalms into his services.

The situation in Geneva, however, continued to deteriorate and some members of the council recognised Calvin had been right. An appeal was made for him to return. Realising he had caused the authority of pastors to be respected, he reluctantly agreed.

Return to Geneva

When Calvin returned he began where he had left off; he set about the task of making Geneva into a 'City of God' and a church modelled upon the New Testament. He taught that both Church and State derived their authority from God; and though each should co-operate with the other, spiritual and civil powers were to be independent of each other.

In his *Ecclesiastical Ordinances* (1541) he laid down how the Church was to be governed: the Venerable Ministry, made up of ministers, to appoint the pastors; and the Consistory, made up of elders appointed by the city council to act as a court of morals. In this way Church discipline would be exercised and the honour of God maintained.

The courts have been criticised as being more like an inquisition, leading to Pharisaism and hypocrisy, imposing an unbearable tyranny upon the city. True, the penalties were determined by the civil courts, but Calvin always urged a gentle approach for the lesser faults while crimes should be punished more severely; for the latter, members were to be deprived of the Lord's Supper until they had shown signs of repentance. Whatever the case, nothing was to be introduced into the Church except that sanctioned by the Word of God, but the question of discipline caused continued unrest.

Death Penalty

Calvin's hard line, however, was most severely criticised in the affair of Michael Servetus, a Spanish physician he had tried to rescue from back-sliding in France, who wrote a treatise in which he denied the Trinity and the true divinity of Christ; he even had the nerve to appear in Geneva to challenge Calvin. Servetus was arrested in 1553 and sentenced to be burned at the stake. Although Calvin tried to have the method of punishment modified, he still consented to the death penalty.

For twenty-four years Calvin laboured in Geneva to maintain the Protestant cause where he preached several sermons a week at St. Peter's Cathedral and lectured every day. In 1559 he founded the Geneva Academy which attracted theological students from all over Europe. He took part in the affairs of other Protestant communities, gave shelter to refugees (including some from England), wrote extensively and, apart from his *Institutes*, produced treatises and Bible commentaries clarify-

---

Erasmus (1469-1536)

Driven by poverty, Erasmus reluctantly joined the Brethren of the Common Life and then in 1486 became an Augustinian monk at Steyn, where he read the Classics and the Church Fathers. Ordained priest in 1492, he moved to Paris and then to Oxford where he studied the New Testament. After a spell in Italy, he returned to England in 1509 where at Cambridge he taught Divinity and became the first lecturer in Greek. The years 1515-1521 were spent in the Netherlands where in 1516 he produced his celebrated edition of the Greek New Testament, which included his own translation into classical Latin. His writings on the Church Fathers revived a knowledge of Christian sources which pro-foundly aided the Reformation. But when he deliberately entered the Reformation controversy in 1524, he spoke out against Luther and defended the Catholic Church, a decision that made enemies for him on both sides.

ing the doctrine of the Reformation and giving it a structure.

Like Luther, he accepted the Bible as the only rule of faith and believed in the sovereignty of God; he taught that salvation was by faith alone through the grace of God, and held the doctrine of predestination and election. But he differed from Luther about the Lord's Supper, believing in the spiritual presence of Christ.

Through Calvin, Geneva was transformed and became a veritable powerhouse of Protestantism. But his influence went far beyond the city. The French Huguenots organised themselves on a Calvinist basis, in 1662 Holland adopted Calvinism as the state religion, and the movement advanced through Europe and reached as far as America when the Puritans settled there.

WILLIAM TYNDALE (1494-1536): Bible Translator

The sixteenth century Reformation was not simply a matter of making changes in the Church, as some from Rome alleged, but was in essence a rediscovery of the truth and power of the Word of God. It was a challenge to the Church to return to its Scriptural origins and to find again a relationship with God through Jesus Christ.

Renaissance

The most important factor in preparing the way for the Reformation, apart from religious reasons, was the Renaissance, a term meaning 're-birth' and referring to the revival of learning that took place in the Middle Ages. When Constantinople fell to the Turks in 1453, many scholars of Greek and Latin literature fled to the West, bringing their learning and ancient manuscripts with them. This triggered off a spirit of enquiry called the New Learning and its disciples were known as Humanists.

The Humanists, through a study of classical literature, aimed at broadening the human spirit by restoring the ancient cultures. The movement began in Italy and quickly spread to the rest of Europe; in Holland and Germany it took on a more Christian character, paving the way for the translation of the Bible.

In England it produced a new zeal for religious education, and several colleges were founded such as Christ's and St. John's at Cambridge, where the new learning might be taught, and St. Paul's School (by John Colet) where 'children should be taught good literature, both Latin and Greek.'

Possibly the most outstanding Christian Humanist was Erasmus (1469-1536) of Rotterdam. For a while Professor of Divinity and Greek at Cambridge, he published his first edition of the Greek New Testament in 1516. Luther used this work as the basis of his translation of the New Testament into German.

In pre-Reformation days in England the Bible had already been translated into English, in separate books, from the time of Bede in the eighth century; and from 1382-88 the complete Bible had been translated into English by Wyclif and his friends and was used by the Lollards. Now it was felt that a new translation was needed,

TYNDALE

this time based on the original Hebrew and Greek texts rather than on the Latin Vulgate. William Tyndale made this the object of his life's work.

Study of Scripture

Tyndale was probably born in Gloucestershire, around the year 1494 and, it was observed, from an early age was 'singularly addicted to the study of the Scriptures'. He was educated first at Oxford where he was converted and in 1515 received his MA degree, then at Cambridge, a university said to be 'infected with Lutheranism'. Here he joined the 'White Horse Inn' group of students who met regularly to study the works of the German Reformer. The ecclesiastical authorities were annoyed by the group's activities and in 1520 arranged a bonfire of Luther's books outside Great St. Mary's Church.

In 1521 Tyndale took up a position as chaplain and tutor to the two sons of Sir John Walsh of Little Sodbury Manor, in the Cotswolds, north of Bath. As well as his teaching responsibilities, he spent time in translation work and in preaching. He ventured as far afield as Bristol, where on the College Green he clashed with a group of preaching friars who objected to his theme of 'justification by faith alone', which to them constituted an attack on their source of income. When they complained to the Archdeacon of Gloucester he was charged with heresy, warned and then released.

Despite his controversial evangelical views, he persisted in maintaining his stance, perhaps to the embarrassment of his employer. Once at Sir John's dinner table, a clerical visitor to the manor was annoyed by Tyndale's use of the Bible as God's law.

'We were better be without God's law than the Pope's,' declared the priest. To which Tyndale replied, 'I defy the Pope and all his laws. If God spare my life, ere many years I will cause a boy that driveth the plough shall know more of the Scriptures than thou dost.'

By now Tyndale had determined to bring out a new translation of the Bible. He wrote that he 'had perceived by experience how that it was impossible to establish the lay people in any truth, except the Scriptures were plainly laid before their eyes in their mother tongue.' In this he agreed with Wyclif, whose translation of the Bible was not widely available and had many inaccuracies.

Tyndale realised the need for a revision based on the original languages and despite the threat of the stake - seven people had recently been burnt for teaching their children the Lord's Prayer, the Ten Commandments and the Apostle's Creed in English - he pressed on.

Hoping to gain the support of Bishop Tunstall of London, he travelled to the capital with an introduction from Sir John. He was able to induce the king's comptroller to speak on his behalf, but received no encouragement from the bishop. However, a Christian merchant, Humphrey Monmouth, took him into his home and supported him for six months.

But England was not a safe place for his work and Tyndale moved to Germany, never to return to his native land. He went to Wittenberg where he probably met Luther and completed his translation of the New Testament, drafted with the assistance of his secretary, William Roye. They took the finished work to Cologne, the centre of printing in Germany, to arrange its publication. The city was hostile to the Reformation and secret plans for printing the book were discovered and reported to the Senate.

An order was placed, prohibiting the printing and ordering the seizure of the paper and type. Tyndale learned in time of the danger and was able to rescue the sheets that had been printed. He fled to the Lutheran city of Worms where the work was completed in 1525. By the following year, copies of the English New Testament were being shipped to London by Monmouth and his friends, soon to reach the cities and universities.

As copies poured into England they were eagerly bought and read by all sorts of ordinary people, who would sit up all night reading and hearing it read. Some gave as much as five marks for a single book, or a load of hay for a few chapters of St. James or St. Paul in English. And although thousands of copies were printed, only two have survived.

The ecclesiastical authorities were furious and Tunstall issued an order that all 'heretical' books should be seized; a few days later they were publicly burned at St. Paul's Cross. The following year the Archbishop of Canterbury even went so far as to purchase as many of the Testaments as he could, and they were destroyed. But the money was filtered back to Tyndale who was able to finance and print a new and revised edition! Not surprisingly, Tunstall claimed he could find 3,000 errors in the Tyndale text, yet it was apparently a remarkably accurate and scholarly piece of work. In fact 90% of the AV New Testament and 75% of the RSV remain as Tyndale wrote it.

Manuscript Lost

With a view to translating the Old Testament, Tyndale set about improving his Hebrew. By 1529 he had completed his translation of the Pentateuch, but the manuscript was lost in a shipwreck as he travelled to Hamburg. A second manuscript was prepared, assisted by his new friend, Myles Coverdale, which reached England in 1530. Later he completed the rest of the Old Testament up to II Chronicles.

Meanwhile Cardinal Wolsey had his agents scouring the Continent for Tyndale, buying and burning all the Protestant books they could find. The king's agents were also searching for him, but failed to entice him back to England where more Reformers were being burnt at the stake.

Tyndale finally moved to Antwerp where in 1535 an Englishman, Henry Phillips, approached him for help. Ostensibly a Lutheran, Phillips was in reality a spy; he managed to entice Tyndale out of the safety of his refuge and had him arrested by the officers of the Emperor Charles V. For sixteen months Tyndale was kept in the castle of Vilvorde, near Brussels, while charges were prepared against him. At one point he wrote to the governor, asking for some warmer clothes, a lamp in the evenings and especially that he would kindly permit him to have the Hebrew Bible, Hebrew grammar and Hebrew Dictionary.

At his trial Tyndale was found guilty of being a heretic, but the authorities then spent two months in trying to force him to recant. In October 1536 he was taken from his dungeon, strangled and his body burnt. His last words were, 'Lord, open the king of England's eyes.'

Back in England, Thomas Cromwell, on instructions from the king, ordered that a copy of Coverdale's Bible, the Great Bible, be placed in every church in England, exhorting the lay people to read it.

Ten years before his death, when his work was being burnt in London, Tyndale wrote: 'In burning the New Testament they did no other thing than I looked for; no more shall they do if they burn me also, if it be God's will it shall be so. Nevertheless, in translating the New Testament I did my duty.' His Bible, completed by Coverdale and published in 1535, prepared the way for the introduction of Reformation ideas in England.

THOMAS CRANMER (1489-1556):
Archbishop of Canterbury

The Reformation in England took a very different shape and course to that in Germany and Switzerland; it began as a political rather than a religious movement, then found its identity not in Luther or Calvin but in a modified version suited to the English scene. For fifty years, from 1521-1571, the country was thrown into confusion by the thrust and counter-thrust of its leaders, when nearly three hundred Catholic and Protestant martyrs went to the stake.

It was not until the reign of Elizabeth I (1558-1603) that there emerged a more stable and united Anglican Church. During this period, one of the foremost architects of the English Reformation was Thomas Cranmer, the first Archbishop of the new Church of England. It was his ideas and guidance that unhurriedly led England in the direction of Protestantism.

Cranmer was born of yeoman stock at Aslacton in Nottinghamshire, and at the age of fourteen was sent to study at Jesus College, Cambridge. He became a Fellow in 1511 and may have been among the group of scholars who met secretly at the White Horse Inn to discuss the new ideas. A quiet, scholarly priest, Cranmer's time at Cambridge was uneventful until suddenly summoned to Canterbury by the king, Henry VIII (1509-1547) who, desperately in need of a male heir to the throne, wanted someone who would support his petition to the Pope for a divorce.

It was probably Cranmer's belief in the royal supremacy, the idea of a 'godly prince' over the Church, that led to his appointment. At his consecration at Westminster Abbey, Cranmer not only swore obedience to Rome, but also read a protestation declaring his allegiance to the king (which explains his willingness to support Henry's divorce plans).

A breach with Rome was looming large as Henry took steps to establish his own authority over the Church. His aim was to have a Catholic Church in England with himself as the head, in order to facilitate his intended marriage to Anne Boleyn. From 1529-1536 the 'Reformation Parliament' put through a series of laws to secure the obedience of the clergy and to destroy papal authority in England. By the Act of the Submission of the Clergy (1532) and the Act for the Restraint of

CRANMER

Appeals (1533) Henry limited the powers of the English Church.

On the 10th May 1533 Cranmer pronounced Henry's marriage to Catherine of Aragon to be invalid, leaving the king free to take the already pregnant Anne as his wife. The Pope excommunicated him and declared his divorce and re-marriage null.

Supreme Head

A series of Acts were passed by Parliament the following year severing the links with Rome, and the Act of Supremacy made Henry 'the only Supreme Head on earth of the Church of England'. In this way the king was given absolute power over the Church - its doctrines, worship and property. These moves affected Cranmer's status as archbishop, and his position was further eroded when Henry made Thomas Cromwell, Earl of Essex, his Vicar-General, to exercise the royal supremacy in ecclesiastical affairs.

Papal power, however, was still in evidence in the country as the monasteries remained loyal to the Pope. Under Henry's instructions, Cromwell arranged for the dissolution of the monasteries between 1536-1539, the lands and wealth of the religious houses were surrendered to the Crown, and were then sold off cheaply to the king's supporters.

Although Henry had rejected Rome, he was still anxious to retain its doctrines, despite growing resentment in the country to the papacy. Many leading figures had Protestant leanings and Cranmer was also coming nearer to the Reformed point of view. The archbishop was not prepared, however, to be hurried into extreme changes; he kept what he felt was good while rejecting some of the excesses.

The *Christian Articles of Religion* (1536), issued after the dissolution of the Reformation Parliament, were mostly his work and show clearly the influence of the Lutheran Diet of Augsburg (1530). They emphasised the authority of Scripture and justification by faith, and excluded the doctrine of transubstantiation.

What was not taught in Scripture, such as pilgrimages, offering money or candles to images and saying prayers over beads, was to be avoided; they also warned against unnecessary holy days and the abuse of images and relics. Yet they allowed other Catholic practices such as the veneration of saints and the belief in purgatory.

In 1538 Cromwell was able, by Henry's command, to order a copy of the Great Bible - so called because of its size - to be placed in every church in England so that the ordinary people could read it. But the king was frightened by the threat of the Reformation and in 1539 published the *Statute of Six Articles*, which restored the old Roman doctrines and, on penalty of death, restricted the reading of the Great Bible to the upper classes.

Cromwell fell out of favour with Henry and was beheaded; Cranmer's hopes were checked, saved by his relationship with the king. His only success at this point was the publication in 1544 of a *Litany in English*, a first step towards an English language prayer book.

Behind the scenes, however, a quiet revolution was taking place. Nicholas Ridley, a member of the White Horse Inn group, was appointed Cranmer's chaplain. His influence on Cranmer was considerable and the archbishop began to change his ideas about the mass. Apart from abandoning transubstantiation, he came to believe that Christ's presence in the mass was spiritual and not real; he also felt that the occasion was not simply for priests alone, but that everyone should be able to take part every Lord's Day.

When Henry died he was succeeded by the boy king, Edward VI, who had been trained by Cranmer. It was during his reign that Protestantism became more firmly entrenched in England. The most important event of his reign was the publication of the first *Prayer Book in English*

(1549), compiled mostly by Cranmer. It was intended to simplify and condense the Latin service book and to provide a guide for the priest and people alike.

Reform

The new *Prayer Book* included the whole of the Psalter and required the lessons to be taken from the Bible only. The term 'mass' was retained, as was the idea of sacrifice at an altar; while the doctrine of transubstantiation gave way to consubstantiation. But the book, written so as not to cause any unnecessary offence to Catholics, was in parts ambiguous and to the uninitiated still looked like the Catholic mass.

On the advice of Peter Martyr and Martin Bucer (from Strasbourg, now at Cambridge), a revised edition was brought out in 1552. The communion service ceased to be a mass and was now celebrated at a table; the invocation of the Virgin and the saints was abolished. The second *Book of Common Prayer*, modified in 1559 during the reign of Elizabeth and revised in 1662, is virtually the one drawn up by Cranmer and was in use until recently.

Finally in 1553, Cranmer and the evangelical Bishop Ridley drew up the *Forty-Two Articles*, a collection of short statements of belief. These were later reduced to *Thirty-nine Articles* and received their final form in 1571. The Act of Uniformity required that all clergy should subscribe to these beliefs, which caused many priests to leave the Church of England.

Regrettably, Edward died prematurely at the age of sixteen, and was succeeded by Mary Tudor, daughter of Henry and a fanatical Romanist. She set out to restore England to the Catholic fold: the authority of the Pope was re-established and Catholic ceremonies brought back; the law against heretics was revived and a terrible period of persecution began, when many Protestants were burnt at the stake.

The first to die was John Rogers, an assistant to Tyndale in Antwerp, followed by Bishop Hooper of Gloucester, and Bishops Ridley and Latimer at Oxford. As they faced the flames, Latimer encouraged Ridley to 'play the man and we shall this day, by God's grace, light such a torch in England as will never be put out'.

After nearly three years in prison, at the Tower and at Oxford, Cranmer was also brought to the stake. The authorities played on his belief in the royal supremacy over the Church in an effort to force him to recant, and under great pressure he gave way. Despite his recantation, Mary went ahead with the execution.

The idea was that Cranmer should make his confession in public in

Great St. Mary's church, but to the anger of his tormentors, the archbishop renounced his recantation and spoke out against the Pope.

Cranmer was pulled down from the stage and led out to the fire. An iron chain was tied about him and the wood kindled. As the fire began to burn, he stretched out the right hand that had signed the papers so that it should be burned first. He was heard repeating, 'This unworthy right hand.' Then finally, 'Lord Jesus, receive my spirit,' and his voice was heard no more.

During Mary's brief reign of five years her policy of persecution stirred up the land against her and the Catholic Church. She deposed over one thousand two hundred clergy and sent over two hundred Protestants to the stake; hundreds more fled to the Continent for safety. But in the end, the Reformation had taken hold in England.

JOHN KNOX (1513-1573): Scottish Reformer

Early Christianity in Scotland had Celtic origins and was based on the monastery rather than the church. Following the Synod of Whitby in 664, when the Roman dating for Easter was accepted, Catholic practices were gradually introduced. By the reign of Queen Margaret, who died in 1093, the process of Romanisation was almost complete.

As in many other countries, the Catholic Church in Scotland degenerated and was given over to ignorance and immorality. Yet by the beginning of the sixteenth century there was a glimmer of hope as the teaching of the Lollards reached western Scotland and the ideas of John Hus were brought home by travellers and students.

The Reformation movement quickly began to take hold in the 1520s, and by 1525 had advanced enough for the government to ban Lutheran books from being brought into the country. In 1528 the whole nation was moved by the martyrdom of the saintly Patrick Hamilton, a student of Luther and a fearless preacher of the gospel. He was charged with heresy and burned at the stake in front of St. Salvator College, St. Andrews.

Others were also charged and put to death, including the preacher George Wishart in 1546. As he was about to be hanged, the executioner fell to his knees and begged to be forgiven. Wishart kissed his cheek and told him, 'That is a token that I forgive thee... do thine office.'

One of Wishart's followers was the unknown John Knox, later to become the focus of the Protestant cause in Scotland. As a result of his leadership, the Roman Church was overthrown and a Presbyterian form of Church government established.

Knox was born at Haddington, near Edinburgh, and became a student

JOHN KNOX

at St. Andrews University soon after the death of Hamilton, when the shock of this event still stirred the nation. He graduated and was ordained priest, but at some point underwent a conversion experience, being moved by reading the seventeenth chapter of the gospel of John.

By 1543 it seems he had espoused the Protestant cause and became a companion and self-appointed bodyguard to Wishart. In fact, he had attended Wishart on the evening before his midnight arrest, when the preacher had dismissed him saying, 'One is sufficient as a sacrifice.'

For a while Knox was tutor to three sons of the Hugh Douglas family. When in 1546 there was a further period of persecution, he took his pupils to the safety of St. Andrews Castle, where other Protestants had taken refuge. At this time Scotland was ruled by the French under Mary of Guise, who was married to the Dauphin, the King of France's eldest son. She was anxious to support both Scotland and the Roman Catholic Church in a fight against Protestant England.

Galley Slave

The Protestants of St. Andrews were besieged by a French army and the castle captured. Along with some of the other prisoners, Knox was sent to be a galley slave on the ship *Notre Dame*. He was in chains for nineteen months before being released in 1549 on the intervention of friends from England.

The next five years were spent in England at the time when Cranmer was establishing a Reformed Church under Edward VI. He ministered first of all at Berwick, near the Scottish border, then in Newcastle. In 1552 he became a royal chaplain and assisted Cranmer in drawing up the *Book of Common Prayer* (1552). His friendship with the Church leaders of the day helped to strengthen his Protestant ideals and also led to his being offered the bishopric of Rochester. He declined, probably because of his views on Church government.

When the Catholic Mary Tudor came to the throne he thought it expedient to leave for the Continent in January 1554. After spending some time in Dieppe and then with Calvin in Geneva, he accepted an invitation to become pastor to a congregation of English refugees in Frankfurt.

His wish to use his own service book in the church led to a disagreement; his was based on Calvin's liturgy, whereas some of his flock preferred the *Book of Common Prayer*. The congregation was displeased and felt that Knox had gone too far. They protested, saying that 'they would have the face of an English church'. To which Knox replied, 'The Lord grant it to have the face of Christ's church.'

The conflict led to Knox's resignation. He returned to Geneva where he ministered at the English Church from 1555-1559. His stay there was one of the happiest periods of his life and he described Geneva as 'the maist perfyt schoole of Chryst that ever was in the erth since the dayis of the apostillis'.

It was during this period that the popular Geneva Bible was produced and Knox published his *First Blast of the Trumpet against the Monstrous Regiment* (reign) *of Women*, a treatise condemning the 'unnatural rule of women'.

Following the death of Queen Mary, Knox was invited to return to Scotland to lead the Protestant cause. He was aware that it involved a risk; he had already been branded a heretic and declared to be an outlaw, and trouble was afoot in Scotland as a result of the burning for heresy of an aged priest. Protestants attacked monasteries, churches at St. Andrews and Perth were destroyed and in Edinburgh images were smashed.

Unrest

When Knox landed at Leith in 1559, he not only faced religious unrest but political unrest as well. The country was ruled first by the Queen Regent, Mary of Lorraine, then from 1560 by the young Queen Mary Stuart. Their firm intention was, with French support, to maintain the Catholic religion.

For the Reformers, a Protestant defence league had been organised in 1557 which accepted Knox as its leader and was supported by many of the Scottish Lords and, reluctantly, by Queen Elizabeth of England.

A 'civil war' situation arose in which Elizabeth despatched an English fleet and the Scottish lords deposed the Regent. A peace was agreed in June 1560 and the Scottish Parliament instructed the Protestant ministers to draw up a Confession of Faith for the nation.

Knox and five others produced the *Scottish Confession* within a space of four days and it was accepted by Parliament as 'hailsome and sound doctrine'. It was mostly the work of Knox (he had worked on the Geneva Confession and also the Thirty-nine Articles) and marked the legal establishment of the reformed Church of Scotland.

The Confession, which ran to twenty-five articles, emphasised the authority of the Word of God; it assumed the doctrine of justification by faith, affirmed the idea of election and condemned transubstantiation. Only two sacraments were recognised: Baptism and 'the Supper or Table of the Lord Jesus'. Reference was also made to the duty of civil magistrates, who were to be 'lieutenants of God', to conserve and purge the Church when necessary.

The next move was to set up a method of Church government, which was embodied in the *First Book of Discipline*. Again drawn up by Knox, it was modelled on Calvinistic ideas and introduced a Presbyterian form of ministry, whereby the Church was governed by presbyters (or elders), the pattern they believed to be laid down in the Scriptures.

The country was divided into ten areas, each with a superintendent (not a bishop), and Church order was to be determined by Church courts, namely Kirk-Session, Synod and General Assembly. There was to be a church and a school in every parish, and education was made compulsory; money was also to be made available for the relief of the poor.

When Mary Stuart returned in November 1561 it was inevitable that conflict would continue. Not only did she want to be an absolute monarch, she also wanted to continue to celebrate mass, albeit privately. As she toured the country, she encouraged the faithful Catholics to disobey the law and to maintain the fight against Protestantism. But the most she was able to achieve was to influence Parliament not to ratify the *Book of Discipline*.

Death Penalty

When Knox preached against the mass, the Queen summoned him to appear before her; after their meeting, he left the Queen in tears and remarked she had 'an indurate heart against God and his truth'. In 1563 Mary thought she had her revenge when Knox was arrested for treason, but the Council acquitted him.

While Knox married happily for the second time (his first wife died in 1560), Mary's two marriages, to Darnley and then to Bothwell, ended in failure.

In July 1567 she was finally forced to abdicate in favour of her young son James VI, later James I of England. The General Assembly of the Church demanded the death penalty for Mary, for murder and adultery; she was imprisoned, but escaped and fled to England, hoping to find shelter with Elizabeth. She was kept in close captivity until she was executed in 1587.

By now the Protestant Church of Scotland was firmly rooted within the country. The *Scottish Confession* had placed the Church on a sound basis and remained in force until replaced by the *Westminster Confession* in 1647.

In his later years, Knox felt his life clouded by troubles and he was further weakened by a stroke. He left Edinburgh for the quieter environs of St. Andrews, where his time was disturbed by the introduction of archbishops and bishops into the Reformed Church; although he did not protest, he did make a plea for safeguards.

After a brief stay at St. Andrews he returned to Edinburgh to die and while on his death bed asked his wife to read 1 Corinthians 15 and then John 17, 'where I first cast my anchor'.

He died on 24th November 1572 and was buried in the churchyard of St. Giles, where for many years he had preached. As his body was laid to rest, the Earl of Morton declared, 'Here lyeth a man who in his life never feared the face of man.'

When the Reformation first appeared in Scotland, it was in a Lutheran form; under the influence of Knox, however, it was modelled on more severe Calvinistic lines. And for over four centuries the faith of Knox has been a major influence in the life of Scotland, creating a strong and vigorous Church and bringing stability to the nation.

IGNATIUS LOYOLA (1491-1556): Founder of the Jesuits

An Italian ambassador writing in the sixteenth century stated, 'in many countries obedience to the Pope had almost ceased, and matters are becoming so critical that, if God does not interfere, they will soon be desperate.'

There were many others also within the Roman Church who recognised the increasing secularisation and corruption of the Church and longed for a return to genuine piety. During this period a number of new religious orders, intent on reviving the Church sprang up all over Italy. Among them were the Capuchins, returning to the high ideals and austerity of St. Francis, and the Barnabites who were specially concerned with the care and education of the young.

The most influential group was called the *Oratory of Divine Love*, set up by a group of clergy and laymen about the same time that Luther was making his protest at Wittenberg. Their aim was to deepen the Church's spiritual life by corporate prayer and works of charity.

Starting in Rome, it quickly spread to other cities and soon found favour with the papal court. The Pope asked the order to prepare a report on the state of the Church, but the resulting document was so outspoken - attacking even the 'Holy Father' - that it was quickly set aside.

One of the society's leading laymen, Gasparo Contarini, was sympathetic to the Protestant ideals. When created a cardinal, he was sent as papal legate to the Colloquy of Regensberg in 1541; he met with Luther's right hand man, Philip Melanchthon, and tried to work out a compromise with the evangelical Reformers. Although the effort failed, it indicated a desire on the part of some Catholics to restore the Protestants to the Church. Despite this failure, the seeds of reform had been sown and the Divine Lady Society had created a positive spiritual momentum within the Catholic Church.

Counter Reformation

This movement, later known as the Counter-Reformation, was chiefly spearheaded, however, by an even more powerful group, the Society of Jesus, founded by Ignatius Lopez of Loyola, in Spain. More than any other, the Society was responsible for establishing the Counter-Reformation within the Catholic Church: it aimed at recovering the Catholic Faith within Europe, taking it to other parts of the world and combating the 'heresy' of Protestantism.

Ignatius was born into a distinguished Spanish family at the ancestral castle at Loyola, south west of San Sebastian. Little is known of his early life, except that he gave no consideration to spiritual matters but was only concerned with the affairs of this world.

He embarked upon a military career and fought with the Spanish army against the French where, at the siege of Pamplona (1521), a cannon ball shattered his leg. His injury forced him to spend some time convalescing and he read all the literature he could lay hold of.

With nothing else to read, he turned to two devotional books, *The Life of Christ* and *The Flowers of the Saints* by Ludolf of Saxony. Through these books he was challenged by the life of the saints and the claims of God upon his life. He determined to become a soldier of Christ and devote himself to serving God, waiting upon him to know what he should do.

Following upon his recovery - except for a slight limp - he visited the famous monastery of Montserrat, set in the mountains above Barcelona. He hung up his sword at the altar and gave his uniform to a pilgrim; clothed as a beggar he spent a night's Vigil of Arms before the statue of Mary and made his confession.

From there he went to the neighbouring town of Manresa; he retired to a cave where he spent a year in prayer and meditation (1522-23). While he was there he experienced 'the dread mysterious dark night of the soul', and emerged into the light, strong in his faith and his determination to follow Christ.

During this time he began to write his great devotional work, *The Spiritual Exercises*, a work he constantly revised though it was not actually published until 1548. The book was a training manual, designed to lead his disciples through a four week induction course into the religious life. Based on his own experience in the cave at Manresa, the exercises considered (1) the fact of sin and the reality of hell, (2) the kingdom of Christ, (3) the Passion of Jesus and (4) the risen Christ.

In order to better prepare himself for his life's work he set out to improve his education. From 1524-28 he endeavoured to study at the universities of Alcala and then Salamanca. His strange ideas attracted the attention of the Inquisition and he was forced to move on. He went to study in Paris (1528-1535) and was a contemporary of Calvin at Collège Montaigu, although the two do not appear to have known each other.

On the Feast of the Assumption, August 1534, at a mass celebrated in a church in Montmartre, Ignatius and six of his friends - including Francis Xavier - took the vows of poverty and chastity, promising to support the Pope in his struggle against the hostile forces ranged against the Catholic Church. To Ignatius, the Church was a society under siege and as a Christian soldier it was his duty to defend it, if necessary by military means.

The Society of Jesus, often known as Jesuits, received official recognition in a bull issued by the Pope in 1540. The constitution of the new order not only enjoined vows of poverty and chastity, but also a special vow of absolute obedience to the Pope. Ignatius gathered around him young men sound in health and intelligent, and formed a military-style organisation. They were neither monks nor priests and did not wear a distinctive dress, yet were expected to develop an inner life based on their founder's *Spiritual Exercises.*

In 1541 Ignatius was elected the first General and spent much time in Rome drawing up the order's Constitution. A cardinal system of training was put into motion, making each Jesuit a loyal and efficient member of the Society. The Jesuit programme majored on three main tasks: education, countering the Protestant 'heresy' and missionary outreach.

The novices were first trained at Coimbra, where a college was opened in 1542; but Ignatius was soon to realise the value of education as a weapon in the battle for the Catholic Faith, and he established further colleges and universities across Europe for the laity. They not only provided a good education, but also created a source of well-trained, intelligent and highly enthusiastic missionaries for the Church. Soon Jesuit-trained students were taking their place throughout Europe in key positions as lecturers and men of power and authority.

They became a strong force in setting up the Counter-Reformation and in leading the attack against Protestantism. On the basis that 'the end justifies the means,' they recaptured some of the areas that had fallen to Protestantism. They were, at times, even prepared to use oppressive means of persuasion, and at one point Ignatius advised that it might be better to execute a few heretics in order to defeat the anti-Catholic teaching.

Missionary Zeal

Since its early days, the Jesuits have been known for their missionary zeal, and travelled to America, Africa and Asia in search of new converts. In the first decades of the Jesuit story, the scene was dominated by Francis Xavier, known as the 'apostle to the Indies and to Japan.'

The son of an aristocratic Basque family, Xavier was one of Loyola's companions at the University of Paris when in 1534 they took vows of poverty and chastity, and set themselves the task of evangelising the heathen. Ordained priest in Venice, he set sail from Lisbon for the East Indies in 1541 and the following May reached Goa (India) where he made his headquarters. After preaching throughout South India, he founded a missionary college before continuing on to Sri Lanka, Malacca and the Molucca Islands. He moved to Japan in 1549 where he made large numbers of converts and established a Catholic community that suffered great persecution.

His great ambition was to revive the Church in China, so after returning to Goa in 1552, he started a journey to China, but died *en route*. Although some of his work was superficial, it is claimed that he baptised around 700,000 converts, and his example proved to be a contagious influence on other Catholic missionaries.

Other Jesuit missions were established in Brazil, where they built the city of Sao Paulo, in Mexico and among the Canadian Indians of Quebec. Attempts to reach the natives of Africa met with little success, and although Portuguese traders were setting up settlements on the continent, there were few converts.

The Society spread rapidly and by 1608 had over ten thousand members, three hundred and six colleges and eighty-six houses and missions. But the cost was high and many Jesuits lost their lives for their cause; in the early days in Japan, churches were destroyed and thousands went to the scaffold.

In addition to the Jesuit contribution to the Counter-Reformation there were other attempts from within the Roman Church to revive Catholicism. The Council of Trent, the most important council to meet since Nicaea in 325, met in three sessions between 1545 and 1563 to draw up a response to the Protestant Reformation. It redefined traditional Catholic doctrines, and dealt with the selection, training and duties of priests and bishops. A number of Protestants were present at the second session (1551-1552), but the two groups could not come to any understanding.

There were two other aids to the Catholic revival: the so-called Roman Inquisition (1542), which used torture and execution as weapons, attempted to coerce 'heretics'; and the restoration of the Index (1559), a list of books which were said to be heretical and dangerous, and were prohibited to the eyes of the faithful.

The results of the revival were soon to be seen: large areas lost to Protestantism were regained, doctrines more clearly redefined, and a new piety emerged. The spread of the Protestant Faith was halted, leaving Europe divided between two opposing religious factions.

In its enthusiasm to regain lost ground, however, the Jesuits became involved in plots and intrigues, and their schemes included plans for the assassination of their opponents. In later years they were banished or suppressed in many Roman Catholic countries, 'complaints and cries' were raised against them, and their 'dangerous results, rebellious and scandals' led to the order being abolished in 1773. This decree was annulled in 1814 when the Jesuits made further gains in Holland, England and the United States.

The Inquisition

This refers to a series of special ecclesiastical courts set up in the thirteenth century to suppress 'heretics' under the sanction of the secular law. They were revived with papal approval in 1479 by King Ferdinand and Queen Isabella of Spain. The purpose was to deal with the Marranos - Jews who under pressure had accepted Christian baptism. Many of these Jews had married into the Spanish aristocracy and enjoyed considerable influence. Secretly, large numbers of them maintained their Jewish faith and the Inquisition was determined to stamp out this heretical tendency. Some 10,000 crypto-Jews were tortured and put to death, usually by being burned. (Ironically, those Jews who resisted conversion were not attacked.) Around 50,000 accepted conversion. In 1492 the Jews were finally expelled and about 90,000 left for Turkey, Italy and North Africa. The Moriscos (Muslim converts) and, later, the Protestants received similar treatment. Portugal expelled the Jews in 1496.

MAJOR PROTESTANT AND ROMAN CATHOLIC DIFFERENCES

DOCTRINES	PROTESTANT	ROMAN CATHOLIC
SCRIPTURE	* The inspired Word of God is the sole authority for Christian faith and life * Every believer, by the Holy Spirit, is able to interpret Scripture * The Apocrypha is not used to establish doctrine	* Church tradition is of equal authority with Scripture * The work of interpreting Scripture is entrusted exclusively to 'the living teaching office' of the Church * Canonicity of the Apocrypha confirmed by the Council of Trent (1545)
SALVATION	* Through the sacrificial and substitutionary death of Christ * Justification is by faith in Christ's death	* Through Christ *and* by the merit of good works * Forgiveness is received at baptism, and grace given to lead a good life. This may be lost through mortal sin, but can be restored by penance
THE CHURCH	* The Church is the Body of Christ on earth, those called by God to salvation * The Pope is the leader of the RC Church, but does not enjoy any 'primacy of honour' * Every believer has immediate access to God through Christ ('the priesthood of all believers')	* The true Church consists of those baptised into the Church of Rome, outside which there is no salvation * The Pope is the vicar of Christ, the vice-regent of God on earth, wielding full and immediate authority over the universal church * The priest is a mediator between man and God
HOLY COMMUNION	* The elements of bread and wine represent the body and blood of Christ, and commemorate his death	* The mass is a sacrifice at which the bread and wine become the actual body and blood of Christ when consecrated by the priest

SIX

The Dissenters

The Puritan Revolt

With the accession of Elizabeth I to the English throne in 1558, Protestantism was restored and Mary Tudor's efforts to re-introduce the Catholic faith were reversed. The Church of England became established as the state Church and the Reformation was secure.

There were many, however, who argued that the Reformation in England had not gone far enough, and they actively worked to further 'purify' the Church of its unscriptural practices; they believed in the maintenance of one national Church of England, but reformed after the model of Geneva. These dissenters were called Puritans, and the movement flourished mainly between the two Acts of Uniformity, from 1559 to 1662.

Elizabeth's religious policy was to steer a middle course between two extremes. Although she had Catholic leanings - she had attended mass and prayed to the Virgin Mary - she felt it prudent to restore the Protestant religion. By the Act of Supremacy she was declared to be the Supreme Governor of the Church of England, and by the Act of Uniformity she restored the second Prayer Book of Edward VI.

Four years later, in 1563, the forty-two Articles of Religion were reduced to thirty-nine, consolidating Protestant doctrine without being distinctly Lutheran or Calvinist. From 1571 the Articles were imposed upon the clergy as a test of orthodoxy, but since 1865 it has only been necessary to affirm a general assent.

As a result of her anti-Catholic measures, the Pope excommunicated Elizabeth, and on 15th May 1570 a papal bull was found nailed to the gate of the Bishop of London's palace. It accused her of usurping the place of Supreme Head of the Church and abolishing the Catholic rites.

Nonconformists

The Puritans, too, were in dispute with the Queen. Since the days of King Edward, their dissenting voice had been heard throughout the land. Bishop Hooper of Gloucester had pleaded in 1550, 'Let the primitive Church be restored' and 'candles, vestments, crosses and altars be removed.' Following Elizabeth's excommunication, they renewed their attack, focusing chiefly upon the Prayer Book which they believed contained many features contrary to the Word of God.

What at first had not been widely realised was that Elizabeth had inserted a clause in the Prayer Book directing the clergy at communion to wear 'a white albe plain, with a vestment or cope', garments used in the mass. This became the Puritans main cause of discontent. Other points at issue included the use of the term 'priest'; kneeling instead of sitting at communion; keeping saints' days; and certain practices linked with infant baptism. They also objected to the wedding ring and the phrase 'with my body I thee worship' in the marriage service, and standing for the reading of the Gospels but not the Old Testament reading.

A further matter for dispute arose when Elizabeth attempted to stamp out the practice of 'prophesyings,' which were unofficial religious meetings for the study of Scripture and for preaching. Her efforts failed, partly because Archbishop Edmund Grindal, a man of Puritan sympathies, refused to co-operate.

Puritan opposition was incensed and strengthened and the Presbyterian Thomas Cartwright (1535-1603), professor of divinity at Cambridge, came to the forefront as leader. He denounced the government as unscriptural and illegitimate, and as a result was removed from his post. He fled to the Continent and remained in Antwerp until he had the opportunity to return in 1585.

Separatists

While the main Puritan party was content to work for reform from within, other groups decided to leave the Church. They became known as Separatists and later met with severe persecution from both Church and State. Under the leadership of Robert Browne, the Congregationalists (or Independents as they were later known) believed that each local congregation must be independent and founded upon a covenant which the believers make with God and with one another.

A break-away group, led by Henry Barrowe, allowed a more substantial authority to the elders chosen by the congregation, and was less democratic. They were the 'Right Wing' of the Congregational movement, and agreed with the Anabaptists that the Church of England was too inclusive and comprehensive.

After the death of Mary Queen of Scots, imprisoned by Elizabeth, there was a further Catholic attempt to take over England. Philip II of Spain organised an attack by 130 ships which made up the Armada

The Thirty-nine Articles

Though all Church of England clergymen have to give their general assent to these doctrinal statements, the laity are not obliged to do so. When an incumbent first officiates in a new parish he has to recite the 39 articles, an occasion known as 'reading himself in'. The articles were first given legal sanction in 1571 when an English translation was approved and published. They reflect a moderate form of Calvinism and represent an attempt to steer a middle way between Roman Catholicism and Anabaptism. When the proposals were submitted to Queen Elizabeth, she struck out article 29 (a reference to the 'Wicked, and such as be void of a lively faith') as being offensive to Catholics, and she amended some of the others; the offending article was restored in 1571. Article 9, 'Of Original or Birth-sin', warns of the fourth century Pelagian heresy.

(1588). Partly as the result of an English naval manoeuvre and partly with the aid of a great wind, the invasion failed.

In 1603 Elizabeth died and James I, son of Mary Queen of Scots, came to the throne. Although brought up as a Presbyterian, he quickly adopted the Anglican cause, to the dismay of the Puritans, who had hoped that he might be sympathetic towards them. They presented a petition - known as the Millenary Petition - to the king as he journeyed from Scotland to England; in it they asked to be relieved from their 'common burden' of Roman rites and ceremonies. It led to the Hampton Court Conference (1604) between the English bishops and the Puritan leaders, to discuss demands for reform. Some minor concessions were made to the Puritans, but their position was not much eased.

The major outcome of the conference was the production of the Authorised Version of the Bible. At the suggestion of John Rainolds, the chief Puritan representative, the king ordered a new translation of the Bible to be made. The fifty-four revisers were instructed to take the Bishop's Bible of 1568 as a basis for their work, but to exclude the marginal notes unless needed to explain Hebrew or Greek words. Sometimes known as the King James Bible, the result was published in 1611 and quickly displaced all previous translations.

The conference is also remembered for the king's outburst of temper. When some idea of Presbyterianism was put forward, James exploded, 'If you aim at a Scottish Presbytery, it agrees as well with a monarchy as God and the devil! No bishop, no king.' The king's dislike of both Presbyterians and Puritans continued unabated throughout his reign.

Once he threatened, 'I will make them conform themselves, or I will harry them out of the land, or else do worse.'

This is exactly what happened, and a group of believers who felt they could no longer worship within the Church of England decided to emigrate. They moved first to Holland and later to America where they founded the colony of Plymouth, Massachusetts. A further attack on the Puritans came when the king issued a proclamation which demanded conformity to the Church of England and acknowledgement of the king as Head of the Church. Nearly two thousand clergy refused; some three hundred of them left their livings and others were imprisoned.

The archbishop at that time was Richard Bancroft, another outspoken critic and opponent of the Puritans, who brought back the use of church ornaments and ceremonies. But James also dealt severely with the Roman Catholics as well, many of whom he put in prison. The Gunpowder Plot, celebrated every 5th November, was in fact a Catholic attempt to blow up the Protestant Parliament. The leaders were discovered and executed.

In 1625 Charles I, James' son, came to the throne and the Puritans

Oliver Cromwell (1599-1658)
The Civil War was (roughly) the king and the Established Church (Cavaliers) against parliament and the Puritans (Roundheads, a reference to their short-cropped hair). When Cromwell (an Independent) was elected an MP in 1640 he supported the Puritan party, and as parliamentary troops were fighting against the Church, church buildings and their treasures were burnt and destroyed. In 1644 he gathered together his New Model Army of 'religious men' who opposed papacy and prelacy. He defeated the king at Naseby (1645) and scattered the Scottish army at Preston (1648) as it moved south to support Charles. After the king's execution (1649) Cromwell subjugated Ireland, routed the Scots and in 1651 defeated Charles' son at Worcester. He dismissed the Long Parliament in 1653 and was installed as Lord Protector. An able statesman and more tolerant than most, he ruled by military authority, which caused much dissatisfaction.

suffered even more persecution. Charles had married a Roman Catholic princess of France, driving a wedge between himself and parliament. He eventually decided that he could rule without their help, which he did for eleven years (1629-40). During this time he was supported in his belief in the 'Divine Right of Kings' - the idea that the king's authority came from God - by a High Church archbishop, William Laud. The archbishop worked to restore something of the pre-Reformation liturgical practice of the Church of England, and he aroused considerable hostility among the Puritans. He turned the communion table into an altar and started the practice of bowing to it.

But the rift between the king and parliament was so wide that it was impossible to heal it; it led to a Civil War (1642-49) which divided the nation and did much damage to both sides. The king's party was known as the Cavaliers, the parliamentary army as the Roundheads, because of their hair style. The parliamentary party enlisted the aid of the Scottish army and in 1643 entered into a Solemn League and Covenant with them, whereby they agreed to bring about a reformation of religion in both countries.

The Westminster Assembly drew up a Confession of Faith, which was adopted by the Presbyterian Church in 1647 as the basis of its statement of belief. It has been recognised as the clearest and most orderly presentation of divine truth ever set forth and is the finest fruit of Reformation theology.

Westminster Confession

The rift between the Puritans and the Established Church concerning Church government and ceremony became increasingly acrimonious. Charles favoured the 'high church' party, and in alliance with Archbishop Laud tried in 1633 to impose the Book of Common Prayer on Presbyterian Scotland, an action which eventually led to the Civil War. In response to the Puritan challenge, parliament convened the Westminster Assembly which met between 1643 and 1649. Its main achievement was the Westminster Confession - intended to replace the Thirty-nine Articles - which reflected a rather more severe form of Calvinism and differed in a number of ways from Calvin's own teaching. The Confession was adopted by the Church of Scotland, replacing the earlier one by Knox; in England, it received only temporary and partial approval.

After some while, the war took a different turn: the parliament and the army parted, and the Scots came to terms with the king. The New Model Army under Oliver Cromwell, who supported the religious and political views of the Puritans, defeated the royal forces; the king was arrested, tried and executed at Whitehall on 30th January 1649.

With no king to rule, a Commonwealth government was set up with Cromwell at its head; but despite Puritan efforts to introduce true liberty of religion - except for 'Popery and Prelacy' - the experiment failed and the House of Stuart was restored to the throne in 1660.

RICHARD BAXTER (1615-1691): Puritan Divine

The Puritan revolt against the Church of England made steady progress during the first half of the seventeenth century. There were many distinguished men among their ranks drawn from the House of Commons and especially from Cambridge University, some of them great preachers and writers whose works have remained firm favourites down to the present.

Yet despite the deep impact the movement had upon the country, there were many who felt that their religion was too narrow: they were later described as 'kill-joys' and accused of using the Scriptures simply as a stern moral code. As a result of their earnestness, they were often mocked and ridiculed; the term 'Puritan', like 'Christian', was originally a term of derision, but the title stuck and became a badge of honour.

Leading Figure

As the century progressed, Richard Baxter emerged as the leading figure within the Puritan movement. He was a prolific writer and his works contained a number of devotional classics and well known hymns.

Born in Shropshire, Baxter was indebted to his father for his earliest religious impressions. The elder Baxter had been addicted to gambling, but when Richard was about nine years old his father was converted 'by the bare reading of Scripture in private', and his life changed. When he began to live a godly life, he was 'reviled commonly by the name of puritan', yet his son always remained grateful for the example set him by his father. It was because of his father that the young Baxter learned to love the Bible and to appreciate the value of other good books.

During his teens he was challenged by reading some of the Puritan authors, especially *The Bruised Reed* by Richard Sibbes, and came to faith when he was about fifteen years old. Plans to send him away to university were never fulfilled and instead he was placed under a few local clergymen at Ludlow.

One in particular, a Rev Baxter, made a deep impression on him, as 'he would never in prayer or confession speak of God or the life to come, but with such marvellous seriousness and reverence as if he had seen the majesty and glory which he talked of.' Happily, this education gave him access to a wider selection of books and his passion for reading increased. His life was dogged, however, by poor health, even at one point facing death, but he survived to continue his studies.

In 1638 he was offered the headship of the Endowed School at Dudley (Worcestershire) and was ordained deacon in order to qualify for the post. He continued his studies while teaching, but had a great desire to lead men to Christ. The following year he became assistant curate in Bridgnorth, and in 1641 was appointed to the living of Kidderminster, the place with which his name has always been associated.

During these years Baxter began to entertain increasing doubts about the validity of some of the Church ceremonies he was required to perform; he even began to re-examine the truth of the Scriptures and the foundation of his Christianity. Yet he came through this period of uncertainty and developed 'a fervent desire for winning souls to God'. He preached with renewed vigour and success, and many were converted as a result.

But his forthright presentation of the gospel, his teaching on sin and the need for a new birth, earned him a number of enemies among the Anglican clergy, for which he was taken to court. Despite opposition, his ministry proved fruitful; but the onset of the Civil War in 1642 forced

RICHARD BAXTER

him to take the side of parliament, and even though he had no sympathy with those who wanted to overthrow the king, he was branded a 'Roundhead'.

Baxter left Kidderminster and became a chaplain in the Parliamentary army, labouring incessantly for the good of the soldiers. When appointed a chaplain in Cromwell's New Model Army (1645-47), he had many conversations with the General, though the two never got on together. For these two years Baxter was attached to Colonel Whalley's regiment; he moved around the country with them, ministering to the wounded and dying.

In 1647 he was again overtaken by ill health and while recovering began to turn his thoughts towards the idea of his first book, *The Saints' Everlasting Rest*, a book still in demand. He completed it on his return to Kidderminster and it was published in 1650. At this point he received a letter with 265 signatures asking him to return to his ministry at Kidderminster. He obviously warmed to the prospect, but was reluctant at the thought of taking away the present incumbent's living, so returned as 'lecturer' which was a Puritan device to secure preachers of whom they approved. In this way he was able to work alongside the vicar, preaching the gospel and acting as a pastor to the flock.

His ministry here fell mostly within the period of the Commonwealth government (1649-1660). With the death of Charles I, the monarchy ceased and England was governed as a 'Free State'. But Cromwell became dissatisfied with this form of government; in 1653 he marched on Parliament with a group of armed men and forcibly took over. He ruled as Lord Protector until his death in 1658, when his son inherited the position.

Tolerant Settlement

During these five years, Cromwell aimed at replacing the Church of England with a more Calvinistic-type religion. There was to be toleration for all believers, except that he had little room for popery and prelacy. He set up an ecclesiastical commission which prohibited the use of the Prayer Book under heavy penalties, and clergymen were deposed. They were replaced with ministers who were approved by a Committee of Triers, made up of men of Presbyterian, Congregational and Baptist persuasion.

Anglican clergy were forbidden to keep schools, preach or administer the sacraments and church buildings were desecrated. Under Cromwell, believers could adopt any non-episcopal system they chose, and there was also room for dissenters. Quakers were ruled out as 'blasphemous', though Anglican and Catholic congregations meeting quietly were not molested.

It was the most tolerant settlement seen for many years. Richard Baxter, normally Cromwell's critic admitted that 'it was his design to do good in the main, and to promote the gospel and the interests of godliness, more than any had done before him'. Permission was also extended to Jewish people to return to England after an absence of some four hundred years, and synagogues were to be opened for worship. Further, an attempt was made to improve public morals: duelling was abolished, and swearing and drunkenness became punishable offences.

Back in Kidderminster in 1653, Baxter introduced a scheme of catechising for his congregation, whereby each member was examined concerning their spiritual well-being. His ministry had a profound effect on the people of the town. 'On the Lord's Day there was no disorder to be seen in the streets, but you might hear one hundred families singing psalms and repeating sermons.'

Another of Baxter's initiatives was the Worcester Association of Ministers, which was a gathering of pastors to discuss doctrine and discipline. As a result of this work he wrote one of his greatest books, *The Reformed Pastor*. This was followed later by *A Call To The Unconverted*, which apparently led to the salvation of whole households.

On Cromwell's death, he worked for the restoration of the monarchy, even though it meant the return to episcopacy and the possibility of imprisonment. In 1660 Charles II promised liberty of conscience, but the

---

Acts of Uniformity

There were four Acts bearing the same title, brought in to strengthen the Established Church:

(1) 1549 - imposed the Book of Common Prayer in all public services;

(2) 1552 - ordered use of revised Book of Common Prayer, absence from church services to be punished;

(3) 1559 - ordered use of 1552 Book of Common Prayer (with modifications), fine of 12p for absence from church;

(4) 1662 - the Book of Common Prayer reintroduced after being banned by Cromwell; all clergy were required publicly to assent to it before St. Bartholomew's Day (24 August), and those who had not received episcopal ordination were to be deprived of their living. Many Presbyterian clergy were ordained in order to retain their benefices, but nearly 2,000 were either ejected or gave up their places. Further laws, known as the Clarendon Code, were enacted (1664-1665) to exercise firmer control over the Church.

persecution of the Puritans soon began. By the Act of Uniformity (1662) clergy were required to give assent to the *Book of Common Prayer*. Nearly two thousand men, including Richard Baxter, were unable to do this and were driven from their livings into Nonconformity.

Pressure upon the Puritans was further increased by the Conventicle Act (1664) which forbade religious meetings in which the Prayer Book was not used, and the Five Mile Act (1665) which prohibited ejected clergymen from coming within five miles of a city or of any place where they had been ministers. Penalties against Nonconformists became more severe and Baxter was soon in trouble. From 1662 to 1687 he had two spells in prison, the second time after a 'trial' before the notorious Chief Justice Jeffreys.

He was released in time to celebrate the 1688 Revolution, when the Catholic King James II was replaced by the Protestant King William of Orange. For the remainder of his life he continued writing and produced some two hundred titles in all. He died in 1691, worn-out by his several bouts of illness and his persecution. With the Act of Uniformity, Puritanism died and the Nonconformist groups came under severe attack; things were made easier by the Act of Toleration (1689), though it did not grant full religious liberty.

Puritanism has exerted a tremendous influence on the life of Great Britain, with its emphasis on independence and democracy, ideas that spread to the colonies of America, while its traits of truthfulness, chastity and industry have lingered on into the present century.

JOHN BUNYAN (1628-1688) Preacher and Author

Following the restoration of the monarchy in 1660, a series of laws were passed reintroducing the use of the Prayer Book and laying down severe penalties for all who refused to conform. These laws, known as the Clarendon Code, signalled the end of the Puritan Revolt and virtually sent the dissenting Church underground.

Some individuals compromised their position and maintained links with the State Church, and a number of groups defied the law and met openly until the local magistrate took action. This happened in East Anglia where, of the thirty-six Congregational churches, only fourteen survived the Restoration.

Many dissenting believers were tortured or even executed for defying the laws; others were more fortunate to escape with a gaol sentence. Among the individuals who suffered imprisonment at this time were the Quakers George Fox and William Penn, who wrote the classic *No Cross,*

No Crown while in the Tower of London. One of the earliest to be arrested, six months after Charles II returned to England, was the preacher and author, John Bunyan, whose time in prison proved to be extremely fruitful.

Humble Parents

Bunyan was born of humble parents at Elstow, one mile south of Bedford, and his baptism is recorded in the parish register on 30th November 1628. The family of Buignon or Bonyon (there are thirty-four different ways of spelling it!) settled in Bedfordshire in the twelfth century, and their property had been gradually whittled down until only a cottage remained, owned by Bunyan's grandfather.

John's father, Thomas Bunyan, was a tinker or brasier, a maker and mender of pots and kettles, and though often regarded as a disreputable trade, the Bunyans were known as steady handicraftsmen who owned their own freehold tenement. At school he learned to both read and write 'according to the rate of other poor men's children', but left his books before he had made adequate progress. He was taken from his primer and copybook to help his father at his trade and what little he had learned, he confessed with shame, was soon lost.

When he was fourteen years old England was plunged into a civil war (1642) and two years later, he was drafted into the parliamentary army. He was one of the 'able and armed men' commanded to garrison Newport Pagnell, twelve miles to the west of Bedford. It appears that he never engaged in battle, though a soldier who stood in for him on sentry duty was shot in the head and killed, a matter he later attributed to God's mercy.

When the forces were disbanded, Bunyan returned to his trade as a tinker. Before long, probably at the age of twenty, he married a young woman who came from godly parents. He and his wife were 'as poor as poor might be, not having so much household stuff as a dish or a spoon' between them. Their only possessions were two religious books which his wife had brought with her, given by her father when he died.

Worldly Ways

The two would sometimes sit together and read the books and talk about them. Bunyan even began to attend church with his wife, twice a day, and joined in heartily with the prayers and hymns. Yet, he confesses, he was often guilty of 'cursing, swearing, lying and blaspheming the holy name of God'. These two books began to evoke in him some desires for

JOHN BUNYAN

religion and he longed to resolve his relationship with God. For the next three years before his conversion he continued his worldly ways; he was buffeted by fears and doubts, and was troubled by his own sense of wickedness. He even began to read the Bible, but found himself tempted by Satan so that he 'would be up and down twenty times an hour'.

One Sunday, after a sermon on the evil of breaking the Sabbath, he was enjoying a game of 'Tip Cat' on the village green, when he heard a voice from heaven: 'Wilt thou leave thy sins and go to heaven, or have thy sins and go to hell?' Bunyan felt as though 'the Lord Jesus was looking down upon me... and as if he did severely threaten me with some grievous punishment'. His attempt to reform his speech and manners amazed his neighbours and he felt proud of his 'godliness'; he thought, 'No man can please God better than I.'

But he was challenged one day as he overheard some poor women discussing the new birth, and from this time began to search for faith and conversion. It was through reading the Scriptures that it dawned on him that he could not make himself right with God, and while meditating as he walked through a field realised that righteousness came from Christ. When he discovered this truth, 'his chains fell off and he went rejoicing for the grace of God'.

In 1653 Bunyan joined the Nonconformist congregation that met at St. John's Church, Bedford, where Mr. Gifford was pastor. Although it was a Congregational church, it practised believer's baptism and welcomed anyone who was a 'visible saint by the Word'. Bunyan's gift of preaching was soon acknowledged, and after his appointment as a deacon in 1657 he began to exercise his ministry publicly while continuing his trade as a tinker in order to support his family. Hundreds of people came to hear him as his fame as a tinker-preacher spread; but while some clergy opened their pulpits to him, others resented his success.

When in 1660 Charles II was restored to the throne and the Prayer Book again authorised for worship, Nonconformists were once more subject to persecution. Bunyan continued his ministry in barns, private houses and out in the open air - wherever he found people ready to pray and listen. Aware of the consequences, he was not surprised to learn that in November of that year a warrant had been issued for his arrest, and he was taken one day as he was about to begin a meeting in a farm house.

The judge was anxious to release him if he promised not to preach, but Bunyan obstinately refused to obey the new law; even an attempt to pardon him on the occasion of the king's coronation failed. He declared that he would stay in prison till the moss grew on his eyelids, rather than disobey God. He was finally indicted for 'upholding and maintaining an unlawful assembly and conventicle, and for not conforming to the national worship of the Church of England'. He was lodged in Bedford gaol where he stayed until 1666.

Released

During his first year, he was allowed out to visit his family and to fulfil preaching engagements; he once even travelled as far as London to preach and visit believers. But his excursions were discovered and swiftly dealt with; afterwards, he was not even allowed so much as to look at the door! Unable to carry on his trade, Bunyan supported his family while in prison by making long-tagged laces, which he sold to hawkers.

And again he took up his pen - he already had three titles to his name- and wrote more books and tracts, including an account of his spiritual biography, called *Grace Abounding To The Chief Of Sinners*, published in 1666. In that year he enjoyed a few brief weeks of freedom before being arrested again for preaching; he was returned to Bedford where he spent a further six years in gaol. His enforced leisure gave him added opportunity for writing and he published more books, including poetry for children.

The congregation in Bedford decided in 1671 to call Bunyan to be their pastor, either as an act of faith or perhaps of defiance. He was

THE PRISON ON BEDFORD BRIDGE

released the following year when the king suspended all penal statutes against Nonconformists. The group met in a barn in the orchard of one of its members, as the Church of St. John had been restored to its rightful owners. He took up his duties as pastor and also continued as an itinerant preacher.

In demand as a preacher, Bunyan paid frequent visits to London where he preached to large congregations. Sometimes as many as twelve hundred people turned out to his services on a winter's morning at seven o'clock; while on Sundays the meeting house could not hold all who wanted to hear him and hundreds were turned away.

But the king's Declaration of Indulgence was short-lived, and in 1675 Bunyan was re-arrested and placed in Bedford bridge gaol, a building which spanned the River Ouse. It was during this six month spell that Bunyan wrote his greatest work, *Pilgrim's Progress*. His cell was the 'den' in which he dreamed his wonderful dream, in which Christian journeys from the City of Destruction to the Celestial City. Part I was published in 1678 and part II, which tells the story of Christiana's pilgrimage, in 1684. His second great work, *The Holy War*, another religious allegory, came out in 1680.

Until his death in 1688, Bunyan continued to minister at the barn in Bedford (it was replaced by a brick building in 1707), later to be known as the Bedford Meeting. He was nicknamed 'Bishop Bedford' because he was the one in charge of organising the churches between Bedford and the outskirts of London.

He became a friend of the Puritan statesman, Dr. John Owen, who greatly admired his preaching gift. When King Charles expressed his astonishment that Owen could listen to an itinerant tinker, the Doctor replied, 'I would gladly give up all my learning for the tinker's power of reaching the heart.'

Despite his lack of a formal education, Bunyan's works reveal a considerable

THE
Pilgrim's Progreſs
FROM
THIS WORLD,
TO
That which is to come:
Delivered under the Similitude of a

DREAM

Wherein is Diſcovered,
The manner of his ſetting out,
His Dangerous Journey; And ſafe
Arrival at the Deſired Countrey.

I have uſed Similitudes, Hoſ. 12. 10.

By *John Bunyan.*

Licenſed and Entred according to Order.

LONDON,
Printed for *Nath. Ponder* at the *Peacock* in the *Po ltrey* near *Cornhil,* 1678.

THE TITLE-PAGE OF THE FIRST EDITION OF 'THE PILGRIM'S PROGRESS'

originality and insight, and they are steeped in the teaching and imagery of the Bible. His *Pilgrim's Progress*, acknowledged as the first novel ever to be written, is one of the best known of Christian books and has been translated into hundreds of languages.

As a gospel preacher, nothing mattered more than the salvation of souls and despite persecutions he refused to accept freedom in exchange for his silence. In the year of his death he published six new books and left sixteen manuscripts ready for the press. He died in London, while on a journey to settle a quarrel between a father and son.

The following year the Act of Toleration brought an end to the persecution of Dissenters who, under certain conditions, were granted freedom of worship. In theory, Nonconformity was still illegal as only the imposition of the penalty had been waived; though allowing only limited toleration, it was a great step forward and marked the beginning of a new era in the treatment of religious minorities.

GEORGE FOX (1624-1691):
Founder of The Society Of Friends

During the time of the Civil War and the Commonwealth, the increasing ferment of ideas produced a number of sects that ran counter to the doctrines of orthodox Christianity and added even more confusion to the religious scene. While some of the new groups were short-lived, others survived and became integrated into the nation's history.

The Levellers, a political and religious party came to prominence in 1647 and gained wide support from sections of the army. They emerged in Surrey as 'the first preaching and practising communists in English history', when they took a plot of public land, to dig and plant it in order to share its fruits in common. The plan was wrecked when their houses were pulled down and their corn trampled underfoot. John Lilburne, their leader, advocated establishing parliament on democratic lines; believing that all were equal in the sight of God, he asserted that everyman had a right to elect his own representatives to parliament - a plea for manhood suffrage. Having already spent time in the Tower, Lilburne was re-arrested along with others of the party and the movement went into decline; it ceased to exist by 1760.

The Ranters, who taught that 'God is essentially in every creature', enjoyed a brief popularity but had disappeared by the time of the Restoration.

Then there were the Seekers, a small Puritan sect which attracted many from the Nonconformist churches, who were waiting for God to ordain new apostles and to found a new Church; and the Sabbatarians who observed the Jewish Sabbath rather than the Christian Sunday.

More disturbing was the revival of the fourth-century heresy of Arianism which denied the divinity of Christ. It began in Poland under the teaching of Faustus Socinus (1539-1604) and by the following century had reached England.

In 1647 a tract published by John Biddle set out twelve arguments against the deity of the Holy Spirit and also denied the atonement and the doctrine of original sin. Biddle was sentenced to death for his views, but was saved by his friends among the Independent parliamentarians. In 1652 his followers began to hold regular Sunday worship meetings, but as the Toleration Act (1689) excluded any who denied the Trinity, their meetings continued to be illegal. The movement was slow to develop and it was not until 1773 that their first place of worship, Essex Chapel in London, was opened. They became known as Unitarians and their position was not finally legalised until 1813.

The Quakers

Of greater importance, however, was the Quaker movement which also had its beginnings at the time of the Civil War. George Fox, the founder, was one of many who were disillusioned with the state of the Church and joined a Seekers' community in the north of England in order to find the 'truth'.

Born in Fenny Drayton, Leicestershire, Fox was the son of Puritan parents; his father, a weaver, was nicknamed 'Righteous Christer' because of his strong convictions, and his mother was 'of the stock of martyrs'.

He appears to have had little education and possessed 'a gravity and staidness of mind and spirit not usual in children'. As a boy of eleven he was said to have been sensitive to God and claimed to have experienced the 'pureness' of the divine presence. His parents intended him for the Church of England ministry, but were persuaded contrary. He was later apprenticed to a shoemaker who also did business as a grazier and wool dealer; soon George became his agent and joined him in the trade.

One day in the company of two Puritans at a fair he was invited to join in a drinking session. He paid his shot but quickly took his leave, shocked at the disparity between their religious profession and their moral behaviour. That night he felt a divine call to leave his work and embark on a spiritual pilgrimage. It was 9th September 1643 and he was just nineteen years old.

For three years he carried on a search for perfection, seeking the advice of clergy and Separatists, but none could satisfy him; he did not appreciate their 'second-hand' answers and could find no assurance of salvation and victory over sin. Turning to Bible reading and prayer, he spent time in lonely places hoping to find an answer, and although he received 'openings' (i.e. revelations) it was not until 1647, at the age of twenty-three, that his spiritual conflict was resolved.

'When all my hope in them were gone, so that I had nothing outwardly left to help me, nor could tell what to do,' he wrote in his Journal, 'then, Oh then, I heard a voice which said, "There is one, even Christ Jesus, that can speak to thy condition," and when I heard it my heart did leap for joy.'

Afterwards he claimed that peace had come to him not through the Scriptures but by direct revelation of Christ: 'Christ it was who had enlightened me, that gave me his light to believe in... and gave his Spirit and grace.' The second-hand answers that had previously left him empty gave way to a heart-warming experience that marked the turning-point in his life.

Before long he began a ministry as an itinerant preacher called 'to go abroad into the world', and was soon much in demand. 'Christ has been too long locked up in the mass or in the Book,' he declared; 'let him be your prophet, priest and king. Obey him.' There was power in Fox's preaching and hundreds were 'convinced' as a result. He preached out-of-doors or at the close of Puritan meetings, and his distinctive message attracted much attention.

Speaking from the Gospel of John, where John the Baptist was sent 'to bear witness to the light', he taught that 'every man was enlightened by the divine light of Christ' and those who were faithful to him 'should come into that state of perfection in which Adam was before he fell'. This idea of attaining to a state of perfection offended the Puritans, but Fox claimed it was a direct revelation from God. For this, he was thrown down church steps, attacked with sticks and hit on the head with a brass-bound Bible.

Prison

His first spell of imprisonment was at Nottingham in 1649 for 'brawling in church' - for interrupting the preacher at St. Mary's. He was arrested again in October 1650 and brought before the magistrate Gervase Bennet at Derby. When charged with 'blasphemy' he bade the official to 'tremble at the Word of the Lord.'

The quick-witted magistrate retorted by nicknaming Fox and his followers 'Quakers', and the title stuck. (Another explanation for the origin of the title is that it arose from their displays of religious emotion, when in their meetings men and women experienced 'such a painful travail' that their bodies shook and they gave out 'groans, sighs and tears.')

The earliest documentary name by which they were known was 'Children of Light' which was superseded by 'Friends of Truth', abbreviated to 'Friends' (John 15:14). May, 1652 is the date which marks the true beginning of the movement. After five years as an itinerant preacher in the north Midlands and Yorkshire, Fox came to Pendle Hill in Lancashire. From the top he saw a place where the Lord 'had a great people to be gathered... (and) a great people in white raiment by a river's side coming to the Lord'. From then his ministry gained momentum and as he moved north thousands were converted. They were mostly drawn from the lower middle classes, from the churches, the Seekers and the Ranters. In 1654 he was able to send out sixty missionaries, travelling in pairs, into the southern counties.

Fox travelled to Wales and to Scotland (1657) and some of his followers visited Ireland, America and the Continent, and even reached the Holy Land and Egypt (1661). At times these sober Quakers resorted to unusual methods of proclaiming their message. Fox walked through Lichfield barefoot crying, 'Woe unto the bloody city,' and James Naylor rode into Wells and Glastonbury with a group of muddy women chanting 'Hosanna' and 'Holy, Holy, Holy,' for which he was imprisoned.

GEORGE FOX

Quakers also drew attention to themselves by their unusual customs and manners. They refused to wear fine clothes, refused to take off their hats before magistrates and used the familiar forms of 'thee' and 'thou' to men who considered themselves their social superiors. They rejected the use of pagan names for days and months and refused to take any oaths. Nor would they join the army, challenging the Church to return to a pacifist policy.

Not surprisingly, they became a much persecuted group: they were beaten by mobs, prosecuted for disturbing public worship and imprisoned for not paying tithes. During this period they suffered two thousand one hundred imprisonments, from which thirty-two Quakers died. Throughout the Restoration, like other Nonconformist sects, the Friends continued as an illegal group.

Even though their meeting places were pulled down, they maintained their worship services - amid the rubble - and their numbers increased. Baxter wrote that 'many turned Quaker because the Quakers kept their meetings openly and went to prison for it cheerfully'. During these years, Fox put the Friends on an organised basis: Monthly Meetings for pastoral care and discipline, Quarterly Meetings and, from 1668, the London Yearly Meeting for the whole movement.

In 1669 Fox married Margaret Fell, one of his converts and a widow

ten years his senior; their union was successful. Her home at Swarthmore
Hall, Lancashire, became his headquarters. Despite increased responsibilities, he produced a steady flow of religious pamphlets to spread his
ideas and wrote many pastoral letters to encourage his missionaries.

Believing that the Friends were called to 'walk cheerfully over the
world', he encouraged his missionaries by his visits to Barbados,
Jamaica, Virginia and New England (1671-73), and also travelled to the
Netherlands and Germany. In 1682 the Quaker William Penn was
granted letters patent to found the colony of Pennsylvania, where all
forms of monotheistic religious worship was permitted.

The central doctrine of the Quakers is the 'Inner Light' which
consists of an inward knowledge or experience of salvation. The idea of
'every man being enlightened' was a repudiation of the Calvinist
doctrine of election, and taught that those who followed the light could
reach a state of perfection. This was made possible by the atonement
which gave victory over sin, leading to an outward change of actions.

One result of their religious convictions was that Quakers became
famed for their reliability as traders; they introduced the idea of a 'just
price' and were successful in banking. They also started schools for their
children, showed a practical concern for the poor, and in Philadelphia
(meaning 'love of the brethren'), Pennsylvania, launched an attack on
the evils of the slave trade.

When Fox died in 1691, the numbers of Quakers had risen to around
100,000, and while the Toleration Act brought relief from persecution,
like all dissenting groups in the following century it suffered a decline.

William Penn (1644-1718)

The eldest son of a famous admiral, Penn was sent down from Oxford in
1661 for refusing to conform to Anglican practises. As the result of a
sermon he heard in 1665 he became a Quaker and began writing in
defence of his new faith. His attacks on orthodox doctrines led to his
imprisonment in the Tower where, in 1669, he wrote his classic work *No
Cross, No Crown*. Acquitted, Penn took up the idea of founding a colony
where Quakers and others could enjoy the religious freedom not available to them in England. In 1681, in release of a debt due from the crown
to his father, he obtained from Charles II by letters patent grants of East
New Jersey and Pennsylvania. He drew up a constitution which allowed
all forms of worship compatible with monotheism and religious liberty.
After founding the town of Philadelphia, he returned to England in 1684
but in 1692 was deprived of the governorship of the colony.

THE PILGRIM FATHERS (1620): the New World

While the Puritans remained within the Church of England, the Separatists withdrew themselves completely, determined not only to set aside 'Roman superstitions' but to found a Church based on a New Testament type of organisation. They took their name from the writings of Paul where he speaks of the need to 'come out... and be separate.' The movement was originally known as 'Brownism,' after Robert Browne, a Cambridge graduate and its first exponent. In the seventeenth century it became the Congregational or Independent Church and boasted Oliver Cromwell as one of its adherents.

A company of Separatists was known to exist in London early in Elizabeth's reign, and in the 1580's another similar movement emerged in the capital under the leadership of a Puritan clergyman, John Greenwood, who was hanged for refusing to acknowledge the Queen as Head of the Church.

To Holland

In 1593 the Conventicle Act provided that anyone over the age of sixteen who refused to attend Church or who attended a conventicle (i.e. house of dissent) and failed to conform within three months, should be banished from the country; if they returned, they should be hanged. This Act caused many Separatists to emigrate to Holland where there was greater freedom of religion. One of the leaders imprisoned was Francis Johnson, the pastor of the 'Ancient (i.e. primitive) Church' of London. His flock was forced to emigrate to Holland but he was not able to join them until his release in 1597.

Another outstanding Separatist leader was John Robinson (1572-1625), a Cambridge graduate, who became a 'lecturer' in the Norwich area where he was 'worthily reverenced of all the city for the grace of God in him'. Though ordained in the Church of England, he became a Puritan and after Norwich joined the 'gathered church' at Gainsborough (Lincolnshire).

In 1606 he moved to Scrooby (Nottinghamshire) to become assistant pastor. It was here that he met up with Brewster and Bradford who, like himself, were later to become leaders of the Pilgrim Fathers. The group had not long been in existence when the government decided to crush the Separatists. Under threat of persecution, the two independent churches determined to leave England for Holland where they could enjoy freedom of worship.

The Gainsborough group managed to escape early in 1607, but when the Scrooby believers tried to follow they were twice arrested, at Boston and Hull, on the grounds that it was illegal to emigrate without government permission. They finally reached Amsterdam by travelling in groups of twos and threes, yet even here all was not well. A breakaway Separatist Church soon formed and, under Robinson and Brewster, moved to Leyden. The group, which grew to three hundred, stayed together until 1620 and it was this church from which the Pilgrim Fathers went out.

Leyden

At first the refugees were penniless but, true to their Nonconformist teaching, quickly established themselves in all kinds of employment: fustian-weavers, tailors, masons and many other occupations. Generally people of good sense and basic intelligence, their solid habits of industry, frugality and independence enabled them at least to become self-supporting.

But there were other problems that disturbed the pilgrims and eventually provoked them to search for another place of refuge. For their children, there were fears that they would be influenced by the habits of their Dutch counter-parts and that the next generation would lose its distinctive character; there was also the possibility that some might have to serve in the Dutch army. But of equal consideration was their 'great hope ... for the propagating and advancing the gospel of the kingdom of Christ in those remoter parts of the world'.

The decision to move on was eventually taken, and they were torn between the possibility of either Guiana or Virginia, where a new colony had been founded at Jamestown in 1607. They chose Virginia, and sent two envoys to England to make   the arrangements. Robinson and Brewster had a contact in London, Sir Edwin Sandys, who was able to help them. Negotiations were difficult - the Separatists were not experienced in commerce or finance - but an agreement was reached with the Merchant Adventurers and the Virginia Company, which gave them access to the British colony of Virginia in America and also advanced them some money.

Surprisingly, the majority of the Separatists decided at this late stage to withdraw from the venture, fearful of the prospect before them and unsure about the terms of the contract. As there were vacancies to be filled, the agents signed on other would-be colonists in London, regardless of their religious convictions, and the final party included both Anglican and Puritan believers.

When the time came to leave, Pastor Robinson, who stayed behind to care for the church, led them in a 'Day of public humiliation'. He preached on Ezra 8:21, they sang a song of praise and thanksgiving, and the pastor blessed them. 'And they all with watrie cheeks, mutual imbrasses, and many tears, tooke their leave of one another'. It was July 1620. Two ships had been chartered: the *Speedwell*, fitted in Holland, and the *Mayflower* hired in London. The *Speedwell* joined the *Mayflower* at Southampton and between them the two boats carried about one hundred and forty passengers.

The Journey

They left Southampton about mid-August but before long the *Speedwell* sprang a leak and they were forced to put into Dartmouth for repairs. After a few more days at sea the *Speedwell* once more began to take in water and they had to return to Plymouth. It was decided to abandon the leaking ship and the remaining 102 passengers crowded aboard the *Mayflower*. After enjoying much kindness and hospitality in Plymouth, the *Mayflower* finally got under way in September.

The journey was one of great discomfort and hardship, and one passenger and four crew died *en route*. It took just over two months to reach America, and due to a navigational error the ship dropped anchor at Cape Cod; the ship's crew refused to take the Pilgrims any further - Virginia was some 200 miles to the south - and they were forced to go ashore. 'Falling on their knees they thanked ye God of heaven who had brought them over ye vast and furious ocean.' The place of anchor is today called Provincetown Harbour.

Because the Virginia Company had no rights there, and therefore no authority, it was essential to draw up some kind of constitution; such a move would also introduce a measure of law and order and prevent some of them from imagining they could do as they liked. All the male passengers on board who were of age were called into the ship's cabin to sign the *Mayflower Compact*.

This document became the basis of a democratic constitution for the new colony and signified the colonists' loyalty to King James and the Crown. It declared their intention to plant a colony (sometimes called a 'plantation') and to draw up all the necessary laws and other legal enactments for the general good and 'for the advancement of ye Christian faith, and honour of our King and Countrie'.

By now it was mid-November and winter was rapidly approaching. Food supplies were scanty and the surrounding area seemed bleak and uninviting. But the faith and courage that had brought them this far did not fail them, and they were determined to overcome the difficulties. They appointed deacon John Carver as the first governor of the provisional government and then began a survey of their new homeland. Over the next two weeks they made several excursions around the bay and finally settled at a place they called Plymouth, in honour of their last port of call. They built their first log huts and celebrated their landing with 'Forefathers' Day' (21st December).

Thanksgiving Day

Conditions over the first winter soon began to take their toll; of the forty-one men who signed the Compact, only nineteen survived to Spring and fourteen out of a total of eighteen married women also died. But the Pilgrims stood firm and mastered their new surroundings; they learned agricultural skills and paid off their debt. In 1621, after they had reaped their first harvest, they held a service of thanksgiving to God and had a celebration meal that included wild turkey.

The practice was continued each year on the fourth Thursday in November and is called Thanksgiving Day. Following the death of Carver, William Bradford was elected governor and was annually returned until his death in 1657. An outstanding leader, he is especially remembered for his work as the Pilgrims' historian.

The Massachusetts Bay Company was formed in 1629 to assist emigration to New England and four hundred Puritans, bringing plenty of supplies, set sail to join them. Within the next twenty years, thousands more crossed the Atlantic to settle there. One was London-born John Harvard who in 1638 gave his name to a 'schoale or colledge' for educating 'the English and Indian youth in knowledge and godliness'.

The Pilgrim Fathers came to America to build a New England and to find a place where they could worship in freedom. But they accomplished much more: their influence in laying the foundations of the United States of America was out of proportion to their numbers, and their stand for democracy, freedom of religion, peace and standards of value is one of the nation's most precious assets. If the New World has cause to be grateful to God, then it is for such people as these who stood at the dawn of the nation's history.

JOHN ELIOT (1604-1690): Apostle to the Indians

The Pilgrim Fathers were by no means the first Christians to set foot on North American soil, and by the time of their arrival a number of missions had already been established. Regrettably, missionary concerns often took second place to commercial interests; the desire to win trading links with the New World attracted a variety of Europeans who exploited the native population and damaged the cause of the gospel.

The discovery of America coincided with the beginning of the Reformation, and the twin phenomena of religious renewal and commercial expansion provided the stimulus for opening up the New World and led ultimately to the founding of the United States.

Under the patronage of the Spanish king, Christopher Columbus sailed westwards in 1492 in the hope of finding a new route to India. Instead he found America and opened up the way for further exploration. As Spain was a Catholic country, one of the aims was to contact the natives and discover 'the manner in which may be undertaken their conversion to our Holy Faith'.

Before England had opened up Virginia, the Catholics had already penetrated Florida and New Mexico, where they established a Catholic university and two theological seminaries; they also began to publish literature translated into the local languages. The French invasion of North America followed later, at the beginning of the seventeenth century. The explorers Cartier and Champlain sailed up the St. Lawrence and opened up vast tracts of land in Canada before moving southwards down the Mississippi River. They paved the way for further Catholic expansion and the Church of Rome made more conquests.

Protestant Christianity

Rather belatedly, Protestant Christianity found its way to America as a result of the founding of the English colonies on the north eastern seaboard. The first colony to be established was Virginia, named in honour of Queen Elizabeth I, and was centred on Jamestown. Outwardly a secular venture, its charter made clear provision for establishing by law an Anglican Church, albeit in Puritan guise.

The charter made twice daily attendance at church compulsory, and there were severe penalties for blasphemy, adultery and violation of the Sabbath day. Though James I had included a clause about propagating the Christian religion, little was done to comply with it. In the early days of the colony, an Alexander Whitaker had shown a concern for the Indians and the Pilgrim Fathers had also endeavoured to preach the gospel, but had been prevented by Indian wars.

When Charles I granted the Massachusetts Bay Company a charter in 1629 it stipulated that the colonists should, by a godly example, 'win and incite the natives of the country to the knowledge and obedience of the only true God and Saviour of mankind and the Christian Faith'.

Missionary Enterprise

Disturbed because little had been done to win 'the natives of the country', a New England minister from Roxbury, near Boston, determined that he would make a beginning of it. While continuing his pastoral work at Roxbury, John Eliot laboured from 1646 to his death in 1690 for the well-being of the Red Indians, and was the first Protestant Christian to establish a missionary enterprise to the natives.

Eliot originally came from Hertfordshire, England, and was the son of a yeoman farmer of Anglican persuasion. After graduating in 1622 at Jesus College, Cambridge, he became an usher at a Grammar School at Little Baddow, near Chelmsford, kept by a Rev Thomas Hooker who introduced his assistant to Nonconformist ideas.

Following his ordination as a Church of England clergyman, his new convictions eventually persuaded him of the need to leave England for the New World. He sailed in 1631 and soon after his arrival was accepted as a 'teacher' in the Church at Roxbury, where he remained with the congregation until his death.

After some years, Eliot's concern for the native Indians began to take a practical turn. With the help of a young Indian who was working as a servant in an English house, he began to learn one of the Indian languages. It was only after two years of study that he felt confident enough to make a pastoral visit to the Indians.

In October 1646 he preached his first sermon to the Pequot tribe, which was camped some miles to the west of Boston. As the Indians showed an interest in the gospel, he was able to continue with his efforts and make return visits. His teaching brought a response and many Indians became believers, soon known as 'praying Indians'. The work won the approval of the Protestant ministers and money began to reach him from well-wishers who were anxious to support his schools for the natives.

News of the outreach reached England by what were known as the Eliot Tracts, which were reports written by Eliot about his work. The Tracts stimulated an interest in the Indians and in 1649 a society was founded in London 'for the advancement of civilisation and Christianity among the Indians'; its title was the 'Corporation for Promoting and Propagating the Gospel among the Indians of New England'.

Evangelising the Indians, however, was no easy task. The language was difficult to learn and each tribe spoke a different dialect; added to which there was no written (i.e. correct) language until Eliot began his work. Further, the Indians tended to be nomadic, so that a sustained teaching programme was not always possible.

But Eliot's desire was not simply to 'save souls'; interwoven with his preaching was a social concern for the Indians, reflected in his efforts to improve their living conditions. He established a number of new townships ('praying towns') for the natives, first at Natick and then throughout New England. He encouraged his converts to build permanent homes, to wear clothes and to get themselves a job; he also set up a simple form of self-government in each settlement.

The Corporation in London sent money to support Eliot's programme and paid for more preachers; schools were founded and an Indian college opened. Later, a number of Indians were sent to Harvard College to complete their education and for some of them to train as preachers. All the work was supervised by Eliot who, while continuing his pastoral duties at Roxbury, visited Natick every fortnight and worked unceasingly for the Indians' well-being.

His most outstanding piece of work, however, was probably his translation of the whole Bible into the Algonquin language, using an alphabet which he himself had devised, which finally appeared in 1663. It was published at Cambridge, New England, and was the first ever Bible to be printed on the American continent. First he published a Catechism (1653), followed by some of the Psalms, then the New Testament in 1661, and finally the rest of the Bible. The New Testament was revised in 1680, and the Old Testament between 1682 and 1685. He also produced an *Indian Grammar* in 1666, and had Baxter's *Call To The Unconverted* and Bayly's *Practice Of Piety* printed as well.

David Brainerd (1718-1747)

Eliot's work among the Indians was followed some hundred years later by that of David Brainerd, who also ministered to the Red Indians. Born into a Puritan family at Hartford, Connecticut, he was converted at the age of 21 while out walking; he experienced 'a new appreciation or view...of God' and his soul 'was filled with light and love'. Three years later he was licensed to preach and was appointed by the Scottish SPCK to evangelise the Indians. Labouring under great difficulties and suffering tremendous deprivations, he lived among the Indians at Crossweeksung, New Jersey, where he had the joy of baptising seventy-eight converts. But his health was poor; he soon became ill and died of tuberculosis. He is reckoned as one of the greatest of all missionaries and his Diary, which reveals his 'passion for prayer', has inspired many others to similar endeavours.

Interned

The number of 'praying towns' increased and by 1674 there were fourteen new settlements with an estimated 3,600 converts. The first church building was erected at Natick in 1660, and later the pastorate of the congregation was taken over by an Indian called Takawompbait. The progress of the gospel was seriously impeded however by the onset of a war.

In 1675-76 an Indian chief known as King Philip attacked the colonists; several thousand of them were killed and half the towns of Massachusetts destroyed or damaged. Despite their loyalty, the 'praying Indians' became victims of suspicion and were interned on Deer Island in Boston harbour. They lived there 'patiently, humbly and piously, without complaining' until allowed to return home two years later. But Eliot's work had been dealt a severe blow from which it never fully recovered. Though the Indians remained faithful, the progress of the gospel slowed down, and by the middle of the following century there was only a single family of believing Indians left.

Although he lived to the age of eighty-six, his wide-ranging responsibilities took their toll: his family commitments, the pastoral work at Roxbury and his concern for the Indians. Towards the end he declared, 'I am drawing home,' and his last words were, 'Welcome joy.' He died on 20th May 1690. Many paid tribute to Eliot's work and he became known as 'the Apostle to the Indians'. Baxter said of him, 'There was no man on earth whom I honoured above him.' Another wrote, 'A nobler, truer and warmer spirit than John Eliot never lived.'

While Eliot had been working quietly among the Indians - and later the Negroes as well - gradual changes had been taking place in America. The population was beginning to expand as more immigrants arrived from Europe: Baptists and Quakers from England, Presbyterians from Scotland, Mennonites from Switzerland and Lutherans from Germany. There was even a nucleus of Jews as well. Yet traditional religious values began to be eroded away and by the following century Churches were settling into respectable indifference. That is, until the 'Great Awakening'.

GEORGE WHITEFIELD (1714-1770): Evangelist

The Great Awakening of the eighteenth century had a profound impact on both sides of the Atlantic, and though it started in America it soon spread to England and Germany. Not only was the spiritual life of the Church quickened and a new impetus given to missionary enterprise, but the social fabric of the nations was touched as well.

The beginnings of the Awakening can be traced to the previous century and to a variety of gradual changes taking place in the colonies. With the influx of European immigrants and the growth of the population, there was a breakdown of traditional religious values; the Church went into decline as colonists lost their religious fervour and church membership dropped.

Though the Puritans maintained the essentials of their Faith, their religion became more and more formal, and moral respectability rather than regeneration became the criterion for church membership. In 1679 a Synod meeting at Boston deplored the decline of 'the power of godliness' and prayed for God to 'pour down his Spirit from on high'. Yet when the first sign of revival came, it was not from within the Puritan movement but among the Dutch-speaking residents of New Jersey. Pastor Theodore Frelinghuysen began to preach the need for regeneration, and in 1726 began to experience a revival with many conversions and a return to godly living.

In the same year Gilbert Tennent of New Brunswick enjoyed similar results, and in 1734 the great theologian Jonathan Edwards began to experience revival at Northampton, Massachusetts. Edwards' account of the revival, *A Narrative Of Surprising Conversions*, was much used of God in America and in England.

Itinerant Preacher

But the most important contribution to the Awakening was probably made by George Whitefield, who became the focus of the revival in the colonies and acted as a link with the Evangelical Revival in the British Isles. For thirty-five years as an itinerant preacher in Britain and America, Whitefield changed the conventions of religious preaching and opened the way for mass evangelism.

Whitefield was born at the Bell Inn, Gloucester, where his parents were the keepers. At school his chief interest was drama and he was apparently a born actor; he took part in a number of school plays and was sometimes invited to make speeches before the town fathers. He left school at the age of fifteen to help his mother run the inn, but three years later was persuaded to enter Pembroke College, Oxford, where as a servitor he gained free tuition by serving his fellow students.

For some while Whitefield had begun to feel a hunger for God and became aware that he had some intention for his life. To prepare himself, he fasted regularly and prayed, and often attended public worship twice a day. At Oxford he planned to enter the Church of England ministry and

.associated with a number of others, known as 'Methodists', who had similar intentions.

The Wesleys had started a religious society, nick-named the Holy Club, to promote the pursuit of personal religion, and Whitefield readily joined in the activities. Realising more and more that his heart was far from God, however, he resolved only to read books that led him 'directly into an experimental knowledge of Jesus Christ'. But it was not until three years later, during Lent 1735, that 'God was pleased... to remove the heavy load and enable me to lay hold of his Son by a living faith'.

Whitefield was twenty-one when he was converted, and when his intention of entering the ministry was made known to Bishop Benson of Gloucester, arrangements were made for him to be ordained before the statutory age. The Sunday following, in January 1736, he preached his first sermon, at the church where he had been baptised. His evangelical fervour was apparent; some mocked but many were impressed. After-

Jonathan Edwards
(1703-1758)
After graduating at Yale in 1720, Edwards studied theology and then took up duty as pastor to a Presbyterian Church in New York. Following two years as a tutor at Yale, he moved to the Congregational Church at North-ampton where he assisted the pastor, his grandfather. He took sole charge of the church in 1729. A Calvinist, Edwards preached justification by faith alone, and in 1734-35 and again in 1740 (with Whitefield), his church ex-perienced revival. But when he tried to tighten membership rules and to exclude all 'unconverted' from communion, he was dis-missed by the congregation. In 1750 he went to Stockbridge as a missionary to the Housatonic In-dians, and for three months before his death in 1758 was President of the College of New Jersey (now Princeton University). His most important work was *Freedom of the Will* (1754), and largely on the basis of this volume he has become known as America's greatest theologian.

wards there was a complaint to the Bishop that his sermon had driven fifteen people 'mad' (i.e. they had been converted); the bishop's response was that he hoped the madness would not be forgotten before next Sunday!

Invitations to preach soon began to reach the young minister, and in both London and Bristol he spoke in churches and at many of the new religious societies that had been formed. But, while his message of the new birth and justification by faith 'made their way like lightning into the hearts of the hearers' conscience', others began to oppose him and refuse the use of their pulpits.

The following year Whitefield sailed for the colony of Georgia to support the Wesleys in their missionary outreach, but by the time he reached Savannah they had returned home. His stay was brief, only long enough to become aware of the need for an orphanage, and he returned to England to raise money for the building.

Open-air

On a preaching tour in the West Country early in 1739, he discovered that many pulpits were still closed to him. At Bath and then at Bristol his request for use of a pulpit was turned down, and it was this refusal that led him to break with tradition and preach in the open-air. In Wales evangelists had already used the method with success, so one Saturday afternoon he determined to speak to the miners of Kingswood on their own ground.

Standing on a hillside, Whitefield preached to some two hundred miners and their families whom, he felt, were 'as sheep having no shepherd'. He was thrilled with the experience and wrote in his diary, 'I believe I never was more acceptable to my Master than when I was standing to teach those hearers in the open fields'.

Anxious to return to America, Whitefield approached the Wesleys and invited them to take over his work in Bristol during his absence. John Wesley, amazed at the large open-air meetings, agreed even though the two preachers began to realise they had deep theological differences. When Whitefield reached the colonies late in 1739, his reputation as a preacher had gone before him. In New England great crowds gathered to hear the twenty-five year old evangelist, and for over a month he spoke to as many as eight thousand people every day. Although opposed by a number of Anglican ministers, his tour was immensely successful and many were converted.

His gift of oratory was greatly admired and he had obviously not lost his youthful skill of acting. Benjamin Franklin, the famous publisher, inventor and writer, spoke enthusiastically of his preaching ability and declared, 'It was wonderful to see the change soon made in the manner of our inhabitants'. Franklin himself once came under the influence of Whitefield's persuasive powers when, following an appeal for his orphanage, the writer - contrary to all his vowed intentions - put all the silver and gold from his pocket into the collection.

The height of the Awakening came in the years 1740-41 when both Whitefield and Jonathan Edwards were ministering in the colonies; thousands were converted and many new churches established as the revival spread South from New England into Virginia. One minister wrote, 'Our lectures flourish, our Sabbaths are joyous, our churches increase and our ministers have new life and spirit in their work.'

On returning to England in 1741, Whitefield found that the situation had changed and there was a breach between him and the Wesleys. During his absence, John Wesley had spoken out against Whitefield's belief in the doctrine of election and predestination, even though Whitefield had asked him to keep their differences private. As Whitefield was supported by ministers from Scotland and Wales, Wesley from then on tended to concentrate his ministry more on England.

But Whitefield always spoke well of the Wesleys, who admitted in later years that he showed them great kindness during this time. In London, Whitefield's supporters provided him with a large, temporary shed - just north of Wesley's Foundry - for his ministry which, in 1756, was replaced by a brick building in Tottenham Court Road.

Over the succeeding years Whitefield visited Scotland on fourteen occasions, the first in 1741. His second visit, the following year, proved

WHITEFIELD PREACHING AT MOORFIELDS

quite remarkable, for revival had broken out at Cambuslang, near Glasgow, and he was able to share in the work of the awakening. The climax of his visit was two communion services held in the open air, one of which attracted 20,000 people.

Servant of All

Whitefield's links with Wales were forged through his relationship with Howell Harris and Daniel Rowland, whose gospel preaching also brought about a revival. Thousands were con-

GEORGE WHITEFIELD

verted and new religious societies founded. Whitefield met with the leaders in 1743 to establish these societies on a regular basis, which became the Calvinistic Methodist Association (now the Presbyterian Church of Wales). When he returned to New England in 1743 there were reports of trouble in the churches.

As he needed to devote more time to America and wanted freedom to assist any evangelical cause, whatever the denomination, he relinquished his leadership of the Calvinistic Methodists. Added to which, he had no desire to face constant opposition from the Wesleys; he decided to retire from the limelight and turn over the work to them. 'Let the name of Whitefield perish and that of Christ be glorified, and let me be but the servant of all!' he declared. He took a particular interest in the work begun by the Countess of Huntingdon, who owned a number of Calvinistic Methodist chapels and in 1768 opened a college for preachers at Trevecca.

A man of immense vigour and zeal, Whitefield maintained a tough schedule of travel and preaching tours, which eventually wore him out. He died during the night of 15th October 1770 at Newburyport, New England, where he was buried.

Happily, his funeral sermon was preached at the Tottenham Court Road Chapel by John Wesley, who testified to Whitefield's tender-heartedness and charitableness, and attributed it to his 'faith in the bleeding Lord... the love of God shed abroad in his heart, filling his soul with tender, disinterested love to every child of man'.

JOHN WESLEY (1703-1791): Founder of Methodism

Although Whitefield was generally acknowledged as the greatest preacher of the eighteenth century Evangelical Revival, it was John Wesley who not only designed a superstructure for the movement, but also gave it some cohesion and a sense of purpose and direction.

The revival began within the Church of England but spread to affect the whole spectrum of Nonconformist Churches; and although Wesley, as an ordained Anglican priest, was anxious to maintain the work within the established Church, it led after his death to the founding of a new denomination.

As a young man Wesley had a conviction that God had a purpose for him in his life. This came about when the Wesleys' home at Epworth (Lincolnshire) was destroyed by fire in 1709. At the height of the blaze the six year old John, who had been left behind, appeared at an upstairs window and was rescued by some farm hands from the village who formed a human ladder to bring him to safety. Afterwards his mother, Susanna, referred to him as a 'brand plucked from the burning' (Zechariah 3:2), which imprinted itself upon the boy's mind.

John's father, the Rev Samuel Wesley, was the rector at Epworth and was a High Anglican by persuasion, though born of Puritan parents. John's mother, who bore the rector nineteen children, was a woman of great courage and strength, and ruled her family with firmness and love. Every day she set aside time with each of her children for teaching them the Bible and Prayer Book, and for improving their conduct.

Good Works

When John and his brother Charles left for school in London, to attend Charterhouse and Westminster, she kept in touch by letter, as she did when they went up to Oxford. Concerned always for their well-being, she plied them with good advice and warned them about the assaults of the world. In this way, Wesley was grounded in Anglicanism and instilled with the idea of achieving 'good works' as essential to salvation. At the age of twenty-two, however, when his father pressed him into being ordained (1725), he began to realise for the first time that 'true religion was seated in the heart', and set himself to attain 'inward holiness'.

At Oxford he became a Fellow at Lincoln College and a tutor in Greek. He was joined by his brother Charles who came up to study at Christ Church, and the two remained at the university for some years. It was Charles who in 1729 founded the religious society nicknamed the

'Holy Club', to encourage like-minded students to pursue their aim of salvation. They spent their time in daily prayer and Bible study, and involved themselves in good works, such as visiting the prisons, helping poor families and caring for the sick. They organised their time so that every minute of the day could be profitably used, and living according to a fixed plan earned for them the name 'Methodists'.

Missionary

In 1734 Wesley felt that God was calling him to be a missionary to the Indians of the newly-founded colony of Georgia. He set sail in October 1735, and on the voyage met a group of Moravian Christians who were emigrating to the New World. In conversations with them it began to dawn on him that he did not have a saving faith, and during a storm rapidly came to the conclusion that he was not yet ready to die.

Wesley tried to impose a rigid discipline on the colonists of Georgia, which they resented; he also failed to make any progress among the Indians. When a warrant was issued against him on an ecclesiastical matter, he left abruptly for England, his missionary hopes dashed. With his heart deeply troubled, he reflected much upon his spiritual condition and wrote in his Journal, 'I went to America to convert the Indians; but oh, who shall convert me?'

Yet God was at work in Wesley's heart and his cry was soon to be answered. Back in London he met another Moravian, Peter Böhler, with whom he had many discussions about the way of salvation. Though yet unconverted - and he was aware of it - he continued preaching the need

HOLY CLUB

JOHN WESLEY

for faith. As Böhler told him, 'Preach faith till you have it; and then because you have it, you will preach faith.'

On the 24th May 1738, Wesley 'unwillingly' attended a Moravian society in Aldersgate Street where someone was reading Luther's *Preface To The Epistle To The Romans*. In his own words, 'About a quarter before nine, while he was describing the change which God works in the heart through faith in Christ, I felt my heart strangely warmed. I felt I did trust in Christ... an assurance was given me that he had taken away my sins, even mine, and saved me from the law of sin and death.' Three days earlier his brother Charles had also experienced a sudden conversion, and the two brothers were now united in their desire to make known their new-found faith in Christ.

Turning Point

This occasion proved to be one of the great turning points in English history; it marked not only the beginning of Methodism but, according to one historian, saved England from the kind of revolution the French were to experience at the end of the century. Within a few months, Wesley met up again with Whitefield, whom he had known in the Holy Club at Oxford. Whitefield, converted three years earlier, had started a gospel work at Bristol and as a result of his open-air preaching a number of societies had been established. He invited Wesley to take over the work in Bristol while he returned to America to build an orphanage.

At first Wesley could not reconcile himself to 'this strange way of preaching in the fields'; he believed in decency and order and thought 'the saving of souls almost a sin if it had not been done in church'. But two days later he followed Whitefield's example 'and proclaimed in the highways the glad tidings of salvation' to about three thousand people. The success of the occasion changed Wesley's mind, and from then on he began to preach wherever he could find an audience, addressing as many as eight thousand at a time. Increasingly he found that pulpits were closed to him, but was happy speaking in the open air to the poorer sections of the population - miners, iron-workers, spinners and weavers

- who would not normally be found in Church.

It was not long, however before the two evangelists realised they had fundamental theological differences. As clergymen, they had both consented to abide by the Thirty-nine Articles, which have a strong Calvinistic leaning. While Whitefield had kept to this, Wesley was more influenced by his Arminian background, which denied predestination and held that the sovereignty of God was compatible with free will, and that Christ died for all and not simply for the elect. Wesley openly attacked Whitefield in a sermon on free grace, and Whitefield responded by writing to ask him not to publish it, a plea Wesley ignored.

When Whitefield returned from America the two agreed that they 'preached two different gospels'; though they parted amicably it led to a permanent division. Whitefield joined Howell Harris and in 1743 founded the Calvinistic Methodist Association of Wales; the following year Wesley formed his 'United Societies' into a nationwide organisation with an annual Conference to decide the best method of carrying on the work of God.

While early Methodism was centred on Bristol, Wesley believed that all the world was his parish; he began an itinerant ministry that included an annual tour of England and twenty visits to both Scotland and Ireland. Travelling mostly on horseback, he covered an estimated 250,000 miles and preached 40,000 sermons; he kept a detailed account of his tours, later published in his *Journal*, as well as writing commentaries on Scripture and editing classical works.

Many bishops and clergy, however, objected to Wesley and his local preachers, and Anglican churches were often closed to them; mobs also took exception to their arrogant claim to salvation, so that homes and meeting places were looted and destroyed and the people subjected to frequent attacks.

Genius

Whereas Whitefield had no vision for establishing his converts, Wesley was a genius at organising his followers into societies and in this way 'preserved the fruits of his labours'. From 1740 he divided each society into classes, each with a leader responsible for pastoral care; the societies were formed into circuits, which were in turn grouped into districts under the supervision of an assistant personally chosen by him. Wesley, in fact, controlled the whole movement: he appointed the assistants, the local preachers and the society leaders; he excluded those who he felt needed to be disciplined and he invited to the annual conference those he needed to advise (and not govern) him.

Acutely aware of the social implications of the gospel, Wesley always had a practical concern for those in need. He visited prisons and poor houses, opened a free dispensary, started the Stranger's Friend Societies to assist the poor, and opposed the slave trade. Like Whitefield, he preached two fundamental doctrines: the new birth and justification by faith. But he also encouraged his converts to aim at Christian perfection, or holiness, and argued that believers should be free from 'outward sin'. In this ideal his views were similar to those of George Fox.

Wesley continued his travels right up to the time of his death, though he acknowledged he was 'now an old man, decayed from head to foot'. He preached his last sermon at Leatherhead in February 1791; five days later he was taken ill. Before he died he was twice heard to say, 'The best of all is God is with us.'

Since 1784, when the Established Church refused to ordain two of his local preachers, he had himself 'laid hands' on candidates for work overseas and in Scotland. And before his death he made similar provision for parts of England where the sacraments were not available. In 1795, Conference decided to allow its preachers to celebrate the Lord's Supper, which in effect severed Methodism's final links with the Church of England and heralded the emergence of the Wesleyan Methodist Church of Britain.

Methodism in America

Methodism was carried to America by an Irish local preacher, Philip Embury, who in 1766 formed a Methodist society in his house in New York. The Movement spread to neighbouring Pennsylvania and Maryland. In 1771 Wesley sent Francis Asbury, a local preacher from Birmingham, to superintend the growing number of societies. Despite the War of Independence (1776-83), the movement continued to expand, from 3,000 members in 1775 to around 60,000 in 1790. Anxious to allow American Methodism to become independent, Wesley tried in vain to have two men ordained by the Bishop of London; when this failed, he himself 'laid hands' on the men and 'set apart' Dr. Thomas Coke as a superintendent to assist Asbury. In December 1784 at the Baltimore Conference, it was agreed to form a Methodist Episcopal Church with Asbury and Coke as bishops, much to Wesley's displeasure.

SOME 18TH-20TH CENTURY REVIVALS

LOCATION	LEADING FIGURES	COURSE OF REVIVAL
NEW ENGLAND, AMERICA (1734-5, 1740s) The Great Awakening	* Jonathan Edwards (1703-58). Pastor, Congregational Church, Northampton, Massachusetts. * George Whitefield (1714-70). British evangelist, visited America 7 times.	* Originated in Dutch Reformed Church 1726 * Edwards preached on 'justification by faith alone' 1734 - many conversions, town 'full of presence of God' * Further outbreak of revival in 1740s following Whitefield's preaching in New England * Out of population of 250,000, over 50,000 added to the church
WALES (from 1735)	* Howell Harris (1714-73). Was refused ordination - became schoolmaster but sacked after conversion * Daniel Rowlands (1713-90). Ordained, then converted while a young curate (1735) under Griffith Jones	* Harris converted Whit Sunday (1735) and immediately began to witness * Became itinerant preacher - hundreds converted * Joined by Rowlands who became a gospel preacher * Whitefield visited Wales and helped with preaching * Revival spread from South to North Wales * Calvinistic Methodist Association founded (1743) - now Presbyterian Church of Wales
ENGLAND AND SCOTLAND (from 1739) The Evangelical Revival	* John Wesley (1703-91). Church of England clergyman with itinerant ministry in Britain and America from 1732. Founder of Methodism.	* From 1739 travelled around Britain, preaching the gospel. - refused entrance to many Anglican pulpits - followed example of Whitefield and preached in open air * Church in Scotland transformed by preaching of both men - revival at Kilsyth and Cambuslang * Converts formed into 'societies': - English Calvinistic Methodist Connexion founded by Whitefield (1743) - Methodist Church only became official in 1794, after Wesley's death
ENGLAND (1800-1830) The 'Ranters' Revival	* Hugh Bourne (b 1772). Born Stoke on Trent. Converted aged 27 and joined Methodist Society at Ridgway * William Clownes (b 1783). With Bourne, became leading preacher in revival	* Bourne became leader of cottage prayer meeting 1799 * Revival spread through Burslem Methodist Circuit * Camp Meetings held at Mow Cop for preaching, prayer and fasting * Meetings disapproved by Methodist Conference - Bourne expelled from church 1808 * May 1811 - founded Primitive Methodist Church * By 1842 there were 1278 chapels and 85,565 members

SOME 18TH-20TH CENTURY REVIVALS

LOCATION	LEADING FIGURES	COURSE OF REVIVAL
AMERICA (1858) The Second Great Awakening (also known as the Prayer Meeting Revival)	* Jeremiah Lanphier (b1809). Converted 1842 in Broadway Tabernacle, New York. Man of Prayer.	* Started Wednesday prayer meeting in Fulton Street, New York, September 1857 * Crowds flocked to daily meetings throughout New York - many conversions followed * Revival broke out in Hamilton, Ontario * Other major cities affected - Boston, Chicago, Washington * Estimated one million people converted.
ULSTER (from 1859)	* James McQuilkin, John Wallace, Robert Carlisle and Jeremiah Meneely. McQuilkin heard of American revival, and he asked 'Why not here?'	* Four men started prayer meeting near Ballymena, September 1857 * Number of prayer meetings grew, church attendance increased * Many conversions and experiences of 'prostrations' * The Holy Spirit at work among children * Southern Ireland affected - Barnardo converted Dublin, 1862
BRITAIN (1859)	* Included such men as W C Burns (Scotland); H R Jones and David Morgan (Wales); C H Spurgeon and William Haslam	* Whole communities experienced revival - Towns and villages - Aberdeen to Inverness - West Wales, the valleys and all the counties - mainly Cornwall and North Devon, few instances in England * Estimated one million converts * Paved way for mission of Moody and Sankey * Created religious climate from which sprang great philanthropic and social causes
WALES (1904-5)	* Evan Roberts (1878-1951) Gave up work as a blacksmith to prepare for entry to Trevecca College. Received anointing for preaching under Seth Joshua, September 1904	* Preached in home village of Loughor, near Swansea, on work of the Holy Spirit * Chapels filled, number of prayer meetings increased - some lasting four hours * Revival spread to Welsh Keswick week at Llandrindod Wells, under F B Meyer * Around 100,000 converted in 2 years
EAST ANGLIA, ENGLAND (1921) NORTH-EAST SCOTLAND	* Rev A Douglas Brown (died 1940) * Jock Troup (died 1954)	* Originated Lowestoft, spread to other East Anglian towns and cities. * Scottish fishermen and wives visiting Great Yarmouth visiting Great Yarmouth - many conversions * Revival continued on return to homes in November

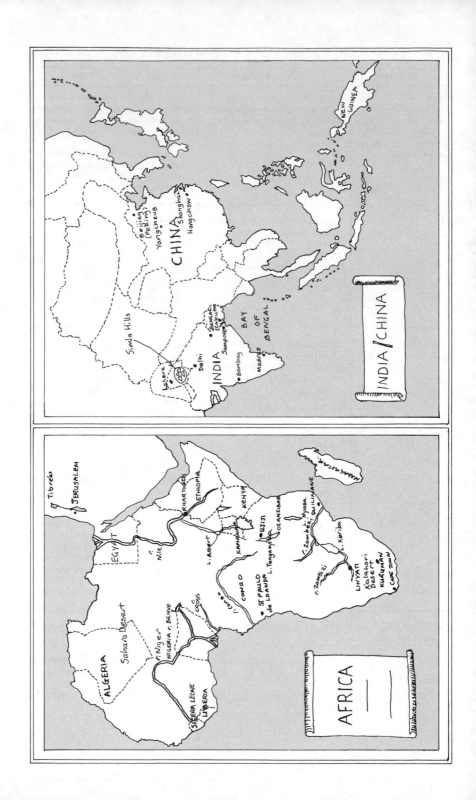

SEVEN

The Nineteenth Century Missionary Movement

In the days of the Early Church, Christians responded with remarkable enthusiasm to the challenge of the gospel and the Great Commission 'to make disciples of all nations'. By the third century much of the Roman Empire had been evangelised and churches established, and Christianity was acknowledged as an acceptable alternative to the pagan religions of the Mediterranean world.

This intense period of activity was followed by a considerable lull in missionary endeavours, and for many centuries little was done to break new territory. Even the impetus gained by the Reformation failed to stir the Protestant Church adequately to evangelism, and it was left to the Jesuits to take the initiative. They established missions in India and the Far East, and made in-roads into South America. In the seventeenth century, further gains were made in Central and North America as a result of conquests made by the Spanish, Portuguese and French armies, opening up vast territories to Rome.

Between the seventeenth and nineteenth centuries there was a gradual build-up of missionary outreach by the Protestant Churches. Up to this date, Christianity had been limited mainly to western Europe, but Protestants slowly began to wake up to the need to take the gospel to the unevangelised nations. Regrettably, it was often linked into a policy of colonisation which, on one hand allowed missionaries freedom of movement, but at the same time gave the impression that Christianity was simply an instrument for civilising the natives.

India

The Protestant Churches on the Continent were first to engage in missionary activity beyond the shores of Europe, though efforts were isolated and lacking in real impact. In 1550 the King of Sweden sent a missionary to Lapland, and in 1620 the King of Denmark encouraged the chaplains of Danish settlements in India to preach the gospel to the Hindus. When the Dutch extended their colonies, they established missions in India and the East Indies. Following the Pietist revival in Germany, the Lutherans organised a mission to India (1705) and the Moravian Church at Herrnhut began sending out missionaries to different parts of the world.

Towards the end of the seventeenth century the Puritan movement in Britain began to show a concern for missionary outreach, and it was the Anglican Church that took the first steps. In 1698 the Society for the Propagation of Christian Knowledge was set up to promote Christian education and the distribution of the Bible. This was followed in 1701 by the Society for the Propagation of the Gospel, founded to provide an Anglican ministry overseas and for the 'conversion of heathens and infidels'.

Although SPCK workers for a while supported the Danish chaplains in India, the SPG was the first missionary society of the Church of England. To a lesser degree, the gospel in India was also represented by the chaplains of the British East India Company, a trading organisation that was the forerunner of the British Empire in the sub-continent.

It was not until 1792 that missionary work was first taken seriously. The credit lies with a group of twelve Baptist ministers, led by William Carey, who met at Kettering (Northants) in the October of that year. They formed the 'Particular Baptist Society for the Propagating of the Gospel', now known as the Baptist Missionary Society. Their decisions to send Carey to India triggered off an explosion of missionary concern on both sides of the Atlantic that led to 'one of the most extensive global movements ever to occur in human history, one that was instrumental in transforming Christianity ... into the world's largest religion' (*Great Christian Leaders*, p. 307).

HOUSE IN KETTERING IN WHICH THE BAPTIST MISSIONARY SOCIETY WAS FORMED

WILLIAM CAREY (1761-1834):
Father of Modern Missions

The son of a weaver who later became the village schoolmaster, Carey's education finished at the age of twelve; he became a gardener and was later apprenticed as a shoe-maker. Though brought up in the Anglican Church, Carey was taken by a friend to Independent services where he was converted. When he discovered he had a flair for languages, he started to study the New Testament and learn Greek; he also taught himself to read French and Dutch, and began to study Latin and Hebrew.

In 1785 he became a lay pastor at the Baptist Church in Moulton, near Kettering, was ordained two years later and in 1789 moved to Harvey Lane Church, Leicester. As a member of the Northampton Association of ministers, he frequently discussed with the fraternity the need to carry the gospel to the unsaved heathens. It was generally held at the time that the Great Commission was for the apostles alone, but Carey thought differently. It is said he was once rebuked for making such a suggestion. 'Sit down, young man,' an older minister told him. 'If the Lord wants to convert the heathen, he can do it without your help.'

To promote his concern, he published a treatise in May 1791, entitled *An Enquiry Into The Obligation Of Christians To Use Means For The Conversion Of The Heathen*, in which he outlined the scriptural teaching and strategy for mission. Three weeks later, in a famous sermon preached at Nottingham, Carey spoke on Isaiah 54:2 and urged the people to 'expect great things from God, attempt great things for God'.

India, rather than the South Sea Islands which had at first attracted Carey, was chosen as a target for their mission. This was because John Thomas, a Baptist and former naval surgeon who had already served in

---

The English Baptists

The Reformation led to a re-appraisal of the practice of baptism. Anabaptists declined to baptise their children and re-affirmed the teaching of believers' baptism; a number of other groups, such as the Swiss Brethren and the Mennonites, followed their lead. In England, two groups of Baptists emerged: (1) The General Baptists originated with the Separatist John Smyth, who led a group from Gainsborough to take refuge in Amsterdam where he re-instituted the practice of believers' baptism. A group of his followers returned to England in 1612 and founded the first Baptist Church at Spitalfields, London. (2) The Particular Baptists, so called because of their belief in a particular atonement, in which Christ died only for the elect, were an off-shoot of a Calvinistic Independent Church; their first congregation was formed in 1633-38 with John Spilsbury as pastor. In the eighteenth century many Baptists lapsed into Unitarianism.

Bengal, was planning to return there. He agreed to join the Baptist Society and Carey volunteered to accompany him and, taking his wife and four children, finally sailed on a Danish vessel in June 1793. The early years in India were times of real hardship: his young son, Peter, died of dysentery, his wife's already poor mental state deteriorated further and Thomas, who often proved unreliable, squandered all their money.

Carey wrote to a friend, 'I am in a strange land, alone, no Christian friend, a large family and nothing to supply their wants.' Yet his faith remained strong and he was able to declare amid it all, 'He is all-sufficient!'

With the turn of a new century and the arrival of new missionaries from England, Carey's circumstances began to improve. Because they were not licensed, the missionaries were not able to operate from British territory and had to accept the offer of a home on a small Danish settlement at Serampore, north of Calcutta. Carey joined them, as he felt the opportunities for ministry would be better. Among the new arrivals were a printer, William Ward, whom Carey had met before, and Joshua Marshman.

WILLIAM CAREY

The three were soon knit together in friendship and the 'Serampore Trio' worked well at translating and publishing the gospel. Up to this point Carey had not experienced the joy of a single convert, but within the year two Hindu men were won to Christ. By 1803 there were twenty-five Indian nationals who had been baptised, and by 1825 over seven hundred had come to faith, some at the cost of their lives. The reason for this breakthrough may have been due in part to a change in the emphasis of his preaching, when he switched from attacking Hinduism to declaring the cross of Christ.

Aware of the urgency for the Bible in an Indian language, Carey devoted most of his time to translation work. The Bengali New Testament was published first, in March 1801; this was followed by Scripture portions in thirty-four languages, with six complete and twenty-four partial translations of the Bible. While the work was obviously hurried and not always accurate, it was a tremendous accomplishment.

Probably as a result of his translation work, Carey was offered the post of tutor in Bengali and Sanskrit at Fort William College, Calcutta. The position was useful in that it provided him with much needed income and also facilitated his work in producing grammars, dictionaries and translations of eastern books. His work received a severe blow and a brief set-back when in 1812 a fire destroyed their print house, entire stock of paper and some of Carey's uncompleted manuscripts. 'In one night the labours of years are consumed,' he wrote ruefully; but his faith was not overwhelmed and he re-wrote the lost manuscripts.

In 1819 he established Serampore College, a Christian school for Indian students. His aim was to prepare Indians to evangelise their own people, but he earned the displeasure of some of his colleagues for accepting non-Christians as day students. The college was nevertheless a success, and in 1827 the King of Denmark granted it a charter to confer its own degrees.

Indian Culture

Carey took a keen interest in Indian culture and customs and was not afraid to become involved in social reform. He strongly opposed the practices of infanticide and child prostitution, and aided Hindu reformers in bringing in legislation (in 1829) to ban *sati*, the practice whereby a widow was burned alive on her husband's funeral pyre.

Although essentially a linguist, Carey was also a pioneer in missionary thinking and some of his ideas were ahead of their time. He believed that as far as possible, missionaries should be self-supporting, and he set an example during his early years in India when he worked as the manager of two indigo factories.

He stressed the need for an indigenous church and believed that with the Scriptures in their own language and proper training, the native peoples would be able to take over their own church growth. He also recognised the need to make use of women missionaries, particularly in India where native women were generally kept out of sight in a male-dominated world and only a female approach was acceptable.

Understandably, Carey became known as the 'Father of modern missions', not simply because of his remarkable translation work but also because he was the author of missionary ideas and philosophy by which future missions were to be guided.

As a result of Carey's work, Protestants were stirred into action and other missions quickly established: the London Missionary Society (1795), the Church Missionary Society (1799) and the British and Foreign Bible Society (1804). Others followed in Scotland, on the Continent and in the United States. Missionaries reached out into previously unknown corners of the world, transforming Christianity into a world religion.

HUDSON TAYLOR (1832-1905):
Founder of the China Inland Mission

Towards the end of his life, Hudson Taylor once recalled the words of an aged minister friend in London, who warned him, 'You are making a great mistake in going to China with no organisation behind you. We live in a busy world, and you will be forgotten, and the Mission won't live for seven years.' The minister was, of course, proved wrong and the China Inland Mission survived and flourished; by 1900 it provided nearly half of the foreign missionaries then in China, and through its work thousands were won to Christ.

When Taylor founded the China Inland Mission in 1865 he started a mission that was quite different to any other that had gone before. It was for example, the first truly inter-denominational missionary society to be founded, and used lay-workers rather than ordained ministers. It was a 'faith' mission, making no appeals for funds, and was not organised from London but from the mission field.

China

The earliest mission to China was launched as far back as the seventh century when an heretical sect settled in the north-west of the country, but the work did not survive long. It was not until the thirteenth century that another mission was set up, this time by the Franciscan friars, aimed at converting the Mongols. But the Mongols eventually went over to Islam and the work declined.

A Jesuit mission followed in the sixteenth century; it was more successful, and in 1692 was influential in winning an edict of toleration for the Chinese Christians. This advantage was lost in 1773, however, when the Pope disbanded the Society of Jesus, and it was another half century before the Church of Rome returned to China.

Protestants had meanwhile begun to show an interest in the country and in 1807 the London Missionary Society sent Robert Morrison to open up a way for Christian outreach. Born in Northumberland in 1782, Morrison left school at fourteen but after his conversion worked diligently to make up his lack of education.

Called to be a missionary at the age of nineteen, he was accepted by LMS in 1804 and set himself to study medicine and astronomy, and in London a Chinese student taught him the rudiments of the language. Because foreigners were not allowed into the interior, he was forced to stay in Canton, one of the five Treaty Ports on the coast. Despite restrictions, he managed to learn the Chinese language and was employed by the East India Company as an interpreter. He eventually published a Chinese grammar, a dictionary and a translation of the Bible.

Other societies soon followed, but it was not until after the Opium Wars of 1840-42, that the interior was finally opened up to missionaries, who were then able to receive official protection. It was at this point, in 1865, that Hudson Taylor founded the China Inland Mission, today called the Overseas Missionary Fellowship.

Medical Training

Hudson Taylor was born in Barnsley, Yorkshire. He came from good Methodist stock which dated back to 1776, when his great-grandfather James had been converted out on Staincross Ridge simply by meditating on a verse from the Bible. The family's Methodist links continued and Hudson's father became a well-known local preacher on the Barnsley circuit. Often the young boy listened to the preachers as they gathered on Quarter Day in the parlour behind the Taylors' chemist shop in Cheapside, discussing foreign missions and especially the needs of China.

HUDSON TAYLOR

When he was four or five, Hudson would often declare, 'When I am a man, I mean to be a missionary and go to China,' but his persistent poor health rather dimmed his hopes. It was not until the age of seventeen, however, that he was truly converted, through the casual reading of a tract.

Before long he began to experience a desire for a deeper relationship with God and as he prayed it through, one evening he heard a command, as if a voice had spoken it: 'Then go for me to China.' From that hour his mind was made up and he was determined to obey God.

He began at once to prepare himself for whatever lay ahead. His Sunday School superintendent gave him a copy of the writings of Luke in the Mandarin dialect and, using his New Testament, he started to work out the meaning of the Chinese characters.

Then the Congregational minister in Barnsley loaned him Medhurst's book *China*, which focused his attention on the usefulness of medical

missions as a means of preparation for the mission field. His next move
was to take a position as assistant to a Dr. Hardey, a distant relation in
Hull, where he studied medicine and - more important - learned to trust
God more, even for his next meal.

During these months, Taylor continued his practice of living frugally
in order to be able to give away two thirds of his salary. He lodged in
a poor home, ate only brown bread and apples for lunch and followed his
father's maxim of 'See if you can do without'. In this way he began to
accustom himself to some of the hardships he would have to face in China.

Faith

Working in the poorest part of Hull, he was called one Sunday evening
to the bedside of a dying woman. After he had prayed, he felt that he
should leave the starving family some money for food. Dipping his hand
into his pocket, he handed his very last coin to the grateful father, and
left wondering how God would provide for his own needs.

The following morning the postman brought him a parcel from an
anonymous donor which contained a pair of gloves and a half sovereign.
'Praise the Lord,' he exclaimed. 'Four hundred per cent for twelve hours
investment - that is good interest!' It was this incident more than any
other that confirmed his faith in God and his determination to go to
China.

Taylor's application to the Chinese Evangelisation Society was
accepted, and following further medical training in London he sailed for
China in September 1853. Hudson Taylor went out as an independent
missionary and spent nearly seven years in the Shanghai-Ningpo coastal
area before being forced to return home because of ill-health. Initially he
made his home in the London Missionary Society compound, but
housing was a constant problem and he had to move several times.

After some months of intensive language study, Taylor began to take
part in distributing tracts and later was able to join in a number of
evangelistic journeys. In time he was fluent enough to begin preaching
at services and to undertake preaching tours, usually with one of his
converts. He also continued his medical studies and was able to work in
the dispensary.

During these years there were three important decisions that he took
that had a considerable effect on his work. First he changed to a Chinese
style of living and adopted the native dress; while he found this made it
easier for him to approach Chinese people, it put a barrier between him
and some Europeans.

Then in January 1858 he married Maria Dyer, a missionary teacher who shared his vision for winning souls. She bore him six children, three of whom died before she herself passed away in July 1870. Finally he resigned from the CES because of their financial policies; for one thing, they had run into debt to the tune of £1,000, which meant that, contrary to his principles, Taylor was living on borrowed money.

He was now completely independent and more than ever looking to the Lord to meet his needs. To encourage his faith he had two Bible words written on scrolls for his sitting room: *Ebenezer* (Hitherto hath the Lord helped us), and *Jehovah-Jireh* (The Lord will provide).

Volunteers

Back in London, Taylor resumed his medical studies at the London hospital with the intention of gaining his degree. He began to work on a translation of the New Testament into the Ningpo dialect, but most of all he directed his energies towards stirring up the hearts of young men and women to volunteer for the mission field in China.

As the number of Protestant missionaries was decreasing, down the previous winter from one hundred and fifteen to ninety-one, burning in his soul was the awareness that in China a million a month were dying without God.

One weekend Taylor had gone alone to stay with friends at Brighton, and on the Sunday morning he took a stroll on the beach. Inwardly he was in agony of spirit, and talking to the Lord about the matter in his mind he prayed for more missionaries. Then he opened his Bible and wrote, 'Prayed for twenty-four willing, skilful labourers at Brighton, June 25th, 1865.'

Two days later he opened a bank account with £10 and named it the 'China Inland Mission'. In a pamphlet to launch the Mission he wrote, 'Our great desire and aim is to plant the standard of Christ in the eleven provinces of China and Chinese Tartary.'

Taylor took eighteen missionaries back with him to Shanghai and began to put this policy into operation. In 1866 two stations were set up, and by 1872 the number had increased to thirteen; by 1884 there were over seventy stations with eighty to ninety missionaries and about a hundred Chinese helpers.

Frequently his prayer to God was for more workers, as he felt the urgent need to take the gospel 'to every creature'. Among the more dramatic responses to his appeal was that of the 'Cambridge Seven', a group of university men of high social standing whose offer to go to

China caused a considerable stir throughout Britain and America.

In 1890 an appeal for 1,000 workers resulted in 1,153 responses, most of whom were women. But Taylor had long discovered the value of women missionaries, who were more easily able to approach Chinese women and break down barriers.

God's Work

The increased number of workers, of course, meant a greater financial burden upon the Mission, and while they often ran short they were never without. Because he believed that 'God's work done in God's way will never lack God's supplies', he refused to appeal for money; he resorted entirely to prayer. News of Taylor's achievements began to spread and support started to come in from Christians of other countries. When he visited America, Sweden and Australia to speak of his work, he received not only gifts of money but men and women responded to the call to China.

Until 1902, Taylor maintained direct control over the Mission from his position in China, though it entailed periodic trips to London for consultations. This whole idea was quite novel and contrary to tradition, but it allowed organisational details to be managed by a 'Council of Christian Friends', thus taking pressure off the Director.

Mission work was often interrupted by opposition from enemies and from civil unrest, but with one exception suffered no loss of life until the infamous Boxer Rebellion of 1900. In the uprising against the 'foreign devils', fifty-eight missionaries and twenty-one children were massacred. Taylor, who was in London at the time, was devastated by the news, though the attack was not entirely unexpected; earlier he had written, 'If the Spirit of Good works mightily we may be sure that the spirit of evil will also be active'.

By now his health was failing him and his life was drawing to its close. When his second wife died in 1904, he returned to China for the last time and died on 1st June the following year. He was buried with other members of the family at Chinkiang.

Probably the best-known of all nineteenth century missionaries, Hudson Taylor's example of faith and devotion to God has been a great source of inspiration for Christians of all denominations.

Towards the end of his life he once reported, 'I have sometimes met people who said: "Trusting God is a beautiful theory, but it won't work." Well, thank God, it has worked and it does work.' Like George Müller before him, his life was a testimony to the reality of a living God.

DAVID LIVINGSTONE (1813-1873):
Missionary and Explorer

Although Africa was long known as the 'Dark Continent' it had in fact been penetrated by the gospel as early as the second century, but it was not until 1,700 years later that any lasting impact was made.

As a result of Livingstone's three journeys into Central Africa, the way was opened up for further Protestant outreach into such areas as Uganda and Zaire, while other missionary societies were at the same time making in-roads into parts of South and West Africa.

Africa

The first positive evidence of Christianity in Africa dates from around 180 when the Church in North Africa was persecuted; it survived until the seventh century when it was almost completely destroyed by Muslim invaders. A Byzantine mission to Ethiopia established a Church there in the fourth century which, despite periods of decline, has continued to this day. Between the thirteenth and seventeenth centuries the Jesuits, the Franciscans and the Capuchins brought Roman Catholicism to a number of coastal areas on the continent which have maintained their hold in face of opposition from Islam.

In South Africa, the Dutch settled in Cape Province in 1652 and set up churches which were cared for by their chaplains; then in 1737 the Moravians sent missionaries to the Cape, and the London Missionary Society opened a mission there in 1799.

Until the nineteenth century few Europeans had ventured into the interior of the continent except for ruthless slave traders who, together with some Arabs, were out to further their own interests. When Livingstone arrived in South Africa, he began to implement the instructions given him by the London Missionary Society directors, to move northwards and set up new mission stations.

Godly Parents

Livingstone was born in Blantyre, a few miles south-east of Glasgow, of poor but godly parents who brought him up in the Kirk of Scotland. At the age of ten he was put into the local cotton mill as a 'piecer', working from six in the morning to eight o'clock at night. He had an unquenchable thirst for education, and after work attended the company's evening school from eight to ten pm and then continued his reading at home until midnight, unless his mother took the book out of his hands. He even found the opportunity to read at work by placing his book on his spinning jenny. Though his main interests were science and travel, he also read many of the classic authors.

After his conversion some time in his teens, he began to consider the idea of becoming a medical missionary to China and set about his preparations. His job enabled him to support himself while attending classes in medicine and Greek in Glasgow in winter, and pursuing a theological course in the summer. He qualified as a doctor and was accepted by the London Missionary Society with a view to going to China as a medical missionary.

DAVID LIVINGSTONE

However, the onset of the Opium Wars prevented his fulfilling this ambition, and he embarked instead for South Africa to join his future father-in-law, the celebrated missionary Robert Moffat (1795-1883). Soon after his arrival at the mission station at Kuruman, he began to turn his attention to the Bechuana people to the north. He first spent six months cut off from all European society in order to learn the language, laws and habits of the natives, a time he always felt to be of incalculable advantage.

Then he attached himself to the friendly Bakuena tribe whose chief, Sechele, became his only known convert. The chief suggested that in order to convert the rest of the tribe he might have them whipped, but the offer was declined! From this base Livingstone began to reach out to other tribes, using his medical skill in healing people and also holding preaching meetings to present the gospel. Possibly because the natives were so much under the influence of the witch-doctors, they refused to respond, as they believed 'God's Word' was responsible for a four year drought they had experienced.

Livingstone soon became aware of the problem of the slave-trade as he saw men, women and children seized and cruelly sold as un-paid labourers, and sent back accurate reports of his findings to England. He came to the conclusion that if it were possible to promote the legitimate sale of Europeans articles in the slave-market then trading in slaves would cease, the Negro family would be introduced 'into the body corporate of nations' and this would lead them into 'the blessings of civilisation and Christianity'.

Marriage

In between his expeditions, Livingstone had married Mary Moffat and they now had a small family to consider. They sometimes accompanied him among the tribes and his wife proved quite indispensable as a 'maid of work'. But by 1852 it was necessary to send them back to the safety of England, and he placed them in a homeward-bound ship at Cape Town.

He was then free to pursue his idea of opening up the interior of Africa for the purpose of trade and was determined to find an alternative route to the Atlantic coast. With twenty-seven porters Livingstone once again crossed the great Kalahari Desert and reached Linyati, the capital-village of the Makololo people. From there he journeyed through country no white man had ever seen before, and finally reached St. Paulo de Loanda on the coast in May 1854. It had taken him two years.

Fever-stricken, Livingstone rested for three months at the home of an Englishman and recovered from his illness. Refusing an offer to return home, he set off again, this time to discover a route to the east coast hopefully by using the great river Zambezi. He reached Quilimane at the mouth of the Zambezi in May 1856 after covering a distance of nearly 2,500 miles. At this point he returned to England and reached home in time for Christmas with his family. He found himself to be a national hero, and was invited to meet Queen Victoria and to receive degrees from the universities of Oxford and Cambridge. He also published an account of his travels, called *Missionary Travels And Researches in South Africa.*

When Livingstone made plans to return to Africa, he was determined to try and stamp out the dreadful slave trade. His aim was 'to make an open path for commerce and Christianity' and he called for volunteers to carry out the work. His appeal led to the founding of the Universities Mission to Central Africa, which was shortly to send an expedition to Nyasaland (Malawi) and the Zanzibar.

Second Journey

Aware that the LMS would not support his ideas of exploration and trade, he arranged to return under the auspices of the British government with status as a consul. He sailed to Cape Town in the spring of 1858, where he left his wife and youngest son, and moved up the coast to the Zambezi. He hoped to prove that the Zambezi was a navigable river and that it could serve as a highway into the interior. But his hopes were dashed when he encountered a huge cataract, and was forced to turn north along one of the tributaries.

This second journey proved to be a failure and the government called him home. His sadness turned to grief when his wife, travelling to meet him, died of a fever. He was cheered, however, by meeting up with Bishop MacKenzie and a group of missionaries from the UMCA and he was able to guide them to Magomero to start their mission.

With little enthusiasm from the government for his plans, Livingstone's furlough was brief, from 1864 to 1865. Equipped by the Royal Geographical Society, he returned to Africa for the last time, as an unpaid consul with little authority. He stopped first in Zanzibar to see the last public slave-market in the world, where today Christ Church cathedral now stands, and from here he began his long walk into the interior, aiming to explore the land between Lakes Nyasa and Tanganyika.

For some years no news was heard of Livingstone, and when natives spread the rumour that he was dead expeditions were sent out to discover the truth. He was eventually found at Ujiji on the shores of Lake Nyasa by H. M. Stanley, a journalist from New York.

What proved to be his last trek was an attempt to find out whether the River Luapula was the source of the Nile or the Congo rivers. But his strength ran out and one morning he was found dead, kneeling at his bedside in an attitude of prayer. The natives cut out his heart and buried it there, at Chitambo; his two helpers, Susi and Chuma, carried his body to the coast for return to England. He died 1st May 1873 and was buried at Westminster Abbey on 18th April 1874.

To most people Livingstone is probably best remembered as an intrepid explorer, while some modern commentators have portrayed him as the pioneer of European colonial rule. But initially he went out as a missionary with the object of setting up mission stations as centres for opening up Africa to the gospel, as he realised it was essential first to chart the unknown territories for missionaries to follow. It is quite likely he would prefer to be remembered for this aspect of his work.

From the start, he was anxious to leave behind the well-established churches of the White Cape colony and to reach out to as many of the tribes as possible, opening up the interior to the influences of both civilisation and Christianity.

Perhaps above all, his hatred of the slave-trade constantly spurred him on to renewed efforts, in the hope that promotion of the right kind of economic activity would eventually replace this evil. Among the last words he wrote were, 'All I can add in my solitude is "May Heaven's rich blessing come down on everyone, American, English or Turk, who will help to heal this open sore of the world".'

MARY SLESSOR (1848-1915): Missionary to the Calabar

When the modern missionary movement came to birth at the close of the eighteenth century it was essentially a male preserve. Married men who were called by God to foreign parts took their wives with them, but the thought of the single women being called to the work was unheard of. It was not until the turn of the century that the idea of female emancipation gradually began to dawn.

As women began to emerge as people in their own right, the way was opened for them to volunteer as missionaries. When Hudson Taylor founded the China Inland Mission in 1865, he was prepared to send single women into the interior of China to minister to other women, and when Mary Slessor applied to join the Calabar Mission in 1875, she had no problem in gaining acceptance. Mission boards were at last wakening up to the realisation that women had a special contribution to make to the spread of the gospel, and soon women candidates out-numbered the men.

Mary Slessor felt she had a double disability when she applied to become a missionary: she was a woman, and she belonged to the working class. But by sheer grit, determination and prayer, she overcame all obstacles and soon allayed any lingering fears there were in sending her out to West Africa, the 'White Man's grave'.

Scotland

Her early years in Scotland were ones of extreme poverty, and she suffered hunger and deprivation. Born the second of seven children, three of whom died, her alcoholic father lost his job and they were forced to leave Aberdeen to seek work in Dundee.

Their new home was one room, with no water, lighting or toilet. There was hardly any furniture, and the bed was a mattress on the floor.

On Sundays they were able to escape for a while when mother took the children to church, where Mary first heard the gospel.

From the age of ten, Mary became a 'half-timer', spending half her day at school and the rest at the mill. At fourteen, she started working full-time, putting in a 58-hour week at the looms.

Her interest in missionary work developed at an early age when a sermon by a missionary from Calabar created a deep impression on her. After she became a Christian, in her teens, she was further encouraged by reading in the *Missionary Record* about her hero David Livingstone.

She realised she would need to improve her education if she was to become a missionary and started to borrow books from the church library. She also joined an evening class for two nights a week.

Her church minister recognised her ability to communicate and persuaded her to help with Sunday School and the young people's work. Later, he persuaded her to speak to adult groups, but she was always conscious of her working class background and became tongue-tied in the company of 'better class people'.

When the news of Livingstone's death came through in 1874, her interest in Calabar was renewed. Yet for a year she tried to forget the idea, thinking she had nothing to offer; but whenever she prayed the word 'Calabar' came back to her mind. In the end, God won; she applied and was accepted as a 'female agent'. In August 1876 she sailed for Calabar, now part of south-east Nigeria, in West Africa.

For a long time West Africa has been associated with the slave trade, and thousands of negroes were transported across the Atlantic to be sold in America and the West Indies. Attempts to counter the trade were begun in 1792 when Sierra Leone was founded as a 'province of freedom' for returned slaves. Later, in 1840, Anglican and Methodist Yoruba missions were started in Nigeria but, because it was not yet a British Territory, no direct action could be taken.

The Calabar Mission was founded in 1846 as an offshoot of the Scottish Missionary Society, and the first missionaries included both whites and Jamaicans of African descent. They found the slave trade to be strongly entrenched in the area and it was the cause of much violence and depravity among the tribes.

The tribes people were animists, which meant they worshipped the gods of the sky, sun and rain, and the spirits of trees, rocks and rivers. They also practised witchcraft, and although the Africans could be kind and hospitable, they could also be extremely cruel and lived in constant fear.

When Mary went to Calabar, her first tour of duty proved quite uneventful and lasted less than three years. In that time she familiarised herself with the area and the other mission stations, visited the women in their homes and taught in the school. She also began to learn the local Efik language and surprised the others at the speed with which she picked it up. She eventually became so fluent that she knew not only the colloquial phrases and the inflections, but their gestures as well. In her second year she contracted malaria badly and although she recovered, was sent home to Scotland to recoup her strength.

Return to Calabar

On her return Mary was pleased when she was given charge of the mission station at Old Town, which enabled her to put some of her ideas into practice. She quickly became involved in outreach: she opened three new out-stations, acted as teacher and district nurse, dispensed medicines and conducted four services each Sunday, walking a circuit of several miles.

An important decision she made at this time was to 'go native', a decision which the Mission did not entirely approve. She abandoned some of her more cumbersome items of clothing and instead wore a simple cotton dress and canvas shoes, though she often went barefoot; she also got rid of her ringlets and wore her hair short. Gradually she gave up eating imported food in favour of the local produce, which saved her both time and money, keeping tea as her only luxury.

Probably as a result of her working class background, Mary felt more at home with the natives than with her missionary colleagues. She found the natives accepted her, and as she shared their difficulties, sought her help and advice. This way of evangelism, she felt, was more effective than preaching.

Much of her time was spent in caring for their physical needs and her simple medical skills came in useful for treating ailments. Invited to cure a dying chief, however, posed a problem - if she failed, she would be accused of his death. First she got rid of the charms and the sacrificed chickens around his bed and gave him some medicine; then with nursing and good soup, the man began to recover. His wives were especially grateful as some of them would otherwise have been killed, so they told her they too wanted to learn about 'God' and 'Book'.

Often Mary felt horrified at the way they treated anyone felt to be guilty of an offence and sometimes she just had to intervene. On one occasion a woman wrongly accused of adultery was to be punished by having boiling oil poured over her as she was tied, spread-eagled, on the ground. Mary stood between the victim and her tormentor, her eye fixed on him until at last he retreated. The people marvelled at this display of the power of the white man's God.

The death of her mother and sister left Mary free to move further inland to reach the dreaded Okoyong tribe, who were still officially at war with the Efiks. The Board finally agreed, and taking only her five orphan children she moved into the village of Ekenge.

For a while she was tolerated by Chief Edem and the other chiefs, and allowed to shelter in the women's compound. It was some months before she was given her own hut, a gesture that indicated they had accepted her.

As with the Efiks at Old Town, Mary gave much attention to treating illnesses and teaching 'Book'; some of the people also wanted to learn to read and write. The more dramatic events, however, took place when she was allowed to attend trials where severe punishments were meted out. At times she challenged the chiefs' decisions and was able to save some from being put to death. The men were amazed at the way she confronted their chiefs and witch doctors, and put it down to the power of her God.

But Mary could never grow accustomed to their cruel ways, rooted in their religion of magic and superstition, and she realised that only the power of God could bring about a change. While the people of Ekenge gradually accepted her, Mary had to admit that trying to teach them the gospel was an uphill struggle.

Throughout all her years in Africa, Mary maintained a cheerful faith.

MARY SLESSOR AND THE CHIEFS

'If I am seldom in a triumphant or ecstatic mood,' she once wrote, 'Christ is here and the Holy Spirit. I am always satisfied and happy in his love.' She kept her close relationship with God, reading her Bible by candlelight and praying alone, often out under the stars.

Because of her intimate knowledge of tribal law and religion she was frequently consulted by government officials, and in 1898 was appointed a Vice-Consul to preside over the Native Court at Akpap. The Okoyong people also held her in high esteem and gave her the title Eka Kpukpro Owa, 'Mother of all the Peoples'.

Over the years, Mary often went down with fever and would either dose herself with laudanum or simply force herself to carry on working.

As she grew older, she became increasingly infirm; in the end she collapsed and as she lay dying was heard to whisper, 'O God, release me.' When she was laid to rest in Duke Town cemetery, all flags were flying at half mast.

Today Mary Slessor's name is kept alive over the hospital erected on her initiative for the people of Calabar. Thanks to her efforts, schools were founded, babies and twins saved from death, regular drunkenness and killings became a thing of the past, and raiding and stealing slaves ceased. Above all the gospel was preached and the tribes taught about 'God' and 'Book'.

Mission to the Pacific Islands

The history of the Church abounds with examples of believers who paid the ultimate price for their faith and laid down their lives for their Saviour. This is particularly so in the story of the evangelisation of the Pacific Islands, where missionaries ventured into territories knowing that their very lives were at stake. Many of them met with an untimely death in the Islands, some in a most barbaric manner, but the gospel triumphed and by 1900 the Pacific Islands had a greater percentage of Christians than either the United States or Great Britain.

The Pacific Islands are composed of three main groups: Polynesia (many islands), situated between Midway Island and New Zealand; Micronesia (small islands) to the south of Japan; and Melanesia (dark islands), largely populated by people of a black skin. It was from Melanesia, and especially New Guinea and Indonesia, that the worst atrocities emanated. Interest in the Pacific Islands was first aroused by the explorer Captain James Cook (1728-79) who circumnavigated the world and was killed by natives while visiting Sandwich Island. Following Cook's discoveries, missionaries and traders began to move into the Pacific: Christian missionaries to spread the gospel, and traders hoping to capture slaves and make their fortune.

In 1776 a Roman Catholic mission was sent to Tahiti, but withdrew after a few months. The London Missionary Society also took an interest and in 1796 sent 'agents' to the Society Islands and the following year to Tahiti.

Soon a steady flow of missionaries from other societies was on its way to the Pacific Islands, including another Catholic group called the Picpus Fathers, known also as the Society of the Sacred Hearts of Jesus and Mary. Named after the Rue de Picpus in Paris where the mother house was opened in 1805, its chief work at first was the education of poor children. When a renewed Catholic attempt to evangelise the Pacific islands was started in 1827 the Picpus Fathers established missions in the South Sea islands, sending its members to Hawaii (1827), the Gambia Islands (1834), the Marquesas Islands (1838) and Tahiti (1841).

The task of the missionaries was a particularly hard one and they faced three main difficulties: communications with the society's headquarters, usually in Europe; tropical diseases; and the savagery of the natives, many of whom were either head-hunters or cannibals. One particular island, Eromonga, in the New Hebrides, became known as 'Martyrs' Isle' because of the many missionaries killed there; even native Christians who went to share the gospel with their fellow Melanesians met with the same fate.

But there were missionaries such as John Paton of Scotland and John Geddie of Nova Scotia who came to no harm and were held in high esteem by their people. It was written of John Geddie, 'When he landed in 1848 there were no Christians here; when he left in 1872, there were no heathens'. The most outstanding martyrs of the Pacific Islands were John Williams and James Chalmers, both of whom were sent out by the London Missionary Society, but whose deaths were some sixty years apart.

JOHN WILLIAMS
(1796-1839): Missionary to the South Sea Islands

Williams was born at Tottenham High Cross in Middlesex and was brought up in a Christian family. As a child he spent much time composing hymns and prayers for his own use, but by the time he reached his teens he had lost the faith of his childhood. When he was eighteen, however, he was converted at Moorfields Tabernacle. Called to be a missionary in 1816, he was accepted by the LMS and appointed to the Pacific Islands.

Taking his young wife, Williams sailed in 1817 with several other missionaries to Society Island, near Tahiti, where a missionary station had already been established. Later, at the invitation of the king of Raiatea, he set up a station in the Leeward Islands. While the natives were happy to adopt Christianity as a state religion, it had only a superficial effect upon them: they had low moral standards and were generally idle and difficult to teach.

Williams tried to encourage them to become more industrious; he instructed them in boat-building and introduced the cultivation of sugar cane. He even set up a printing press and published the Gospel of Luke and some elementary books in their own language in order to stimulate their interest in education.

JOHN WILLIAMS

But Williams was anxious to move on and reach the heathens on other islands; when his Mission turned down the idea, he decided to take the matter into his own hands. With money from an inheritance he purchased a schooner, the *Endeavour*, and set off to explore the islands of the South Sea, financing the expedition by trading with the natives. His first aim was to find the island of Rarotonga (where the people were said to be the most ferocious in Polynesia) then he spent the next eleven years (1821-32) sailing the South Seas and planting mission stations.

Although financial constraints forced him to sell his ship, he was determined to continue his travels; with considerable ingenuity he built his own boat in a space of fifteen weeks and set off once more. He visited Tahiti, the Savage Islands, Friendly Islands and Samoa before returning to Rarotonga to complete his translation of the New Testament.

When he went home on furlough in 1834, he discovered that news of his adventures had made him famous and the LMS was now prepared to support his commercial activities, voting to purchase a new ship for him. They also offered to advance him money with which to build a theological college at Rarotonga and a school at Tahiti.

On his return in 1837, he continued to tour the islands, reinforcing the work where a mission had been established; he even ventured as far as the New Hebrides where he hoped to open up a new station. Some of the islands in the group had already been evangelised by John Paton and John Geddie, both of whom survived to see the fruits of their labour. But when Williams and his colleague James Harris landed at Dillon's Bay, on Eromanga, on 20th November 1839, they were killed and eaten by natives. It was in retaliation, it is believed, for the cruelties previously perpetrated by the crew of an English Ship. The missionaries' remains were collected by Captain Croker of *HMS Favourite* and buried at Apia, on the island of Upolu, Samoa.

Williams is recognised as one of the most successful missionaries of modern times. Despite his lack of education and proper training, he was able to learn the languages of the different races he encountered and to adapt himself to the varying cultures of the South Sea Islands. His single-minded zeal for the well-being of the native peoples earned him a permanent place in the hearts of the South Sea islanders.

In addition to his translation work, William published, in April 1837, *A Narrative Of Missionary Enterprise In The South Sea Islands, With Remarks On The Natural History Of The Islands, Origin, Languages, Traditions And Usages Of The Inhabitants*, a work which received high praise from scholars and scientists alike. His findings proved of immense value to succeeding missionaries, one of whom - James Chalmers - met with a similar fate.

JAMES CHALMERS (1841-1901):
Missionary to New Guinea

James Chalmers, a Scotsman and a Congregationalist, decided as a teenager to become a missionary after hearing a letter read in church from a missionary in Fiji. The pastor ended by asking, 'I wonder if there is a boy here who will by-and-by bring the gospel to the cannibals?' The young James resolved in his heart that he would be that boy.

Some ten years later, in 1866, Chalmers and his young bride sailed for the Southern Seas, only to be ship-wrecked on Rarotonga. As he was carried ashore, a native asked him in pidgin-English, 'What fellow name belong you?' 'Chalmers', was the reply. Struggling to imitate the sound, the native announced him as 'Tamate', the name by which he became known among the islanders.

Chalmers settled on Rarotonga where he gradually learned the

JAMES CHALMERS

language and grew acclimatised to the culture and the climate. But his thoughts often turned towards New Guinea, where he knew there were tribes without the gospel. 'The nearer I get to Christ and his cross,' he once wrote, 'the more do I long for direct contact with the heathen.'

In May 1877 Chalmers sailed for Papua, south-east New Guinea, and was warmly received into a cannibal village called Suau. The people responded to his kindness and he established a good relationship with them. Although at one point some of the natives turned against him, his life was saved by the chief. He made no attempt to preach to them, but simply concentrated on living a normal Christian life.

When a small steamer was given him by the Mission he embarked upon a series of journeys up and down the coast, visiting 105 villages and staying where he could to establish a gospel work. He recorded his observations in a notebook, marking villages where he could safely return or send a teacher. Once he was surrounded by a band of natives who demanded tomahawks and knives - or they would kill both him and his wife. 'You may kill us, but never a thing you will get from us,' he retorted, and they let him be. The following day they came back to apologise, and became friends.

In 1879 his wife died after a prolonged illness and for a while he was devastated. But rather than go home on furlough, he moved to Port Moresby and immersed himself more fully in his work. 'Let me bury my sorrow in work for Christ,' he told his friends. He was now convinced that his main aim was to be a 'fore-runner', travelling among the tribes, making friends and preparing the way for others to follow him.

All along the coast the name of Tamate became well-known and respected as much as for his courage as for his concern for the natives. He was invited into villages to speak, often preaching in their heathen temples. On one occasion, one of his assistants preached all night (Chalmers fell asleep!) but at the close the people declared, 'No more fighting, Tamate, no more man-eating, we will strive for peace.' By 1882 Chalmers could report that in the area where he worked there were 'no cannibal-ovens, no feasts, no human flesh, no desire for skulls'.

Twice Chalmers returned to England on furlough, in 1886 and again in 1894 for the centenary of his Mission. Each time he felt compelled to return, saying, 'I cannot rest with so many thousands of savages without a knowledge of God near us.'

On 7th April 1901, accompanied by Oliver Tompkins and a band of assistants, Chalmers sailed to the island of Goaribari. The following morning as he and Tompkins went ashore to visit the natives, the situation looked dangerous; armed warriors took over the ship as natives escorted the two missionaries to a large building. Once inside the two men were knocked to the ground with stone clubs, and killed; their heads were cut off and their bodies hacked to pieces, ready for cooking that same day.

The world was shocked at the news of their deaths, but others were inspired to volunteer to take their places. 'Tamate is dead,' was the cry, 'but others will carry on his work.'

The Middle East

Since the seventh century the countries of the Middle East, including Palestine - the cradle of Christianity - have been under the domination of Islam, creating a barrier which Christians found almost impossible to penetrate. It was not until the nineteenth century that under the impetus of the Evangelical Revival, missionaries attempted to break through to reach the people of both Islam and Judaism, and gain a foothold for the gospel.

One of the earliest missionaries to venture into the Islamic stronghold was Henry Martyn, a Cambridge scholar and expert in linguistics. After a period of service in India, he moved to Persia in 1811 where he spent a year at Shiraz translating the New Testament before dying at the early age of thirty-one. Between 1821 and 1841 Joseph Wolff, a Jewish Christian, made four exploratory journeys around the Middle East, visiting Jewish communities and preaching the Good News. American missions also took an interest in the area, and introduced medicine and founded many schools in Turkey and Syria; they also founded the Syrian Protestant College (now the American University) of Beirut.

The Church Missionary Society established a work in the Middle East, chiefly in Egypt, where their aim was to strengthen and invigorate the older Christian churches. But for many Christians, attention has been focused mainly on the Holy Land which for centuries had virtually been a closed door. It has taken nearly 1800 years for the Church to arouse itself and present the claims of the Messiah to the Jewish people.

Following the destruction of Jerusalem in AD 70 and the dispersion of the Jews - including the predominantly Jewish Church - access to Roman Palestine was limited. Interest in the holy places was revived during the reign of Emperor Constantine the Great, but in 638 the country came under Arab rule. Jerusalem became the third holy city of Islam after the Dome of the Rock was built (685-705) on the Temple Mount, giving the Muslims an entrenched position in the Holy City.

During the Middle Ages, the Crusades were mounted from western Europe in an effort to protect Christian pilgrims and to recover the Holy Land from Islam. While Jerusalem was captured and brought under Christian control (1099-1187), the expeditions failed to have any lasting success and the Arabs regained control in 1291.

Chosen People

There was no attempt to evangelise the minority group of Jews in Palestine or those encountered en route; the Crusades were entirely military expeditions and the Jews were regarded as 'Christ-killers'. Tragically this attitude persisted down the centuries and it was not until 1809 that the London Society for Promoting Christianity amongst the Jews was formed specifically to evangelise the 'Chosen People'. The new mission, an offshoot of the London Missionary Society, was remodelled in 1813 as an Anglican society and is today known as The Church's Ministry among the Jews.

Although the number of Jews in Palestine during the nineteenth century was relatively small - there was an estimated 24,000 in 1880 - Lewis Way of the London Society went out to the Holy Land in 1823 to make a tentative beginning to missionary work. By 1833 the home of a missionary called Nicolayson was being used as a place of worship and preaching, and though the mission was tolerated by the Turkish government, it was viewed with suspicion.

In 1835 the Society decided that it was necessary to build an Anglican church in Jerusalem; work commenced in 1841 but because of opposition was not completed until five years later. When a decision was taken to create an Anglican bishopric, the Protestant King of Prussia proposed a joint undertaking between the Prussian and English Churches, the bishop to be nominated alternately by the two Crowns. The idea was accepted, and appropriately the first Anglican bishop in Jerusalem was a Jewish Christian, the Rev Michael Solomon Alexander, formerly a Prussian citizen.

MICHAEL SOLOMON ALEXANDER (1799-1845):
Bishop in Jerusalem

Born near Posnen (now in Poland), Alexander's parents were strict Jews and his father an orthodox rabbi. He was trained in the principles of orthodox rabbinical Judaism and at the age of sixteen became a teacher of the Talmud. But he began to question the nature of his Jewish faith and as a result, after his father died, was forced to leave home. At the age of twenty he came to England, his father's native country, and found a post in Colchester as a private tutor to a Jewish family.

It was here that for the first time he was introduced to the New Testament, which filled his mind with further doubts and questionings. Appointed Rabbi at Norwich and afterwards Prayer-reader and Schochet (responsible for the ritual slaughter of animals) at Plymouth, he managed to resist the thoughts, but only for a while.

When asked to give Hebrew lessons to an Anglican curate, which involved a study of such passages as Psalm 22 and Isaiah 53, Alexander was once again faced with the claims of the Messiah. Secretly, he thought, he began to attend evening prayer at an Anglican church, and when his fiancée learned that he was considering becoming a Christian both she and her family were alarmed.

Surprisingly the wedding was allowed to go ahead but within a year the young rabbi had come to believe that Jesus was the Messiah. He was suspended from office and it was suggested he go before the Ark in the synagogue and curse the God of the Christians.

Determined to make a public witness, he was baptised before a large congregation at St. Andrew's Church, Plymouth, in June 1825. Five months later his newly-wed wife also came to faith in Jesus and was baptised at Exeter. As it was no longer safe to remain in the area, Alexander took up a post as a Hebrew teacher in Dublin; he spent time studying his new faith and in December 1827, following the suggestion of the Archbishop, was ordained a priest in the Church of England.

The rabbi-turned-priest had a burning desire to take the Good News of Jesus to his own people, and as he prayed about his next move he wrote, 'I desire to be resigned entirely to his holy will'. The way soon opened for him to join the London Society for Promoting Christianity among the Jews, and in company with the Rev W Ayerst was posted to the land of his birth.

He was thrilled to be able to spend three years in and around Posnen where he was 'engaged as a humble, but unworthy instrument to preach the glad tidings of salvation' to his brethren. And his delight was completed with the opportunity to be reunited with his brother and three sisters, who received him warmly.

In 1830 Alexander was recalled to England to work among the Jews of the East End of London. He preached at the mission house in Petticoat Lane and at the Episcopal Jews' Chapel in Palestine Place, Bethnal Green. The services attracted large numbers of Jews, and many of them remained afterwards to engage in discussion and debate.

A great honour was bestowed upon him in 1832 when he was appointed Professor of Hebrew and Rabbinic Literature at King's College, London. Yet despite his high position, he continued his preaching among the Jews of the East End; sometimes he visited them in their homes or they called on him. He never missed an opportunity of speaking to them about 'the great truths of religion', sending them away with a suitable tract or portion of Scripture.

He was also involved at this time in revising the Hebrew translation of the New Testament and in making a Hebrew translation of the Prayer Book, which proved an asset both in London and in Jerusalem.

When the decision to appoint a bishop in Jerusalem was made, the position was first offered to Dr. McCaul, one of the Society's missionaries, but he declined and suggested that the Jewish Christian, Alexander, would be a more appropriate choice. It was agreed, and Alexander was consecrated bishop at Lambeth Palace in November 1841.

Jerusalem

The arrival of the bishop and his family in Jerusalem in January 1842 was an occasion of considerable importance; there was a salute of guns at the Jaffa Gate, and the Pasha (Military ruler) declared the bishop to be 'the apple of his eye'. The Jews regarded the appointment as one of great honour to their race, and were pleased - until they realised more fully the nature of the mission.

Despite primitive conditions and lack of facilities, the work soon began to bear fruit. The building of the new church - Christ Church - had already begun, and preaching services were meanwhile held in a temporary chapel. In March Alexander held his first ordination, in May he baptised a Jewish family, and in October he confirmed eight Jewish children and conducted the marriage ceremonies of two new Jewish Christians.

Further conversions followed, including those of three rabbis, which resulted in a deputation of Jews being sent from Tiberias to put pressure on the apostates to return to Judaism. For their help and protection, he

MICHAEL SOLOMON ALEXANDER

opened a school for converts and a 'House of Industry' to provide them with work; he also set up a Bible depot for distribution of the Scriptures, while in 1844 the dispensary was replaced with a 'Hospital for Poor Sick Jews'.

Sadly his life was brought to a close in November 1845 when, as he journeyed to Egypt making a tour of the southern part of his diocese, he suffered a heart-attack and died. Though his episcopate was brief, thirty-one Jewish Christians in Jerusalem were moved to write to his wife, 'We feel that we have lost not only a true Father in Christ, but also a loving brother and most kind friend'.

When the former rabbi came to faith in Jesus as the Messiah, he made a sacrifice that for most Gentiles is quite alien - he became a *meshumad*, an apostate or traitor to Judaism, separated from his family and community. His brother and sister at first disowned him, and when his wife believed in Jesus an attempt was made to kidnap her.

But throughout his life, like the apostle Paul, his 'heart's desire and prayer to God for the Israelites was that they may be saved'. Alexander never lost sight of the roots of his religion and, steeped in Judaism and rabbinic literature, he preached to his own people with a new conviction, quoting their own Scriptures as well as the Talmud.

He was the first and only Jewish bishop in Jerusalem, and left behind him a reputation as 'the brightest earthly star'.

WELLESLEY BAILEY (1846-1937):
Founder of the Leprosy Mission

One of the marks of true missionary endeavour has been the close link between evangelism and a concern for people's physical well-being. When Jesus sent out his twelve disciples he gave them power and authority not only to preach the kingdom of God, but also to heal the sick. Holding to traditional Hebrew thought, he regarded body and soul as an essential unity; he did not come simply to save souls but to minister to the total man.

Since its inception, the Church has also been under the same obligation to fulfil the two-fold command of Christ, and whilst maintaining an emphasis on preaching the gospel, Christians have shown a practical concern for those who were sick or in any other kind of need. This has been especially evidenced in the establishment of a wide variety of caring organisations where people with different needs could find help.

While from the first century the Romans had private infirmaries, it was the Church that took up the idea in the fourth century and developed it. In 361, a wealthy Roman Christian used her home as a refuge for sick pilgrims, and in 370, a hospital was opened for the poor people of Edessa (Syria); other hospitals were to be found at Caesarea (Cappadocia) and Constantinople, where seven hospitals provided for cripples, invalids, orphans and old people. The movement spread to the West, where the work was continued, usually by members of specialist religious orders.

Leprosy

Leprosy was the first disease ever to be singled out for particular treatment, and a hospital was opened for leprosy patients at the end of the fourth century in Caesarea (Cappadocia) by the local bishop, Basil. He is also reputed to be the founder of the Order of Lazarus, an order dedicated to the care of lepers. During the Middle Ages, the Order of Lazarus set up numerous 'leper-houses' in France and throughout the rest of Europe, and Franciscans also engaged in the work by tending victims already being nursed by another Order, the Crucifieri.

For the Protestants - who mostly lived in lands free of leprosy - it was the Moravians of Germany who pioneered leprosy work. In 1732 County Zinzendorf established a missionary organisation called 'The Order Of The Mustard Seed' which, among other projects, started a work among sufferers in a lovely valley of South Africa's Cape Colony. They also built a leprosy hospital outside the walls of Jerusalem which was intended to serve all the victims in Palestine.

In India, isolated attempts were made to care for leprosy victims in such centres as Calcutta and Benares, but it was not until 1869, when the young missionary Wellesley Bailey paid his first visit to a leprosy asylum, that a concerted effort was launched.

Something Worthwhile

Bailey was born at Abbeyleix, south west of Dublin, where his father was agent for the Stradballey Estate. Along with his three brothers, he was baptised into the Church of Ireland and was converted to Christ at the age of twenty. It happened on the eve of his departure for Australia, as he was waiting for his ship at Gravesend. His efforts to make a fortune 'down-under' failed and he returned to Ireland, where his father urged him to find something worthwhile to do.

Believing that God would now show him what to do, he sailed for India where his brother was an army officer. His intention was first to learn Hindi and then to take a commission as a police officer, but this was never to be. While staying at the home of a German CMS missionary, the Rev Reuther, he began to notice the great needs of the poor people around him, and wondered whether God would have him as a missionary rather than a policeman.

Finally convinced of the rightness of such a change, he applied to the American Presbyterian Mission and was accepted as a teacher at their school in Ambala.

The leader of the mission station was the Rev Dr J H Morrison (one of the founders of the January 'Week of Prayer') whose example in prayer considerably influenced the young missionary. It was while accompanying his senior that Bailey first visited a leper asylum, where some forty lepers were being sheltered and cared for. They lived in three rows of huts under a clump of trees, close to a main road and yet out of view. Deeply moved by what he saw, Bailey concluded that 'if ever there was a Christ-like work in this world it was to go among these poor sufferers and bring to them the consolation of the gospel'.

Caring Ministry

Bailey made frequent visits to the asylum, becoming more aware of their needs: first the gospel, but also the want of proper living accommodation, good food, clothing and medical care. As a result of his caring ministry a number of leprosy sufferers were converted and baptised.

In 1871 he was joined by his fiancée, Alice Grahame, and after they were married the two of them continued their visits to the asylum. But the work soon told on Mrs. Bailey's health and in 1873 they were forced to return to Ireland. Invited to speak at a meeting at the Friends' Meeting House in Monkstown, Dublin, Bailey spoke of his work among leprosy-patients. Listening to his address were three sisters, the Misses Pim, and moved by his account they offered to collect a sum of at least £30 a year in support of his work, an amount that was quickly exceeded. All the gifts were carefully listed and banked in an account called 'Lepers in India'.

In order to be able to pursue his concern for leprosy sufferers, Bailey joined the Church of Scotland Missionary Society, and when he returned

WELLESLEY C BAILEY

to India in 1875 was posted to Chamba in the foothills of the Himalayas. Together with his wife he opened up a small leprosy asylum, encouraged by the news that the state government would go halves with the expenditure.

Within a short space of time Bailey began to emerge as the driving force behind efforts to provide adequate care for leprosy sufferers, initially in the northern parts of the sub-continent. He first teamed up with a missionary friend, a Dr Newton, so they could give each other mutual support. Short of money, the American doctor asked Bailey for financial aid, and from his missionary fund Bailey was able to respond, and help set up a poor-house at Sabutha in the Simla Hills.

In 1879 Bailey moved from Chamba to Wazirabad where he started a new work, but his asylum was later taken over by the state. Meanwhile pleas for help were beginning to come in, such as the one from a German missionary in East India who wanted advice in treating his leprosy patients, and another request from Purulia where they needed new huts for shelter.

As the work of Lepers in India grew, the organisation continued to be staffed by unpaid helpers; the time was coming, however, when a more permanent structure would be needed. When the Baileys returned to England it was decided that he would become the first Secretary to the 'Mission to Lepers in India'. Instead of operating from the field, Bailey took over the responsibility of running the Mission from Edinburgh, keeping in touch with the work by making extended tours.

Following his first tour to India as Secretary (1886-87), the work expanded even further. A variety of Christian missions began to look to Bailey for support in different ways and the mission commenced operations in other parts of India, especially the south where there were also many leprosy sufferers. One particularly pleasing development was among the care of children, where homes were established for healthy children of leprous parents.

The year 1889 was a significant one in the life of the Mission. In April the death of Father Damien of the leper island of Molokai evoked a widespread stirring of sympathy and conscience and the work of the

Mission was brought to the public's attention. In the same month, following an appeal from the Wesleyan Methodist Mission, Bailey was able to open up a Home for Lepers in Burma, the first venture beyond the boundaries of India. Next there was an appeal from the CMS hospital at Hangchow in China, where Dr. Duncan Main had no room for leprosy sufferers coming to him for help. A home was set up, and by the end of the century the Mission was supporting seven stations in China. Further requests for help came from Japan (1894), South Africa (1894), South America (1895), Sumatra (1900) and Korea (1908).

Because of the international nature of the Mission, auxiliary bodies were started in America, Canada and Australia; financial support from these countries enabled the Mission to continue to expand its work. In India, state governments also made contributions to support their own peoples, in some cases establishing their own Homes. Despite advancing years, the Baileys made further tours of the work, their last one in 1913-14.

When he resigned in 1917, Bailey declared, 'God does not make the burdens heavy, he makes them light. I have had his blessing in carrying it on and he has fitted the back to the burden.'

For hundreds of years, people have been afraid of leprosy; drugs have now been developed that can arrest the disease and prevent deformity. But often it was the social effects that were more disturbing, and The Leprosy Mission, as it is now called, has had to deal with both aspects of this need. Today there are an estimated twelve million people worldwide suffering from leprosy, but only three million receive any treatment. Yet the battle continues, as governments and the World Health Organisation join the Leprosy Mission in fighting the disease.

Father Damien (1840-1889)

A Belgian Catholic priest who achieved posthumous fame as a result of his sacrificial labours among the leprosy sufferers on the island of Molokai, Hawaii. He was sent to Hawaii in 1863, and for nine years was a parish priest before volunteering to serve the leprosy settlement. The bishop told the islanders, 'I have brought someone who will be father to you all. He loves you so much that he has come to live and die with you.' Aged 33, the young priest rebuilt the settlement's church, comforted the dying, made coffins and dug graves (about 1,600 in the first six years alone), laid on a fresh water supply and built new homes; he also opened a hospital, a school and an orphanage. News of his death brought in gifts of medicine and money for the work, and for the first time people around the world began to pay attention to leprosy reports.

C T STUDD (1862-1931): Founder, WEC International

The closing years of the nineteenth century proved to be amongst the most fruitful and exciting times experienced in the history of the Church in England. The 1859 Ulster revival spread throughout the British Isles, influencing all classes of society and releasing a wave of philanthropic and charitable works that expressed Christian principles in many practical ways.

It is estimated that as many as three quarters of the total number of voluntary charitable works that existed in the second half of the century were evangelical in character. Many of them were inspired by the preaching of men like Spurgeon and Moody, whose message gave new impetus to social outreach.

Yet of greater importance was the new lease of life that broke through the respectability of the Victorian Church. The gospel touched the hearts not only of the unchurched, but also those who for many years sat undisturbed in their pews, so that church membership increased and the moral fibre of the nation was revitalised.

The Studd family

Among the many thousands who came under the power of Moody's preaching was the Studd family of Tedworth Hall, Wiltshire. Edward Studd, a retired planter from India, was soundly converted in 1875; a year later his three eldest sons, who became well-known cricketers at Eton and Cambridge, also received Christ.

The most famous of the three was Charlie (or CT) who later founded the Heart of Africa Mission. He became one of England's greatest all-rounders and played in Australia with the MCC team which recovered the 'Ashes' during the tour of winter 1882-83.

Three months later, after six years as a backslider, CT was restored to God at one of the Moody meetings in Cambridge. Now with a 'vision for souls' he endeavoured to win his friends for the gospel; he even persuaded some of the English XI to go to hear Moody, and at least two of them were converted. Aware that he still lacked power in his life, he finally realised that he had not fully yielded his life to Christ. When he did, he had a deep experience of the Spirit of God and was 'perfectly at peace'. From then on, his life took a completely new course.

Called to China as a missionary, he was accepted by Hudson Taylor (who was in England at the time) as an associate member of the China Inland Mission. Unknown to him, his Cambridge friend Stanley Smith was also led to offer for China, and they were soon joined by five other

C.T. STUDD

young men of similar social standing. The men, soon known as the Cambridge Seven, launched a series of evangelistic meetings around the country, making a great impact especially upon the students at Edinburgh University. C T Studd's name was by now a household word, and though he was an indifferent speaker, his personal testimony captivated the crowds and many volunteered for overseas missions.

The Cambridge Seven sailed for China in February 1885, landing at Shanghai. In accordance with CIM policy, they adopted Chinese dress and wore a pigtail. CT, with his big feet, had to have shoes specially made for him, which became a great joke among the people. Despite the hardships, CT revelled in his missionary calling; his correspondence home reveals how God moulded him through the circumstances of those early days in China and he rapidly matured in his Christian commitment.

On his twenty-fifth birthday CT came into a large inheritance, which in the light of Christ's teaching he decided to give to Christian work. On 13th January 1887 he sent off four cheques of £5,000 each - to Moody, Müller, Holland of Whitechapel and Booth-Tucker of India. Other cheques went to Barnardo, Archibald Brown and the Misses McPherson and Smyly, plus some of the remainder to CIM.

A few months later he married Priscilla Stewart, a CIM missionary, and they gave the rest of their money away, leaving five dollars and some bedding. They intended to start their married life by obeying the Lord and living by faith.

Their early married years, from 1887 to 1894, were tough; they went about in fear of their lives and were taunted as 'foreign devils'. They survived, and eventually a break-through came when they found the magic lantern to be an especially useful tool in their evangelism, and many were won to Christ. CT also spent much of his time running an Opium Refuge where over a period of seven years he cared for about 800 addicts.

Poor Health

Throughout his life Studd was dogged by poor health. Both he and his wife were ill during their years in China, and in 1893 CT nearly died. Scilla gave birth to four girls during this time, each one delivered without the care of a doctor. Always they prayed and each anointed the other with oil when they were ill but, strained and undernourished, they returned to England in 1894. During their four years' furlough, Studd spend eighteen months touring colleges in America at the invitation of Moody. The student revival had spread there following the call of the Cambridge Seven.

He wanted to return to China, but when this door closed he decided it was his opportunity to fulfil a family responsibility and take the gospel to India, where his father had made his fortune. Between 1900 and 1906 he spent six months in Tirhoot, north India, and then took up a pastorate at Ootacamund in south India, ministering mostly among expatriates. The highlight of this period was the conversion of all their four daughters, who were baptised on the same day, in a baptistry specially dug in their garden; and a large crowd - which included Amy Carmichael - gathered to witness the event.

Once again the Studds were forced to return to England, this time as a result of CT's frequent severe asthma attacks. Now aged fifty and in poor health, he might have stayed at home. But an amusing notice in a Liverpool window, 'Cannibals want missionaries', drew his attention to the needs of Africa. He discovered that while traders, hunters and officials had ventured into the interior, there were areas where no

---

The Cambridge Seven

The announcement in 1884 that seven young men of high social standing - six of whom were Cambridge graduates - had chosen to abandon their all to serve with the China Inland Mission caused a tremendous stir. At a meeting with Hudson Taylor at Cambridge, fifty more undergraduates offered for the mission field. After further meetings in London, Edinburgh and the North of England, forty Cambridge missionaries were present at a meeting at Exeter Hall to say 'Farewell' to the Seven. They sang, *Tell it out among the heathen that the Lord is King*, and each of the Seven was given a Chinese New Testament. The best-known of the Seven, C T Studd, famous as an England cricketer, had earlier said, 'What I would have you gather is that God does not deal with you until you are wholly given up to him, and then he will tell you what he would have you do.' Another was Dixon Hoste, who succeeded Taylor as Director of CIM. The Seven left for China the following day, 5th February, 1885.

Christians had taken the gospel. At the end of 1910 he set off alone to reconnoitre the situation in southern Sudan. As he left Liverpool, God spoke to him and said, 'This trip is not merely for the Sudan; it is for the whole unevangelised world.'

In the Sudan, Studd made contact with missionaries from the Church Missionary Society, including Bishop Gwynne of Khartoum. He found that beyond Sudan lay Belgian Congo (now Zaire), where there were vast numbers of people without the gospel.

He determined that this, the heart of Africa, was where the Lord wanted him to start a new crusade. Studd returned to Africa in 1913 and although his wife approved, she was not well enough to accompany him; instead he took a young Cambridge graduate called Alfred Buxton. They entered the Congo through Kenya and Uganda, escorted by porters and where possible, riding their bicycles. (This remained Studd's chief form of transport until in his later years he accepted the use of a motor car.)

A mission was established at Nala, the centre of an area teeming with people, and where ten years previously soldiers had been killed, cooked and eaten by the natives. Despite language problems there were many conversions, but Studd's heart condition made it necessary for him to return home to rest. His wife had not been idle during his absence and had organised the new work on a sound basis. A headquarters was established at Upper Norwood, south London, and an appeal launched for help in reaching the unevangelised.

Sacrifice

In a magazine article, Studd wrote that 'Christ's call was not to 'scoffers', but sinners to repentance... to raise living churches of souls among the destitute, to capture men from the Devil's clutches and snatch them from the very jaws of hell, to enlist and train them for Jesus, and make them an almighty army of God. But this can only be accomplished by red-hot, unconventional, unfettered Holy Spirit religion... (and) by reckless sacrifice and heroism in the foremost trenches'.

Studd did not mince words; he demanded and expected total dedication to the Lord and to the new Mission, and always set his crusaders an example. When he left for the Congo in 1916 he was accompanied by eight new missionaries, including his daughter Edith, all of whom were prepared to be 'lively heroes for Christ'. For the remainder of his time, Studd centred his work on Nala and later at Ibambi. The Mission flourished; thousands accepted 'the way to heaven' and were baptised, and further stations were opened.

After Buxton and his new wife Edith returned home in 1919, Studd went through a severe testing: ill-health, lack of new workers and, above all, missionaries backsliding. Yet there were encouragements among the Africans, particularly through the 5am prayer meeting that he started; and he was thrilled to see Africans becoming leaders in their churches and others going out as evangelists.

Studd pushed himself to the limit to overcome his physical weakness, doing all he could to win souls while there was still time. Such was his dedication that the committee back home was disturbed, and the Heart of Africa Mission was described as 'one of the craziest missionary societies'.

In 1922 the Mission expanded and opened up mission fields in other parts of the world - South America, Central Asia and West Africa - and took the new title of World Evangelisation Crusade. In more recent years the work has spread to India, and has further branched out to include Christian Literature Crusade.

After a separation of twelve years, Mrs. Studd paid a two week visit to her husband at Ibambi, the last time they were together before her death. It was then that some of the Christians realised the sacrifice their Bwana Mukubwa ('Big Boss') had paid to bring them the gospel.

During his last two years, Studd's health deteriorated rapidly; he contracted fever and suffered a number of heart attacks. One Sunday he conducted a five hour meeting for the Africans, and died the following Thursday.

Studd's emphasis on the absolute necessity for practical holiness in the lives of all believers and his demand for a willingness to pay the supreme sacrifice, eventually caused some discontent within the ranks of his missionaries. But the Mission survived and Bwana saw the fulfilment of his desire for a Spirit-filled church in the heart of Africa.

MISSIONARY SOCIETIES

MISSION and DATE	FOUNDER(S)	MINISTRY
BAPTIST MISSIONARY SOCIETY 1792	* Group of Baptist ministers, at Kettering (Northamptonshire)	* India, Brazil, Caribbean
COUNCIL FOR WORLD MISSION 1795 formerly LONDON MISSIONARY SOCIETY	* Group of Congregationals, Anglicans, Presbyterians and Wesleyans	* Pacific Islands, India, South Africa, Hong Kong
CHURCH MISSIONARY SOCIETY 1799	* Church of England, Independent and Presbyterian ministers	* Africa, Indian sub-continent, Middle and Far East
SOUTH AMERICAN MISSIONARY SOCIETY 1844	* Captain Allen Gardiner	* South America, Spain and Portugal * Evangelism, church planting, education, and medical work
INTERSERVE (formerly BMMF) 1852	* Offshoot of Zenana Bible and Medical Mission	* South Asia, Middle East and North Africa; also among Asians in Britain * Cooperation with national churches and other agencies to build up the Church
OVERSEAS MISSIONARY FELLOWSHIP (formerly CIM) 1865	* J Hudson Taylor	* Far East * Evangelism and church planting
ARAB WORLD MINISTRIES (formerly NAM) 1881	* George Pearse	* North Africa, Middle East and Europe * Friendship evangelism and caring ministry
QUA IBOE FELLOWSHIP 1887	* Samuel Bill	* Nigeria, plus - in partnership with Action Partners - Ghana and Chad * Evangelism, church planting, theological training, medical care
SIM INTERNATIONAL 1893	* Dr Rowland Bingham	* Sudan, West Africa; also South America, India and Asia * Evangelism, church planting and medical work

MISSIONARY SOCIETIES continued

MISSION AND DATE	FOUNDER(S)	MINISTRY
AIM INTERNATIONAL 1895	* Peter Cameron Scott	* Central Africa (12 countries), plus Comoro and Seychelle islands * Evangelism, Bible teaching, medical care, education, famine relief
OMS INTERNATIONAL 1901	* Charles Cowman	* Far East, South America * Evangelism, church planting, training national Christian leaders
JAPAN EVANGELISTIC BAND 1903	* A Paget Wilkes and Rev Barclay Buxton	* Japan, some Commonwealth countries and USA * Evangelism and church planting
ACTION PARTNERS (formerly SUM) 1904	* Dr Karl Kumm	* Nigeria and Sudan; plus partnerships with indigenous churches and missionary agencies in other countries * HQ at Bawtry Hall developed as centre for inter-mission cooperation
EUROPEAN CHRISTIAN MISSION 1904	* G P Raud	* Western and Eastern Europe * Church planting in areas of little spiritual life; training church leaders, radio ministry
ASSEMBLIES OF GOD OVERSEAS MISSIONS 1909	* Assemblies of God	* Europe, Africa, Far East * Evangelism, church planting, training national leaders, medical and agricultural work
WEC INTERNATIONAL (formerly Worldwide Evangelization Crusade) 1913	* C T Studd	* Worldwide * Evangelism, church planting

MISSIONARY SOCIETIES continued

MISSION AND DATE	FOUNDER(S)	MINISTRY
INTERNATIONAL NEPAL FELLOW-SHIP (formerly Nepal Evangelistic Band) 1940	* Dr Lily O'Hanlan	* Nepal * Health and development programme includes leprosy and tuberculosis work, community health care and training nurses
CHRISTIAN LITERATURE CRUSADE 1941	* Kenneth Adams	* Worldwide * Christian literature distribution, book sales via own outlets
TRANS WORLD RADIO 1954	* Dr Paul Freed	* Operates from France, Bonaire Island, Cyprus, Swaziland, Guram, Sri Lanka and Uruguay * Evangelism, encouraging believers in isolation
WYCLIFFE BIBLE TRANSLATORS 1955	* Cameron Townsend	* Worldwide * Bible translation, training in linguistics at annual Summer School
OPERATION MOBILISATION 1958	* George Verwer	* Worldwide * Evangelism, Bible and Christian Literature distribution * Floating education exhibition on two ships, *Logos* and *Doulos*
ASIAN OUT-REACH 1960	* Paul Kaufman	* All Asian countries * Evangelism, church planting, leadership training, publishing
YOUTH WITH A MISSION 1960	* Loren Cunningham	* Worldwide * Evangelism - short-term (mostly student) volunteers; Bible training schools; two ships - *Anastasis* and *Good Samaritan*

EIGHT

Social Reformers of the Nineteenth Century

Probably the greatest influence for good during the Evangelical Revival was a group of Christians known as 'The Saints', later termed the Clapham Sect. They were not a sect in the normal usage of the term, but a band of well-to-do Anglican evangelicals who lived in the village of Clapham, three miles south west of Westminster, and worshipped at the parish church.

It was largely as a result of their efforts, and especially those of their leader William Wilberforce, that the 'odious traffic' of slave trading was abolished in the British Empire at the beginning of the nineteenth century.

WILLIAM WILBERFORCE (1759-1833):
Philanthropist and Reformer

Wilberforce was born in Hull, Yorkshire, which in those days was a prosperous and important port. His family could trace its ancestry back to Saxon times; they were successful merchants, and his grandfather had twice been mayor of the town. As a child he was rather delicate and short-sighted, but blessed with intelligence. He was sent to the local grammar school at the age of seven where he was taught writing, French, Arithmetic and Latin, and his elocution was said to be a model for the rest of the school.

When his father died the following year, he was sent to live in Wimbledon with an aunt and uncle who were staunch evangelicals. But when the young boy became interested in Methodism his mother brought him back home, while his grandfather threatened that 'if Billy turns Methodist he shall not have a sixpence of mine'. In order to divert him from the religious life he was introduced, at the tender age of twelve, to the social life of the principal families of the town: theatre, supper parties, cards and race meetings at York. The manoeuvre succeeded, at least temporarily.

His education was completed first at Pocklington School and then at St. John's College, Cambridge. Although possessed of a quick intellect and a good memory, he was not encouraged to work hard, but spent much time in playing cards and gambling. It was here that he met William Pitt, later to become the Prime Minister. At the age of twenty he became MP for Hull in 1780 and while he took his responsibilities seriously, he also entered fully into London social life. He received frequent invitations to the homes of the aristocracy and the rich, and became a firm favourite at supper parties. Possessed of great charm, he was amusing, quick-witted and had a good singing voice.

WILLIAM WILBERFORCE

In 1784-85 he made two tours of the Continent in the company of Isaac Milner, a Christian school master from Hull, when they spent time reading the Bible together. By the end of his second trip Wilberforce was able to declare that he 'fully believed'. He decided to place himself completely at God's disposal, and dedicated his life and fortune to the service of God. As his life took a new direction, news of his decision became known and even people like Pitt expressed their admiration for him. In Hull, his mother was disturbed as she had heard reports that he had gone mad; she soon discovered the truth and was not displeased.

From the beginning Wilberforce was supported by Christian friends such as the Thorntons of Clapham; and he sought the advice of John Newton at St. Mary Woolnoth, London, who urged him to use his position for God and wrote prophetically, 'It is hoped and believed that the Lord has raised you up for the good of his Church and for the good of the nation'.

After two years considering how best to serve God, he recorded in his diary, 'God Almighty has set before me two great objects, the suppression of the slave trade and the reformation of manners (i.e. morals)'. These two causes were his main occupations to the end of his life, and he maintained his position in Parliament in order to be best able to fight the battles.

Wilberforce was already at this time in association with The Saints who met for prayer and Bible study at the Thorntons' house in Clapham; they were bound together by their common desire to further the gospel and, above all, to bring about the abolition of the slave trade. Aware of the power and influence of Wilberforce in the Commons, the group urged him to assume leadership of the Anti-slavery Movement; when encouraged also by Pitt, he accepted. In 1787 they formed an Abolition Committee and began to prepare their case.

A serious illness in 1788 prevented him from raising the question in the Commons, but the following May he spoke to the House for three and a half hours, outlining the evils of the trade. His speech was afterwards described as 'impressive and eloquent'. Support for the cause began to grow, and eminent people such as Jeremy Bentham, Lord Canning and the Duke of Gloucester allied themselves with his aims. John Wesley wrote to him from his death-bed, urging him 'in the name of God' to oppose 'that execrable villainy'.

Slave trading had been carried on by British ships since 1713 and the number of slaves transported across the Atlantic reached an estimated 100,000. In 1771 it was reckoned that 50,000 slaves were carried in British ships alone. The mortality rate for this 'Middle Passage' was high - the final total could be as much as 40% - and many of the crew also died or else deserted the ship.

Parliament
From 1791 a bill was presented almost every year in Parliament and the abolitionists were out-voted eleven times, once by a mere seventeen votes (some of their supporters had gone to see a new comic opera!). The slavery lobby in the House was firmly entrenched and persuaded MPs that there would be an economic collapse should the bill be passed. But the movement gradually gained ground and in 1807 the House of Commons finally passed a bill to abolish the slave trade by 283 votes to 16.

During these years a project was set up by the Clapham Sect that did much to further the abolitionist cause. As well as the thousands of slaves in the colonies, there were some 14,000 slaves in England; should they be set free, they needed somewhere to settle. At their suggestion, the colony of Sierra Leone was founded in West Africa for freed slaves; its capital became known as Freetown. Despite initial disasters and problems, the young colony survived and was reinforced in 1792 by the arrival of 1,131 former slaves from America.

Meanwhile, Wilberforce's other great object, that of fighting vice and immorality, also continued to occupy his time. He concluded that severe punishments such as hanging did little to deal with the root cause of the problem, but that it was better 'to repress that general spirit of licentiousness which is the parent of every species of vice'. With the support of the king, he founded the Proclamation Society in June 1787, the aim of which was to enforce existing laws on duelling, lotteries, drunkenness, blasphemy and other 'unacceptable' forms of public behaviour. Soon Wilberforce became a sort of guardian of public morals and after the success of the anti-slavery bill was regarded by many as a guide to the nation's conscience.

In Parliament he worked unceasingly for a variety of humanitarian causes and strenuously opposed anything he felt would lead to a misuse of Sunday. Although this meant he was responsible for limiting the pleasures of the poor, his efforts ensured that they did at least have one rest day a week.

Rather later in life than most, he got married - at the age of thirty-eight - to Barbara Spooner, the daughter of a country banker, and they went to live in Broomfield Road, Clapham. Though in some respects it may not have been the best match, she gave him thirty-five years of 'undiluted happiness'.

Abolition

After the abolition of slavery, there was yet a further battle to be fought, to abolish the institution of slavery and set free those thousands of captives held in the West Indies. The war with France (1793-1815) prevented much progress being made, but at the Treaty of Vienna in 1815 the powers agreed to condemn the trade and resolved to end it as soon as possible.

By now Wilberforce was growing older, and though still an MP gave over the control of the Emancipation Movement to Fowell Buxton MP, who was already working for penal reform. In 1825 he was forced by illness to retire from politics, but despite failing strength continued to maintain a fatherly interest in the campaign.

After ten years of parliamentary struggle, the bill for the Abolition of Slavery in the British colonies was passed in July 1833, largely as a result of support from new MPs elected under the Reform Bill. Due to Wilberforce's insistence, a clause was inserted giving the slave owners £20 million compensation, which he felt was only right.

The news was conveyed to the dying Wilberforce, who said, 'Thank God that I should have lived to witness a day in which England is willing to give twenty millions sterling for the abolition of slavery.'

He died four days later, and his body was laid to rest in the north transept of Westminster Abbey, near to that of his friend Pitt. The two

Houses suspended business to attend his funeral and among the pall-bearers were the Lord Chancellor and the Speaker of the Commons.

Although Wilberforce did not initiate the opposition to slavery - the Quakers were probably first to begin the agitation - he was the obvious choice to spearhead the movement, and his charm, popularity, perseverance and faith helped him win the day.

Despite his success, he had his enemies who accused him of hypocrisy, in that he failed to espouse the cause of the 'slaves' at home, in factories and the mines, but they were in the minority. In fact he supported a wide variety of humanitarian causes and was generous in giving to charitable organisations and to individuals in distress.

Impetuously generous, his transparent kindliness and simplicity made him lovable, it was said, even to his opponents, and he came to occupy a unique position in the nation as one who was respected by people of all walks of life. As a result of his anti-slavery work, a doctrine developed known as 'The Three C's', Christianity, convenience and civilisation, which helped shape future missionary activity in Africa.

ELIZABETH FRY (1789-1845): Prison Reformer

Many of the great humanitarian reforms of the past two hundred years or so have mostly been achieved as a result of private enterprise, and the state has been conspicuous by its absence. What usually started as a personal campaign at the initiative of ordinary people was later taken over by the state in order to accomplish the matter by legislation. It could probably be argued that unless individuals had first pioneered a cause, the state would have attempted nothing unless forced to do so by some disaster or other.

The question of the condition of prisons serves as a useful illustration of this point. The reform of the penal system made hardly any progress until the findings of people like John Howard and Elizabeth Fry provoked the state to take action.

The institution of prison dates back to the ancient civilisation of Egypt and is frequently alluded to in the Bible. Jesus taught that visiting the prisoner was one of the marks of 'the righteous', yet for hundreds of years it seems to have been a neglected aspect of Christian ministry.

In England, the plight of the prisoner received scant attention until the eighteenth century. In 1701 the Society for Promoting Christian Knowledge attempted to expose the evils of the system, but made little progress. A number of Methodists, including Wesley and Whitefield, visited prisons; they collected money to provide for some of the bare necessities of prisoners, preached to the unsaved and comforted the condemned.

The most important prison reformer of the century was an evangelical, John Howard, the High Sheriff of Bedford, who witnessed at
first-hand the plight of prisoners. He travelled widely and his report,
State of Prisons (1777), resulted in some reforms being made, though
they proved to be of only a temporary nature. It was left to Elizabeth Fry
early the following century to bring attention to the appalling state of our
prisons, and it was as a result of her efforts that more permanent reforms
were achieved.

Quaker Stock

Elizabeth Gurney, as she was then, was born into a wealthy family; her
father was a successful merchant banker, while her mother also came
from a banking family, the Barclays. Coming from long established
Quaker stock, they worshipped every Sunday at the Friends' Meeting
House in Goat Lane, Norwich, though they did not take their religion too
seriously.

Their home at Earlham Hall, on the banks of the River Wensum, was
one of the centres of Norwich society, and Elizabeth enjoyed wearing
bright clothes and attending parties, where she never lacked dancing
partners. The Gurneys, not surprisingly, were known as 'Gay' Quakers
rather than 'Plain' (who frowned on the social round and wore only grey
or brown clothes), but the children still found their family religion a
discipline they could not easily endure. On Sundays, the two-hour
service with its long sermon proved boring, and Elizabeth was always
glad when it was over.

In her teens, however, Elizabeth became what the Quakers called a
'seeker'; she felt that religion should make a difference to a person's life
and she longed to know God for real. At the age of seventeen she
recorded in her diary that she had no religion and it seemed as though her
search was at an end.

Within a year, however, her life was changed. Listening to William
Savery, an American preacher, she was deeply impressed by the gospel;
for the first time she realised there was a God and that Jesus had died to
save her. When some months later it was prophesied of her in a Quaker
meeting that she was to be 'a light to the blind, speech to the dumb and
feet to the lame', she felt that God must have a special work for her to do.

Looking around for ways of being useful to God, she undertook a
number of charitable works in and around Norwich: she started a Sunday
School at Earlham Hall for the poor children who lived near the estate,
visited the sick in Norwich and read the Bible to them, and made clothes

for the poor. Influenced by her stricter Friends of Coalbrookdale in Shropshire, she became a 'Plain' Quaker and gave up her social life to adopt the more severe form of Quaker dress and cap, which she wore for the rest of her life.

At the age of twenty she married Joseph Fry, a London tea, coffee and spice merchant, and they went to live in the capital. She became a dedicated wife and mother, but as the years passed she grew restless and was saddened by her failure to lead a more 'useful' life. When, in 1808, the Frys moved out of the city to Plashet (Essex), she was able once again to find opportunities of serving people on the estate. She opened a school

with a paid teacher, set-up a 'soup-kitchen' and tended the sick. In 1811 she was 're-corded' by the Friends at Barking (Essex) as an (un-paid) minister and soon received invitations to speak in different parts of the country where she enjoyed preaching on 'the grace of God to all'.

It was in 1813 that her attention was first drawn to prison conditions by an American Quaker called Stephen Grellet, who had visited Newgate. Shocked by what he discovered, he reported the situation to Elizabeth Fry who reacted

ELIZABETH FRY ENTERING NEWGATE

immediately. With a group of Quaker ladies she went to the prison with clothing for the sick women and children, and paid the turnkey (keeper) to provide clean straw for them to sleep on.

The Women's Side at Newgate contained three hundred women and children, crowded into four rooms, where they slept, cooked and ate what little food they had. During the day they were allowed to mix with the male prisoners, and with nothing better to do, spent their time in gambling, drinking, fighting, dancing and singing. Innocent and guilty alike were thrown together, and many of them came out more hardened than when they went in.

Return to Newgate

Because of her family and other responsibilities, Elizabeth was not able to return to Newgate until January 1817, when she began regular visits to the prison. Her opening move was to suggest starting a school for the children, to which the women responded with enthusiasm. Before long the women and older girls asked that they too might have lessons, and classes were started where they were taught to knit and sew. They were divided into groups of twelve, each with a 'monitor' to supervise them; they learned to make clothes for their children, and other items which were sold to give them a small income. In this way the women learned a little self-respect.

With their earnings they were able to purchase luxuries such as tea and sugar at Mrs. Fry's prison shop, and they began to take more pride in their hygiene and personal appearance. A committee of Quaker ladies was formed to raise money for the school and to ensure that at least one member visited the prison each day.

For Elizabeth, the most important habit she established in the prison was that of reading the Bible; every day a bell was sounded at 9 am and 6 pm to summon the inmates together for prayer and to listen to Mrs. Fry read the Scriptures. It was said she spoke with marvellous effect, and that the pathos of her voice melted even the hardest criminals.

Although not all the women responded equally to her efforts, the scheme was a success and news of the changes were reported in the press. Ladies' committees were set up around the country to provide help in other prisons, and Elizabeth travelled as far as Scotland combining her preaching engagement with inspection visits to prisons.

Transportation

A convict could be sentenced to transportation for life for crimes such as stealing an apron or a side of bacon, and to fourteen years for stealing 1lb of potatoes or a pair of shoes. Until 1776 they were sent to the American colonies, after that to Botany Bay, Australia. Women convicts were chained together and carried to the ships at Deptford in open carts. During the long voyage to Australia they were kept in unhealthy conditions with no medical attention. At the penal colony, they were treated as slaves and given neither accommodation nor decent employment. All these abuses she set right: the women were taken to the ships in closed Hackney carriages, and on board their chains were removed; she saw to it that they had a Bible, and gave each of them a parcel of needles and materials to enable them to sew and knit; urgent changes were also made at Botany Bay. She aroused such feelings against the system that it was eventually stopped.

She later set down her findings in a book, *Observations On The Visiting, Superintending And Government Of Female Prisoners*, but her novel ideas were expensive and not immediately taken up. Elizabeth was a pragmatist, and whatever the theorists said, she knew the job had to be done there and then.

As a result of her success at Newgate she was invited in 1818 to give evidence of the state of prisons before a House of Commons select committee, and then before the House of Lords. Later, she received invitations to tour the Continent and travelled as far as Russia. She met King Louis-Philippe of France, and the King of Prussia came to regard her as 'his friend'.

It was in the summer of 1818 that she first discovered the evils of the system of transportation, when a batch of women from Newgate was due to sail to Australia. She persuaded the governor, who was by now her friend, to treat the transports more kindly. As a consequence of her more humane treatment, the women went quietly and maintained the dignity which they had developed in the prison.

A report later reached Mrs. Fry that when the transports reached Botany Bay, however, they had once again to endure terrible hardships. The government responded immediately to her complaint, providing employment and proper living accommodation for the women.

Over a period of twenty-five years, except for times of illness, Elizabeth visited every convict ship leaving London that carried women, which amounted to 126 ships carrying a total of 12,000 prisoners. After her efforts, the number of transports began to decrease from 1837, and ceased altogether in 1854.

Although getting on in years, Elizabeth continued to look for other ways of making herself useful to God and was responsible for setting up a number of humanitarian projects. Already she had founded a Nightly Shelter for the Homeless (1819) and a series of District Charity Societies (1824); she also opened a Nurses' Training Home and founded the Protestant Sisters of Charity (1840). Worn out by her continual labours, she died peacefully at Ramsgate and was buried in the Friends' burial-ground at Barking.

Inspired by her faith in God and her conviction that all human beings should be treated with respect, Elizabeth Fry encouraged a more humane form of treatment within British prisons, and many of her proposals were adopted both here and on the Continent. But it may be that it was her appeal as a woman reformer that finally persuaded governments to accept the changes.

GEORGE MULLER (1805-1898):
Founder of Children's Homes, Bristol

Following the dissolution of the monasteries in 1536-40, there were few medieval charitable bodies left in existence to assist the poor, while at the same time social problems were further heightened by a population drift from the countryside into the towns. Some towns attempted to meet the needs of their more distressed citizens by instituting homes and schools for children, hospitals for the sick and relief for the aged, but it was ultimately left to the government of the day to draw up a national policy.

Under the terms of the Poor Law, 1601, apprentice schemes were set up for homeless children which also provided them with accommodation, but the Act fell short of its intentions. By the nineteenth century an increasing number of children were being made homeless, and many of them preferred the freedom of the streets rather than endure the cruelty of the workhouse system.

Despite the humanitarian spirit of the Evangelical Revival, which gave birth to charity schools and the Sunday School movement, it was not until 1836 that the first of the great orphanages was established by George Müller, in Bristol. The success of his work was an inspiration to many Christians, especially Dr. Barnardo, and proved to be the beginning of an attempt to meet the needs of thousands of children made destitute by the Industrial Revolution.

On The Side Of Christ

Müller was born and brought up in Prussia where he was baptised and confirmed into the Lutheran Church. But his religion was superficial, and from an early age he developed traits of dishonesty and deceit. While a teenage student at the Cathedral school at Halberstadt, he once spent three weeks in prison for fraud, but failed to learn his lesson. Despite all his resolutions, he was unable to let go of his irresponsible habits. At Halle University where he was training to become a pastor, he was taken one evening to a Bible meeting which marked a turning point in his life; from then on he put away his 'sinful practices' and 'stood on the side of Christ'.

Thinking he should become a missionary to the Jews, Müller came to England in 1829 to train with the London Society for Promoting Christianity among the Jews (now the Church's Ministry among the Jews), but changed his mind and became pastor of Ebenezer Chapel, Teignmouth, Devon. Three weeks after marrying Mary Groves of

Exeter, he and his wife decided that 'they should depend on God alone for all their needs'. Instead of drawing a salary, a box was placed in the chapel and from then on they made known their requests only to God.

Invited by his friend Henry Craik to preach in Bristol, Müller - who was one of the leaders of the early Brethren Movement - afterwards 'felt fully persuaded that Bristol is the place where the Lord will have me to labour'. In 1832 the Müllers settled in Bristol where he shared the ministry with Craik at Bethesda Chapel, Great George Street, on the understanding that they would never run up a debt. The work flourished and at the end of the first year they were able to report an increase of 109 in the membership, including 65 by conversion.

GEORGE MULLER

Encouraged, Müller decided in 1834 to found what he called the *Scriptural Knowledge Institution for Home and Abroad*. It aimed to promote the spread of the gospel by way of education, literature and missionary efforts.

The following year, the idea of opening an orphanage began to develop in his mind, though he told no one about it. In both Teignmouth and Bristol he had been aware of the large number of ragged children running wild in the streets, and a cholera epidemic in 1832 had left even more children homeless.

After being 'very much in prayer respecting it', he put his plan into action and prayed for premises, for £1,000, and for the right people to care for the children. But his motive was not simply one of compassion; he desired above all to show that God is still the living God, and that he is faithful to those who put their trust in him.

Müller determined that the children would be provided with everything they needed by prayer and faith, without making an appeal for money to anyone but God. He laid the matter before his congregation in December 1835, and they approved. By the following April the first Home was opened for thirty girls between the ages of seven and twelve years, a second Home for infants was ready by November and third Home for boys over seven opened the following September. All three of them were situated close together in Wilson Street, Bristol.

During the first two years, enough money came in to finance the project without undue delay; but then began a number of trials which went on for over ten years. At times they were down to their last coin or even out of funds before God answered prayer. The most famous occasion when help came at the last moment happened one morning at the breakfast table. With no food in the larder and no money, Müller said grace: 'Dear Father, we thank thee for what thou art going to give us to eat.' As he finished, the baker arrived with a supply of fresh bread, for the Lord had told him during the night that it was needed. Then the milkman turned up; his cart had broken down and he asked them to relieve him of his milk so that he could carry out repairs!

By now Müller had one hundred and thirty children to care for each day, and whilst their style of living was of necessity simple, perhaps even frugal, the orphans never went without. In fact, they probably enjoyed a more secure life than many other children of their day, and letters from ex-orphans testify to the high level of care and the sound Christian education they received. As far as possible, when boys and girls were old enough to leave the Home they were set up in work with Christian people who were able to keep an eye on them. Not all placings were successful, however, as some of the employers' references were misleading; but for the most part the children were able to make a satisfactory start to their adult life.

New Home

In 1845 a polite complaint from a Wilson Street resident that the Homes were an 'inconvenience' to the neighbours moved Müller to re-examine the situation; it occurred to him that it would be better to have a different location where the children would have more space. He and his wife prayed about the matter before sharing the new vision with some of his fellow-workers. Whereas the properties in Wilson Street were rented, it was decided to pray for £10,000 with which to build a new Home for three hundred children.

As the money came in, land was purchased on Ashley Down, on the outskirts of Bristol, where there was plenty of open space and country air. When the full amount was realised, the Home was built to be opened in June 1849, fully-fitted and furnished, with a balance of £776. Further Homes followed, and by 1870 there were five large Homes - complete with schools - caring for 2,050 children. All five buildings were paid for, and the money came directly in response to prayer.

Following his wife's death in 1870 Müller began to delegate more of the responsibilities for running the Homes; after his second marriage, he gave over the work to his co-director, his son-in-law James Wright. This left him free to pursue a long-cherished desire to travel and preach the gospel in foreign lands. At the age of seventy he started a series of tours that over the years took him to all corners of the world. His purpose was not to collect money, but to preach the gospel to the unconverted and to benefit Christians, especially young believers.

Müller was scrupulous in his financial affairs and adhered strictly to the principles he first laid down in 1834. To avoid scandal, he always declared the monies received; the total from 1834 to his death in 1898 amounted to almost £1,400,000, most of which was donated for the orphans. His personal income between 1831 and 1886 varied between £151 in 1831 and £4,260 in 1877; he kept £300 a year and gave the rest either to suitable Christian causes or even to non-believers in need, a total of £81,000.

All this was not achieved without much prayer, which was one of his major occupations, both with his wife and in secret. His *Narratives* are illustrated with numerous examples of God's provision, and he claimed to have had over 30,000 answers to prayer on the very day they were made. His faith in God has been an inspiration to thousands of believers; men like Hudson Taylor, Barnardo and Spurgeon sought his counsel, and so the influence of his ministry was widespread.

Through the work of the Scripture Knowledge Institution, his efforts quietly benefited a number of Christian enterprises that might otherwise

---

The Scriptural Knowledge Institution for Home and Abroad
Müller recorded in his diary on 25 February 1834, 'I was led again this day to pray about founding a new Missionary Institution, and felt still more confirmed that we should do so.' It had Four Objects: (1) to assist day, adult and Sunday Schools where teachers were professing Christians, by receiving and distributing gifts of money; (2) to sell portions of Scripture cheaply, or to give them free of cost; (3) to aid missionary effort by gifts of money to individual, free-lance missionaries; (4) to circulate tracts in English, and in various foreign languages. A fifth object was added later by Müller, which related to his other great project, the orphan homes. The founders decided not to involve any unconverted people in the work nor to seek money from them; nor would they contract debts. Success would be reckoned by God's blessing (in proportion to the extent in which they prayed) and not by statistics.

have floundered. In the early years of the China Inland Mission he was the main financial benefactor behind Hudson Taylor, and for many years supported 189 missionaries. In addition, he entirely funded 100 schools with 9,000 pupils, distributed about four million tracts and sent out thousands of copies of the Scriptures.

In Bristol, he was responsible for feeding and housing 2,050 children for every day of each year, together with the upkeep of the buildings. Up to the time of his death, 10,024 orphans had been cared for, educated and given a firm grounding in the Christian Faith.

Of course, Müller had his critics. Some accused him of being too strict, others that he was 'educating the poor above their station' (really a compliment) or that the Homes were 'religious forcing grounds'. The fact is that thousands of destitute children were given a start in life that otherwise they would have been denied.

An entry in Müller's Journal from 1874 underlines his continued faith in God: 'God who has raised up this work through me; God who has led me generally year after year to enlarge it; God who has supported this work now for more than forty years, will still help, and will not suffer me to be confounded, because I rely upon him.' Müller's faith is a challenge to the 'respectable' Christians of every age, and provides a visible reminder of the reality and faithfulness of God.

THOMAS BARNARDO (1845-1905):
Founder of Children's Home

There was a startling rise in the number of homeless children in England during the course of the nineteenth century. Although no firm statistics are available, it was once reckoned that in the East End of London alone there were about 30,000 boys and girls under sixteen living on the streets. On any one night there would be another 15,000 who had no home but were not able to afford the cost of a lodging house. A further large number of 'street urchins' were to be found in the boroughs immediately south of the River Thames, in places such as Lambeth and Southwark.

It was the work of the ragged schools and the city missions, along with the writings of Charles Dickens, that increasingly drew attention to the plight of homeless children in the second half of the nineteenth century. A number of Homes were founded as the result of evangelical missions, such as Mr Fegan's Homes for destitute boys (1870), in Deptford, south east London; Shaftesbury Homes (1843) at St Giles; Mrs Smyly's Homes (1852) in Dublin; William Quarrier's Homes

(1864) in Scotland; and the Manchester and Salford Refuges (1870) which started out as a ragged school work.

Other Homes were linked to denominations such as the National Children's Home (1869), founded in Lambeth by Dr Bowman Stephenson, a Wesleyan minister; others include Spurgeon's ·Homes (1867), the Church of England Children's Society (1881) founded in south Lambeth by the Rudolph brothers, plus a number of smaller homes founded by Roman Catholic and High Church sisters.

Missionary Training

It was in Dublin that Thomas Barnardo, of Italian ancestry, was born into a prosperous fur-trading family. His parents were regular worshippers at St. Andrew's Church, where Barnardo was confirmed; but although religion played an important place in their lives, at the age of sixteen young Thomas declared himself to be agnostic.

Within a short time, however, he was soundly converted to Christ. He joined the Open Plymouth Brethren with two of his brothers and for four years devoted his considerable energies to working among the poor of his city; he taught in a Ragged school and visited the slums sharing the gospel. After a personal conversation with Hudson Taylor when he visited Dublin in 1865, Barnardo accepted the challenge to become a missionary.

Just before his twenty-first birthday, in April 1866, he went to London to join a group of recruits sailing for China, but Taylor persuaded him to stay behind and first train to become a doctor. Disappointed, Barnardo registered at the London Hospital in Whitechapel and rented two rooms just off Commercial Road. During a cholera epidemic, the medical students joined the doctors in visiting the poor in their homes, and in this way Barnardo got to know Stepney and all its horrors.

He joined the Plymouth Brethren in Sidney Street, and spent Sundays as well as two evenings a week distributing Bibles and preaching on street corners and in pubs. Despite his shortness (he never grew to be more than five foot three inches) he was a determined young man and would not allow threats to discourage him.

Ragged School

Later in the year he opened a ragged school in a rented shed that had been used as a donkey stable. It was soon crammed with eager pupils, some of them older than their teacher. It was here that Barnardo met ten-year-old Jim Jarvis and first became aware of the problem of homeless children. But he felt unable to tackle the problem with his meagre resources.

The problem of homelessness was due to a combination of low wages, unemployment and alcohol. Some children were forced to beg, or were even sold by their parents as cheap labour to supplement the family income. Other children were turned out of their homes, and thousands simply took to the streets where many of them died before they reached their teens.

Barnardo went on to found what became the East End Juvenile Mission, in two cottages opposite the donkey stable. As well as holding

gospel services, he helped the boys and girls to find jobs, but realised this was not the complete answer to their problems; a more radical solution was necessary. In any case, he still thought in terms of going to China and his heart was set on becoming a missionary.

One day he received an offer of £1,000 from an MP for his work among the slum children which seemed to be the sign he had prayed for. He kept the news to himself for ten days, and then accepted the offer. Barnardo now set aside the idea of joining the China Inland Mission and was able to concentrate on his mission to the young people of the East End.

THOMAS BARNARDO

While continuing his medical studies, Barnardo preached three times a week at the Mission and held nightly prayer meetings for anything up to five hundred young people. By the Spring of 1870 over one hundred and fifty converts had been baptised, but he became increasingly uneasy as each night he realised that many of them probably had nowhere to sleep.

After hesitating for some while, he rented a large house on Stepney Causeway as an orphanage, and with his Mission helpers prepared the place to receive their first inmates. He appointed a 'godly brother' and his wife to act as houseparents, and spent two nights searching the slums for boys willing to accept his help. (As a bachelor, he felt it wiser to limit his care to homeless boys.)

In the early days Barnardo determined never to get into debt, and limited the Home to twenty-five boys until his funds increased. But one of the boys he had to refuse, called 'Carrots', was a few days later found dead, due to 'frequent exposure and want of food'. Barnardo was stunned and blamed himself for the tragedy. He declared that never again would he refuse a single destitute child, 'even though there should not be one shilling in my purse or a loaf in the larder'. Shortly afterwards, a large notice was fixed to the outside of the Home: *No destitute child ever refused admittance*. From then on, every bed was kept filled.

People's Church

His next great project was to open a People's Church in the heart of the East End. Alarmed at the terrible effects of alcohol on the poor, he started an evangelistic campaign close to the biggest 'gin palace' in the neighbourhood, the *Edinburgh Castle*. It was so successful that the pub had to close down. Barnardo raised the necessary purchase price and in 1873 re-opened the building as a church, complete with a coffee bar where the poor could buy cheap meals.

The church, which had a membership of three hundred, voted Barnardo as their pastor; he conducted weekly services and sometimes spent as much as four hours a day in visiting his growing congregation. Attendances at Sunday services rose to 2,000 and there were many conversions. The Castle became a unique social centre and probably contributed much towards tackling the problem of poverty and destitution in the East End.

In the same year, Barnardo married Syrie Elmslie of Richmond, and together they opened the first Barnardo Home for girls at Ilford. But he soon realised that the barrack-style home was not the best idea for girls and they would benefit more from a family-type environment.

In answer to prayer he was able to open a Village for Girls at Ilford where they were grouped in separate cottages, each one with a 'Mother' to care for them. The family-home idea proved successful and he decided to expand the scheme. For some years he had placed a number of his charges with foster-parents, and in 1886 he launched a programme of boarding-out children between the ages of five and nine with recommended people living in carefully chosen villages where they could enjoy fresh country air.

As a medical man, Barnardo was specially concerned for the children's health. In 1876, when he qualified as a surgeon, he opened a hospital for sick children close to the Stepney Causeway home, and two years later started a medical mission with a free clinic. Mrs. Barnardo formed a nursing organisation staffed by deaconesses, who nursed the sick and visited the poor in their homes.

Over the years, Barnardo responded to every need that came to his attention, and the wide variety of his concerns is quite astonishing. In addition to other branches around the country, he opened a home for Babies in Kent (1883), two homes for 'cripples' (1887), a home for incurables (1894) and a Nautical Training School for Boys (1903).

Some of the older children were given the offer of a new life abroad in countries such as Canada and Australia. Since the days of Jim Jarvis, Barnardo had obtained places for some of his children under a private scheme run by Miss Annie Macpherson, but in 1882 he started his own emigration programme. Within six years he had settled 2,400 children in countries of the Empire, and many grew up to become successful farmers, businessmen and lawyers.

Barnardo's financial support came by prayer and appeal. He had quite a flair for publicity, and though he always prayed about his needs, he also kept his supporters informed about his projects and what funds were required. With his expanding commitments, the financial needs were considerable. Even though the income came to a total £150,000 a year, this was not enough to keep him out of debt. On one occasion his trustees had to take a firm line and insist he attempt to reduce it.

Despite his success, or perhaps because of it, he attracted much criticism, and his enemies (among them some churchmen) made false accusations against him. A special tribunal set up to examine the charges not only exonerated him, but heaped high praise upon his efforts. To his staff, he was a hard task-master who was not always easy to get on with; but despite his faults they respected him and he inspired them to great efforts.

Above all, his desire was for the well-being of the children, many of whom adored him; he provided not only a roof over their heads but also cared for their spiritual needs, without which he felt his life's work would have been in vain. He carried demanding responsibilities as Pastor of the People's Church and Director of the Children's Homes to the end, and when he died it was from sheer exhaustion.

WILLIAM BOOTH (1829-1912):
Founder of The Salvation Army

Evangelicals in 1883 were challenged by the author of a penny pamphlet entitled *The Bitter Cry of Outcast London*. Published by the London Congregational Union, the pamphlet pointed out that while Evangelicals were building their churches, the poor had been growing poorer, and the gap between them and the churches and the chapels had been widening.

Although the gulf between the classes was evident throughout the nation, it was most obvious in the East End of London. During the second half of the nineteenth century there were an estimated five hundred philanthropic agencies at work in the East End, pouring in an annual £3.5 million in charity, yet unable to stem the rising tide of poverty and misery.

While the main body of Christian churches made little or no attempt to evangelise the poor and the down-and-outs, it was the radical approach of the Salvation Army that made the gospel meaningful to the thousands of unchurched.

As a result of the publicity, the social conscience of the Church was touched and some of the denominations were moved to begin a similar social work themselves, though on a much smaller scale.

East End

The Army began in the East End of London and was originally known as the East London Christian Mission. It started in 1865 as the result of a mission headed by William Booth, an ex-Methodist New Connexion minister, who had resigned to work as an itinerant evangelist. Based first of all in a tent on a disused Quaker burial ground, Booth's mission attracted many of the worst elements of the area, especially when he preached outside the Blind Beggar public house. He withstood the assaults and by the end of the year had gathered a group of sixty converts round him, including characters like the boxer, Peter Monk and Mother Moore, a drunken charwoman.

Early on, Booth learned two vital lessons that were to transform his ministry and pave the way for a truly working class movement. First he discovered that he needed to change his presentation of the gospel. Booth had always dressed and preached as though he was facing a chapel congregation, but after inviting a recently-converted gypsy hawker to give his testimony he changed his style. Over the years he came to approach evangelism in an almost theatrical manner, which appealed to the working classes.

Next, he attempted to return his converts to the churches, but found that they could not settle there. With the help of his energetic wife, Catherine, he set up 'stations' (as he called them) where the new Christians could be nurtured in the familiar environment of the East End.

Soon after he started the Mission, Booth took his family to live in Hackney so that he could be closer to the people he wanted to reach. He opened his headquarters at 272 Whitechapel Road, which also served as a social centre.

On Christmas morning 1868, after preaching in Whitechapel, he returned home feeling dejected; he had seen the poor celebrating the festival by getting drunk and was determined that it should not happen again. The following year he organised three hundred Christmas dinners for the poor, most of them cooked by Catherine and an Army helper in their home kitchen. This marked the beginning of the Mission's social work.

Realising that people don't respond to the gospel on an empty stomach, he opened a 'soup kitchen' selling hot drinks at all hours of the day. He also set up five 'Food-for-the-Million Shops' where cheap three course meals were available.

The Christian Mission, as it was now called, produced militant-type Christians who almost from the beginning began to use military-style terms. They were 'fighting for God' in the 'Hallelujah army', and Booth was their 'General'. In 1878 Booth described the Mission as a 'Volunteer Army', but his lieutenant, George Railton, protested. Booth replaced the term 'Volunteer' with 'Salvation' and the title stuck.

By early 1879 converts could be counted by the thousands, and the Army had eighty-one stations manned by one hundred and twenty-seven full-time evangelists and holding 75,000 services a year. Yet Booth still felt that there was an unexplained element missing. The solution came at an Army meeting in Salisbury. Faced with the possibility of trouble at an open-air meeting, Salvationist William Fry and his three sons offered to act as bodyguards.

Army Bands

They brought their musical instruments with them to accompany the singing, and the first Army band was formed. For a while the General was not attracted by the idea of a band but was eventually forced to declare, 'Why should the Devil have all the best tunes?' Soon the band was to accompany Booth on his tours and was often a means of attracting people to his meetings.

Before long, the Army added other features which promoted the military image. Instead of a conference, the Army was now governed by a 'Council of War'; ranks and titles came later. In 1878 Catherine Booth designed a flag for the station at Coventry which became the Army standard; it had a crimson background with a sun in the centre, later replaced by a star with the words 'Blood and Fire'. And in 1880 a standard uniform was introduced to take the place of the imaginative outfits worn by the first converts; this included the distinctive bonnet for the women, still worn today.

Army music

The intention of the first Army band, formed in 1878, was simply to accompany songs (the word 'hymn' was banned as too 'churchy'), using an odd assortment of instruments: cornets, hunting horns, banjos and tambourines (very popular). Under Richard Slater, former first violin with Sir Arthur Sullivan, many hit tunes of the day were appropriated (no copyright problem) and became Army songs - 'The Old Folk At Home' became 'Joy, Freedom, Peace and Ceaseless Blessing', and in Scotland 'Here's to Good Old Whisky' was adapted to 'Storm the Forts of Darkness'. Booth was not fully convinced about their use until at a Worcester theatre in 1882 he heard 'Champagne Charlie sung as 'Bless His Name, He Sets Me Free', which elicited his famous remark about the Devil not having all the best tunes. Within a year the Army had its own Music Department, and there were four hundred bands with a repertoire of eighty-eight hit tunes.

As the Army success gathered momentum, so did the opposition - the decade beginning in 1880 witnessed a period of assaults more violent than anything experienced in the early days. In one year alone (1882), six hundred and sixty-nine Army soldiers were attacked and sixty buildings wrecked. All over the country Army processions were broken up, meetings disrupted, while at Hastings one woman was kicked to death.

The most prolonged battle was fought at Worthing, on the south coast. There in 1884 a 'Skeleton Army' some 4,000 strong launched a series of attacks that went on over a period of three months. In the end, order was only restored when troops were called in from Brighton. By about 1890 the troubles began to die down as magistrates took a firmer line with offenders, and the Army won the right to parade the streets of England without being molested.

Now with a wider vision of his work, Booth declared that his intention was 'to get his arms right around the world', but the initial step came about as if by accident. It happened in 1878 when Amos Shirley from Coventry emigrated to America in order to find a job. With his wife and daughter, he rented a disused factory in Philadelphia and started Army-type preaching services to packed meetings. Two years later, George Railton sailed to New York and opened up a centre for the Army, followed by ten others in different parts of the country.

Next, the General's eldest daughter, Kate Booth, led an 'attack' on France in 1881, and Major Frederick Tucker - fluent in three native languages - sailed to India the following year to begin a crusade among Hindus and Sikhs. Other centres were opened as far away as Australia

---

The Church Army

The Anglican response to Booth's work was the Church Army, formed under the leadership of Wilson Carlile (1847-1942), a successful businessman of Scottish Presbyterian background. Ordained into the Church of England in 1878, Carlile had been impressed by Moody's campaign in 1874, and his use of the testimonies of ordinary young men. He gathered together a group of working class laymen in Kensington, London, and began open-air meetings and lantern slide services. In 1882 he joined up with two like-minded Anglicans to found the Church Army, calling for volunteers 'full of fire and hard work, ready to give up all for the Lord Jesus'. Modelled along the lines of the Salvation Army, the stress was always on evangelism but linked to a constructive social programme designed to help the destitute and the homeless. In 1926 Carlile toured the United States and Canada to launch a North American branch of the Army.

---

and New Zealand, while on the Continent, Army soldiers moved into Switzerland, Germany, Holland and Scandinavia. By 1891 there were 10,000 officers working in twenty-six countries, with much more ground yet to be captured.

At home, Booth never missed an opportunity for dealing with a problem whenever he saw the need. Crossing London Bridge late one night he discovered men lying at the side of the road, covered with newspapers and trying to sleep. Next day he called his son and told him to do something about it. Bramwell rented a warehouse by the West India Docks which became the Army's first hostel for the homeless, complete with a food shop serving cheap meals. In England at that time there were an estimated three million poor people - people who were starving and homeless.

In order to publicise their circumstances, Booth co-authored a book with W T Stead, a newspaper editor, called *In Darkest England and the Way Out*. The book described how the poor lived and outlined Booth's ideas to remedy their plight.

He called his plan the 'Cab-Horse Charter', pointing out that just as every cab-horse was given food, shelter and work, so people should enjoy the same rights. In order to achieve this aim he called for a public subscription of at least £100,000, and another £30,000 every year to maintain the scheme.

The public responded with enthusiasm and his target was reached. The idea, however, was attacked by a number of leading figures, including the aged Lord Shaftesbury and Sir Thomas Huxley, who described it as an 'impractical Utopia'. But with the support of people like Winston Churchill and Cardinal Manning he decided to go ahead. He realised it was not the complete answer, but at least it was a start.

The scheme, which foreshadowed the Welfare State by some twenty years, provided for a job centre, a bank which advanced small loans, a farm for training workers and a missing persons bureau. Within nine years, the Army had found jobs for 9,000 workers and every night gave lodging to over 3,000 men and women.

In 1890 Booth was devastated by the loss of his wife who had been his closest companion, but his work went on unhindered. He now felt freer to make a series of tours to see the Army at work and visited many parts of the globe. Between 1904 and 1907, he made three motor tours of Britain, covering over 5,000 miles and addressing nearly 400 meetings.

The saddest episode in the General's work occurred when Bramwell and W T Stead tried to overturn a prostitution racket involving girls as young as thirteen years, some of whom were smuggled abroad and sold. While his efforts resulted in the age of consent being raised from thirteen to sixteen years, the plan back-fired and Stead was jailed for attempting to procure a young girl, a totally misplaced accusation.

Throughout his career, Booth remained essentially an evangelist; but he not only preached the love of God, he put it into action. Like Barnardo, he viewed evangelism and social action as two sides of the same coin, and he could never separate them. It is reported that when the two men once met, Booth told Barnardo, 'You look after the children and I'll look after the adults, and together we'll convert the world.'

When Booth died his funeral service was held at Olympia, West London. Unknown to anyone, Queen Mary slipped in quietly and sat at the back beside a shabby but neatly-dressed woman who afterwards confessed to the Queen that the Army had saved her from prostitution. As the coffin passed down the aisle, the woman slipped three faded carnations on to the lid. Curious, the Queen asked the woman, 'What brought you here to the service?' 'Well,' the woman replied, 'he cared for the likes of us.'

CATHERINE BOOTH (1829-1890):
Mother of The Salvation Army

The Salvation Army might never have been born had it not been for the contribution made by Catherine Booth. While William Booth is usually regarded as its founder, it really owes its origins and success to the combined efforts of husband and wife. This is all the more remarkable considering that women at the time were only just awakening to the idea of the 'equality of the sexes'. The campaign for the emancipation of women surfaced about the middle of the nineteenth century, and in 1851 Catherine Mumford, as she was then, first took up her pen to defend the new cause.

Inspired by the life's work of Florence Nightingale, the writings of the Brontë sisters and the radical John Stuart Mill, the pursuit of equality was at that stage merely a theory. As the century progressed the idea of equality spread, permeating some of the professions such as nursing and education.

For the most part the Church resisted the idea of women in the pulpit, and while Catherine's calling to preach met with opposition, there were many women who not only enjoyed the novelty, but also appreciated her gift. She stood her ground, convinced both of the biblical basis and of the urgency of her divine commission, and went on to become one of the most famous preachers of her day.

William Booth came to recognise that women converts were just as effective as men and once remarked, 'The best men in my Army are the women.'

In 1880, a training programme was started for women officers who were put in charge of scores of Army stations. Some of their names have gone down in Army history: Captain Ada Smith of Worthing who for three months defied the Skeleton Army; Captain Abbie Thompson of Kingston (Canada) who preached every night to 12,000 people; and Mrs. Susannah Beaty of Hastings who in 1882 was the Army's first martyr.

Army 'Orders and Regulations' ceased to distinguish between 'he' and 'she', and any lassie was entitled to become chaplain, editor - or even the General, a position currently held by an Australian, Eva Burrows.

Expelled

When Catherine came to faith at the age of seventeen, just after the Mumford family moved from Lincolnshire to live in Brixton, south London, she determined to spend her life in 'loving God with all her heart'. She joined the Brixton Methodist Church and was considerably helped by her class leader to gain confidence in praying aloud and in speaking in public. Following a dispute, however, she was expelled from the Methodist Church and joined a nearby congregation of the 'Reform Movement'.

It was here that Catherine met William Booth, who himself had recently been driven out of the Wesleyan Church. They were engaged the following year and married in July 1855 at Stockwell New Chapel. During the intervening years, and later when they were again parted, the two exchanged long and moving love letters, and Catherine's writings have been described as 'quite outstanding in literature'. Not only did they confide their deepest feelings for each other, but they discussed serious matters of faith and life, establishing principles that were later to serve as a foundation for their life's work together.

WILLIAM AND CATHERINE BOOTH

William Booth joined the Methodist New Connexion Church and spent some years as an itinerant evangelist, but quite contrary to his hopes was then appointed Superintendent of Brighouse and later Gateshead Circuits. It was here that Catherine first had the opportunity to display her gifts: she taught classes of children and adults, engaged in open-air preaching and took the important step of starting door-to-door visitation, reaching those whom the Church frequently passed by.

The leaders at Gateshead were so impressed with Catherine that they issued an unprecedented invitation for her to address a special prayer meeting. Because it was contrary to convention, she refused; afterwards, however, she felt rebuked and determined she would obey God the next time she had an opportunity to minister.

Such a prompting came at the Whit Sunday Service in 1860, as William was concluding his sermon. Fighting off the Devil's attempts to dissuade her, she mounted the pulpit. When she told her husband that she wanted to 'say a word', he was taken aback, but had enough sense to make way for her. The congregation was much moved by her address - many were weeping audibly - and so William announced that his wife would speak again at the evening service.

News of her preaching spread round the North and she received many invitations to speak at other chapels. When William was forced to spend nine weeks recuperating from an illness, she took his place and acted as superintendent for that time. From then on, Catherine and William shared their preaching engagements; they now enjoyed each other more and their relationship deepened as they worked together. Catherine continued to receive invitations as a speaker in her own right and her reputation spread.

Anxious to take up his work again as an evangelist, William made a third application to be released by the New Connexion Conference, but it was refused. When a compromise solution was proposed, Catherine - who was at the conference, seated in the gallery - rose to her feet and called out 'Never!' William resigned and the New Connexion denied him further use of their chapels.

Despite the dispute, the Booths were invited to Hayle in Cornwall for revival meetings, and were able to find other places for their services. More than 7,000 people professed conversion during the campaign. During these meetings the Booths learned the value of using the testimonies of new converts, who were able to influence their former companions, and of allowing greater freedom of individual expression in their meetings.

London

The Booths arrived in London in March 1865 with many invitations to speak, but they often separated to cover different occasions. Catherine's meetings attracted many unchurched people whose attention was caught by the handbills calling them to 'Come and hear a woman preach'. There followed a number of remarkable conversions, some of whom became members either at Spurgeon's Tabernacle or at Rotherhithe Chapel. While William went to the poor of the East End, Catherine often preached to the upper classes of the West End, and it was the gifts she received that brought in their support in the early days.

The term Salvation Army was now being used to describe their organisation and some of the wealthy people who heard her continued their financial support of the Army for many years. Within three years the Booths had set up thirteen preaching stations in the East End and Catherine had ventured further afield to set up additional stations at places such as Croydon, Ramsgate and Hastings. Other invitations led to continued expansion as far north as Edinburgh, where thousands more were converted.

Responsibility for the work fell equally upon both their shoulders, but Catherine was in addition the mother of eight children. She could undertake her frequent journeyings only because she had help at home, and despite her busyness always made time for her family. They were all highly devoted to each other and the children took a ready part in serving the Army.

Over the years both Catherine and William suffered from bouts of illness, and living in the East End they were in constant danger of such diseases as cholera and typhoid.

When William contracted typhoid fever in 1870, Catherine had to conduct the opening services at the new People's Mission Hall. But when Catherine was seized with another attack of angina in 1875, William spent nearly five months at her side, which gave them the best rest they had had in years.

Recognised as 'the Army Mother', Catherine took a practical interest in the follow-up of their converts and with William worked to foster a sense of family feeling among their soldiers.

They instilled in them the conviction that each one must become his 'brother's keeper' and great bonds of sympathy were formed throughout the Army. When she visited a local corps she counselled the officers and enquired about their living conditions, health and happiness.

Women Officers

Not surprisingly, women figured largely in the work of the Salvation Army. From the beginning, Catherine insisted on the right of women workers to preach, yet it was not until 1874 that they were allowed to be present at the annual conference and take part as delegates. Two years later came a decision to put women evangelists in charge of stations, whereas previously they had only acted as assistants.

Typically, it was Catherine who saw the need to train women officers as well as men. A training home for women cadets was set up under her second daughter, Emma, and Catherine regularly visited the home to give lectures. During the 1880s when the Army passed through a period of severe persecution, the women suffered just as much as the men. In fact the Army's first martyr was a woman from Hastings, who was kicked to death in a dark alley. Others, like Captain Ada Smith of Worthing, braved fierce odds to maintain the Army witness, and were pelted with rotten eggs and paint.

Catherine's power in preaching was a direct result, she believed, of the 'full salvation' she received as a young Christian in 1861 by her total surrender to God. Sometimes referred to as the baptism of the Holy Spirit or a second blessing, it was linked to the teaching of the holiness movement that influenced sections of the Church during the nineteenth century, and for Catherine resulted in a new release of God's power in her life. She held weekly 'holiness meetings' for their soldiers in order to encourage them to go on further with God, but met with criticism by some sections of the Church. When Catherine preached it was from the fullness of her heart and thousands responded to the gospel.

As the work expanded, the weight of the responsibility increased and Catherine sometimes saw little of her husband. On occasions she was at times fatigued and even depressed, but insisted in pressing on. At one period, someone was deputed to tug at her coat when she had preached for long enough, to help preserve her strength. In Bristol in February 1888, after she preached one of her last sermons and where eight hundred answered her call, it was first realised she had breast cancer. Despite the latest treatment available, the cancer spread.

When death came most of the family were able to gather at her bedside; they sang some of her favourite hymns and prayed. In the afternoon of 4th October 1890 her life ebbed away, her hand clasping that of her beloved William. The Mother of the Salvation Army, Mother of Nations, had gone home.

William Stead wrote of her: 'No woman before her exercised so direct an influence upon the religious life of her time... She and her husband built up out of recruits gathered in the highways and byways of the land what is to all intents and purposes a vast world-wide Church... The Salvation Army is a miracle of our time.'

SOCIETIES WITH CHRISTIAN ORIGINS

ORGANISA-TION	FOUNDER(S) AND DATE	ACTIVITY
PILGRIM HOMES	Committee led by James Bissett, 1807	* Accommodation and care for elderly evangelical Christians over 60 * 13 sheltered and/or full-time homes
RSPCA	Richard Martin, 1822	* Animal welfare
ROYAL HOSPITAL HOME, PUTNEY	Rev Andrew Reed, DD, 1843	* Medical, nursing and rehabilitation for people suffering from severe physical disability * Offshoot: British Home and Hospital, Streatham
YMCA	Sir George Williams 1844	* Housing and hostel accommodation for young people in context of Christian faith * Branches worldwide
BAND OF HOPE	Mrs Ann Jane Carlisle and Rev Jabez Tunnicliff 1846	* Preventative alcohol and drug education for children and young people
YWCA	Lady Mary Kinnaird and Emma Robart 1855	* Cares for homeless teenagers, ethnic groups and victims of violence * Youth and community projects * Branches in 80 countries
RED CROSS	Henri Dunant 1864	* Care of wounded prisoners in war time * Disaster relief
WILLIAM QUARRIER'S HOMES	William Quarrier 1864	* Child care in Scotland
JOHN GROOM'S ASSOCIATION	John Groom 1866	* Care of the disabled - residential care, employment, holidays
RNIB	Dr Thomas Armitage 1868	* Residential homes, education and training for the visually handicapped * Braille materials

SOCIETIES WITH CHRISTIAN ORIGINS continued

ORGANISATION	FOUNDER(S) AND DATE	ACTIVITY/RESPONSIBILITY/ FUNCTION
NATIONAL CHILDREN'S HOME	Dr Thomas Bowman Stephenson 1869	* Counselling and support for children and their families * Residential schools for handicapped youngsters * Support unit for young offenders
SANDES HOMES	Elise Sandes 1869	* Soldiers and Airmen's Centres for recreation and refreshment
MR FEGAN'S HOMES	J W C Fegan 1870	* Daycare facilities for children * Bed-sit accommodation for 16-18 year olds * Counselling services
ROYAL SAILORS' HOMES	Agnes Weston 1876	* Provides for the moral, social, and spiritual welfare of Navy personnel and their families.
THE CHILDREN'S SOCIETY (CHURCH OF ENGLAND)	Edward and Robert Rudolph 1881	* Care for the material, physical, mental and emotional needs of young people
MISSION TO DEEP SEA FISHERMEN	Sir Wilfred Grenfell 1881	* Ministry to spiritual, material, and physical needs of fishermen and their families
CHURCH ARMY	Rev Preb Wilson Carlile 1882	* Evangelism and social concern
NSPCC	Rev Benjamin Waugh 1884	* Child welfare

NINE

Great Preachers Of the Nineteenth And Twentieth Centuries

Preaching is the chief means ordained by God of communicating the message of the Bible. The Lord and his disciples proclaimed the gospel to whoever would listen, as did the apostle Paul, though the spread of the gospel has often been the result of the personal testimony given by ordinary believers.

In the early days of the Church, preaching was mostly in the open-air, but the onset of persecution in the Roman Empire made it a hazardous practice. When Christians were free to erect their own places of worship, it was often limited to the pulpit. Yet Christianity has spread to become a world-wide religion, mostly by missionaries and evangelists who moved outside the confines of a church building in order to reach the masses.

Since the Reformation there have been many fine men - and some women - who have earned for themselves a niche in history as a consequence of their preaching ministry. At times of spiritual decline, God raised up men who through the preaching of the Word restored a measure of health and strength to the Church and helped to keep the Faith vibrant. This was especially so during the nineteenth century, when the Church was challenged by the teaching of evolution and weakened by the onslaught of Higher Criticism from the German universities. It was only by a return to sound biblical doctrine that the Church recovered.

History has shown that wherever the Word of God is believed and proclaimed, albeit by the humblest of his servants, then people are drawn to listen and God responds by doing great things. One of the great names of this era was that of the popular preacher Charles Haddon Spurgeon. Thousands were attracted to listen to his sermons. He was a staunch defender of the evangelical Faith.

C. H. SPURGEON (1834-1892):
Pastor, Metropolitan Tabernacle

Spurgeon has been called 'the last of the Puritans'. The title is misleading, for the Puritans have had more recent heirs, but it expresses the conviction that Spurgeon belonged to an important tradition in English

Christianity. The Puritan movement, in effect a revolt within the Church of England, flourished for about a century until ended by the 1662 Act of Uniformity. This required all clergy to assent wholly to the *Book of Common Prayer*. But the spirit of the Puritans lived on; it recovered in the following century in the preaching of Whitefield and Wesley and the Evangelical Revival, and then found nineteenth century expression in the preaching of Spurgeon.

Spurgeon was steeped in the writings of the great Puritans and they shaped his theology. His preaching, like theirs, was based on the authority of Scripture and aimed to set forth the Saviour. It has been said of him that 'he had nothing to say if he could not speak of Jesus', and in his first sermon at the Metropolitan Tabernacle declared that 'the subject of the ministry of this house shall be the person of Jesus Christ, the only mediator between God and man'.

Formative Years

Born and raised in rural Essex, Spurgeon came from a line of solid, dissenting ancestors, and both his father and his grandfather were Independent ministers. Brought up during his formative years by his grandparents, he returned at the age of seven to his parents' home where his mother lovingly taught her children the Scriptures and prayed for them individually. For Charles she prayed, 'O that my son might live for thee'.

Her prayers were answered in 1849 when Charles was aged fifteen. Under the conviction of sin and anxious to know forgiveness, he found himself one Sunday morning in a Primitive Methodist Chapel in Colchester. The local preacher could hardly read the Bible and his sermon was simple and brief. But his text, 'Look unto me and be ye saved', spoke to Spurgeon's heart and he was converted.

Baptised in the River Lark in May 1850, he vowed to spend his life 'in the extension of Christ's cause, in whatsoever way he pleases'. He preached his first sermon at the age of sixteen before a small congregation of farm labourers and their wives in a thatched cottage in Teversham, and as a result was soon in demand.

Despite his lack of years, the villagers at the Waterbeach Baptist Chapel, near Cambridge, were impressed with Spurgeon, and invited him to become their pastor. Conversions followed and the membership swelled from forty to one hundred. Spurgeon habitually rose early each day for prayer and Bible reading. His knowledge of the Word of God increased, and he quickly grasped the fundamentals of the Faith. He considered pursuing a theological training, but the idea came to nothing.

After two years at Waterbeach his fame as a 'boy preacher' had spread to London, and he was invited to become the pastor at the New Park Street Baptist Church, Southwark. Aged nineteen, Spurgeon began his pastorate at the rundown church in March 1854 and remained there until his death some thirty-eight years later.

Conscious of his youth and inexperience, he prayed that 'these may not hinder my usefulness'. Modelling himself on his hero Whitefield, he soon became the most popular preacher in London and cabbies used to speak of taking their fares 'over the river to Charlie'. Numbers at the services swelled to fill the church, and it was soon necessary to extend the premises. For three months the church met at the Exeter Hall in the Strand where crowds of people went each Sunday, filling all 4,500 seats. Despite the extension, there was still not enough room.

The meetings were switched to the Music Hall in Surrey Gardens while the possibility of building a new church building was discussed. The first Sunday an estimated 22,000 people tried to gain entry, but there was seating for only 12,000 within the Hall. The occasion ended in tragedy when a hoax cry of 'Fire!' caused panic; seven people died and twenty-eight were seriously injured. Spurgeon, carried fainting from the pulpit, was taken to a friend's house in Croydon to recover. Although slandered by the press, he was able to resume his preaching within two weeks to even bigger crowds.

Metropolitan Tabernacle

Proposals to build a new church were agreed in 1858. At Spurgeon's request, its design was to be in the Grecian style, for 'Greek is the sacred tongue'. When the Metropolitan Tabernacle was opened in March 1861 it was the largest dissenting place of worship in the land, seating over 5,000 people. Sadly, it was considerably damaged by fire six years after Spurgeon's death, and had to be rebuilt yet again after its destruction during the Second World War.

During his ministry, attendance at services averaged over 5,000 and at first members were only admitted by ticket. There was no organ for many years, and a man with a tuning fork led the singing. For most, the highlight of the service was Spurgeon's sermon, which he delivered with a rich, deep voice, heard throughout the auditorium. Sometimes the occasion took a dramatic turn when, pacing up and down the rostrum, he acted out his words. His habit of waving his handkerchief irritated some, but he used it to illustrate a point.

Hundreds responded to the gospel in his early years and his future wife, Susannah Thompson, was among them. Membership of the church showed a healthy growth, from 232 in 1854 to 4,417 in 1875. By the time of Spurgeon's death the number had reached 5,307.

His sermons, which he prepared on Saturday evening and Sunday afternoon, were taken down each Sunday in shorthand, revised on Monday morning and published every Thursday. They were translated into several languages and even sold in Australia and America (though references to the anti-slavery movement were erased). The sermons were issued weekly until 1917, by which time sales totalled over 100 million copies.

Throughout his ministry Spurgeon proved to be a prolific writer. He edited a monthly magazine *Sword and Trowel*, wrote several books and commentaries, and produced sermon notes and lectures for students. He maintained his doctrinal position on Calvinism and consistently preached the doctrines of grace, which he stoutly defended to the end.

On two occasions he became involved in doctrinal controversy and was subject to attacks from churchmen for his outspoken views.

The first concerned the 'error of baptismal regeneration' which he attacked in 1864 during a sermon on Mark 16:15-16. Spurgeon called attention to the teaching of the *Book of Common Prayer* where it speaks of a child being made regenerate by baptism. He claimed that evangelical clergy in the Church of England who did not accept baptismal regeneration were being dishonest by remaining in the Church. 'Children,' he declared, 'were brought to Christ and not to the baptismal font.'

Another more serious issue, which threatened to split the Baptist Union, arose in 1887 and was known as the 'Down-grade controversy'. It came about as the result of Spurgeon's attack on the spread of modern biblical criticism among some Baptist ministers, churches and theological colleges. He claimed that the new liberal theology rejected the authority of the Scriptures, denied the deity of Christ and weakened the Calvinistic doctrines for which he felt the Baptist Union stood.

Many people wrote to Spurgeon urging him to do something about the situation, as there was no machinery whereby the Baptist Union could resolve the problem. He wrote articles in the *Sword and Trowel* defending the Puritan position and attacking the 'enemies of our faith'.

At the Baptist Union Assembly held at the City Temple, April 1888, a large majority approved what Spurgeon regarded as a vote of censure against him. Some observers considered the Union had condemned 'the greatest, noblest and grandest leader of the faith'. Although forsaken by many of his friends, a meeting of the Evangelical Alliance was called to support him and testify to the fundamental truths of the gospel. There was a suggestion at the time that another denomination should be founded, an idea Spurgeon rejected. But the Fellowship of Independent Evangelical Churches, formed in 1922 under E. J. Poole-Connor, attracted some who had left the Baptist Union with Spurgeon.

To further the work of the gospel, Spurgeon established the Pastors' College at Camberwell for students who could not gain entrance to other Baptist colleges, due to lack of qualifications. He made himself responsible for a weekly lecture there and later published his notes in *Lectures to My Students*. After his death it was renamed Spurgeon's College and relocated in South Norwood.

Orphanage

In 1866 a gift of £20,000 enabled him to found an orphanage at Stockwell, providing a home and education for five hundred homeless boys and girls. In the same year he formed the Colportage Association to give country people the opportunity to buy Christian books at low cost. In one year alone, the ninety-six colporteurs sold 23,000 Bibles.

C. H. SPURGEON

As a mark of their esteem, the members of the Tabernacle presented him with a testimony of over £6,000 after twenty-five years as pastor. With the money he bought a house and small estate off Beulah Hill, Upper Norwood, away from the smog and grime of the city. The house, called 'Westwood', had wonderful views over Surrey and he was so grateful to God for it that he spent his last years there, lovingly tending his rose garden.

Following the Down-grade controversy, Spurgeon's health continued to deteriorate and he was forced to spend some time recuperating in the south of France. He died at Mentone in January 1892 and his body was brought back to England for burial in West Norwood cemetery, close to that of the missionary Robert Moffat.

It is not without reason that Spurgeon was dubbed the 'Prince of Preachers'. Writing in 1898, a Free Church editor declared that his sermons 'will continue to be studied with growing interest and wonder, and will ultimately be accepted as incomparably the greatest contribution to the literature of experimental Christianity that has been made in this century'.

THOMAS CHALMERS (1780-1847):
Scottish Theologian and Philanthropist

One of the key tenets of Evangelical religion is the need for a new birth; the experience of repentance towards God and of faith in Christ's atoning death is crucial to becoming a Christian. When Thomas Chalmers experienced such a conversion he was already the minister of Kilmany Church, Fife, but his parish ministry was significantly transformed. He emerged as a powerful preacher of the gospel, with a renewed sense of responsibility towards his parishioners; it changed his attitudes and priorities, and strengthened his family relationships. And whereas without Christ he may well have remained in obscurity, he became the leading churchman in Scotland during the nineteenth century.

Chalmers entered the University of St. Andrews at the early age of twelve, following a rather indifferent performance at the parish school at Anstruther, Fife, the village where he was born. His first two sessions were spent mostly in sporting pursuits, but under the influence of Dr. James Brown, the assistant professor of mathematics, his latent intelligence was quickened by a mental 'awakening'; his literary tastes widened, he became keenly interested in ethics and politics, and he made great strides in the study of mathematics.

In 1795, intent on fulfilling a boyhood dream to become a minister, he enrolled as a Divinity student. Deeply stirred by the writings of Jonathan Edwards, he came to an intellectual grasp of the wonder of the Godhead, but was otherwise unmoved. Although licensed by special dispensation as a probationer in 1799, he maintained a consuming interest in mathematics and went to Edinburgh where he spent two sessions furthering his studies in mathematics and chemistry.

For some years, Chalmers managed to combine his two interests in mathematics and theology without any undue worry. In the winter of 1801-02 he accepted a position as Assistant in the Mathematics Department at St. Andrews, and about the same time was elected to the living at Kilmany, Fife, where his induction took place in May 1803.

As a teacher he aroused the enthusiasm of his students and 'secured in a singular manner the confidence and attachment of his pupils'. But he made an enemy of his professor who later dismissed him for 'inefficiency'. Chalmers returned to St. Andrews the following session and opened rival classes, and his success compelled recognition both of his ability and his sincerity. Although he discontinued them after two sessions, he had proved himself a force to be reckoned with.

At Kilmany, a short distance from St. Andrews, he discharged his

Sabbath duties as a minister, but spent a minimal amount of time in the parish. It took him an hour or two on Saturday evenings to prepare his sermons, then after the Sabbath 'enjoyed five days in the week of interrupted leisure'. One parishioner complained to him, 'I find you aye busy sir, with one thing and another, but, come when I may, I never find you at your studies for the Sabbath.'

Crisis

In the year 1809 Chalmers found himself facing a crisis. An older brother and sister both died within a short space of time, and they had drawn much comfort from their Christian faith. Suffering from a severe illness himself from which he did not expect to recover, he was forced to consider 'the magnitude of eternity'.

His mind was further focused by his reading Pascal's *Thoughts on Religion* and Wilberforce's *Practical View of Christianity*, which spoke of the depravity of man and the need for atonement. He experienced a new birth as unmistakable as his intellectual rebirth had been, and he gladly recognised God's claim to rule the affections of his heart and command his life's obedience.

News of the minister's conversion spread round the parish and people flocked to his Sunday services. Chalmers' preaching was transformed and he continually urged his congregation to accept God's gift of new life. Before long there was a religious awakening throughout the area as God's Spirit laid hold of the people. He began pastoral visits in earnest, started a branch of the Bible Society in the parish, with a subscription of a penny a week, and became a devoted student of the Scriptures.

In 1814 the living at Tron Church, Glasgow, fell vacant and the magistrates elected Chalmers to the position, though not without opposition. From his pleasant rural parish he turned his attention to the problems of a growing industrial city, where he was minister to some 11,000 parishioners. He not only established his name as a preacher, but further developed the role of the minister; whereas previously it had simply consisted of conducting Sunday and weekday services and administering innumerable charities, he took practical steps to deal with the problems of poverty and ignorance prevalent among his people.

Like Wesley before him, he made use of the laity; he revived the office of deacon and organised his elders to co-operate in the parish work. He commenced a programme of house to house visitation and, accompanied by a church elder, visited every house in the parish over a period of two years, although the visits were of necessity brief. Sabbath evening schools were started in each of the forty districts, and day schools were built for which he had the task of finding the teachers' salaries. When he tried to set up a project for supporting the poor by means of voluntary contributions, however, the scheme failed because of legal obstacles.

Chalmers' plea for twenty more city churches received a muted response from the magistrates, but they agreed to build St. John's Church - and then invited him to become the minister. Tempted by the promise of freedom to organise the church with minimal interference from the city authorities, he accepted the offer and began work in 1819, before the building was completed.

In his vision of a Christian Scotland, Chalmers believed that every congregation should serve the area in which it was situated, to bring the light of the gospel to bear on every aspect of life. As at Tron, he started Sabbath School work and, to cater for the many children unable to read, built a number of day schools which, by the time he left, catered for seven hundred pupils. Women were trained in housecraft and work was found for the unemployed. With the elders, he went out to meet the people of the parish, to help them with their spiritual and moral problems, while the deacons served the people's material needs.

He persuaded the magistrates to set aside the Poor Law for the parish, in order to try his method of dealing with pauperism. The plan involved receiving voluntary contributions from his congregation and distributing the money to the poor by his unpaid assistants. Each parish was divided into districts, with a deacon who investigated individual cases on the spot and made suitable provision. The scheme appeared to work - the better off were encouraged to give willingly and the poor received support when in need; costs were reduced and pauperism became a decreasing quantity. Under his ministry there was a revival of true religion, and many were won to Christ and gave themselves to Christian service.

The work in Glasgow made excessive demands upon Chalmers, and when in 1823 he received an invitation to return to St. Andrews as Professor of Moral Philosophy, he saw it as an opportunity of wider usefulness. His lectures, which always began with prayer, attracted many students who often greeted his eloquence with applause. In the town, he undertook more visitation, started a Sabbath evening school and associated himself with missionary work. At the end of his first session, he returned to St. John's and spent six weeks helping and encouraging in his former parish.

Foreign missions

Chalmers was a fervent supporter of foreign missions. When in 1812 Carey's printing house and paper stock at Serampore were destroyed, Chalmers was invited to preach the annual missionary sermon at Dundee, where the collection was towards Carey's work. In 1817 he organised a petition at Kilmany in support of Wilberforce's attempt to persuade Parliament to reject the East Indian Company's prohibition on missionary activity in India. The London Missionary Society invited him to preach their anniversary sermon in the capital on 14th May 1817, and at seven in the morning, the chapel was crowded to excess. At St. Andrews, he was associated with several societies and presided at the ordination of Alexander Duff, the first Church of Scotland missionary in India. He supported the Moravian missionaries and was responsible for raising £500 for their work; he was also concerned for Jewish missions, under the banner of the Church of Scotland and, later, the Free Church.

When the Chair of Theology fell vacant at Edinburgh, he was unanimously elected to fill the position; he accepted the offer and lectured there from 1828 to 1843. During this time, which proved to be one of the most momentous and harassing periods of the Church of Scotland's history, he continued his interest in the problem of poverty

DR. THOMAS CHALMERS

and advocated the right use of the parochial system. Under his leadership, a system of church-planting was begun to keep pace with the growing population, and resulted in the building of over two hundred new churches.

But in the 1830s there was a split in the Church of Scotland concerning the question of patronage. Under the Patronage Act of 1712, a landowner had the right to bring a minister to a parish, even though he might not be acceptable to the people. In 1834 the General Assembly passed the Veto Act, reasserting its right to reject unacceptable nominees. The dispute was brought to court where the Church lost its case, a judgement which was upheld by the House of Lords.

When, in May 1843, the government refused to give the Church its freedom, over 470 ministers, with over 400 elders and their congregations together with all the missionaries serving abroad, left to form the Free Church of Scotland. They surrendered all the buildings, cut themselves off from the state and looked only to God.

As Chalmers had been mostly responsible for influencing the direction of events that led up to The Disruption, and because of his standing in public esteem, he was called upon to be the first Moderator of the Free Church. He resigned his Chair at the University and devoted the remaining years of his life to setting the new Church on a firm foundation. Money had to be found for supporting the ministers and sites were needed for new church buildings; he was appointed Principal and Professor of Divinity at New College, the Free Church Theological Institute, with the task of preparing the Church's future pastors.

At the end of the college session in 1847 he visited London on Church business and returned home to prepare for the General Assembly the following Monday. He retired to bed, saying, 'I expect to give worship tomorrow morning,' but died during the night.

Chalmers had great academic gifts and was a powerful orator, but will probably best be remembered for his parish concept, that it was the duty of every local church to serve the people around it. Under his guidance, the love of God was translated into practical terms that bore an impressive witness to the working people of Glasgow. 'I long to see the day,' he wrote, 'when every parish shall have a Christian society - when not a district shall be left uncultivated, but shall yield a produce to the cause of the Saviour.'

The Church in Scotland
In the Middle Ages the Church of Scotland was under Roman domination and resisted attempts by Canterbury to influence it. Following Knox's return to Scotland in 1559 a Reformed Church of Scotland was established on Presbyterian lines, with authority entrusted to elders rather than bishops. During the seventeenth century attempts by the Stuart kings to make the Kirk episcopal failed, until 1660, when the 'Drunken Parliament' in Edinburgh gave in to the wishes of Charles II. At the Revolution Settlement of 1689-90, the Presbyterian Church was re-established and the sovereign obliged to recognise it. The Westminster Confession of Faith was accepted as expressing the creed of the Scottish Church. After the Disruption, a number of unions took place, including, in 1900, that of the United Free Church and the Free Church of Scotland to form the United Free Church, which in 1929 rejoined the Church of Scotland, with the exception of some congregations.

D. L. MOODY (1837-1899): American Evangelist

Dwight Lyman Moody, more than any other, can be said to be the founder of the modern mass evangelism movement. While Whitefield and Wesley before him had attracted large crowds, it was Moody who pioneered evangelistic campaigns with a planned itinerary and funding, had meetings booked at specific venues, arranged publicity, introduced the inquiry room and, with Sankey, broke new ground in the use of religious songs.

The Moody family lived in the farming community of Northfield, Massachusetts, and were left to struggle as best they could after their father died of too much whisky. Their determined mother, a Unitarian by religion, sent her children to school, but the need to earn money often kept young Dwight at home. Such was his lack of education that throughout the rest of his life he was never able to spell properly and sometimes felt ill-at-ease in the company of educated people.

At the age of seventeen he left home and persuaded his uncle to give him a job in his Boston shoe shop. The following year, during revival meetings at the Congregational Church, his Sunday School teacher visited the shoe shop and urged Moody to come to Christ, which he did. The decision was immediate and real, and Moody was a new man. In 1856 he moved to Chicago with an ambition to become rich. He found work as a travelling salesman, joined Plymouth Church and immersed himself in evangelism, often filling the front pews with men he had pulled in from the streets.

Keen to reach children for Christ, he became a Sunday School teacher at the Wells Street Mission and on his first morning rounded up eighteen slum boys from the streets. Though the meetings were frequently noisy, the children enjoyed the talks and the singing, but were specially captivated by Moody's compassion, good humour and winning ways. As the numbers grew to around six hundred, Moody gave up his job to devote himself to full-time evangelism.

He started week-night meetings for both children and adults, and during the day worked as a missionary for the newly-formed YMCA. Eager to win souls for Christ, he became known in Chicago as 'Crazy Moody'. During the years of the Civil War (1861-65) the scope of his ministry widened still further. His Sunday School developed into an Independent Church, on Illinois Street, and as a YMCA worker he held preaching services for the troops at Camp David; later he ministered at the battlefront to the wounded on both sides, as well as to the freed slaves.

In 1862 he took time off to get married to English-born Emma Revell, whom he considered to be a cut above himself; throughout all their life together they were 'so perfectly one... completely wrapped up in each other'. Mrs. Moody often accompanied her husband on his tours, but their first trip to England was taken on doctor's orders. Emma had developed asthma and was advised to take a long sea voyage, so the Moodys took the opportunity to visit the 'Old Country'.

There were a few speaking engagements, mostly in Brethren halls, but the visit had more far-reaching consequences than Moody could have expected, through meeting Harry Moorhouse, a converted pickpocket from Lancashire.

The following year, Moorhouse turned up at the Moody home in Chicago and offered to preach at Illinois Street Church. As Moody had to be away, he reluctantly agreed for him to speak at a mid-week meeting. The church was highly impressed with Moorhouse, as his message was different to that preached by the pastor; whereas Moody declared that God hated the sinner as well as the sin, Moorhouse preached from John 3:16 that God loves sinners.

When Moody returned, his prejudice was shattered; the character of his message had to be revised, and he even learned from Moorhouse how to read and study the Bible. Later that year at a Convention, he told his listeners how they had to 'conquer by love; for if a man has his heart full of love and a little common sense, he will succeed'.

In October 1871 a great fire destroyed much of the city of Chicago, including the Moody's home, the church and the new YMCA building. But Moody saw the hand of God for him in this terrible tragedy, and he felt led to give up the Mission and undertake a much wider ministry.

Feeling dried up inside and lacking in power, he prayed for some weeks that God would 'baptise him in the Spirit'. His prayer was answered one day when he was walking down a street in New York; as in his heart he surrendered to God, he was overpowered by the Spirit and from that moment his life took a completely different turn.

Return to England

In order to have some time for rest and study, Moody paid a return visit to England in the summer of 1871. He accepted invitations to preach at a couple of churches in London, with startling results; after a week's meetings one of the churches received four hundred new converts into membership.

Impressed by his ministry, three prominent Christians quite independently suggested he should return for a preaching tour and they would help with expenses. In Dublin, Henry Varley told him, 'The world has yet to see what God will do with a man fully consecrated to him.' Moody felt challenged by Varley's words, and determined that he would allow God to use him. Already he had persuaded a gifted singer called Ira Sankey to join him and lead the singing at his Chicago church. The two of them came to England in 1873, assuming that preparations were in hand for a campaign; but as Moody had not formally replied to the invitations, nothing had been arranged.

Plans were hurriedly drawn up for meetings at York, where Moody had contact with the YMCA secretary. The local clergy were suspicious of the two Americans, but with Moody's informal preaching and Sankey's rousing songs there were many conversions. A starchy young minister, F B Meyer, was especially astonished by the pair and his ministry was transformed by what he learned from them.

D L MOODY

After York they visited Sunderland and then Newcastle, where they met a Free Church of Scotland minister who invited them to Edinburgh. Moody was rather apprehensive about the idea but decided to take the risk. Six weeks of meetings were arranged and crowds of people came to hear them.

Aware of the strong Calvinistic doctrines held north of the border, Moody preached that God desired that all men should be saved, and he expected results. At the end of each meeting, he invited any who wanted their lives to be changed by the power of God to move into the 'inquiry room', where a 'personal worker' would give further counsel. Many left their seats to give themselves to Christ, and wealthy young men abandoned their careers and comforts to become missionaries or to work in the slums of London's East End.

Fame

The two Americans shot to fame as revival spread out from Edinburgh to Dundee, Glasgow and the north of Scotland. Invitations to Ireland and other parts of England soon followed, culminating in a triumphal visit to London. Despite opposition and criticism from churchmen, the meetings in Islington's Agricultural Hall were crowded. Moody later

---

Sankey

Ira D. Sankey (1840-1908), a Methodist church choirmaster with a fine voice, was invited by Moody in 1870 to join him in Chicago. In 1873-75 the two of them toured Britain where Sankey's new, rousing gospel songs were a great success. A sixteen page pamphlet of *Sacred Songs and Solos* was published in September 1873 at sixpence a copy, and an enlarged edition appeared 1st January 1875. Royalties for the first six months' sales totalled £5,600 and were given to complete the building of Moody's Chicago church. Because of copyright, *Sacred Songs* could not be published in America and was replaced by *Gospel Songs*; they sold 50-80 million copies in fifty years. Later, a Trust was set up into which the royalties were paid to fund Mount Hermon School and other projects; the two men relinquished a great fortune. For a brief period, in 1879, Sankey parted with Moody, but his visit to England was not a success and their partnership was resumed. By the 90s, Sankey's voice was wearing out and he went blind, but he survived his partner by nine years.

---

moved into the East End; then, at the suggestion of Lord Shaftesbury, to the Queen's Opera House in the Haymarket. As a result, both poor and rich alike were able to hear the gospel. The meetings at the Opera House were particularly successful and many wealthy and influential people were converted.

Moody's informal, anecdotal style of preaching proved a breath of fresh air to churchgoers in England, and Sankey's 'human hymns', which sometimes presented the gospel in a story-telling format, had great appeal. The English Church benefited not only by increased membership, but by the added impetus given to a variety of social concerns encouraged by Moody's support and advice.

In America, Moody and Sankey undertook a number of evangelistic campaigns between 1864 and 1881, focusing their efforts on great cities such as New York, Philadelphia and Boston. Following his tour of England, Moody's preaching had matured and he was more polished; wherever he spoke, the fires of revival began to blaze and he became a national hero. He set up his home base back at Northfield, his birthplace, and it became the centre of his ministry.

In 1879 he opened a school for girls from poor families, and two years later the Mount Hermon School for boys, both of which were funded by the royalties from Sankey's *Sacred Songs and Solos*. An annual Northfield conference was also established where 'all the hungry Christians' could meet to wait upon God.

A second Moody and Sankey tour of England in 1881-84 was less spectacular, but still of note. While London was again taken by storm, it was the meetings at Cambridge University that proved to have far-reaching consequences.

Despite an almost disastrous opening to the week, the mood changed and on the last night two hundred students stood to acknowledge that 'they had received a blessing'. As a result of these meetings the 'Cambridge Seven', a group of university undergraduates, caused a stir throughout the nation when they volunteered for missionary work in China.

Back in America, a student conference at Northfield in 1886 was greatly moved by this news. One hundred students signed a declaration of willingness to serve overseas as missionaries; their motto was 'The evangelisation of the world in this generation'. This Student Volunteer Movement spread across America and to Europe; in England it led to the founding of the Student Christian Movement and later the Inter-Varsity Fellowship. Two other institutions founded by Moody were the Moody Bible Institute in Chicago (1886) and the Moody Press (1895), which started out as a mobile Gospel wagon selling paperbacks.

Moody's later years were taken up by further tours of America and a visit to England; but the pressures of his work and his problem of overweight led to a heart ailment. He was taken ill in Kansas and died back at Northfield at the age of sixty-two.

His contribution to English Christianity was not only the large numbers of conversions he won; he was also the inspiration behind many individuals and organisations whose ministry counted for God in succeeding generations.

SMITH WIGGLESWORTH (1859-1946)
Preaching and Healing Ministry

Towards the end of the nineteenth century a movement developed within Christianity that was to have an increasingly profound effect upon Christians, the implications of which are still being felt today. The movement, originally known as Pentecostalism, placed an emphasis on the 'fullness (or baptism) of the Holy Spirit', teaching that the apostles' experience on the Day of Pentecost, neglected for many centuries, should be the right of every believing Christian.

Sometimes referred to as a second blessing, Spirit-baptism recovered the gifts of the Spirit, especially those of speaking in tongues and healing. It generated opposition from some of the older denominations, but also brought a breath of new life to the Church and led to the formation of many new church fellowships.

It is generally acknowledged that Pentecostalism began with the Azusa Street revival in Los Angeles, in 1906, but the teaching was not unknown in England. In the eighteenth century John Wesley experienced the Holy Spirit when his 'heart was strangely warmed' and what happened became an essential element in his message. Later, the Booths and C T Studd began to experience the gifts of the Spirit in their ministry and to encourage other Christians to seek them for themselves.

For half a century the Holy Spirit movement was largely confined to the Pentecostal group of churches. Then in the 1950s Christians from other denominations began to experience a baptism of the Holy Spirit for themselves. This neo-Pentecostal, or charismatic, movement brought about widespread renewal, influencing Roman Catholic and Protestant groups alike. There has been a reappearance of the miraculous powers experienced in the early Church, and believers have discovered a deeper love and joy than they had previously known.

One of the new Pentecostal churches was the Assemblies of God, now the largest Pentecostal denomination in Britain. It was founded in 1924 following a series of meetings at All Saints Parish Church, Monkwearmouth, Sunderland, under the leadership of the Rev Alexander Boddy. Today, there are over six hundred ministers and nearly as many churches, with missionaries around the world sent out from local assemblies.

One of the most powerful exponents of Spirit-baptism was Smith Wigglesworth, an evangelist associated with the Assemblies of God, whose world-wide ministry knew no denominational boundaries. When people learned of the wonderful conversions and healings that accompanied his preaching, he received countless invitations to minister in churches of many kinds. Although he had long known the power of God upon him, it was not until after his 'Pentecostal baptism' that he went on into a new phase of ministry.

Only Believe

Wigglesworth was born into a working class family in Yorkshire at the time of the 1859 Ulster revival. His parents were good-living people but were not Christians, and it seems that the greatest religious influence in his impressionable years was his grandmother, a Wesleyan Methodist. As a young boy he often accompanied her to meetings and it was at one of those, at the age of eight, that he first realised that Jesus had died for his sins. 'I saw that God wants us so badly that he has made the condition as simple as he possibly could - "Only believe".'

From that day he became a soul-winner, and the first person he won for Christ was his mother. His father had no religious inclinations, but sent their four children to the local Anglican church where Smith was confirmed at the age of ten. When the bishop laid his hands on him, he was 'filled with the consciousness of God's presence', an experience he never forgot.

When Smith was thirteen the family moved to Bradford and he began to move deeper into the spiritual life; his zeal to bring people to Christ increased and he often tried to share the gospel with other boys of his age. He linked up with the recently-formed Christian Mission, later known as the Salvation Army, because he felt they had great power and were concerned for the unsaved. After a spell in Liverpool, he returned to Bradford where he set up in business as a plumber.

At the age of twenty-three he married a Salvation Army officer, Polly Featherstone, who had to resign her commission. Together they opened a mission in a part of Bradford where there was no Christian witness. A keen evangelist like her husband, and a popular preacher, Polly preached while Smith stood at the penitent form to lead souls to Christ.

One severe winter, Smith was in so much demand as a plumber that while his business prospered his love for the Lord grew cold; he was restored by the prayers and quiet faithfulness of his wife. Their mission work recovered and they were forced to move into larger premises in Bowland Street. It was at this point that the Wigglesworths discovered the possibilities of 'divine healing'. When Polly was ill, Smith took her to a healing meeting in Leeds. After she was restored, Smith also was completely healed of haemorrhoids, a complaint from which he had suffered for some years. They determined from then onwards they would no longer make use of either medicines or doctors.

The decision, however, was soon to be tested, when Smith was gripped with severe pains at a meeting and had to be brought home. Believing that it was his home-call, he told Polly to call the doctor, as they had agreed, in order to avoid having to hold an inquest.

The doctor informed them that he was suffering from a severe case of appendicitis and there was no hope of recovery. But when a believing woman and young man came to see him, they felt it was of the devil; they laid hands on Smith and cried, 'Come out devil, in the name of Jesus!' Smith was immediately relieved of the pain, went downstairs and told his wife, 'I am healed.' He learned that there was a call for a plumbing job and went off to work.

Speaking in Tongues

For over twenty years the two of them ministered in Bradford, preaching in the open-air and at the mission, and praying for the sick. But when Smith heard that in Sunderland people were being baptised in the Spirit and speaking in tongues, he felt that he needed to have these gifts for himself. After four days of meetings at an Anglican church in Monkwearmouth, as he was about to return home, he received 'the real baptism of the Holy Spirit as they received on the Day of Pentecost'.

It proved to be the turning point of his ministry and from then on he endeavoured to live and walk even more closely in the Spirit than before. Soon afterwards his wife had a similar experience, and before long they were receiving invitations from all over the country to speak to groups and individuals.

As a result of the demands now being made upon him, he gave up his business and began to live 'by faith'. He laid down a condition before God that he would never appear 'down at heel' or wear trousers with the knees out! His faith was rewarded and he was always able to present himself smartly dressed, a matter he felt important when presenting the gospel.

Wigglesworth began to experience greater liberty in his preaching and his reputation as an evangelist soared. He took every opportunity he could to point people to Christ; even the informal moments of everyday life were to him God-given openings, such as walking in the park or travelling on a train. But he was equally at home when speaking to large crowds, where his preaching technique was quite unique. He would invariably take off his coat and preach in his shirt sleeves, and even critical audiences would soon be enthralled by his message.

Faith in God

His main theme was the need for faith in God. He taught that a definite faith brought definite results, and urged his listeners, 'Ask for what you want; believe, receive from God, and thank God for it.' His gift of healing greatly increased his reputation and thousands came to his meetings for this reason alone. He had a great compassion for the sick and as he prayed for them would 'burn with a holy anger'.

Over the years he saw the lame walk, the deaf hear and the blind see; demons were cast out, cancers cured and the dead raised. Some of his methods were controversial, but his object was to set forth the power of God. He often sent handkerchiefs to the sick and there were reports of numerous healings. After praying for anyone who was lame, he would tell them to drop their sticks and walk or even run round the hall.

After his wife's death in 1913, Wigglesworth began to travel more widely, and without any organisation behind him held missions in many parts of the world. Each time he would arrive unannounced, and before long his preaching attracted attention and tours were hastily arranged. In this way he visited all five continents and saw thousands converted or healed.

In times of personal illness he constantly refused the aid of a doctor,  even when at the age of seventy-two he suffered from gall-stones; as always he relied solely on prayer. In this instance he was in much pain over a number of months, before the stones finally passed through his system. He maintained good health and vigour - and a full set of teeth - until his death at the age of eighty-seven.

Once described as 'God's gentleman', Wigglesworth not only took pride in his appearance, but was also known to be courteous, un-

SMITH WIGGLESWORTH

selfish and generous, and wherever he went was said to be 'an aroma of the presence of God'. At his funeral, Joseph Smith, Dean of the Elim Bible College, said, 'We often hear the remark "he's gone", but in this case he has arrived. Brother Wigglesworth was not an ordinary man, and it was his faith in God that made him so.'

DR. MARTYN LLOYD-JONES (1899-1981):
Westminster Chapel, London

The term 'Evangelical' is used to describe those Protestant Christians who base their doctrines pre-eminently on the New Testament and who emphasise the need for salvation through faith in the atoning death of Jesus. The use of the term achieved popularity in the eighteenth century when revival spread through many of the Protestant churches, and has continued to be used to denote Christians who maintain the fundamental truths of the Bible.

Evangelicals

The revival touched not only the Nonconformist churches but the Anglican Church as well, where the term 'evangelical' was first applied. Whereas previously it had been used by Bishop Berkeley to describe an inward and spiritual religion (as opposed to one of hypocrisy and superstition), by the end of the century it was widely employed of a number of key figures within the Anglican Church who constituted the 'Evangelical Party'. Among the leaders were such men as Wilberforce and the members of the Clapham Sect, Samuel Walker of Truro, Henry Venn of Huddersfield and John Newton of Olney.

Yet there were believers from other denominations who were of the same persuasion and the term 'Evangelical' was later applied to them as well. Though Evangelicals differed on certain points of doctrine and in some of their practices, Nonconformists and Anglicans alike were united in their efforts to further the cause of the gospel.

Although Evangelicalism's key emphasis was a spiritual one, converts often began to engage in charitable enterprises, as well as to share their faith with others. As a result, the nineteenth century proved to be a golden era; it was the age of the modern missionary movement and of the great Christian societies, covering a remarkable range of philanthropic and social concerns, and the growth of Christian literature.

Since the evangelical beginnings, whole generations of Christians have enjoyed a continuity of the great truths expounded by preachers such as Charles Simeon of Cambridge and C H Spurgeon of the Metropolitan Tabernacle.

In recent years a leading exponent of the evangelical faith was Dr. Martyn Lloyd-Jones of Westminster Chapel, London, a preacher of Calvinistic-Methodist background and a 'latter-day Puritan'. His pastorate at the Chapel, where he succeeded Dr. Campbell Morgan, lasted for twenty-nine years, but his influence spread far beyond the bounds of his pulpit.

Interest in People

Martyn Lloyd-Jones qualified in medicine at St. Bartholomew's Hospital, London, under the leading physician of the day, Sir Thomas (later Lord) Horder, the royal physician. It was his training at Barts that laid the foundation of his preaching technique and pastoral work, and he believed it was God's preparation for the ministry.

Horder ingrained into his students the Socratic method of diagnosis - to collect the facts and then reason through them until they reached a correct conclusion. It was this approach that Lloyd-Jones used in his preaching, or when dealing with people's spiritual problems and giving advice to ministers.

In 1922 he was appointed as the chief clinical assistant to Horder and the prospect of a lucrative career in Harley Street seemed assured. But he realised that he was more interested in people than in their physical diseases, and when he was called to the ministry, though he had to wrestle with the decision for eighteen months, he finally knew he had to accept.

At the age of twenty-seven, without any formal theological training, he became pastor of the Bethlehem Forward Movement Mission Church in Sandfields, close by the docks of Port Talbot in his native Wales.

From the beginning, Lloyd-Jones was determined to win people to Christ through preaching the gospel and not attempt to attract them by social activities. He believed that working-class people were just as capable as anyone else of listening to a reasoned sermon, and he adopted his distinctive 'medical approach' whereby he appealed to his listeners to think through the reasonableness of Christianity.

Though he made no appeals for converts, many were won to Christ under his preaching. Seventy were converted at the Mission in 1929, and one hundred and twenty-eight in 1930. During his twelve years at Sandfields the membership grew from ninety-three to five hundred and thirty, and attendances at the Sunday services reached about eight hundred and fifty.

In 1935 he began an association with the Inter-Varsity Fellowship (now the UCCF) which was to last for the rest of his life. Though reluctant at first to address its annual conference, he finally agreed and in 1939 became its president. During those years he gave the IVF a new image. By providing a solid doctrinal basis of Scripture, he weaned the students away from a sporty, anti-intellectual type of Christianity, and with his emphasis on the mind encouraged them to think about their faith. He also taught the students how to relate their faith to the subjects they studied, and suggested that they enter all the mainstream professions and not just the traditional callings of medicine or full-time Christian work.

As president of IVF he influenced the setting up in 1939 of the International Fellowship of Evangelical Students, an umbrella organisation for bringing together student Christian groups from many different national and denominational backgrounds. From 1947 to 1959 he acted as chairman and was asked by the IFES to draw up their basis of faith and action, which many of his friends acknowledged as one of his greatest achievements. The statement also included a declaration of the evangelical view of 'the true Church', an issue later to cause much controversy.

The Doctor

But for most people Martyn Lloyd-Jones is remembered as the minister of Westminster Chapel where he was affectionately known as 'the Doctor'. He became joint minister with Campbell Morgan in 1939, and then took complete responsibility for the Chapel in 1943 when his colleague retired. During the war the chapel was damaged and the congregation sorely depleted. After 1945 the situation began to normalise, and congregations soon began to average 1,500 on a Sunday morning and over 2,000 in the evening.

His preaching was based solely on Scripture and on a systematic study of the biblical text; he stimulated the minds of his listeners, but also strove to satisfy their spiritual needs. His sermons contained no jokes or anecdotes - although he was said to have an enormous sense of humour - but they were always relevant and up-to-date. He preached a pastoral sermon on Sunday mornings and an evangelistic one in the evenings. No appeal was made for decisions, though a note in the pews invited anyone in need of spiritual help to meet him in the vestry - which they did, week after week. For many years he conducted a Bible study each Friday evening when he preached through *Ro-*

DR. MARTYN LLOYD-JONES

mans and *Ephesians*, verse by verse, to hundreds of city workers and people from the suburbs.

There were two other involvements that gave the Doctor great satisfaction while at the Chapel. One was a ministers' fraternal where, as chairman, he became the pastors' pastor. The other was the Puritan Conference where every year he delivered the final paper. His feeling was that believers should never forget their Protestant doctrinal foundations, and he stressed that Christians should know Church history.

The Doctor disappointed many Christians by his refusal to take part in Billy Graham's evangelistic crusades, and was the only minister of a major London church to decline; he also decided not to participate in the 1966 Berlin World Congress on Evangelism. The reason was his unhappiness at organised campaigns and also the system of inviting people to 'get up out of their seats'. What was more essential, he argued, was a revival, a visitation of the Holy Spirit. He suggested that campaigns did little to improve the spiritual condition of the Church; to him, this approach relied ultimately on techniques rather than the power of the Spirit.

From 1966 the Doctor was involved in a controversy that reverberated throughout the evangelical world. In an address to the National Evangelical Assembly he declared his new position on the doctrine of the true Church. He had become alarmed at the in-roads being made by such movements as the World Council of Churches and felt obliged to sound a note of warning to his fellow Evangelicals.

He argued that loyal Evangelicals could not continue to belong to denominations which denied the basic tenets of the evangelical faith. They should face up to the issues raised by the biblical doctrine of the Church rather than being 'more concerned to maintain the integrity of their denominations'. When later he removed Westminster Chapel from the newly-formed United Reformed Church, he was followed by many other evangelicals into the Fellowship of Independent Evangelical Churches, though very few Anglicans responded.

Ill-health forced the Doctor to retire from Westminster Chapel in 1968 and he spent the remainder of his life publishing his books and travelling to small churches in order to bring them encouragement. The day before he died, he stopped his treatment and cancelled his newspapers. 'Don't try to hold me back from the glory,' he told his family, and on St. David's Day he died peacefully in his sleep.

Martyn Lloyd-Jones' grandson and biographer, Christopher Catherwood, claims that the Doctor cannot really be understood in human terms apart from his Welshness, his Calvinistic-Methodist background plus a rare combination of great intellect and fiery emotion, which gave his sermons a wide appeal. Certainly he did more than anyone to restore to evangelism the art of systematic, expository preaching and he explained Puritan, Reformed doctrine to twentieth century Christians in a language they could understand.

BILLY GRAHAM (born 1918):
Evangelist and Christian Statesman

Protestantism in both Britain and America flourished during the nineteenth century and the 1859 revival inspired a remarkable variety of philanthropic and social causes. Yet at the same time seeds of religious scepticism were being sown by writers such as Charles Darwin and John Stuart Mill, while the German theologians' new critical approach to the Bible began to unsettle even the ordinary churchgoer.

The spread of liberalism continued into the twentieth century. Theologians such as Karl Barth and Emil Brunner appeared to be leading the Church back to the Bible, but their views were far from orthodox. Much traditional Christian teaching was held up for questioning; evangelicals especially were alarmed by the 'God is dead' heresy and by Bishop John Robinson's book *Honest to God* which rejected the notion of a God 'up there'.

Despite these assaults, evangelical Christians responded to the challenge. In 1928 the Inter-Varsity Fellowship of Evangelical Unions was founded as a rallying point in the universities, and a further impetus was given to the movement when in 1939 the International Fellowship of Evangelical Students was set up under the leadership of Dr. Lloyd-Jones. From the early 1940s a biblically-based theological movement arose aiming to restore the Bible to its rightful position as the Word of God and encourage the growth of a more orthodox faith.

Without doubt the most outstanding leader to emerge during the post-war years was the American evangelist, Billy Graham. Acclaimed not only as the greatest evangelist since D L Moody, he has also become the movement's recognised ambassador, and is acknowledged as a Christian statesman of international repute. His stand on the authority of the Word of God has won thousands of people to Christ and has helped re-establish evangelism to its rightful place in Christian thought and teaching.

Street Preacher

Billy Graham was a country lad, raised on the family farm near Charlotte, North Carolina; he cleared out the cow stalls, forked manure, pitched hay and was taught how to milk and herd. Both his mother and father were descended from Scottish pioneers of Presbyterian persuasion, and Billy Frank, as the family called him, was brought up to be a regular churchgoer. He was converted to Christ at the age of sixteen during a crusade in Charlotte led by a white-haired evangelist, Mordecai Fowler Ham.

Following a short period of study in a strictly-run Bible school, Billy moved to the Florida Bible Institute, Tampa, where he had his first experience of street preaching. Persuaded that this was his vocation, he was ordained a Baptist minister at the early age of twenty-one then entered Wheaton College, Chicago, where in 1943 he graduated in anthropology. That same year he married Ruth Bell, the daughter of a Presbyterian missionary surgeon in China, who was a year ahead of him at college.

For two years he pastored a small Baptist church on the outskirts of Chicago, where he gained a reputation as a 'preaching windmill'. It was here that he received his first break, when Pastor Torrey Johnson, a professor at the Northern Baptist Seminary, invited the young preacher to take over his Sunday evening radio programme, *Songs in the Night*. In 1945 Johnson founded Youth for Christ with an emphasis on bright Saturday night rallies, appointing Billy as its full-time evangelist.

After touring America, Billy made a brief trip to England and Europe in 1946. He stirred up enough interest for him to be asked to return, and in the winter of 1946-47 he and Cliff Barrows visited twenty-one British cities and held three hundred and sixty meetings.

Back home, the idea of an evangelistic team began to take shape, and Billy invited Cliff Barrows, Grady Wilson (who was converted at the same crusade as Billy) and a singer called Bev Shea, with whom he had worked in Chicago, to join him on a series of city-wide campaigns. Though the meetings were not a success (two were virtually a 'flop') the team stayed together and sorted out the reasons for their failure.

The turning point in Billy's ministry came at a Los Angeles tent campaign in 1949. The men had thought through some of their failures and Billy had come through a spiritual crisis from which he was able to preach with renewed vigour and authority. The campaign was scheduled to run for three weeks, but public response persuaded them to extend their stay to eight. The sensational conversions of Stuart Hamblen, a top radio personality, and Jim Vaus, who worked for gangster Micky Cohen, brought Billy wide media coverage and propelled him to instant fame.

New Image
Now in demand in other parts of the States, Billy realised the need to create a new image for mass evangelism and to place his organisation on a proper footing. In 1950 he formed the Billy Graham Evangelistic Association, later setting up his headquarters at Minneapolis. He brought

in two new team members and decided they should all receive a fixed salary rather than depend on the unsatisfactory method of taking up a love-offering. He adopted the terms 'crusade' instead of campaign, and 'counsellor' rather than personal worker; he also decided never to work in a city without first having an invitation from a majority of local church representatives.

A key development was the new way of following up enquirers at his crusades. He realised that mass evangelism could become little more

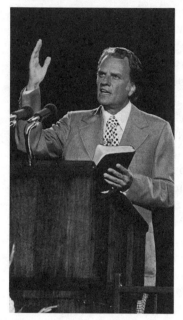

BILLY GRAHAM

than a wave of religious emotion, and that giving new converts a better start to their Christian life needed more thought. He persuaded Dawson Trottman of the Navigators to draw up an improved scheme of support that could replace the 'five hints' normally given to enquirers. In future, counsellors were to be specially chosen and trained and an effort would be made to link new believers with a local church.

Two crusades held around this time were important for other developments. At the Washington Crusade in 1952, where a unique closing service was held on the steps of the Capitol, Billy won the high regard of a number of influential political leaders, including two future presidents Richard Nixon and Lyndon Johnson. Billy appreciated the value of Christian leaders and encouraged men like Presidents Eisenhower and Kennedy to do all they could to call Americans back to God.

The following year, in Tennessee, he gained a significant victory when he insisted on holding his first racially integrated crusade, more than one year before the famous 1954 Supreme Court decision which banned segregation in state schools anywhere in the USA.

Still in his mid-thirties, Billy was established as America's leading evangelist and was now able to develop other avenues of media outreach. His radio programme *Hour of Decision* was successfully launched, he started a weekly *My Answer* column in a daily newspaper, published his best selling book *Peace with God* and went into film evangelism with *Mr. Texas* and *Oiltown USA*.

In March 1954, at the invitation of the Evangelical Alliance, Billy began a three-month crusade at the out-door Harringay arena, London. The churches, suspicious of Americans, were hesitant in their support and the Press was highly antagonistic. Before long, however, both the Press and the public warmed to this honest, down-to-earth preacher, and they were won over.

Further British crusades were held in 1955 when he visited Scotland, London (Wembley) and Cambridge University. In London he met the Queen Mother and Princess Margaret, and was invited to preach before the Queen at Windsor Castle. Since then he has held crusades in Manchester (1961), Earls Court, London (1966), Sheffield (1973) and in five regional areas during Mission England (1984). His appearance at Mission '89 in England followed an invitation signed by over five hundred church and civic leaders. The meetings were held at three centres in the capital, and those from Earls Court were relayed live by satellite to fifty-one centres in Britain as well as to thirty countries on the continent of Africa. A similar mission was held in Scotland in 1991, when he preached in Glasgow and Aberdeen.

Global Mission
From 1959 onwards Billy had begun to travel more widely: Australia and New Zealand (1959), Africa (1960), Japan and India (1966), Singapore (1968), Brazil (1974) and the Far East (1975). His first ever visit to a Communist country was to Yugoslavia in 1966, then later to Hungary (1977), Poland (1978) where he was invited to preach in a Roman Catholic cathedral, and to East Germany and Czechoslovakia (1982). For many Christians, his 1982 attendance at a Moscow inter-faith conference on the 'Nuclear Catastrophe' was a serious error, for which he was severely criticised.

To further promote the cause of evangelism, he initiated the World Conference on Evangelism in Berlin (1966) and conceived the idea that led to the Lausanne Conference (1974) which drew together a large number of world Christian leaders to discuss the issues of evangelism and social concern. In addition, he convened the 1983 Amsterdam Conference for 4,000 itinerant evangelists, mostly from Third World countries, in order to encourage them.

Billy admits that he has made mistakes, but has learned to admit them and apologise when wrong. He has been criticised for his readiness to share his platform with men who did not hold to fundamentalist views, while others have accused him of failing to preach a social gospel.

Although he has received several invitations to enter politics where, with his incisive mind and good looks, he could easily have made his mark, he chose to remain faithful to his calling. As a result, the Christian Faith has been made credible to millions of people, many of whom have gone on to become full-time workers or to take up other positions of responsibility.

The significance of his work is summed up in a comment he wrote in 1959: 'The result of these crusades is not in the changing of a city's life, but in the individuals whose lives are permanently changed, the many churches which are revived and ministers who received a new vision.'

LUIS PALAU (born 1934): Argentinian Evangelist

Throughout the history of Christianity several movements have arisen attempting to return to the doctrines and practices of the early Church. In the second quarter of the nineteenth century, with many of the mainstream churches considered spiritually dead and the Evangelical Revival on the wane, one such attempt was the emergence in 1827 of the Christian (Plymouth) Brethren. The leaders of the movement were mainly evangelical Anglicans who held to strong Calvinistic doctrines, and wanted a return to a simple form of Christian worship and communion. Between 1830 and 1835 the movement spread and meetings were formed in England and Ireland, centred on Plymouth and Dublin, as well as in Switzerland, Germany and France.

Soon, however, two opposing factions arose within the movement, which in 1849 resulted in a permanent rift between the 'Open' and 'Exclusive' Brethren. The Open Brethren had a firm commitment to missionary work, and at one point something like 1% of their British adherents became missionaries. Some Brethren emigrated to other parts of the world, motivated by their zeal to spread the gospel. Meetings were established in countries such as New Zealand, southern India and Zambia, and in Argentina they formed the second largest Protestant group in the country.

One such missionary was Charles Rogers, an executive with the Shell Oil Company who emigrated to Argentina on purpose to plant local bodies of Brethren assemblies. It was as a result of his ministry that Luis Palau's parents were won to Christ and that Palau began to put down spiritual roots. Later in life, he acknowledged that his Brethren upbringing and the experience of his Anglican day school had given him a wide denominational perspective.

Luis Palau was born in a township on the outskirts of Buenos Aires, the capital of Argentina, where his family attended the small Brethren assembly. His father owned a successful construction business, and after his conversion used his trucks at weekends to run believers to neighbouring towns in order to witness and hand out tracts.

The young Luis soon acquired an evangelical fervour, and at school and in the street experienced the jeers and taunts often hurled at the adults. Converted at the age of thirteen, he fell away from the Lord after the early euphoria had died down. Finally aware of an emptiness and discontent within him, he made what he says is the second most important decision of his life.

During Carnival Week in Buenos Aires, at the age of sixteen, he determined 'to serve only Jesus Christ and to give my life to working for him'. This proved to be the beginning of a new commitment, and his determination to serve the Lord remained firm from then on. When he left school the following year he took a job with the Bank of London, where he was able to use his ability to speak both Spanish and English.

Wondering one night what his future might be, he heard the evangelist Billy Graham on the Christian radio station HCJB, based in Quito, Ecuador, and his boyhood dream of speaking to people about Jesus came back to him. He prayed, 'Jesus, some day use me on the radio to bring others back to you, just as this programme has strengthened my commitment to you.' A short time later he moved to Córdoba to be with his widowed mother and sisters, and linked up with a lively Brethren assembly.

As well as becoming Sunday School superintendent, he plunged into a variety of outreach activities; he joined a small team that held street meetings and tent campaigns, and developed a seven-minute local radio programme called *Christian Meditation*.

Deadline

Despite his frenzy of activity, he was conscious of a lack of victory or powerful living and he spent whole nights in prayer seeking an answer from God, but nothing happened. Perhaps, he thought, I am too big a scoundrel for the Lord to work with? He finally gave God a deadline: either God would bless him or he would stop preaching. Nothing dramatic occurred, but God impressed upon him that he was just a vehicle and that it was the Holy Spirit who did the convicting.

Palau's thoughts about his future now began to become clearer and he was impressed by reports of Billy Graham's crusades. He had a vision that the Lord wanted him to take the gospel to the people of Latin America and that one day he would preach to great crowds.

As a first step he left the bank to join SEPAL, the Latin American division of the American-based Overseas Crusades. He took part in an experiment in church-planting in the small Argentinian town of Oncativo, where no evangelical church existed. The team set up a series of meetings at which Palau was the preacher.

On the first night when he invited the seventy-five-strong congregation to decide for Christ, thirty-five people raised their hands. Afraid that they had not properly understood him, he spent a further half hour explaining what was involved; at a second count, thirty-seven hands went up. By the end of the week, a church of seventy believers had been established, who later went on to plant churches in other nearby towns.

Although eager to continue with his evangelistic work, Palau was persuaded to undertake a formal course of theological training at the Multnomah School of the Bible in Portland, Oregon. His first trip to the States was not easy; he was homesick, had to learn to cope with the American culture, and also realised that there were areas in his personal life that needed to be dealt with. His host, Ray Stedman, treated him almost as a son, even to the extent of rebuking him and pointing out a few home truths. During his time at Multnomah, Palau met and married Pat Scofield, a student in his class.

After leaving Bible school, they were sent by Overseas Crusades for further training at a church in Detroit, and then he was seconded to work with Billy Graham for two and a half months as interpreter in the Fresno Crusade. The following year he was posted by Overseas Crusades to Columbia, to train nationals in evangelism and church-planting, though he considered the work simply as a stepping stone to his goal of mass evangelism.

While in this frame of mind, he accepted an invitation from HCJB Radio of Quito, Ecuador, to begin regular gospel broadcasts, which reached an estimated twenty million in the Spanish speaking world. He followed this up with a TV counselling programme, *Responde*, which enjoyed similar success.

Now turned thirty years old, Palau was eager to move towards his cherished ambition and an opportunity shortly presented itself. A group of Christians in Columbia invited him to lead a crusade in the capital Bogotá. Palau preached for four nights and 865 decisions were recorded. At last he had achieved his breakthrough and was finally freed from anxious wondering about when his chance would come.

Mexico

Following a spell of deputation work, Luis Palau drew together a team of men for outreach in Mexico; they staged a series of fourteen campaigns which attracted over 104,000 people. For the new team, however, it was a time of learning: how to organise a crusade, together with counselling, follow-up, keeping records - and how to trust God for

finance. From Mexico they moved into other Latin American countries where with the exception of a few outside trips, they stayed until 1978.

In that year Palau resigned from Overseas Crusades to begin his own independent team and felt free to accept invitations from Europe, the Far East and the United States. He has since visited all five continents, preaching in fifty-two countries to more than 8.2 million people.

His two-phase mission to England in 1983 and 1984 was his longest yet crusade, and his *Tell Wales* tour lasted five weeks in which 78,000 people heard the gospel. He was also able to hold a rally in Budapest, Hungary, where 12,000 people turned out to hear

LUIS PALAU

him and nearly 1,000 responded to his message; and at a meeting in the USSR he spoke to 40,000 and 8,500 responded to the gospel.

Some critics of mass crusades are troubled about the lasting value of such decisions. According to Palau, independent surveys showed that as many as 84% of those who responded still attended church two years later. He also stressed that crusades make an impact on society at large, at all levels of civic and national life, but even more so on individuals whose lives are transformed.

If you were to ask him the secret of his success, he would probably refer to Galatians 2:20, a verse frequently quoted by Major Ian Thomas of the Torchbearers, his tutor at Bible School. When the truth of this text eventually dawned upon him - that God could not use him until he came to the end of himself - his ministry was transformed. 'My biggest spiritual struggle was finally over. I would let God be God, and Luis Palau be dependent upon him.'

TEN

Into the Twentieth Century

While the nineteenth century is usually regarded as the great century for missionary expansion, it was not until after 1875 - the year the Keswick Convention was founded - that the movement began to gather momentum. The reason for this has to do with the Second Great Awakening, which started in North America in 1857 and moved across the Atlantic to Britain and other parts of the globe. No doubt stirred by the example of Hudson Taylor's faith mission (the China Inland Mission was founded in 1865), it was further assisted by the preaching of Moody and the formation of the Student Volunteer Movement in 1886.

By the beginning of the twentieth century most regions of the world had been penetrated by Protestant or Catholic missionaries. The new Protestant missions, operating mostly in Africa, India and Asia, were inter-denominational in character and aimed at setting up indigenous churches. But in addition to preaching the gospel they founded schools and colleges, opened clinics and hospitals, introduced more advanced methods of farming, reduced the native language to writing and began translating the Bible.

Missionary efforts have meanwhile been sustained and new openings have arisen for communicating the gospel to unreached millions. Using modern technology and methods of evangelism, the mandate to make disciples of all nations has continued as the Church's primary task.

India

Christianity was slow to take root in India. Despite the pioneering work of men like William Carey and Henry Martyn, it was not until the middle of the nineteenth century that the larger missionary societies were firmly established on the sub-continent. By then there were less than five hundred missionaries, and the Indian Protestant community, found chiefly in the Madras area, numbered only about 100,000. Further expansion took place during the second half of the century and today the number of adherents (including Roman Catholic and Orthodox Churches) totals twenty-seven million, eleven million of which are Protestants.

The churches founded in the nineteenth century were western in style and their schools provided a traditional English education. Leadership

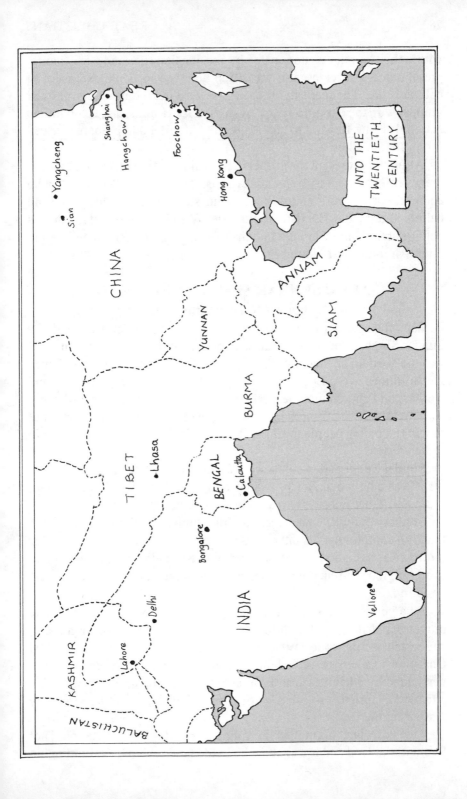

INTO THE TWENTIETH CENTURY

CHINA

Yangcheng
Sian
Shanghai
Hangchow
Foochow
Hong Kong

ANNAM
YUNNAN
SIAM
BURMA

TIBET
Lhasa

BENGAL
Calcutta

Bangalore

INDIA
Delhi
Lahore
Vellore

KASHMIR

BALUCHISTAN

within the Church was dominated by the missionaries and Christianity, presented in a foreign garb, was often believed to be an extension of colonial rule. The majority of converts were from outcaste or animist groups, with the exception of a few high-class Hindus, and so no Indian nationals came forward to challenge the old order and prepare the way for an Indian Church.

Attempts to present the gospel in an Indian setting were first made in the seventeenth century by a Catholic missionary, Robert de Nobili, who adopted native dress and customs, and studied Hindu literature and beliefs. Later, the Baptist missionary, William Carey established a college at Serampore to train Indians to evangelise their own people and establish indigenous churches.

SADHU SUNDAR SINGH (1889-1929/33):
Evangelist to India and Tibet

Perhaps the most striking plea for a truly Indian Church was made by Sundar Singh, a converted Sikh, who protested that the Church in India was too western and had lost its way. The services, the hymns and even the buildings were English; the converts adopted western ways and clothes, and church members relied on the missionaries for leadership and direction. The Church in India was in effect a western Church, but to win the Indian people to Christ it would have to present the gospel in Indian terms.

Sundar Singh parted company with the organised Church and spent his life as a holy man, a Christian sadhu, travelling mostly in northern India and Tibet in order to reach the people he loved most.

Sundar's family, who came from the Punjab, held high rank within the Sikh community; his father was a chieftain and a landowner, and his mother was honoured as a *bhakta*, or saint. She believed there was good in all religions and encouraged her son to seek the truth wherever it could be found.

As a young boy, Sundar used to rise early with his mother to recite prayers, and they paid a fortnightly visit to a Hindu holy man who suggested he might one day become a sadhu. His mother also welcomed Christian teachers to their home, though the two of them were not persuaded by what they heard. Indeed, Sundar who as a boy of twelve attended a Christian mission school, once ended a Scripture lesson by tearing up the Bible.

Two years later his mother died and his world collapsed; he could not live without God and it was she who made God real to him. Finding no help from the holy man, he vented his anger on the Christians: he became violent, attacking believers and disrupting their meetings, and with a gang of other boys stoned the preachers in the bazaar and shouted down those who protested. The climax came when he bought a copy of the New Testament, and in front of his friends contemptuously ripped it apart and burned it page by page.

Vision

For three days and nights Sundar stayed in his room, praying that God would reveal himself; if not, he planned to end his life by throwing himself under an express train that passed through his village every morning at five o'clock. A short while before the deadline, a great light filled his room and out of the brightness came the figure, not of Krishna or one of his own gods, but of Jesus. 'How long will you persecute me? I have come to save you. You were praying to know the right way, why do you not take it? I am the way,' said the Lord.

His family were shocked to learn of his vision. 'Now I am a Christian, I can serve no one else but Jesus,' he declared. Despite threats, attacks and personal abuse, Sundar remained true to his decision. Rather than suffer any further family disgrace his father turned him out of the home, telling him he would have no more to do with him. Sundar's last meal was spiked with poison and the following morning he began to vomit, while blood oozed out of his mouth; he managed to crawl to the safety of a pastor's house in the next village, where he recovered.

On his sixteenth birthday, 3rd September 1905, he was baptised a Christian at the Anglican Church at Lahore, then left for the Simla Hills where he spent almost a month seeking God's will for his future. He turned his back on the security of a western Church and decided to don the yellow robe of an Indian sadhu. His aim was to revitalise the Indian Church by presenting the gospel in Indian terms. What better way could he achieve this than by becoming a Christian sadhu?

His first act was to return to his home village to reach the people there, but although he was welcomed into some of the high-caste homes, his family still rejected him. In later life, however, he had the thrill of hearing his father tell him, 'I too love Jesus'.

From the beginning, Sundar longed to take the gospel to Tibet which was virtually a closed country. His first tour was into the foothills of the Himalayas, where he learned some of the hard realities of his calling. Often honourably received into homes along his route, he would be driven out again and again when he spoke of Jesus. But when he did not curse or revile his attackers, as many other sadhus would have done, they asked his forgiveness and invited him to return.

Eighteen months after his baptism, Sundar made his first trip to Tibet. Two Moravian missionaries taught him something of the language and lent him a young interpreter to accompany him. The two of them tramped from village to village, only to be rejected when they preached about Jesus; the one exception was at a monastery where the Lama gave him permission to speak to the monks. After this, he returned to Tibet every year between 1908 and 1929. Some of the adventures he experienced on these journeys seem almost impossible and people often asked, 'Can they be true?' He was beaten, imprisoned and left to die on several occasions, yet escaped to continue his preaching.

Once he was arrested by monks and thrown down a well, where he was left to die among the putrefying remains of previous victims. On the third night he was secretly rescued, even though the only key to the lock was kept by the Grand Lama himself. At least three times he was similarly saved from death by unknown rescuers who proved to be members of the Sannyasi Mission, a group of secret disciples of Jesus and one of the strange underground Christian movements of modern India.

On another occasion he was travelling with a stranger over a mountain pass in winter. Hearing the cries of an injured man, Sundar went to the rescue while his fellow-traveller quickly moved on to avoid the approaching storm. He later found his former companion frozen to death, while he and the injured man survived.

College

In 1909 he was persuaded to enter St. John's College, Lahore, to study for the ministry; he believed that he could give the Church a vision which no one else at that time could pass on. But he refused ordination when he realised it would mean remaining in the one diocese and no longer travelling to Tibet. While college gave him some idea of the work of a minister, it confirmed him in his belief that western-type Christianity was not suited to India.

While at college, Sundar was much influenced by Thomas à Kempis' *The Imitation of Christ*, and wanting to share in his Lord's sufferings determined to spend forty days in fasting, hoping to quicken his spiritual awareness. When he did not re-appear, his death was announced, only for him to be discovered in an emaciated state in a jungle clearing. He soon recovered, ready to begin his annual trek to Tibet, and later claimed that the experience of being absorbed into the Spirit of God had given him new power.

Sundar Singh's fame began to spread beyond India, and between 1919 and 1922 he toured the Far East and visited Europe, America and Australia. He was greatly disappointed with the West; he found it to be materialistic and utterly indifferent to all spiritual values. He was especially distressed by the divisions and disunity of the churches. 'How do Christians expect to live together in Heaven when they cannot live together on earth?' he asked.

For three years, from 1925 to 1927, Sundar was forced to rest and he spent his time in the Simla Hills, writing books and pamphlets. He attempted to reach Tibet in 1927 but illness caused him to turn back. His last attempt came in April 1929, when he finally disappeared without trace. Some believe that he had joined the Christian hermits in the Kailas Ranges, others that he had been martyred for the sake of the gospel. No one knows, and his death is still a mystery. In the end he fulfilled his oft-repeated prophecy, 'I never expect to return from Tibet.'

DR. IDA SCUDDER (1870-1960):
Founder of Vellore Medical College

Nineteen year old Ida Scudder's dreams for the future were rudely shattered one night by a sequence of events that was to shape the remaining seventy years of her life. For God spoke to her so dramatically through these experiences that she could not but see the hand of God pointing her in the direction she was to take.

Visiting her missionary parents in south India in 1890, the desperate need for women doctors was brought home to her when three men - a Brahmin, a Muslim and another Hindu - each came separately to beg her to save their teenage wives who were in labour. As she had no medical knowledge or skill, she felt unable to help them, but instead offered to call her father, the mission doctor. All three of them refused, as the Brahmin explained, 'It is better that my wife should die than that another man should look on her face.'

When Ida found out the next day that all three women had died, she was devastated; here were dying women within her reach, yet it had been impossible for her to do anything about it. There was only one response she could make. She told her parents, 'I am going to America to study to be a doctor, so that I can come back here and help the women of India.'

Perhaps this outcome is not so surprising, for Ida Scudder came from a long line of missionary doctors. In 1819 her grandfather had become

the first medical missionary from the United
States to India; since then
over thirty members of
the Scudder family have
given nearly 1,000 years
of missionary service.
Her father worked with
the Arcot Mission,
founded by his three
brothers, and Ida in-
tended to follow in his
footsteps. Supported by
her church mission
board, Ida enrolled in
1895 at the Women's
Medical College in Phila-
delphia, but transferred
to the Cornell Medical

DR. IDA SCUDDER

College for her final year. After the end of her academic course, she
went to get practical experience under her father, who was
developing the use of the new cholera inoculations.

Knowing her concern, the mission board suggested she open a
hospital for women in Vellore, where her father worked. There were
thousands of Hindu and Muslim women who would only accept
treatment from another woman, so there was an urgent need. Ida was able
to raise the necessary funds and left for Vellore in 1899.

Gaining people's confidence as a woman doctor was not easy, for the
natives preferred her more familiar father. But eventually she was called
out to her first patient, an elderly lady who was dying. She tended the
patient lovingly and to the gratitude of the family made her final hours
comfortable.

Soon after Ida arrived back in India, her father died and she was
forced to open a new dispensary without any help. People were still
unwilling to trust her and it was many days before a patient finally
ventured to her bungalow for treatment. Within two weeks there was a
steady stream of patients with all sorts of ailments - TB, typhoid, leg
ulcers, eye infections, cancer and, of course, leprosy; cholera and
malaria were also common diseases, but were more treatable.

The main causes of the majority of sicknesses were malnutrition, over-crowding and lack of sanitation. Besides these deprivations there were other problems to face. Ancient superstitions, quack remedies and ignorance took a heavy toll of life and often patients were only brought to her as a very last resort.

Even intelligent, high-caste Hindus were subject to fears and taboos, and Ida's patience was frequently stretched to the limit. In one home, a young girl with facial paralysis was treated by killing a dove and letting the blood fall onto her head. In another case, after cleaning a wound, Ida found the injury covered with holy ashes. And when certain feast days came round, patients never turned up at the dispensary for their medicine.

Women's Hospital

The women's hospital at Vellore was opened in September 1902. Called the Mary Taber Schell Hospital, after the main benefactor, it initially had thirty beds in two wards, one for poor patients admitted free and the other for caste people who could afford to make a contribution. Working only with the help of Salomi, her native helper, Ida performed twenty-one major operations, four hundred and twenty-eight minor ones, and treated 12,359 patients in the first year alone.

It was about this time that she had to face two disasters which strained the hospital's resources. First there was a famine, following ten years with hardly any rain; then bubonic plague killed four hundred people within three weeks. Despite her offers of help, many natives flocked to the shrine of Kale, the goddess of death, with prayers and gifts for healing.

After two years the hospital had expanded to forty-two beds and Ida was joined by another doctor and a trained nurse. She had further help from eleven young Indian women, whom she had gathered around her to train as nurses. At this time her two main aims were to start a school of nursing and to organise a programme of village medical work, which would let her treat men and women in a more familiar environment.

During a furlough in the USA she raised enough money to open a small nursing school which had an initial intake of fifteen students. Within four years there were eighteen nurses in the hospital, four of them qualified and three enrolled in a mid-wifery class.

The gift of a motor-car enabled her to begin a regular programme of village visiting, limited previously through lack of adequate transport. Each Wednesday was set aside for her visit and she had as many as fifty villages on her itinerary, known simply as 'Roadside'. After the usual initial fears, villagers were eager to take advantage of the mobile dispensary and would line up at certain recognised stops along the route. They came with all kinds of ailments and conditions: dysentery, blindness, scabies, lameness, abscesses, broken bones, elephantiasis, leprosy and tumours. All were treated prayerfully and lovingly, and soon the rich and high-born were waiting their turn next to the outcastes.

Amazed that she cared so much for people, one of the villagers pronounced Ida to be an *Atvar*, 'an incarnation of the god Vishnu'. 'You think so?' queried one of her companions. 'Did you ever hear of one of the Atvars doing any good in the world?' 'No,' admitted the villager thoughtfully.

Occasionally she was stopped between villages by people needing emergency help, like the half-delirious man with a fearfully infected hand. Ida set up an operating table at the roadside and successfully treated the infection. The following week the patient was waiting for her with a large bag of rice for the hospital.

As the work progressed, the hospital proved to be far too small and Dr. Ida began to visualise the need not only for a new hospital but also for a medical college, which seemed an impossible dream. The proposal was met with scepticism - 'Train Indian women in medicine?' and 'The denominational boards would never agree!' But the scheme was approved and Ida Scudder was to be the college's first principal. The plan was delayed by the outbreak of war in 1914, and it eventually opened in 1918. There were seventeen students on roll, later reduced to fourteen, all of whom graduated, six as prize-winners. These results far surpassed those achieved by the men's colleges.

The Vellore hospital continued to grow, with more wards added and improved facilities. It was not until 1924 that Dr. Ida won her battle to

---

The caste system
Although caste discrimination is legally forbidden in India, it is still socially important for the majority of the population. The Hindu caste system was originally a matter of varna, or colour, but developed into a series of sub-divisions according to occupations. Every Hindu was born into a jati (birth caste group) and a varna (occupational class), and had to follow the dharma (duty) of that position. There are four classes: (1) Brahmins, the priestly class; (2) Kshatriyas, warriors and rulers; (3) Vaisyas, farmers, merchants and minor officials; (4) Sudras, unskilled workers. In addition, there are the 'pariahs' - the outcastes or untouchables - who do the menial tasks. Hindus were expected to marry within their own jati, but the religious leader Gandhi (1869-1948) did much to undermine the system and today old customs are being eroded by new ideas.

rebuild the hospital on a two hundred acre site outside the town. It was dedicated by the governor of Madras in March 1928. Today's modern hospital complex would do Dr. Ida justice, as it boasts 1,300 beds, a research building, a new operating complex of fourteen theatres and a new Schell eye hospital.

Her dream was to upgrade the medical school to a college where degree courses could be offered instead of the Licensed Medical Practitioner's Diploma, a plan that assumed a greater urgency when the government decided that the diploma course was no longer acceptable. The scheme met with considerable opposition from the mission board in America when members realised the new college would be for both men and women students.

Many of Ida's friends felt betrayed by the woman who had struggled so long for the cause of women. The plan, debated for many years, at last began to gain ground. In 1942 permission was granted for a women's degree class to go ahead, and in 1947 the new college was affiliated to Madras University and male students were also admitted. The courses on offer gradually expanded and today there are eighty recognised training programmes in paramedical, nursing and medical fields.

When in 1938 a missionary asked if she could be allowed start a world-wide Prayer Fellowship to support Vellore, Ida wrote back, 'I feel that the great burden which was upon me has been lifted.' There is now a British branch of the Friends of Vellore which makes the hospital's needs known and shares in its work.

Today, Vellore has an international reputation and doctors from all parts of the world come to learn some of the new medical techniques pioneered at the hospital. It is widely renowned for its leprosy rehabilitation programme where Dr. Paul Brand has developed new operations to restore crippled hands and foot distortions, and to correct facial contours.

Following her retirement from her post at Vellore, Dr. Ida continued to take a keen interest in all the new developments as well as conducting her long-established Tuesday Bible class. She died in May 1960, in her ninetieth year, a 'Great Soul' who was truly loved and respected by all her patients and students.

AMY CARMICHAEL (1861-1951):
Founder of the Dohnavur Fellowship

Hinduism has been entrenched as the native religion of India for several thousand years and over 80% of its population is influenced by the caste system. Christianity first reached India in the fourth century, but made little impact upon the country, and the attack of Islam began in the eighth century. Hinduism has withstood these monotheistic assaults and in some areas remains as a fatalistic force that still impedes social and medical progress.

Modern India is a secular state that allows freedom for all religions to practice their faith, but there has been strong pressure from Hindu militants, at a state and central level, to prevent proselytisation. Popular Hinduism is an idolatrous practice, though it has a philosophical and mystical element that has a growing appeal in western countries. Today Christians account for a mere 2.6% of the total population, while Muslims constitute 12%. As nineteenth century missionaries discovered, higher-caste Hindus show little open response to the gospel and most converts are from among the 'untouchables' (or 'pariahs') who are sometimes seeking to escape the caste system. The Muslims are the most accessible group for Christian witness and many of them are known to have come to Christ.

Life Work

When Amy Carmichael reached India in 1895 she immediately encountered the full impact of the country's religious barrier. At the mission school where she was stationed, the missionaries did not expect - or indeed experience - any converts from either Hinduism or Islam. And at another school, the parents had no fear of losing their children to the Christian religion as no one of their caste, with the exception of two some fifty years earlier, had ever gone over. This failure was compounded by the lack of Urdu-speaking Christian teachers, which meant the schools were staffed by Hindu, Muslims and unconverted 'Christians'.

In 1901 the young missionary began what proved to be her life-work, rescuing Temple children, both girls and boys, who were condemned to be 'married' to the gods for vile and immoral purposes. When knowledge of this evil traffic circulated it was received with horror in both mission and government circles, leading to a determination to strengthen the law to defeat the practice.

Amy was born into a middle class family in Northern Ireland and her parents were God-fearing Presbyterians. From her childhood, she had a love for God and recollects how at the age of three she used to pray in bed, 'Father, please come and sit with me.' But it was not until the age of sixteen that she was truly 'drawn into his fold' and settled once and for all the pattern of her future life.

Fired by socialist ideas, Amy's many activities included the founding of Welcome Hall, a mission among mill-girls or 'shawlies' as they were known. It was here that she learned the principle of looking to the Lord alone for financial and other needs, which remained with her all the rest of her life.

When the Carmichael family moved to Manchester, Amy once again immersed herself in slum work and joined Frank Crossley at Ancoats. In 1888 she paid her first visit to the Keswick Convention and became a life-long friend of Robert Wilson, one of the co-founders. As a result of this link she was chosen as the first Keswick-sponsored missionary, though she was not fully sure whether she should go to China or Africa. Following the principle of 'knocking on doors', she sailed for Japan in 1893, which at the time seemed the right thing to do. But after a year, illness forced her to return to England.

Then in 1895 she was accepted by the Church of England Zenana Missionary Society to work at Bangalore in south India where the climate was healthier, though again she was not aware of any distinct call. She settled in the Tinnevelly District, towards the extreme south of the sub-continent, where she joined the Rev and Mrs Walker in evangelistic work among the villages.

Amy soon gathered around her a group of converted women who formed a Women's Band, which she called the Starry Cluster. They travelled around the villages, visiting homes and speaking to women and children who were willing to listen to the gospel. When two teenage girls who wanted to become believers escaped from their homes and came to the Walkers' bungalow for refuge, the threat of violence forced them all to move to Dohnavur.

Temple Child

It was here in 1901 that Amy rescued her first temple child, a seven year old girl found one night by a Christian women. Preena, a high-caste girl, went to bed hungry that night as she would not break caste by eating the Christian lady's food. When taken next morning to Amy, who put her on her lap and kissed her, the girl wondered, 'Who is this person who kisses me like my mother?' Preena had already escaped from the Temple once before, but had been torn from her mother's arms and taken back; as a punishment, both her tiny hands had been branded with a hot iron.

Temple women had tried to scare her with talk of the 'child-catching Missie Ammal' (i.e. 'lady', a reference to Amy), but the girl felt this would be better than remaining in her prison. It was not long before some of the temple women appeared to reclaim the child, but Preena declared firmly, 'I won't go with them.'

From that day on Amy became her new mother and she stayed for the rest of her life. Shocked by the stories of life in the temples, Amy began to gather facts about these helpless children who were destined for a life of prostitution. She discovered that they were usually given to the temple either by couples with an

AMY CARMICHAEL

unhappy marriage, or by a deserted wife or widow; others were a gift, hopefully to induce the god to grant recovery from illness.

There were to be trained as dancing and singing girls, to perform before gods carried in procession, to carry the sacred light and to fan the idols with oxtails. Worse still, they were there to satisfy the lusts of men, including practices that Amy felt too evil to be described.

As news of her crusade became known, babies in danger of being taken into temple service were brought to her for care. Her Women's Band shared her concern and helped in mothering and training the children. A suitable spot outside Dohnavur was bought for building the first home; later, as more children arrived, the number of homes increased and new centres were opened up in other parts of the District, one of which was strategically placed next to the London Missionary Society hospital at Neyyoor. By 1906 the family numbered seventy, though ten babies died that year in an outbreak of dysentery. By 1913 it totalled one hundred and forty.

Other building projects included Forest House, a retreat in the mountain forest above Dohnavur where workers and children could take a break, and Three Pavilions, a home for physically and mentally handicapped children, beautifully situated near the coast with views of both mountains and sea. Later, a House of Prayer was added to the mission compound and the grandest project of all, a new hospital known as the 'Place of Heavenly Healing'.

All her life Amy was a learner in the school of prayer and from her early days in Belfast had discovered the secret of trusting God. Without any appeal except in prayer, all her needs were met and her diary is full of answers to prayer. When the hospital was built, workers and children alike prayed for £10,000. Amy later wrote in a log book which they all signed: 'Asked for, and received according to 1 John 5:14-15, £10,000 for the Place of Heavenly Healing'.

As the new hospital was built, Amy saw in it an answer to the fulfilment of another need concerning the future of the children. The hospital was eventually made up of Dohnavur's own boys and girls 'trained to serve, evangelists, lovers of souls'. But in the early days Dohnavur had attracted helpers from many parts of the world, although there were sometimes those who, despite their goodwill, had to withdraw: a few were spiritual casualties, others could not cope with the physical strain and some simply did not fit.

In 1925 Amy resigned from the CEZMS - it had always been understood that she would work independently of the parent body - and formed the Dohnavur Fellowship. Its objects: to save children in moral danger and to make God's love known to the people of India. What in fact Amy created was a family and she was Amma, 'mother', the term by which she was known by children and workers. She bathed her children and cared for them in sickness; she played with them and took them on walks into the forest where she taught them to love animals and appreciate nature.

Invalid

On the morning of 24th October 1931 Amy was especially in prayer about her work. 'Do with me as thou wilt. Do anything that will fit me to serve thee and help my beloveds,' she implored. In the afternoon she fell and broke a leg and dislocated an ankle; complications set in which, added to her thirty-six years unbroken service in India, left her an invalid for the rest of her life.

For the next twenty years Amy was more or less confined to her room, yet from her bed - often lying completely flat - she continued in her role as Amma to her family. She kept in touch with the outside world through her correspondence and, with help, wrote thousands of letters. Already the author of many books, she wrote a further thirteen works during this period, as well as revising her other titles and producing more poetry.

Although the practice of 'marrying' children to gods is now illegal, it has not completely died out and the Fellowship's homes are still open to receive unwanted children. The work Amy started continues to exemplify the love of God, and the staff at Dohnavur, with one exception, are all Amy's grown-up children, fulfilling one of her dearest wishes.

Throughout her struggles in India, Amy was always aware that a battle was being fought, yet in it she learned 'to know Christ, in the power of his resurrection, and in the fellowship of his sufferings'.

China

The Church in China has been subject this century to a barrage of violent attacks, resulting in the deaths of hundreds of missionaries and Chinese Christians. Persecution under Communist rule since 1949 has caused untold agonies, but the Church has grown. Since 1977 many millions have come to faith in Christ, and by now there may be more Chinese Christians than Communist Party members. The most radical result of persecution, however, has been the emergence of an indigenous Chinese Church, free of domination by foreign missionaries, something which might not otherwise have been achieved.

After the death of the last Emperor in China, the Manchu dynasty was replaced by a republic under a Protestant leader, Dr. Sun Yat-sen, whose life had once been saved by a British missionary. In the political turmoil after his death in 1925, a Nationalist government was established under the Christian general, Chiang Kai-shek. Growing anti-British and anti-missionary feelings led to more deaths, however, and a civil war broke out between the Nationalists and the newly-emerging Communist party under Mao Tse-tung. In the 1930s the situation was further complicated by a Japanese attempt to overrun China, which was defeated in 1945. Meanwhile, the Communist Party triumph in 1949 forced Chiang Kai-shek to withdraw to Taiwan, where he set up an alternative Chinese government.

Until 1951 thousands of foreign missionaries had worked throughout China often against immense difficulties, establishing churches, schools, universities and hospitals. With the exception of the China Inland Mission, missionaries were from denominational societies and represented the Anglican, Baptist, Methodist, Presbyterian and Congregational churches, together with an active Catholic presence.

There were some Christians however, who were anxious to build a strong Chinese Church and were ardently working towards this end; among them was Ni Shu-tsu, better known as Watchman Nee, leader of the Little Flock movement.

WATCHMAN NEE (1903-1972)
Chinese Pastor and Preacher

Born into a nominally Christian family, Nee was converted at the age of eighteen while still a student at Trinity College, an Anglican high school in Foochow. Abandoning any prospect of a university education, he gave himself to Bible study and evangelism, and many students were won to Christ.

Before long he began to display two gifts which were to mark out his ministry as something special, and he became well-known both as a preacher and a writer. His gift as a preacher lay in his ability to make the gospel clear and simple for his listeners, and as a Bible expositor, his teaching was lively, full of anecdotes and humour, that led his hearers back to the fundamentals of the New Testament.

In his early days he produced a magazine called *Revival*, later changed to *The Christian*, which mostly carried his own sermons plus extracts from other devotional writers. His books, based on his own sermons, included *The Spiritual Man, The Normal Christian Life* and *Sit, Walk, Stand*, regarded by many today as Christian classics.

In 1928 Nee moved from Foochow to the treaty port of Shanghai, which was to be the centre of his ministry for the remainder of his life. Here, in the international settlement, he established a small meeting on a lane called Wen Teh Li. As the work expanded, the premises were extended to include offices and hostel accommodation.

Brethren Links

When in 1930 Nee met a British business man, Charles R Barlow, associated with the 'London Group' of Brethren, links were forged between them.

This resulted in Nee travelling to England in 1933 to seek their advice and support, unaware that they were 'Exclusive' and under the leadership of James Taylor of New York.

During his stay, Nee took the opportunity to visit the Christian Fellowship Centre at Honor Oak, south London, where he broke bread with the believers there. When the London Group discovered this, they wrote that he had 'compromised the fellowship' and felt obliged to withdraw from him. His relationship with Honor Oak, however, continued and he found their pattern of worship helpful.

Nee was not happy with the denominational Chinese churches that he had so far encountered, and wanted to build a fellowship based on a less rigid pattern. Influenced by a number of Open Brethren writers, he established a Sunday evening act of worship around the Lord's Table where anyone present was free to offer individual prayers of adoration and praise to God. He felt this was closer to the New Testament ideal.

The numbers in the Shanghai congregation grew and it became necessary to make further changes; the church was divided into fifteen 'families' (house groups), meeting three times a week, for the breaking of bread, for prayer and for teaching. Each family consisted of up to two hundred believers and was sub-divided into sections of fifteen or so members. In this way, fellowship and the use of spiritual gifts were encouraged.

Under Nee, the church was ruled by a number of elders and each 'family' was cared for by a brother or sister. There were full-time apostles - as many as two hundred at one point - who travelled to the unevangelised parts of the country to win converts and plant new churches. In the 1940s there were four hundred and seventy groups in fellowship with the Shanghai church; they were nicknamed 'The Little Flock', after the title of the Brethren hymn book that they used in their worship.

WATCHMAN NEE

The Little Flock was one of several movements in China - including the Jesus Family, the Spiritual Gifts movement and the True Jesus Church - which preferred to develop independently of foreign missions, aiming to return to New Testament origins. For them, the denominational churches were too westernised and tended to divide rather than unite the body of Christ.

One special feature of the Little Flock churches was the emphasis on evangelism; every believer was expected to do the work of an evangelist, and was encouraged to witness to at least one person a day. Another form of evangelism, for which they found a principle in the Acts of the Apostles, was migration, which they developed in the 1940s. Groups of believers, selected to represent a cross-section of trades, moved into remote areas of the country and were supported by the church for an initial three months. Their purpose was to win converts and establish churches; and although the scheme was not a complete success, some new fellowships were started.

War

With the Japanese occupation of Shanghai in 1941, the church came under severe pressure; restrictions were placed on members and funds were reduced, placing some of the apostles under great hardship. To meet the need, Nee felt that God was leading him to set up a business, and with the help of his brother, a chemist, he established a pharmaceutical company. The business flourished, but it took Nee away from his church; his elders were puzzled and eventually asked him to discontinue his preaching at Wen Teh Li.

Nee continued to minister in various other places and after the war was able to plough back some of the company's profits into the church at Shanghai; later the church became prosperous as he and other members handed over their businesses for the benefit of the work. But it was not until 1948 that Nee was at last reconciled with the elders and welcomed back into the fellowship.

When in October 1949 the Communist Party overthrew the Nationalist government and set up the People's Republic of China, it was clear that the church's commercial activities would attract attention. At first they were hopeful that they might be able to enjoy limited co-operation with the new régime, but after two years, the situation began to change when the Communists unfolded plans to take the Chinese Church under its control.

Through the Three Self-Reform Movement, the government aimed to make the Church self-governing, self-supporting and self-propagating; it was placed under the Bureau of Religious Affairs which brought pressure on the Church to persuade missionaries to withdraw from the country, thus getting rid of all 'imperialists'. Christian schools, hospitals and other properties were confiscated.

During this period, the Little Flock and the Jesus Family house churches strongly resisted joining the National Christian Church, regarded as a puppet organisation, and thousands of their members were either killed or imprisoned. All churches were forced to hold meetings, often infiltrated by Communist stooges, to encourage self-criticism and reform. Pastors and leaders were accused of being 'running dogs' of the foreigners and Nee was charged with being the leader of a large secret system disseminating anti-revolutionary poison.

False Accusations

He was arrested in 1952 and for four years was subjected to harsh treatment and attempts to 're-educate' him, by means that can only be imagined. At his trial in 1956, many false accusations were brought against him, including some by believers who had gone over to the other side. Together with other church members he was sentenced to fifteen years imprisonment, which he served in the First Municipal Prison in Shanghai. Little is known of his years in prison, except that his physical condition deteriorated and he continued faithful to the Lord.

Instead of being released after his time, however, his sentence was extended. He should have been allowed out in 1967, but it was the year of the Cultural Revolution when there was another furious attack on the Church; services were discontinued and all religious buildings were to be 'secularised'. The Communists offered to release Nee if he was prepared not to resume his preaching, but it was an assurance he could not give; even the idea of a ransom refused to change his mind. Nee was moved to another prison inland where he died in his sixty-ninth year.

Many missionaries spoke warmly of Watchman Nee's excellent Bible teaching and of the true Christian fellowship they found among his members, though the movement was criticised for setting up what appeared to be another denomination, and there was a tendency towards an authoritarian control over the church. Nevertheless, Nee was an outstanding Christian leader whose vision of an indigenous Church in China prepared believers for the onslaught of Communism and the fiery trials which followed.

GLADYS AYLWARD (1903-1970): Missionary to China

In 1900 a savage onslaught was launched against Christians in China when hundreds of believers - both missionaries and native Christians - suffered dreadfully. The secret society of the 'Righteous and Harmonious Fists', otherwise known as 'Boxers', stirred up hatred against all foreigners in China, especially against the believers. Wielding long curved swords, they rampaged through towns and villages, destroying churches and mission homes, killing missionaries and their families, as well as hundreds of Chinese Christians.

The progress of the rebellion was limited to the northern provinces by the quick thinking of a Chinese sympathiser who changed one character in a message sent to the south; instead of saying 'Kill all Christians', it read '*Protect* all Christians'. The worst affected province was Shansi, to the south west of Peking, where much missionary work was concentrated. China Inland Mission stations had been opened there by C T Studd and Stanley Smith of 'Cambridge Seven' fame, and there were missions operated by the Baptists, the Swedish Holiness Union and the Catholics. While Chinese believers did their best to hide the victims, at the risk of their own lives, one hundred and eighty-eight missionaries and their children were slaughtered - many of them beheaded or hacked to death.

After the rebellion, Christians returned to the province and there was a revival; in the next six years the number of Protestants doubled and the Boxer martyrdoms bore fruit for decades to come. Yet the violence was not over, and in the uneasy political situation of succeeding years the believers faced death at the hands of the Communist revolutionaries and Japanese invaders.

Inspired

It was to Shansi province in 1932 that Gladys Aylward, an intrepid twenty-seven-year-old parlourmaid came, independent of any missionary society and without church backing or financial support, inspired by a God-given compulsion to 'preach the gospel of Jesus Christ'. Like earlier missionaries, she went about under the threat of death, but survived to recount thrilling tales of her adventures for Christ.

Converted at the age of twenty-six, Gladys spent her spare time in a number of evangelistic missions but soon became fixed on the idea of taking the gospel to the millions of Chinese who had never heard about Jesus. She was turned down by a missionary society, concerned about her lack of theological training and convinced she would never master the language.

Gladys was determined to go out alone, and when she heard of an elderly missionary in China who was in need of an assistant she felt that this was God's work for her. Despite all odds, she travelled by train across Europe and Russia, twice avoiding capture in the Sino-Russian war, before eventually arriving at the home of seventy-three year old Jeannie Lawson in the walled town of Yangcheng.

Yangcheng, situated in the southern part of Shansi province, was the cradle of Chinese civilisation. It was here that Mrs Lawson and Gladys opened an inn for

GLADYS AYLWARD

muleteers, where each night they told the men Bible stories and introduced them to Jesus. During the day the two women travelled around the villages preaching the gospel, and though often regarded with suspicion as 'foreign devils' they were gradually accepted by the people.

Despite gloomy predictions, Gladys quickly learned the local dialect and was able to assist with the preaching; she also adopted Chinese dress, ate Chinese food and apart from her European appearance was able to pass off as a native. Such was her love for the country that after four years she became a naturalised Chinese subject and took as her official name *Ai-weh-deh*, 'the virtuous woman', a title accorded her by the people.

After the death of Mrs Lawson, Gladys was left alone to carry on the work. As the inn was not paying she was glad when the local Mandarin, wanting someone to carry out the demands of a new law, offered her a job as 'Foot Inspector'. Her responsibility was to visit the villages and untie the bound feet of little girls; in this way, she was able to earn some extra income and teach about Jesus as well.

There were many converts, and Gladys opened a large room at the inn as a mission hall; in the villages, groups of new believers met together to form churches. Whenever Gladys returned to a village, she declared the day to be a Sabbath and they met for worship and teaching. Each year there was a convention when Christians from more distant parts came together for prayer and Bible study. The meetings, led by Chinese leaders and evangelists, also attracted believers and missionaries from denominational mission stations and proved a great encouragement to them all.

Gladys is best remembered for her care of orphans, many of whom were abandoned by their parents or made homeless by the war. She bought her first child from a child-dealer for nine pence and before long more children were added to her family; eventually she had almost one hundred boys and girls dependent upon her. The Chinese people could not at first understand why Gladys was prepared to care for the children when they were often pleased to be rid of them. But if she had not done so, they would either have been sold into slavery or left to die.

Prison Riot

Another area of involvement was among the prisoners in the town gaol, to which she had a dramatic introduction. A riot had broken out and an inmate, seizing an axe and going on the rampage, killed two men. No one dared go inside the prison to quell the disturbance and so the governor sent for Gladys, since she claimed that her God looked after her.

Fearful of facing the deranged man, she went in and was able to calm him down; she tended the wounded and persuaded the prisoners to return to their cages. Afterwards, she prevailed upon the governor to give the men work to do, that would enable them to earn some money and gain a little self-respect; she became a regular visitor to the prison and was able to share the gospel with the men.

In 1931 the Japanese army invaded China and advanced into Shansi province. As the soldiers moved south, Yangcheng came under attack and bore the brunt of the battle, for the town was seized by the enemy and then re-occupied by the Nationalists. Gladys was badly injured during the first air-raid on the town, but was pulled out of the rubble and struggled to render first-aid to the wounded.

The threat of the Japanese advance and the news that she was on their 'wanted' list finally persuaded her that she must leave Yangcheng. The Mandarin gave a farewell dinner party, at which he announced before all the guests that as a result of what he had seen of Gladys' God, he too wanted to become a Christian. With two soldiers to act as guards and enough food for three days, Gladys set off with her children to walk over the mountains to Sian, where Madame Chiang Kai-shek had an orphanage.

It seemed a foolhardy journey to attempt; to conduct nearly one hundred children through unknown mountainous country while in danger of meeting enemy troops was to court disaster. But God wonderfully protected them and provided for their needs. After five and a half weeks' journey they reached their destination. At the end of it, Gladys collapsed, near to death; she recovered in the Baptist Hospital at Sian and then spent time with CIM missionaries for convalescence. Unable to return to Yangcheng, she stayed at Sian where she worked with the New Life movement, to start a church for the refugees pouring into the city.

The God Who Loves

Her most remarkable experience here was a meeting with five hundred Tibetan Lamas while on an evangelistic trek in the north west of the country. One of the Lamas had once been given a tract quoting John 3:16, which had given them all a longing to know 'the God who loves'. They believed one day this God would send them a messenger to tell them more, and when Gladys arrived she seemed to be the one. She stayed with them for more than a week and taught them the gospel but never knew what happened to them afterwards, for the Communists drove them away and destroyed the lamasery.

As the Japanese advanced, she felt it necessary once again to move on, this time to Boa Chi, one of the resistance centres of the Nationalist army. She devoted much of her time caring for patients in a leper colony and also gained access to the prison, the second largest in the country, where many hardened criminals became Christians.

Worn out after nearly twenty years without a break and still suffering the effects of illness and a beating from Japanese soldiers received several years before, it was made possible for her to return to England. She did not want to leave China, for all her 'family' were there as well as her five legally adopted children, but it seemed the right thing to do.

Gladys was saddened to see the changes that had taken place in England during her absence - the carelessness concerning morals and the apathy of the Church - and wondered how this so-called Christian country would react if seized by a Communist power. Unable to return to her beloved China because of the Communist take-over, she spent eight years serving the best way she could. She travelled hundreds of miles, telling people the story of the Church in China, helped form a Chinese Church in London and became second mother to hundreds of Chinese students from Hong Kong and Singapore.

In 1957 Gladys left England for Taiwan where many Chinese people had fled, and where she found some of her orphan children now grown up, with families of their own. She spent the remaining years of her life on the island caring for a second family of orphans, and died in Taiwan, among the people she loved and for whom she had spent her life.

GEOFFREY BULL (born 1921):
Missionary to Tibet

In 1950 Tibet was over-run by the People's Liberation Army and became a vassal state of Communist China. The Dalai Lama, the Buddhist leader of Tibet, fled over the border to India along with thousands of other refugees. Others were not so fortunate; leading members of the ruling class were put to death and hundreds of others sent to prison for 're-education'. Among the victims who also lost their lives were a few hundred Christians; those who survived were said to be living in virtual slavery.

Tibet, one of the nations more resistant to the gospel, is situated on a high mountainous plateau to the north of the Himalayas. In the past access to the country was difficult, not only because of the nature of the terrain, but also because entry was possible only by government permission. In the late 1940s fighting along the Sino-Tibetan border caused political unrest which made an attempted entry hazardous.

Christianity was first introduced into Tibet by a Jesuit missionary in 1626, but he died of poisoning eight years later. Other missionary efforts also failed and it was not until the beginning of the present century that the first evangelical church of baptised nationals was established. Later attempts resulted in a few converts, though the Buddhist authorities maintained a firm veto on missionary activity. Even Sundar Singh, who visited the country almost annually between 1908 and 1929, gave no indication of converts during his tours.

With George Patterson

Geoffrey Bull's call to take the gospel to Tibet began to crystallise in September 1941, but it was a further six years before he was able to leave for Central Asia. He teamed up with George Patterson, another freelance missionary, and the two left for China in March 1947. At Shanghai they stayed with missionaries from the China Inland Mission before moving up the Yangtze River to Nanchang.

Rather to their surprise, the two men realised that many of the missionaries appeared to practise the 'compound-system', which meant that they stayed in one centre, building up a local church without venturing too far into the surrounding region. Both Bull and Patterson were determined to follow what they believed to be the apostolic practice of moving around, establishing churches and then passing on to another place.

Their next destination was Kangting where they spent eighteen months learning the language and making valuable contact with Tibetans who lived in the region. They became friends with the two Pangda brothers, powerful nobles who invited Bull to their stronghold at Po, a village on the Chinese side of the River Yangtze which formed the Tibetan frontier. He continued his study of the language, taking the Tibetan New Testament chapter by chapter, and with a working knowledge of the language, began to preach the gospel.

But his eyes were fixed on Tibet and it was time to move on. By January 1950 the vanguard of the Chinese Red Army was advancing towards the border and he was anxious to move into the country ahead of them. Despite the political crisis building up, Bull felt it right to continue his efforts to gain entry to the mountain kingdom, and after Patterson left him to recruit more workers from India, he moved into the Pangda's stronghold. Looking for more open opportunities of proclaiming the gospel, he started by befriending the locals and opening a dispensary.

In Demand

His services were quickly in demand, and though his medical skills and supplies were limited he was able to cope with simple wounds, infections and eye complaints. Many of the men came for treatment for syphilis and gonorrhoea, a result of their custom of sharing their women around; others needed minor surgery in order, for example, to prevent gangrene spreading. Some of his patients were in a critical condition and on one occasion he was able to save the life of a woman who had been severely burned.

He was alarmed, however, when he discovered that his patients had afterwards called in the Lama to invoke the spirits' help as well. On one such occasion he decided to explain his 'Jesus doctrine' to the Lama and the patient, showing that God would not allow his work of healing to be attributed to demons.

Not sure how long he would have at Po, Bull resolved to extend his log cabin and add a room for a meeting house. He decorated it with Bible texts and pictures, which particularly attracted the attention of the children. When he was joined by two Chinese evangelists who were passing through, he was able to hold his first worship service there.

He then returned with two believers to Batang in western China, where he spent some time building up the small church and helping its people to sort out some of their problems. He reported his presence to the Communist authorities and was allowed to continue his work, which may have given him a false sense of security; this was the calm before the storm.

When in May 1950 news that the main body of the Red Army was approaching, he returned to the stronghold of Po, but before long advanced units of Chinese soldiers reached the village. Again he made himself known as a Christian missionary and was left alone, yet as a foreigner he was obviously under suspicion. Still hoping to fulfil his call and cross the border into Tibet, he waited for the right opportunity to move. At the end of July the Communists left and he crossed the Tibetan frontier and made for Markham Gartok, a frontier fort on a plateau about 14,000 feet above sea-level. He waited there for permission to proceed further inland to the capital Lhasa, where he hoped to start a medical mission.

During the months among the Tibetan people he had been conscious of the opposition to the gospel exerted by the powers of Buddhism and Communism. He had observed their Buddhist rituals and festivals, and had confronted their Lamas whom he felt to be demon-possessed; he had learned of Communist brutality towards missionaries and knew of their insidious ways of attacking the mind. Soon, he too was to face satanic attacks, more devastating than anything he had so far imagined and threatening the very foundations of his faith.

Arrest

By October, permission to advance had still not come and the People's Liberation Army had moved across the border into Tibet. The governor of Gartok had no option but to surrender to superior forces; Bull was arrested and kept under guard before being escorted back to Batang for interrogation.

Despite his protests, he was accused of being a 'British imperialist' and a spy. His captors even went so far as to suggest that he might be shot. For two days he was in agony of mind at the thought of going out 'like a candle' when only twenty-nine, but he came through this attack and was never again in bondage to the fear of death.

It was after this threat, while still at Batang, that the Lord indicated to him that he would be in prison for three years, a prospect he felt hard to bear at the time. He had his Bible with him and was allowed freedom to read and pray, so his faith was strengthened; but it was more difficult later, when his Bible was taken away from him and he was not allowed to kneel for prayer. At this stage, he kept his faith alive by going over in his mind all the portions of Scripture he knew, and praying while lying down for sleep.

Altogether he spent forty-five days in solitary confinement at Batang before being transferred to Chungking, a forty-four day journey in the middle of winter. Day after day at Chungking he was interrogated by army officers about his life and work and the people he had met; his diaries, letters and papers were scrutinised for further evidence against him. For five months he was subject to continual bombardment, but his captors' efforts at 'thought reformation' proved ineffective.

In July 1951 Bull was transferred to a newly-built prison 'to make a proper confession'. He was given Marxist textbooks and newspapers to help his reformation and further interrogation took place 'to determine what his crimes were against the Chinese people'. For almost a year now he had been kept apart from other prisoners and the solitude became almost unbearable. Other prisoners were eventually moved into his small cell; but this was a change of tactic, not a lack of space.

Interrogations

A cell-leader was appointed to lead daily group discussions and help each prisoner 'progress' towards reform. Each one had to review his life-history, while the others criticised him and pointed out his errors. For Bull, his faith was always identified as a hindrance to progress and he was accused of using religion to mask his real work as an 'international spy'. After admitting once to being critical of imperialism they felt he had made a big step forward, but not enough; new pressure began and he was subject to even more interrogations and criticism meetings as once again he was forced to review his attitudes.

Always the pressure was on the mind, and by 1953 he was mentally fatigued and hardly able to meditate on Scripture or pray. One last great assault was made upon his faith, and he seemed on the verge of collapse and at the very brink of apostasy. But he realised that thousands were praying for him and God on his throne intervened: 'Thus far and no further'.

On the 11th November he was told he was going to be moved, and on 2nd December - the anniversary of God's promise - an official indicated that a decision was imminent. Nine days later he was brought before the governor who read out his sentence: he was to be expelled from the People's Republic of China, forever. Before Christmas 1953 he had reached Hong Kong and freedom.

Geoffrey Bull spent six weeks in the British colony re-adjusting to the idea of freedom. Mentally and physically he had changed, but he felt he was still the same person underneath and despite over two hundred brain-washing sessions his faith remained sure.

As he looked back over his three years in captivity, during which time he had been 'spiritually and psychologically bludgeoned', he was so aware that it was God, and God alone, who had brought him through. Although in the crisis he had found his faith and love at times too weak to hold him fast, yet God's love had not let him go, and 'he had kept that which he had committed unto him'. At the end, Geoffrey Bull was freed, and he had proved God's Word to be unbreakable.

JACKIE PULLINGER (born 1944):
Missionary to the Walled City

Evangelical activity in Britain greatly increased around the middle of this century, and the Church was further renewed in the 1960s by the arrival of the charismatic movement. Starting among the Anglo-Catholics in California, the movement gradually penetrated the older Protestant denominations and within a few years had become a significant force even within Roman Catholicism.

Often associated simply with speaking in tongues, it resulted in a recovery of spiritual gifts, especially of healing, and also led to an outburst of worship and praise expressed in music, dance and art, unequalled since the days of Wesley.

In many areas the movement has cut across the denominational divides and brought a new unity within the body of Christ, though in some cases it has created controversy and erected barriers. Nevertheless, the faith of thousands of individual Christians has been renewed and churches have experienced a remarkable growth in love and power through the renewing of the Holy Spirit.

Holy Spirit

One such Christian was Jackie Pullinger whose life was radically transformed by being baptised in the Holy Spirit, and her ministry in the Walled City of Kowloon, Hong Kong, took on a new dimension. Despite all the zeal of a young missionary, Jackie had met only with scorn and contempt when she tried to speak about Jesus; but after her Spirit baptism she discovered that when she witnessed to people they believed, addicts came off drugs and she began to experience wonderful answers to prayer.

Jackie, an ex-student of the Royal College of Music, was too young and unqualified to be accepted by some of the missionary societies to which she applied, while others did not want musicians; but she still felt drawn by God into missionary work. 'Trust me, and I will lead you,' God had said.

Following the advice of an Anglican minister, she just went; she took a one-way ticket to China and disembarked from the boat at Hong Kong around the time that the cultural revolution was starting in China. She found a part-time teaching job at a mission school in the Walled City, and played the harmonium at the Sunday services. Not much, she felt, but it was a start.

When Jackie arrived in 1966 her first move was to open a youth club for the Walled City's teenage gang members; and she did more - she also helped them find jobs, went with them to court and became involved in helping their families.

When news of her willingness spread, other people in the city began to approach her as well. They assumed that as a Westerner she could get anything for them, and while she was unable to meet many of their demands, she was prepared to be used in this way. Her hope was that by 'walking the extra mile' she might be able to show them something about Jesus.

But the club seemed a failure and her attempts to speak about Jesus met with blank stares, or a nod and a 'Yeah, yeah, that's nice'. She was

---

Drugs

From the eighteenth century, the Chinese government's policy on opium had been to ban it; one reason was the country's estimated ten million addicts, but it was also the cause of a national fiscal crisis. In 1839 the Chinese government embarked on a crusade to suppress the trade and that year confiscated 20,000 chests of the white poppy plant. The British, anxious to keep the lucrative drug traffic, sent 4,000 troops and a force of warships to regain the initiative and restore trading rights. After the Nanking Treaty, the trade continued to flourish and Hong Kong became a centre for drug trafficking, and it was not until 1940 that opium was declared illegal. In the 1950s heroin became popular; it was cheaper, it could be injected as well as smoked and had a more traumatic effect. Originally imported from India, supplies now come from Thailand, Burma and Laos. Since 1981 the Hong Kong government has spent over £20 million a year to fight the drug trade, but expects its treatment centres to be open for many years yet.

JACKIE PULLINGER

further troubled by the attitude of some of the more established missionaries on the Island, who no longer appeared to expect to see anyone won to Christ.

Encouraged by two Chinese Christians, Jackie experienced a baptism of the Holy Spirit and received the gift of speaking in tongues. There was nothing emotional about it, and it was six weeks before she began to notice that something remarkable was happening - now that she let God have a hand in her prayers, Chinese youngsters began coming to Christ.

To provide for the new converts, Jackie started a weekly Bible study at the Mission and on Sundays took them along to the evening service. The congregation, however, did not take too kindly to these unkempt young people, so on the advice of an old missionary she started her own worship services on a Sunday morning. Later, she began a Saturday evening prayer meeting which attracted a wide range of Christians and proved to be the 'power house' behind her ministry. The room where they met was called 'The Well' and it provided a focal point for her Walled City work.

Much of her outreach was directed towards the Triad gangs who controlled life in the Walled City. These secret societies had originally been formed in the seventeenth century to overthrow the Manchu dynasty; today they are criminal gangs who make money by controlling gambling and opium dens. Jackie's first contact with a Triad gang came the night after her youth club had been broken into and vandalised and the 14K Triad leader, Goko, sent his 'fight-fixer' to guard the club against further trouble.

Opium addict Winsom stationed himself at the club door each night, but refused to be drawn into the club itself. Over the weeks however he listened to the talks Jackie gave to the gang members and one night declared himself ready to give Jesus a try. When he prayed with Jackie, he was immediately baptised in the Spirit and - without knowing anything about the experience - immediately began to speak in tongues. Within half an hour he had come completely through opium withdrawal without any of the usual symptoms, the first junkie Jackie saw painlessly set free by the power of God.

Goko, the Triad leader, was amazed at Jackie's 'power' to get his gang members off drugs and agreed to release any of his boys who wanted to follow Jesus. But it was not until ten years later that Goko finally admitted his own need to change and agreed to trust Jesus.

Jackie's mission is not only to the Triads, however; she works among the poor and the destitute, street sleepers, prostitutes and drug addicts. She looks for the 'poor in spirit and body', to show them that they are loved and can find new life and hope. Most of them are addicts and she has led many of them to Christ. Hong Kong has long been a centre of the drug trade and there are an estimated 40,000 addicts in the colony.

One junkie she met was sixteen year old Ah Tsoi, who had been living on the streets since he was eight. Jackie spent many days and nights

THE KOWLOON WALLED CITY

trying to bring him off drugs, but failed. If nothing else this encounter taught her that addicts could only come off drugs if they wanted it for themselves.

Her next step was to provide a home and family environment in which ex-addicts could avoid the temptations of going back to their old ways, and instead begin to grow in their Christian life. At first she was forced to take a group of the boys into her own flat, but the strain of looking after them was too much, and she eventually heeded advice to find her own place into which she could escape to regain strength and enjoy some peace. When word got around that addicts could receive a power enabling them to kick drugs painlessly, there was a constant queue to be admitted to the boys' home and two further homes were set up to cope with the demand.

In order to establish an official body through which to operate, it was decided to form the Society of Stephen (sometimes shortened to 'Stephen' or even to 'SOS'). A full-time worker, an ex-nun, was brought in to supervise the homes, leaving Jackie more time to work in the City. Instead of having to carry the burden of the work alone, helpers of many nationalities came alongside her as the project developed. More encouraging, some of the 'Stephen' boys began to play an active role; they welcomed the newcomers, gave them practical support and prayed with them. For the first time, Jackie admits, she appreciated the true meaning of the phrase 'the body of Christ'.

Caring for addicts, however, is a long-term job and she has realised that the boys need at least six or even twelve months in which to become established in their new life. By 1979 the drug problem in the Walled City had become less serious and Jackie started to spend a great deal of her time working at Tuen Mun refugee camp, caring for some of the thousands of refugees who had fled from Vietnam. She assisted a

---

The Walled City - its Chinese name means 'darkness' - was originally a fortified area of Kowloon on the Chinese mainland, opposite Hong Kong but still part of the British colony. No longer surrounded by walls - they were demolished by the Japanese during World War II - it retained its semblance as a fortress; covering an area of only six acres, it was surrounded on its four sides by high-rise blocks of flats, penetrated only by dark narrow alleys guarded by watchmen. Inside, some 30,000 people lived in crowded, unhygienic conditions. Without any form of law-enforcement, the Walled City had become a haven for criminals, drug addicts and gamblers.

missionary doctor, Donald Dale, who opened a clinic at the camp, and held daily classes for anyone who wanted to learn English or receive Bible teaching.

In the early 1980s, however, the drug problem worsened, and once again she felt it necessary to give more time to the Walled City. The Hong Kong government loaned her the use of a temporary housing area consisting of fourteen long, tin huts. Hang Fook Camp was renovated by the believers and provided new homes for ex-addicts as well as for poor people from the city.

Over the years God has wonderfully provided for the work and Jackie has at times been amazed to see how income has grown as her 'family' increased; gifts of money and in kind have come in, often anonymously. Asked one day by a persistent questioner, 'Where does your money come from?' they were both startled when someone knocked at the door bearing an envelope for Jackie which contained a hundred dollar bill. The questioner was suitably impressed!

Jackie's mission to the Walled City continued for a time, until it was demolished and the land made into a park. Those residents who had legal status were rehoused or given financial help. For over twenty-five years Jackie has served the inhabitants of the Walled City, but her ministry has expanded far beyond its bounds: while some of her boys have taken the work to other parts of Hong Kong and to nearby Macau, she has travelled to many parts of the world to give her testimony of God's grace. Her work among drug addicts has happily been recognised by the Queen who made her an MBE.

Jackie Pullinger's ministry in the Walled City was distinguished by two features: love and power. By her care for people she has put the love of Christ into action, but has recognised that only by the power of God's Spirit are the miracles of conversion and healing accomplished. If the Church is to bear witness to its Saviour and fulfil its role in the world, then these are the two elements of the gospel that need to be recovered in the lives of ordinary Christians.

ELEVEN

The Suffering Church Of the Twentieth Century

When Jesus sent out the twelve disciples he warned them he had not 'come to bring peace, but a sword'. This, of course, was to be the *effect* of his mission, rather than the purpose. His prophetic words came true, for since the days of the early Church the followers of Jesus in every era have been subject to persecution, and there is a great roll of honour of those who have suffered because of their faith in Christ.

Our present century is no exception; in fact it has been claimed that more Christians have died for their faith this century than in all the previous centuries combined (*By Their Blood*, J & M Hefley). In some cases, Christians surrendered their lives rather than deny the Lord, and experienced true martyrdom; others were killed rather as a consequence of their witness for Christ. Many believers have suffered for their faith through imprisonment, torture, starvation and beatings, but by the grace of God have survived.

The fiercest opposition has been from atheistic Communism, which for almost a century pursued believers in an attempt to wipe out the Church. In Africa, Christians have come under attack from the forces of heathenism, where rebels endeavoured to extinguish the work of the gospel. And in Europe, Christians lost their lives during the Holocaust as they opposed the Nazis and attempted to save Jewish people from extermination in the death camps.

As in previous centuries, the words of Tertullian still ring true: 'The blood of martyrs is the seed of the Church'.

Eastern Europe

The Bolshevik revolution of 1917 brought to power a Communist government that was intent on suppressing the Christian Church in Russia. Although in theory every citizen was free to profess the faith of their own choosing, the laws were weighted heavily against believers.

The Orthodox Church resisted the new régime and consequently became the target of Communist attacks; its churches were burned, monasteries pillaged, and clergymen and laymen brought to trial for crimes against the state. No final numbers are available, but thousands of priests and bishops are known to have been killed and many thousands of Orthodox churches confiscated or closed.

In 1928 the Law of Religious Association was passed, signalling a new attack on the Church. It said that religious groups had to be registered with a government committee, children's and young people's activities must end, and clergy could only preach in designated 'prayer buildings' leased from the government. The law virtually strangled the life of the Church, and believers found they could be arrested for almost any reason a Communist official could care to find.

The following year Stalin became Premier; he increased the NKVD (Secret Police, later called the KGB), and made greater use of concentration and forced labour camps. Evangelicals, who had so far avoided persecution, now found themselves under scrutiny. Pastors and priests in particular were the special target of the NKVD, and many met their deaths in a most brutal manner.

THE VINS FAMILY IN RUSSIA

With the aim of corrupting the Church from the inside, apostate Christians were appointed to positions of leadership under pressure from the secret police, and they were used to betray fellow-believers. When Peter Vins, a minister of the gospel from Siberia attended an Assembly of Russian Baptists in Moscow in 1930, he was invited by Communist officials to support the nomination of two government-chosen members to the Baptist Union Board. He refused, and within a few days was arrested and spent three months in Butyrki prison under investigation. In the end, he was sentenced to three years in a labour camp and sent to Svetlaya Bay in the Far East.

At this time his son Georgi, who was just two years old, used to kneel down with his mother and pray, 'Jesus, bring Daddy back!' Peter Vins was released in 1933; his passport was taken from him - which made it difficult for him to get a job - and he was given the status of an exile.

The family lived in poverty for a year before he received permission to move to another town, and they found a home at Omsk where the Baptist church had been closed. They met with the believers in a house on the outskirts of Omsk and Peter Vins once again took up his pastoral work, visiting and encouraging those who were fearful or weak in the faith. Despite the ban on meetings, the number of believers grew and by 1936 there were around 1,000 Christians in the town.

When a new wave of arrest started, Peter Vins was kept under surveillance and it was inevitable that he would be re-arrested. His wife, Lidia, cut a Gospel into parts and sewed sections into her husband's coat lining and trousers. One evening NKVD agents knocked on the door and produced a warrant for his arrest. The officer in charge of the search looked around the poorly-furnished room with surprise. 'I had expected to see the luxurious flat of an American missionary,' he remarked, 'but this is poverty.'

The agents searched the home and took away a Bible, personal letters and photographs. Lidia had a bag of dried crusts waiting for him to take, he put on warm clothing and they had a final prayer together. As his father was driven away, young Georgi ran into the yard behind the shed and wept, 'Mother, I don't want to live any longer!'

The investigation into Peter's case lasted for nine months, before he was brought to trial, along with ten other believers. The witnesses, however, retracted their evidence at the last moment and the men had to be set free. Thin and smelling unpleasantly of prison. Peter was able to join his family for another few years of freedom.

Arrested Again

In 1937 he was arrested again and taken to Omsk prison. For a while the family had contact with him; he was able to look out of his cell window and wave to them in the street below, and they were allowed to take him parcels. But when he received a ten year sentence, he was sent to a closed labour camp for socially dangerous prisoners and all contact ceased. They learned that he died in the camp on 27th December 1943 - cause unknown. He was forty-five years old.

The Germans invaded Russia in 1941, and Stalin ordered the NKVD to stop persecuting the churches to gain their support in the name of national unity. When the war was over, the policy was continued and believers had further relief from persecution. After the death of Stalin in 1956, however, Kruschev took power and three years later began a new round of attacks against the Church.

The aim was to eradicate all religion from the country by 1980. Once again, old laws were rigidly enforced and new laws enacted; one of them was the so-called 'anti-parasite law' which laid down that anyone considered socially unfit by government officials could be imprisoned, a law that was often applied to full-time Christian workers. During this reign of terror, thousands more Orthodox churches were closed and taken over for public use; believers were arrested, tortured and killed, and some were confined to mental institutions. A government-controlled committee of bishops issued new regulations, further

GEORGI VINS IN PENAL CAMP

strengthening state control over the churches.

Attention was soon focused on the evangelical Baptists, and certain leaders of the All-Union Council of Evangelical Christians and Baptists were persuaded to adopt a similar document. Called 'New Statutes', it aimed at controlling church affairs and checking growth among evangelicals. The rules laid down that only congregations registered by the state could belong to the All-Union Council, making all other churches illegal; tighter restrictions were placed on work among children and young people, and 'unhealthy missionary tendencies' were to be restrained.

The New Statutes brought together many evangelical churches in a challenge to the government. Georgi Vins, Peter's son, and Gennadi Kryuchkov headed the formation of a new Council of Churches of Evangelical Christians and Baptists. Hundreds of churches from the AUCECB joined the new organisation, causing a major split.

Georgi, pastor of a Baptist Church in Kiev, emerged as one of the leaders of the new ECB Church, often referred to as Reform Baptists. From its foundation, the new Church became the target for KGB attacks; meetings were broken up, and from 1961 there were usually about two hundred Reform Baptists in prison at any one time. An All-Union Conference of Baptist Prisoners' Relatives, led by Lidia Vins, was formed in 1961 to support the prisoners and their dependants. It was the first organised movement behind the 'Iron Curtain' to fight for prisoners' rights.

On 16th-17th May 1966, five hundred Baptist representatives staged a public demonstration at the offices of the Central Committee of the Communist Party. Vins and Kryuchkov presented a petition on behalf of the CCECB requesting religious freedom for the new Church. The five hundred representatives were beaten up and taken off to prison: Vins and Kryuchkov were rounded up later and put on trial.

Their contrived trial, on false charges, was brief, finishing at 2 am on the second day. The two men were sentenced to three years' imprisonment in a 'special régime' camp, the maximum permitted under the relevant article of the Penal Code. The Baptist Prisoners' Relatives Committee published the plight of Christians in prison by writing to the Secretary of the United Nations Organisation, asking him to intervene.

Labour Camp

As a result Lidia Vins, who was their President, was arrested and sentenced to three years in a labour camp. The believers were concerned for her condition, as she was an older lady in poor health. She survived her sentence and was released in 1974. Her son, Georgi did not fare so well, and when released needed two operations to treat a complex hernia. Meanwhile, his family also had to suffer: his wife, who held a degree in foreign languages, had to take a job selling ice cream, their daughter was terrorised at school and their son Peter also served two prison sentences.

During the 1970s persecution continued to centre on believers from unregistered churches, and there are records of horrendous treatment meted out to arrested Christians. But there was increased publicity abroad about human rights violations and the Soviet Government became more sensitive to world opinion, especially after the Helsinki Agreement of 1975.

Georgi was once more summoned under suspicion as a criminal, but he evaded arrest by going into hiding. He was finally arrested in 1974 and charged with being a 'parasite'. Appeals on his behalf included one to the World Council of Churches and another to Amnesty International; even the renowned academician Dr. Sakharov, founder of the unofficial Human Rights Committee in Moscow, took his case up.

In 1975 Georgi was sentenced to five years' labour camp and five years' exile in Siberia. Half way through his sentence he was transferred to a prison in Moscow; on 27th April 1979 he was stripped of his Soviet citizenship and exiled to the United States in a transfer deal. His family was able to join him in America six weeks later.

Vins now lives and works in America and his life is dedicated to helping Christians in what was formerly the Soviet Union. Only time will tell whether ex-President Gorbachev's recent promise to the Pope to allow complete religious freedom will truly be fulfilled, though the signs are promising. Since the collapse of Communism in eastern Europe in 1989, there has been a continued demand for Bibles, and many intellectuals are expressing an interest in Christian ideas and spiritual values. The Iron Curtain appears to have been drawn back - but for how long?

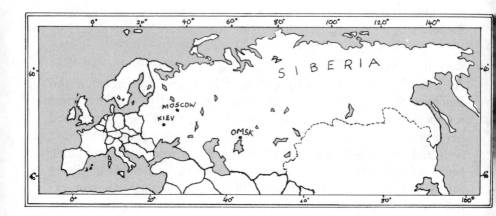

RICHARD WURMBRAND (born 1912): Romanian Pastor

The rise of Nazism in the 1930s culminated in the conquest of almost the entire continent of Europe and the elimination of some six million Jews. In January 1939 troops of the Third Reich swept through Eastern Europe and down towards the Balkans, where Fascist governments were set up to support Nazi policies. But by 1945 they had been over-run by the Russians, who formed Communist governments in all the countries they 'liberated'.

After the horrors of the Nazis' anti-Jewish holocaust, the Soviets introduced their own form of repression, and thousands of Christians were tortured and put to death in a Communist attempt to eradicate religion. Among those who suffered more than any others were the Jewish Christians, who became the target of attacks under both the Nazi and Communist régimes. One of the best known stories to emerge from this sacrificial period of Church history is that of Richard and Sabina

Wurmbrand, a Romanian pastor and his wife, who risked their lives to witness for Christ and endured terrible suffering under Communist rule.

The Wurmbrands were brought up in Jewish Orthodox families, but they abandoned the faith of their forefathers and became 'militant atheists'. After their synagogue wedding, they determined to live life to the full; Richard was a successful businessman with plenty of money to spend and together they set out on a round of night clubs, theatres and parties.

Within a year Richard had developed tuberculosis and was taken into a sanatorium up in the mountains for fresh air and rest. In a nearby village he met an old carpenter who gave him a Bible and introduced him to Jesus. Back in Bucharest, he continued his search for God and began to attend meetings held under the auspices of the Church's Ministry among the Jews where he was eventually converted and baptised. His wife rebelled against his decision, protesting they were Jews and should have nothing to do with Christianity. She decided that on the day of Richard's baptism she would commit suicide, but her attitude changed and she too was won to Christ.

The two new converts were anxious to share their faith with their fellow-Jews and took every available opportunity, whether on a train, in a park or in the street. Richard started by telling the rabbi who conducted their wedding service and was rebuked for having read Isaiah 53, which was forbidden; on other occasions he visited synagogues on Friday evenings, the beginning of the Sabbath, to speak with Jewish people about the Messiah.

As World War II approached, the Romanian government remained neutral, but a strongly anti-Semitic, pro-Nazi puppet government took office in November 1940. Immediately Jews were arrested, tortured and deprived of their businesses, and the persecution only ceased on the payment of an enormous bribe.

The following year Nazi troops arrived in Romania and the pogroms started again. One of the worst affected towns was Jassy where there was a community of Jewish believers. Over 4,000 Jews in the town died as a result of the killings and deportation, and by the end of the war, out of a total of 600,000, some 260,000 Romanian Jews had been put to death. The capital Bucharest where the Wurmbrands lived was largely unscathed in these attacks, and people were imprisoned for weeks rather than years.

The English mission church was closed and the pastor forced to leave; Richard became the new pastor, and the congregation was placed under the protection of the Norwegian and Swedish missions. In this way Richard was able to continue preaching, visiting and witnessing to both Jews and Gentiles. When the German army arrived in the city, he even had a special edition of John's Gospel printed for free distribution to the soldiers. On three occasions he was arrested but was never in prison for more than two or three weeks, as each time a suitable bribe secured his release.

Underground Church

These years saw the beginning in Romania of what became known as the 'Underground Church', a reference to assemblies without government permission to meet, so that believers were forced to gather secretly in each other's homes. During one illegal meeting, the secret police knocked at the front door of a home, and while the leader kept them talking the believers slipped out of a window at the back!

Richard gained access to the Minister of Ecclesiastical Affairs to ask permission for his church to restart their meetings publicly. Although he was refused, with typical Wurmbrand audacity he began to speak to the Minister about the gospel, and the man's attitude changed; from then on he became their friend and protector.

Much of the anti-Semitism faced by Jewish believers came from sections of the Church, and Richard was always prepared for a hostile reaction from some churchmen. On one occasion he was given permission to sell Bibles outside an Orthodox church, but when his Jewish identity was discovered people cried out, 'These dirty Jews have desecrated our church and our gospel,' and demanded their money back.

Yet Richard personally knew church leaders who were truly godly men with a deep concern for Jews, and some Orthodox and Lutheran bishops risked their lives to support them during persecution. In every denomination there were true believers who formed 'the invisible church', with whom he felt a real sense of brotherhood - people who did not succumb to Nazi intimidation, but remained faithful witnesses to the gospel.

Throughout the war the Wurmbrands worked to help the Nazis' victims - Jewish orphans, Romanian Protestants and gypsies. Then ironically during the advance of the Russian army in 1944 they even sheltered Nazi officers, helping them escape back to Germany.

That summer marked the start of a new régime under Communist rulers. At first the authorities made suitable overtures to the Church at a Congress of Cults, saying that Communists were in favour of religion;

they declared they would even continue to pay clergy stipends. Bishops and pastors among the 4,000 participants stood to praise the new government and chose Stalin as honorary president.

Prompted by his wife, Richard made the one lone protest of the Congress and was applauded by the audience; the Minister of Cults was furious and cut him short. After that, he found that his church meetings were infiltrated by hostile youths who jeered and interrupted the services, and Richard became a marked man.

For many years Richard had longed to be able to witness to Russians brought up on atheist propaganda. There were now a million troops in Romania and his moment of opportunity had arrived. Again he was quick to seize any opening to preach the gospel. Once, in a shop, he met a Russian captain with a woman officer and invited them to his home; both were converted that day and then helped in his underground ministry to the Russians.

There were many others who came to Christ as a result of his secret preaching in army barracks. Under the Communists, the Church was once more subject to persecution and believers were forced underground. Yet despite restrictions, evangelism continued and literature specially designed for Communists was printed.

Disappeared
Walking alone to church on Sunday 29th February 1948, Richard was seized by the secret police. His identity papers and belongings were taken away and he was given a new name. As a result he 'disappeared' and for eight and a half years was impossible to trace. At first Sabina was told he had absconded with money intended for famine relief work, then later that he had died in prison.

Between 1948 and 1956 Richard was frequently interrogated and subjected to terrible forms of torture. He was hung upside down and beaten on his feet, placed in an ice-box 'refrigerator cell', beaten till his bones were broken and had eighteen holes burned in his body. When his captors could not break him, they let him go; he had lost much weight and was in bad shape, and it was a miracle that he was still alive. Imprisoned again after three years' freedom, he was finally released five and a half years later, during a general amnesty in 1964.

During these years Sabina was also imprisoned and, without trial, sentenced to three years' hard labour. She was interrogated and placed in a carcer, a narrow cupboard with air holes designed to break down a prisoner's resistance. And while helping to dig a canal, she had two ribs

RICHARD AND SABINA WURMBRAND

broken when thrown into the River Danube by the guards. Their son, Mihail, was left an orphan for three years, and the two ladies caring for him were seized by the police, beaten and left permanently crippled. At school he was twice expelled for daring to speak out against Communist indoctrination, and lost two years of his education.

Realising the danger of further imprisonment, the Norwegian Israel Mission paid the Romanian Government £2,500 for the Wurmbrands to leave the country. Richard concluded that it would be better to continue his work from outside, and decided to live in the United States where he could be the 'voice' of the Underground Church in the Free World. He founded the *Christian Mission to the Communist World*, through which help could be channelled to believers in Communist lands.

When he came out of prison in 1956, his son - who became a Christian as a result of his parents' witness - asked him, 'What have you learned from all your suffering?' His father replied, 'First, that there is a God; second, Christ is our Saviour; third, there is eternal life; and fourth, love is the best way.'

Return to Romania

During their years in exile, the Wurmbrands founded the Christian Mission to the Communist World through which they have endeavoured to be 'the voice of the Underground Church' to the Western World. After twenty-five years they were finally able to pay a return visit to Romania, on 14th May 1990. Groups of friends and acquaintances who had suffered with them gathered at the airport to greet them, including believers who had been in prison with Richard, and there were tears of joy at the reunion. The crowd prayed openly and sang hymns, including one that the hymn writer Moldoveanu and Richard had composed together in prison. Bystanders were moved by the occasion, and soldiers and police looked on in amazement. 'Who are these people who are received with such overwhelming joy?' they asked. But despite the relaxation of religious laws the Christian Mission to the Communist World believes there is much work still to be done.

BROTHER ANDREW (born 1928):
Ministry To The Communist World

When Karl Marx declared, 'Give me twenty-six lead soldiers and I will conquer the world,' he realised that in the battle for people's minds the most powerful weapon he could use was the written word. Since then, Communists have deliberately set out to disseminate their ideas through the widespread use of literature. By the 1960s they had more full-time literature distributers in south east Asia alone than the West had Christian missionaries in the entire world.

The Christian Church had increasingly become aware of the importance of making the Scriptures available on a world-wide basis, but not until recent years was there any sense of urgency about the task. In 1804 the British and Foreign Bible Society was established to complement the work of the newly formed missionary societies. The first such society to be founded, its aim was to print and distribute Bibles, and to make the Scriptures available in other languages. Other groups were set up later to meet specialist needs, notably the Scripture Gift Mission (1888), The Gideons (1899), Wycliffe Bible Translators (1934) and, more recently, Open Doors with Brother Andrew.

Suffering For The Gospel

The plight of Christians in Eastern Europe first came to Brother Andrew's attention on a visit to Warsaw in the summer of 1955. Invited to a Communist Youth Festival, he was able to break away from the main

party and secretly visit five churches in the capital. After preaching at a
Baptist church the pastor told him, 'We want to thank you for being
here... we feel at times as if we are alone in our struggle.'

The struggle referred to was the Church's fight for survival behind
the Iron Curtain, and for the first time it dawned on Andrew that here was
a part of the Body of Christ that was suffering for the gospel and was in
desperate need of help. Thinking about this situation he opened his Bible
and his eyes fell on a verse in Revelation: 'Awake, and strengthen what
remains and is on the point of death'. It came as a clear call from God
to minister to this remnant Church, in a mission field seemingly without
labourers.

On a second trip behind the Iron Curtain, Andrew paid a visit to
Czechoslovakia and found the situation worse. There was not only a
shortage of Bibles, but the government put great pressure on the Church
to conform to the state; those who refused were imprisoned. At the last
church where he spoke, in Prague, he was given a brooch in the form of
a cup - it was the 'Cup of Suffering', to remind Christians in the West
of the suffering Church in Czechoslovakia.

One-man Mission

Yet in the next few years he discovered there were believers in other
lands enduring a far worse fate, many of whom paid the ultimate price
for their faith. Determined to do what he could, Andrew began what was
for a number of years a one-man mission to the Communist world, taking
Bibles, encouraging Christians and preaching the gospel.

Backed by a prayer group in Holland, his first trip was to Yugoslavia

---

The ethics of smuggling

Christians sometimes questioned the morality of Andrew's smuggling
activities, and argued that it was breaking the law. He admits that when
his book *God's Smuggler* appeared he was not altogether happy with the
title, as smuggling was associated with illegal activities such as contraband
or drugs, but maintained that as the agent of 'a government not of this
world' his aim was 'to promote the cause of our sovereign Lord,' whether
done openly or under cover; it was a matter of obeying God rather than
man. The very first principle for any Christian work, he believed, was
that the Lord had commanded his people 'to invade this enemy-occupied
world and reclaim it for God.' When taking Bibles behind the Iron
Curtain, Andrew always prayed for God's protection and always spoke
the truth, though sometimes he imparted only partial truth or concealed
information that was not strictly required of him. His argument was that
we are not facing an ethical issue but a loyalty issue.

in 1957, in a car crammed with Bibles and tracts. The literature was not hidden in a secret compartment, but was distributed among his camping gear and personal belongings. As he approached the border guards, he prayed his now-famous prayer, 'Lord, when you were on earth, you made blind eyes see. Now, I pray, make seeing eyes blind.'

When questioned, he did not tell any untruths but gave carefully worded answers that avoided arousing their suspicions, and was allowed through. He spent seven weeks in the country and was able to travel about freely. During his stay, he preached at eighty meetings, including a Catholic church, and distributed the Bibles.

Before long he paid a return visit to the country and found that the situation had worsened. Many of the pastors had spent time in prison and ordinary church members were cautious, aware of continual police surveillance. Unable to preach for fear of reprisals against Christians, Andrew developed other techniques; he was allowed to bring 'greetings' from the West and from the Lord, which provided an opportunity for teaching the Scriptures. Then he used 'funeral and wedding' evangelism, the only two occasions where it was possible to present the gospel briefly.

As he travelled around Europe he discovered that the Communists were introducing their own techniques for putting pressure on young people especially, to woo them away from the Church. The believers called it the 'Counterfeit Church', as it was an attempt to substitute patriotism and the state for allegiance to God, by offering state ceremonies as an alternative to Christian rites. In the Lutheran Church of East Germany, there was a state Welcome Service as an alternative to Baptism, and for young people a Youth Consecration instead of Confirmation. A Wedding and Funeral Service was also on offer, when a state official extolled the virtues of socialism. While at first the Church refused to compromise, it gradually eased its position; only the Catholic Church resisted the state, to the admiration of many Protestants.

According to Andrew's information, the two countries where persecution was most intense were Bulgaria and Romania. Despite this, he had no problem in obtaining visas and set off with his car heavily weighed down with boxes of Bibles. Of the two countries, Romania took the harder line and was referred to by the believers as the 'greenhouse of atheism'. There was a more rigid control over the Church, worship services were restricted and evangelism prohibited.

His first attempt to pass on his Bibles met with a refusal, as the church leaders were fearful of the consequences of being discovered. During the second week, however, he met believers with whom he was able to share fellowship and who were thrilled to receive his gift. Perhaps his most moving impression of this trip was the occasion when the congregation of one church realised there were believers abroad who cared, and they were not alone in their struggle.

Now married with a small family, it seemed necessary for Andrew to have a partner with whom to share the workload. Hans Grubar, a Russian-speaking Dutchman, was the first of several men who came to work alongside him, and his language gift provided them with an opportunity to minister to the Soviet Church.

On a previous exploratory visit to the Soviet Union Andrew had met a Baptist Union official in Moscow, so already had a contact within the country. When he returned to the same church with Hans, he had a remarkable encounter with a Christian from Siberia who told him the Lord had sent him 2,000 miles to find a Bible for his Church. It was also arranged for Andrew to meet another believer and, within a short distance of Red Square, transferred one hundred Bibles to the Russian's car. 'By this time next week,' his contact told him, 'these Bibles will be in the hands of pastors all over Russia.'

BROTHER ANDREW

The success of this mission encouraged Andrew to organise a print of a further 5,000 Bibles for Russia and in 1964, with the support of the Dutch Bible Society, he was able to make an initial supply of six hundred and fifty available for the Underground Church.

Struggling Church

From this point on his ministry began to expand to the Suffering Church in other corners of the world. In 1965 he visited Vietnam, China and Cuba, and two members of his team managed to enter Albania; in all cases they found a struggling Church, in need of help yet fearful to make contact with western Christians. Increasingly since 1974 his attention has turned to Africa, an area of turmoil and political instability, where revolutionaries have attacked the Church and thrown out the missionaries.

In recent years countries such as Mozambique, Ethiopia, Uganda and Angola have formed battlegrounds for rival factions, with the Suffering Church caught between the two. Again, his aim has been to strengthen the Church and supply it with Bibles. More recently he has visited parts of Central and South America where the Church is facing similar problems, and needs to be prepared for the hard times to come, he asserts.

Brother Andrew explains that the battle will not be settled by governments and generals; it is a spiritual battle in which the weapons are prayer, intercession and commitment, and every Christian can play a part in winning it. Open Doors is still seeking to fulfil the original vision given to Andrew in 1955, to support Christians who are suffering for their faith. Its title is taken from Revelation 3:8, where Jesus declares that he has set before us 'an open door which no man can close', and encourages believers to respond to the challenge.

In recent years his vision has widened and he has been engaged in mission to the Muslim World; he is actively involved in the Middle East where a new prayer campaign has been launched, and he reminds Christians that 'Prayer changes everything; it is God who is at work, it is he that is carrying out his plans.'

Ecuador, South America

Latin America proved to be the area of greatest success for Roman Catholic missionaries during the sixteenth and seventeenth centuries, when both Franciscan and Jesuit priests gained a strong foothold in the wake of the Spanish and Portuguese conquerors. But the loss of Spanish supremacy and the suppression of the religious orders left the Catholic missions weakened, and by the nineteenth century the Roman Church had suffered many losses.

At this point, the Protestants began to take an interest in the region. Led mostly by undenominational 'faith missions' they won many converts and pioneered elementary education among Indians and people of mixed race. But there were still millions of Indians unreached by any form of Christianity, some because they lived in lands cut off by high mountains or dense forests, others who fiercely resisted every advance made by white men and remained isolated and ignorant.

One of the three countries in Latin America where Protestants found it difficult to gain a foothold was Ecuador, a land of mountains and forests on the western sea-board. Catholic missionaries first entered the country in the sixteenth century but made little progress, and when in 1667 a Jesuit priest attempted to penetrate the interior he was killed by Auca Indians. Between 1875 and 1925 rubber-hunters plundered and burned Indian homes, turning the tribes people even more against the white man and closing the door to any hope of missionary enterprise.

In 1945, while still young missionary candidates with the Gospel Missionary Union, Frank and Marie Drown responded to a call for a couple to open up a mission station among the Jivaro Indians of Ecuador. They reached their centre at Macuma, an area where the Gospel Missionary Union had been working since 1903, some three years before the arrival of Nate and Marj Saint at nearby Shell Mera.

The Drowns were fully aware of the dangers of taking the gospel to hostile Indians - they knew of the intertribal warfare and the Jivaros' reputation as headhunters, and they had been warned of the unending fight against loneliness, disease, pestiferous insects and poisonous snakes. Yet they had a vision of an indigenous church that would be self-supporting, self-governing and self-propagating, and believed the Lord would bring them through. Over the years, they saw their mission station grow and become an efficient gospel nerve centre, where Indians conducted their own services, experimental farm and schools.

While a number of Protestant missionaries had managed to establish contact with the Jivaro and Quichua tribes in Ecuador, the feared Aucas remained beyond their reach. It was not until the 1950s that renewed attempts were made to establish contact with these savage killers, attempts which resulted in the death of five young Americans.

NATE SAINT (1923-1956): Mission to Headhunters

The senior member of the group was Nate Saint, an ex-US Air Force pilot, who joined Mission Aviation Fellowship almost at the time of its inception. He went to Ecuador in 1948 with his wife, Marj and operated a small Piper aeroplane from Shell Mera, an abandoned Shell Oil Company base 150 miles south-east of the capital, Quito.

With his ingenious turn of mind, he was able to devise new techniques to make flying safer and missionary work easier. Two ideas of particular value were an alternative fuel system, essential for his small aeroplane, and what he called his 'spiralling-line technique', a method of lowering a canvas bucket from an aeroplane still in full flight into the

NATE SAINT

hands of a person on the ground. This second invention played a significant part in their efforts to reach the Auca Indians, as well as being useful for supplying mission stations with some of their everyday needs.

Nate's arrival at Shell Mera marked the beginning of a new way of life on the isolated jungle mission stations. Missionaries had previously been cut off from the outside world, with supplies and medical aid often taking days to reach them; now their needs were only minutes of flying time away. It led to an improvement in the quality of life for the missionaries and they were safer, healthier and more efficient.

God's Choosing

In 1952 two friends, Jim Elliot and Pete Fleming sailed together for Ecuador, convinced that this was the place of God's choosing for them. They formed an incongruous partnership - Jim was the school champion wrestler and Pete was an academic who was expected to become a college professor, yet they were drawn together in a determination to serve Christ.

Both of them had finally focused their attention on Ecuador as the result of hearing missionaries speak of the challenge of taking the gospel to the Indians. Although initially their attention was directed to the Jivaro and Quichua Indians, they began to hear of the Aucas (whose name means 'savage') and wondered whether some day they might have a part in winning them to Christ.

Later in 1952 Ed McCully, a college athlete and championship footballer, arrived in Quito with his wife, Marilou. They were due at Shandia to join Jim and Pete in outreach to the Indians. Their move to the mission station was delayed when severe flooding destroyed the

---

Mission Aviation Fellowship

The MAF was founded by a number of Christian RAF officers at the end of World War II. New Zealander pilot Flight Lieutenant Murray Kendon was appalled by the destruction cause by aircraft during the war, and wondered why they could not instead be used to spread the gospel of peace. He shared his vision with the Movement for World Evangelisation and an aircraft was purchased in 1947. A survey was made of the needs of missionaries in central Africa, and in 1950 regular operations began in Sudan; the work spread through Africa to other Third World countries. There are now 17 autonomous MAF groups around the world, with over 300 pilots and ground staff operating 140 aircraft in 25 countries. MAF America was founded in 1946, and it was from here that Nate Saint flew out to Ecuador where he 'changed the lives of missionaries'.

whole of the mission compound. Ed joined his two friends in a re-building programme and by the following September they were all resettled in their new homes.

The final addition to the team was Roger Youderian who was crippled by polio at the age of nine but had gradually overcome the effects of his disability. At high school he was able to play basketball, and at the age of nineteen enlisted as a paratrooper, being decorated in 1944 for his action in the invasion of Europe.

With his wife, Barbara and six-month old daughter, he arrived in Ecuador in January 1953. They settled at the mission station at Macuma where Frank and Marie Drown were the senior missionaries, working among the Jivaros. Like the other men, Roger found that he had to spend much of his time doing routine jobs such as construction and mainte-nance work, which appeared to distract him from the essential nature of his calling. But in these months he was able to learn the language, spend time getting to know the natives and work with them on language development.

In September 1955 the missionaries joined forces to begin what they termed 'Operation Auca'. From then on, regular searches were made for signs of the Indians' whereabouts, but it was not until October that they at last found their 'neighbours'. The village was only fifteen minutes away by plane from Ed's new base at Arajuno, on the edge of Auca territory.

The Aucas

The men were now convinced that the Lord was leading them to do something about the Aucas, but they were faced with two problems: one was that of language, and the other was how to make contact with the Indians without scaring them away. Jim Elliott recalled meeting an Auca woman called Dayuma who had escaped from the tribes and felt she might help. He went to talk with her and she supplied them with a number of useful phrases such as, 'I like you' and 'I am your friend'.

For the second problem, they decided to begin a series of gift-drops, using the spiralling-line technique devised by Nate. In this way, they could show the natives that they had the power to give or to retain the gift and that it had not simply fallen out of the plane's 'stomach'. Over a period of two months they made a series of drops to different village clearings, sending gifts such as a kettle with beads inside, an axe or items of clothing. Sometimes the drops were accompanied by broadcasting the Auca terms they had learned, using a loud-speaker.

As the Aucas became used to the plane, their response seemed to be more and more favourable. In one clearing they built a platform, evidently with the intent of reaching up to the plane, while in another place an even higher one was erected. Twice the missionaries received gifts in return, placed in the bucket, including a headband of feathers and later a parrot.

By the end of November the missionaries were agreed that the time for meeting the Aucas on the ground was fast approaching and they began to make their final plans. The men, together with their wives, gave much thought and discussion to the issues involved and declared themselves 'ready to die for the salvation of the Aucas'; the women also appreciated the risks and were prepared to accept they might become widows.

With these matters settled, they went ahead with their preparations. A suitable landing strip, which they nick-named 'Palm Beach', was chosen on the banks of the River Curaray, a short distance from the Auca village. Provisions were gathered, a pre-fabricated tree-house constructed and various other necessary items (including guns) were packed for their stay among the Indians.

The day chosen was Tuesday, 3rd January 1956. After prayer and singing their favourite hymn, *We rest on thee*, the mission got under way. Before the end of the day, all their gear had been transported to Palm Beach, and Nate flew over the village inviting the Indians, 'Come tomorrow to the Curaray'.

Silence

It was not until Friday that three Aucas ventured to meet them; they spent most of the day on the beach and seemed quite at ease. One even risked a trip in the plane. On Sunday, Nate spotted a group of ten men making their way towards the river and radioed his wife that he would contact her with more news at 4.30 that afternoon. But at 4.30 there was only silence.

As time passed by, the women began to imagine what might have detained them and their fears started to mount. At 7 o'clock on Monday morning a search was set up; Nate's plane was spotted on the beach, but there was no sign of life. The civil authorities were alerted and the US Air Force Rescue Service brought in to help. Over the next few days, four of the bodies were recovered, speared to death; there was no trace of Ed McCully. The men were buried together in a common grave on the spot where they had waited to greet the Aucas.

To the world at large, their deaths seemed a terrible waste of life; yet their sacrifice made a tremendous impact on many other lives. Even several of the Quichua Indians surrendered themselves to God for his use among their own people. The work of reaching the Aucas continued, to try and show them that the missionaries' intentions were good.

Three years later Elizabeth Elliot, with her little daughter Valerie and Nate's sister, Rachel Saint, was invited into the Auca village. For nearly a year she lived and worked among the men who killed the missionaries, including her own husband.

She must often have pondered during these difficult days words written by Jim in 1949 when a Wheaton College student: 'He is no fool who gives what he cannot keep to gain what he cannot lose'. For her they had gained a whole new meaning.

Uganda, Africa

After David Livingstone died in 1873 the American newspaper correspondent Henry Stanley made an appeal for missionaries to serve in Uganda. On his journey from Lake Tanganyika to the coast he had met King Mtesa who told him, 'I am like a man sitting in darkness. All I ask is that I be taught how to see.' Stanley's letter to the *London Daily Telegraph* resulted in the Church Missionary Society sending a party of eight missionaries, headed by a Scottish engineer called Alexander Mackay. The first missionaries reached the king's court in January 1877 and carried with them the 'book' Mtesa was anxious to learn about. But he was unable to make up his mind and vacillated between Anglicanism and Catholicism; when he died suddenly in 1884 he had still not made any commitment.

He was succeeded by his son, a youth easily influenced by the Muslims. They turned him against Christianity, and afterwards the Church was subject to violent attacks in which hundreds of believers were put to death. On one day alone, thirty-two boys were tortured and then roasted alive for their faith in Christ.

The persecutions ended in 1894 when Uganda became a British Protectorate, with a Ugandan head of state as a figurehead ruler. During the period of peace that followed, the number of Christians continued to grow, until 60 to 70% of the population claimed allegiance to either the Anglican or the Catholic Church.

In 1962 Uganda gained its independence and became a sovereign state within the British Commonwealth, a move that led to a further period of unrest. Prime Minister Milton Obote deposed the President and assumed full executive authority over the government, but he too was overthrown in 1971 when General Idi Amin seized power.

JANANI LUWUM (died 1977): Archbishop of Uganda

From the beginning, Amin embarked upon a reign of terror. It reached its climax in February 1977 with the massacre of thousands of soldiers and civilians in retaliation for an unsuccessful army rebellion, and then with the killing of Janani Luwum, the Anglican Archbishop of Uganda. The archbishop's murder stirred up renewed fears among Ugandan Christians and many fled across the eastern border into Kenya. Among those who escaped were the archbishop's wife and children, and three black Anglican bishops who were able to give details of the killing to the outside world.

Janani Luwum was born into the Acholi tribe whose homeland was in northern Uganda, close to the border with Sudan. Though destined to become a tribal chief, lack of family funds forced him to enter a missionary-run training college, where in 1942 he graduated with highest honours as a teacher. His conversion to Christ came in January 1948 as a result of hearing the evangelist Yusto Otunno and his wife. At the end of the meeting, Janani stood up to declare his response to the gospel and prophetically announced, 'I am prepared to die in the army of the Lord'.

Back at school he felt that he had to share his faith with his students, and once climbed a tree in order to preach, telling them to repent and turn to Christ. He was thrilled when later he discovered that a number of boys had been converted as a result of his sermon. He became so caught up with the new charismatic revival movement that he was dismissed from his post by the Church authorities who found his message of repentance was upsetting. Yet his enthusiasm was not dimmed and he continued the work of evangelism. Once, after an open-air meeting, he was arrested and thrown into prison with eight other believers, charged with disturbing the peace.

Within a matter of months, Janani began to realise that God was calling him to be a pastor. Reluctantly at first, he set aside his teaching career and his family's hopes of his becoming a chief, and made plans for the Anglican ministry. He was not ordained until 1956 and, because he showed such promise, was sent to England for further theological training - to St. Augustine's College, Canterbury (1958-59) and the London College of Divinity (1962-65). In between he spent three years as a priest in what his bishop considered to be the most difficult parish in his diocese, and for one year acted as principal of an Anglican College at Buwalasi.

Higher Office

By now Janani was obviously destined for higher office. In September he was appointed Provincial Secretary, the senior administrative officer for the Church, and in 1968 he attended the Lambeth Conference as an overseas consultant. On his return, it was decided that the diocese of Northern Uganda should be divided and that Janani should be Bishop over the Langi and Acholi people.

He was consecrated in January 1969, the first member of the Acholi tribe to hold that high office. The Anglican Church was weaker in Northern Uganda than in any other part of the country: it lacked a committed leadership, congregations had dwindled and church buildings had fallen into disrepair.

Janani's first task was to visit every parish, to encourage the people and strengthen the Church. He took a great interest in leprosy work in Acholi, where a new clinic was opened with financial support from West Germany. He tried to develop a Christian agricultural centre where church members could receive training in Christian leadership and find help with new farming methods, and he worked on a scheme for providing accommodation and support for homeless girls.

Neither of the projects was the success he had hoped for and when he left Acholi he had to entrust the work to less capable hands. Perhaps his greatest concern was to build up a people who were totally committed to Christ, which culminated in a diocesan mission in April 1970. Supported by over a hundred missionaries from other dioceses, the mission succeeded in bring new hope and determination to many of the Acholi Christians.

Yet these were difficult times for Uganda and the state of the nation was threatened by political disorder. An attempt to assassinate President Obote failed, and in January 1971 General Amin took the country by surprise when he seized control of the government. He quickly suspended parts of the constitution, dissolved parliament and forbade political activity.

Initially there was a sense of elation for some Ugandans when Amin promised free elections, but fear soon spread throughout the country when Amin showed himself in his true colours. At his command, property was confiscated and a number of prominent Christian leaders were murdered. Hundreds of dissenting army officers, soldiers and

JANANI LUWUM

Langi and Acholi tribesmen were killed. In 1972 the dictator expelled
55,000 Asians who held British passports, as well as fifty-eight European missionaries.

Janani was the leader of a delegation of bishops that protested to the
President about the killings, and with three other members of the World
Council of Churches wrote a letter of protest to him about his treatment
of the Asians. His opposition to Amin's policies placed him in great
danger and his friends feared for his life.

When the Archbishop of Uganda retired in 1974, Janani Luwum was
his obvious successor, and despite doubts in some quarters about the
reality of his faith, he was duly elected. His enthronement took place at
Namirembe Cathedral, Kampala, in June 1974. He saw his immediate
task as that of healing the many divisions within the Church and working
with Catholics and non-Christian groups alike towards reconstructing
the nation.

He increasingly became the focal point of protest towards Amin. After a student demonstration was ruthlessly put down in 1976 and many students killed, the country's religious leaders met together to discuss the situation. Led by Janani, they drew up a list of concerns to present to the President, but he refused to meet them.

Marked Man

From this time Janani was a marked man and was seen by the governing authorities as leader of the opposition. For some time, Janani had been in touch with Obote in exile, making plans for an attempt to overthrow Amin's government. But when arms were smuggled into Uganda, Amin's security forces learned of the plot and raided Janani's home hoping to discover them. Incensed by the incident, the Anglican and Catholic bishops met together in February 1977 to make a determined stand against the President and a memorandum was drawn up, signed by the Archbishop and fifteen bishops.

Again Amin refused to meet them, but instead sent for the Archbishop alone. His wife tried to dissuade him from going, but he felt he had to do what he could to resolve the situation. He was released that day, but recalled three days later to attend a conference of the country's leaders and administrators. Janani was escorted away separately and the two bishops with him dismissed; they never saw him again.

In the evening Radio Uganda announced that the Archbishop and two cabinet ministers had been arrested. The following morning it was reported that the three men had been killed in a road accident, a clumsy cover-up that aroused a loud outcry in the world's capitals.

From evidence gleaned afterwards, it appears that Amin had tried to force the Archbishop to sign a confession stating that he had plotted to overthrow the dictator, but had refused. He was then tortured and personally executed by the President. Another source reports that the two cabinet ministers were executed by Amin's security forces who then shot the Archbishop to stop him from informing the outside world.

A Statement made by Kenyan church leaders afterwards probably summed up the feelings of many Christians: 'We confess that we have too often kept quiet when we should have identified ourselves with the suffering and persecuted peoples of the Continent of Africa and Uganda in particular. It only remains for good men to do nothing for evil to flourish.'

In 1981 a guerrilla force invaded Uganda and deposed the dictator Amin.

Western Europe

In July 1938 a conference held in the French town of Evian on the shores of Lake Geneva discussed how the nations could rescue the Jews from Hitler's persecution. Of the thirty-two countries represented at the talks, only three of them agreed to accept any more refugees - the Dominican Republic, Denmark and Holland. America refused to increase its immigrant quota and Britain would only accept some children.

A German newspaper which reported the conference ran the headline: 'Jews for sale, who wants them? No one.' Hitler realised that he would be able to proceed with his plans for a 'Final Solution'.

That year the Nazis intensified their anti-Jewish measures - concentration camps were enlarged to accept more prisoners, Jewish businesses were closed down and properties forfeited. And in one terrible night known as Kristallnacht ('The Night of the Broken Glass'), 9th November, Jewish homes and shops in Germany and Austria were attacked and burned down, and in Vienna alone over forty synagogues were destroyed.

By this time more than 200,000 Jews had left Germany and found a refuge in Palestine, America, Britain and a few European countries. But as more and more Jews fled their homes, some governments began to place restrictions on the numbers they were prepared to admit, though Denmark and Holland continued to keep an open door.

CORRIE TEN BOOM (1892-1983): Ambassador For Christ

Among the 'righteous Gentiles' who risked their lives to save Jewish refugees was the ten Boom family of Holland. The ten Booms lived in the beautiful old Dutch town of Haarlem, between Amsterdam and the North Sea. For many years the family had had a love for the Jews, God's chosen people, and their sympathies were known in the town. When the Nazis over-ran Holland, many Jews knew where they could turn for help, and the local rabbi brought all his Jewish theological books to Corrie's father in the hope of preserving them for future use.

As early as 1937 ten Boom's son, Willem, had opened a home for elderly Jews fleeing from Germany, and as the places filled up he had to find other homes among Christian families. During the first year of occupation there were only minor attacks on Jews: anti-Jewish graffiti on walls, signs in shop windows stating 'Jews will not be served' and orders forbidding Jews the use of parks, theatres and restaurants. And all Jews were ordered to wear the yellow Star of David with the word 'Jew' in the centre.

Before long, Jewish people began to disappear and their shops closed. It happened to some Jews living opposite the ten Boom watch-shop, when their furriers was ransacked by German soldiers. Fearful of further trouble, Corrie arranged for the couple to stay at Willem's house in Hilversum. This incident drew Corrie into working with the Dutch underground movement. But first she gave thought to the ethics of the matter: how far, she wondered, should a Christian become involved in this kind of intrigue? She finally accepted the challenge and was able to pray one evening: 'Lord Jesus, I offer myself for your people. In any way. Any place. Any time.'

In May 1942 the ten Booms took in their first Jewish fugitives, and Willem was able to take them on to a safe haven after Corrie had found a means of obtaining ration cards for them. Her contact, in fact brought her not three but a hundred ration cards, an invaluable asset for future refugees. Now deeply involved in the underground movement, it was necessary for her to be introduced to some of her compatriots who could be of assistance to her.

At a specially arranged meeting she was introduced to one man who could supply her with false identification cards, and another who could arrange for her to have an official government car. Most important, she met an architect who suggested that she needed a secret room where her guests could hide in case of a Gestapo raid. Corrie's room at the top of the house offered the ideal place, and when the hide-out was completed no-one would have guessed there was anything behind the seemingly stained old wall.

The number of guests staying with the ten Booms increased to nine and there was much coming and going at the watch-shop. As their home

---

The Holocaust

The word is derived from Greek and means 'a whole burnt offering, a wholesale sacrifice or destruction'. The term is used to describe the period from 1933 to 1945, when the Nazis of Germany systematically put to death six million Jews. Adolf Hitler blamed the Jewish people for Germany's social and economic problems and vowed to annihilate the Jews from Europe. Beginning with Germany, Jews in all countries under Nazi control were eventually affected. No city, town or village escaped; death camps, labour camps, mass executions, forced marches and starvation all took their toll, but it was the concentration camp at Auschwitz in Poland 'where barbarism reached its most diabolical depths' and three million people, nearly all of them Jews, were killed. Not surprisingly, many Jews have often asked the question, 'Where was the Church during the Holocaust?'

CORRIE TEN BOOM

was a mere hundred yards from the police station, it was essential to take precautions. At one point, neighbours heard them having a singsong and warned Corrie to be careful; it was obvious more people knew about their activities than she realised. Her worst fears seemed to be confirmed when one day she was summoned to see the Chief of Police. She was relieved, however, to find that the man was a believer and was actually seeking her help.

It was only a matter of time before the Gestapo detected her mission. One Wednesday in February 1944 the house was raided by Gestapo officers and two Dutch Nazis. They searched the building thoroughly for any Jews who might be in hiding, but failed to find the secret room. Despite being beaten, Corrie and her sister, Betsie, gave nothing away and the raiders were forced to admit defeat. Guards were deployed around the house in order to starve out any who might still be in hiding there, and the ten Booms plus some innocent visitors were taken to the Gestapo headquarters at The Hague. Eventually the prisoners were released except for Betsie and Corrie, 'the ringleader'; their father collapsed and died in hospital ten days later. Four days after the arrests all the Jews in the secret room were rescued and led to safety.

Corrie and Betsie were transferred to a prison in Scheveningen which marked the beginning of a ten month ordeal in captivity. Facing the prospect of suffering and even death, the two sisters were strengthened by their faith and in many ways discovered that God had not forsaken them. At Scheveningen, Corrie was separated from the other prisoners and kept for four months in solitary confinement. Interrogated by a sympathetic German officer, no verdict was ever pronounced, but she was transferred to a concentration camp in southern Holland to begin her sentence.

Re-united with her sister, the two of them remained together for the rest of their internment. During the following months it became increasingly clear to them that the Lord had allowed their circumstances so that they could minister God's Word to the prisoners. As they met secretly each evening with believers, they were able to encourage them in their faith. Camp life was grim; over-crowding, inadequate food, long days working at a nearby factory and the frequent sound of the firing squad all took their toll. In September, news of the Allied advance through France and Belgium spread around the camp and everyone became excited at the thought of an early release.

Ravensbruck

Instead they were transferred to Germany, where at Ravensbruck camp they endured circumstances far worse than any experienced before. At the camp reception Corrie managed to conceal a small Bible and a bottle of vitamin drops sent into prison by their sister Nollie. She carried them in a pouch slung round her neck, and both items proved to be life-savers in the months to come.

Each evening the Bible became the centre of a meeting for worship and study; barriers of nationality and denomination were of no account as Catholic, Lutheran and Orthodox Christians met together to seek God. The fact that the barrack room was swarming with fleas kept out the guards so that the women were not disturbed.

With the approach of winter, daily life became increasingly arduous: a roll call sometimes lasting several hours on a cold, dark morning; an eleven-hour working day, sustained by a meagre food ration; terrible working conditions and lack of proper medical care.

Betsie's physical condition gave Corrie cause for concern, but she was able to treat her with drops from the bottle of vitamins. Used sparingly, it gave as many as twenty-five doses a day - including other prisoners as well - and like the widow's cruse of oil, never seemed to fail. But on the day one of the prisoners 'removed' a small supply of yeast from the camp hospital, the drops gave out.

Despite her illness, Betsie's faith grew stronger; she proved to be the one on whom they were all able to lean, and her infectious faith generated a more caring attitude in the barrack room. But her condition deteriorated and near the end she was admitted to hospital.

Not long before she died, Betsie had a vision in which she saw a concentration camp in Germany and then a large house in Holland where she felt they were to work, caring for people who had been damaged by the war. She also told Corrie that the Lord had said they would be out of prison by the first day of the new year. Betsie died and three days later Corrie was informed of her discharge - she was released on the last day of December 1944. Without seeking it, both dreams were fulfilled for Corrie, exactly as her sister had envisaged them.

After the war Corrie travelled extensively, speaking of her experiences and sharing the gospel. At a church in Munich, in 1947, she was confronted by a man whom she recognised as one of the most cruel guards at Ravensbruck. It seems that he had become a Christian and knew that God had forgiven him - but would she? Corrie had already faced the problem before when, with hatred in her heart, she had forgiven the man who once betrayed them; now she was being challenged again. After a long pause and a great struggle, she was able to respond, 'I forgive you brother, with all my heart.'

In 1968 Israel honoured her for her work in aid of the Jews and she was invited to plant a tree in the Avenue of the Righteous Gentiles, Jerusalem. She must have recalled her father's words when he once witnessed Jews being deported: 'I pity the poor Germans, Corrie. They have touched the apple of God's eye.'

AVENUE OF THE RIGHTEOUS GENTILES, JERUSALEM.

SOME EXAMPLES OF 20th CENTURY PERSECUTIONS

COUNTRY	BACKGROUND	PERSECUTIONS
CHINA	* The Boxer Rebellion, 1900, started when members of a secret society attacked and killed Chinese Christians and foreign missionaries, who were blamed for three years of crop failures * After a few years, resentment towards Christians revived. In 1920s and 30s, the Communists invaded China and began attacks on the Church	* Worst massacre in capital of Shansi province - 32 adults and children from the BMB and CIM societies, plus 12 Catholic priests and nuns were beheaded * Ten Swedish missionaries and their children were stoned to death * In all 188 foreign missionaries and children were murdered, plus hundreds of Chinese believers * Many Chinese Christians killed in Szechwan and Kiangsi provinces during 1927 * John and Betty Stam of CIM were beheaded in 1934; their baby daughter survived * Between 1949 and 1958 over 700 Chinese priests died in prison
KOREA	* First the Japanese (1910), then the Communists (1948) conquered the land, and attacked the Church.	* Two young brothers, sons of Pastor Son, were shot for refusing to deny Christ * Many believers fled to South Korea
USSR	* After the 1917 Revolution, the Communists set out to destroy the Church. In January 1918 attacks began on Orthodox churches and priests were killed	* In 1921 Bishop Gemogen was found weighted with an 80 lb rock and thrown into a river * From 1929, Stalin sent thousands of believers to concentration camps where they died in terrible conditions * Private 'Vanya' was tortured and died for his faith while a conscript in the Russian army during the 1970s

SOME EXAMPLES OF 20th CENTURY PERSECUTIONS
continued

COUNTRY	BACKGROUND	PERSECUTION
GERMANY	* Hitler and the Nazis came to power in 1933; soon afterwards attacks began on Jewish people, their properties and synagogues	* Dietrich Bonhoeffer, a Lutheran pastor, opposed Hitler's policy towards the Jews. He was arrested in 1943 and executed two years later, shortly before the end of the war
POLAND	* In 1939 the Nazis invaded Poland from the West, while the Russians moved in from the East	* Over 3,600 Catholic priests and an unknown number of Protestant pastors were sent to the concentration camps where they were shot or gassed * Fr Maximilian Kolbe took the place of a condemned man and was starved to death in an underground cell
SUDAN	* Following the outbreak of civil war, the Muslims in power expelled all missionaries in 1964	* Numerous attacks made on Sudanese Christians * Christian schoolboys were rounded up by soldiers and their teeth pulled out * In 1970, Christians in the village of Banja were massacred in their church and the building set alight
ZAIRE	* In 1964 rebel forces known as Simbas, attempted to take over the former territory of Congo, killing hundreds of foreigners in an attempt to stamp out Christianity	* About 50 Protestant and Catholic missionaries were found, cut to pieces and parts of their bodies thrown into the river * Dr Paul Carlson was shot while helping a colleague to escape * Never have so many missionaries been killed in one year since the Boxer Rebellion

ACKNOWLEDGEMENTS

The Publisher gratefully acknowledges the co-operation of these sources, whose illustrations appear in the present work.

Assemblies of God, 267; Baptist Missionary Society, 180, 182; Barnardo's Photograph Archives, 234; Christian Herald, 340; Christian Mission to the Communist World, 322; Church Ministry Among the Jews, 206; Church Missionary Society, 336; Church of Scotland, 196; Dohnavur Fellowship, 286, 292; Evangelical Library: 51, 55, 90, 103, 120, 124, 128, 141, 144, 149, 151, 156, 167, 169, 170, 173, 190, 199, 201, 220, 229, 253, 257, 261, 270; French Government Tourist Office, 19; German National Tourist Office, 79, 106, 108, 112; Celia Hanks, 83; Geoffrey Hanks, 71; Hong Kong Government Office, 310; Irish Tourist Board, 66; Israel Government Tourist Office, 342; Dr Angus Kinnear, 296; The Leprosy Mission, 209; Mission England, 274; Mission Aviation Fellowship, 329; Open Doors, 326; Overseas Missionary Fellowship, 185, 300; Luis Palau Evangelistic Association, 279; Jackie Pullinger, 309; Radstock Ministries, 316; The Salvation Army International Heritage Centre, 243; Tunisian National Tourist Office, 27; WEC International, 212.

Geoffrey Hanks lives with his wife, Celia, in Worthing on the south coast of England. Prior to his retirement, he was head of RE at one of London's largest comprehensive schools. He was Co-Editor of the Faith in Action series of biographies for young people. In addition he has written several series for the Christian Herald on the subjects of Church History, Christian Social Organisations, Christian Missionary Societies and Revival.